HEGEMONIC
MIMICRY

HEGEMONIC
MIMICRY

KOREAN POPULAR CULTURE OF
THE TWENTY-FIRST CENTURY

KYUNG HYUN KIM

DUKE UNIVERSITY PRESS · DURHAM AND LONDON · 2021

Printed and bound by CPI Group (UK) Ltd, Croydon,
CR0 4YY
Designed by Matthew Tauch
Typeset in Huronia Pro and Quadraat Sans Pro by
Westchester Publishing Services

Library of Congress Cataloging-in-Publication Data
Names: Kim, Kyung Hyun, [date] author.
Title: Hegemonic mimicry: Korean popular culture
of the twenty-first century / Kyung Hyun Kim.
Description: Durham: Duke University Press, 2021. | Includes
bibliographical references and index.
Identifiers: LCCN 2021000875 (print)
LCCN 2021000876 (ebook)
ISBN 9781478013587 (hardcover)
ISBN 9781478014492 (paperback)
ISBN 9781478021803 (ebook)
Subjects: LCSH: Popularculture— Korea(South)— History—21st
century. | Mass media and culture— Korea (South) | Popular
culture and globalization. | Glocalization— Korea (South) |
K-pop(Subculture) | Popu lar music— Korea(South) | B ISAC:
SOCIAL SCIENCE / Popular Culture | HISTORY / Asia / Korea
Classification: LCC DS923.23. K474 2021 (print) | LCC DS923.23
(ebook) | DDC 306.095195— dc23
LC recordavailableathttps:/ /lccn.loc.gov/2021000875
LC ebook recordavailableathttps:/ /lccn.loc.gov/2021000876

Cover art: Tiger JK (*left*) and Yoon Mi-rae during a concert,
2019. Photo by Kyung Hyun Kim.

For Yourim Lee

CONTENTS

Writing Pop Culture in the Time of Pandemic

One of the greatest lines in Korean cinema is delivered by venerable actor Song Kang-ho playing a gruff and frustrated country cop in *Memories of Murder* (dir. Bong Joon-ho, 2003), a film based on a true story and set in 1986. "You know why American FBI [agents] insists on [forensic] investigation?" Song yells. "Because they've got to deal with the US, where the land mass is too friggin' big!" Implied in Song's drunken declaration is that South Korea is much smaller than the United States and does not yet have the technological resources to allow police investigators to use DNA analysis for solving murder mysteries. Fast-forward three and a half decades, when South Korea is a global leader in many areas, including information technology (IT), participatory democracy, and popular culture. During the recent global pandemic, South Korea set an example to the rest of the world with its response to COVID-19.[1] Ironically, it was locally manufactured polymerase chain reaction (PCR) test kits (commonly known as swab test kits) based on an RNA/DNA analysis method invented by American biochemist Kary Mullis in the previous century that enabled Korea to quickly put in place systematic measures to effectively contain the virus without resorting to border closures or full-scale lockdowns. Whereas in the 1986-set *Memories of Murder* a serial killer eludes police investigation largely due to the unavailability of forensic DNA analysis test kits, in 2020 Korea has been able to suppress the COVID-19 infection curve by deploying convenient testing sites for the general population, implementing effective contact tracing, and, most important, reappropriating American scientific inventions to create a testing infrastructure on its path toward global leadership in disease prevention.

That South Korean medical technology today is largely borrowed from twentieth-century America is perhaps no surprise: the best biomedical and pharmaceutical research centers are still located in the West. However, in many ways, what most experts reporting on Korea's success story in controlling the spread of COVID-19 failed to recognize was that the playbook of Korea's response to the pandemic closely resembled that of the K-pop industry. By redeploying essentially American scientific innovations such as PCR, global positioning systems (GPS, developed by the National Aeronautics and Space Administration [NASA]), and Code Division Multiple Access (CDMA, licensed by Qualcomm) to test, trace, and effectively quarantine COVID-19 patients as well as potentially exposed individuals, and then emphasizing the public's trust in its health experts, South Korea was perfecting a system that followed a path from mimicking and pirating the West to establishing an authority of its own. If K-pop moguls borrowed the genres and beats of the West in order to craft their own immaculate dancing idols for global consumption, Korea's COVID-19 response redeployed Western medical technology and tracing tools to effectively control the virus in such a way that would serve as a model for the rest of the world. Just as South Korea had nurtured its domestic pop talents—sans songwriting genius—before developing them into overseas export items, it had now seized on its domestic success with COVID-19 to become a major global exporter of medical devices and equipment—sans recognized scientific innovation in the field.[2]

In this book, I have sought to understand the blurring of boundaries between innovation and plagiarism and between hegemony and underdevelopment that has occurred over the past several decades of the postcolonial, ultracapitalist era by studying and analyzing the question, "How did South Korea achieve so much success without necessarily developing its own unique technology, styles, and culture in the twenty-first century?" I was amazed to learn that even during the COVID-19 pandemic, when concerts and public events throughout the world came to a screeching halt, South Korea dominated headlines not because it was a medical technology innovator but because it was able to quickly adapt to the crisis and deploy the tools innovated elsewhere, first for local application and then for mass foreign export. South Korea is a country of only fifty million people, so for any domestic mass production to succeed, whether of refrigerators, K-pop CDs, or virus test kits, external markets must be found. While writing this book, I was constantly reminded of the words of Stuart Hall, who claimed that the logic of capital "would translate everything in the world into a kind of replica of itself."[3] South Korea continually excelled, not by repackaging its local cultures for the necessities of modern life but by surreptitiously and implicitly referencing its own cultural impulses while reenacting American styles, music, and trends.

Most people, including academics, who still remember Korea as a backward country that suffered from dire poverty and military dictatorship throughout the twentieth century may find perplexing the fact that during the first two decades of the twenty-first century, both the most successful non-English-language film (*Parasite*) and the best-selling non-English-language pop star (BTS) in the United States have been from Korea. The year 2020, which most people will remember as one of the worst years of their lives, was ironically a noteworthy year for Korean culture, as the country's film industry was recognized for its achievements by the US Academy of Motion Pictures and Sciences and its pop music industry produced three No. 1 tracks on the US Billboard Singles chart (BTS's "Dynamite," "Savage Love [Laxed-Siren Beat]," and "Life Goes On")—a feat rare for a group of foreign artists associated with neither a major studio deal nor a major US-label contract. These cultural products, however, exemplify the condition of "hegemonic mimicry" that I have termed for this book as a description of the Korean cultural condition of the past several decades, which is deeply connected with both the commercial and military ascent of the United States and the decline of a monolithic and unitary assertion of whiteness associated with Pax Americana.[4] South Korea also experienced a good portion of what Henry Luce once referred to in *Life* magazine as the "American Century"—that is, taking part in the same political, economic, and linguistic sphere as the Americans, with the nation's elites growing up learning English for more than two generations.[5] What the success of *Parasite* and BTS indicated was that South Koreans had come of age, which signaled both the end of the old American Century and the beginning of a new era where American-ness had to embrace, among others, Korean-ness.

Throughout this book, I make the case that Korean cultural products of the past several decades became ambivalently hegemonic through their creative praxis of mimicry, a practice that is both unique, due to its effectively opaque underscoring of traditional cultural identity, and ordinary, because on the surface it in no way differs from other cosmopolitan neo-American aesthetics and styles commonly seen on YouTube and in shopping malls around the world. When, for instance, *hallyu* actress Song Hye-gyo and K-pop idol BTS are featured on billboards and department store advertisements around the world alongside Keira Knightley, LeBron James, and Lionel Messi, this no longer comes as a surprise to most passersby. The Korean faces are just as familiar and nondescript as those of any other famous person gracing a Louis Vuitton or Clinique advertisement. Some Korean stars today generate a much larger fan following outside Korea than at home and have themselves become hegemonic—and this has come about in the absence of the linguistic power or military dominance associated with many of the more culturally powerful nations. K-pop glitter today represents an ideal of Asian affluence and glamour that is just as commodifiable as the porcelain beauty of a British film star, the hip-hop cool of black rappers from the 'hood, or the sensuality of Latin American music icons. The authentication of K-pop is both vouchsafed from the American capitalist hegemony of the past century as well as uniquely isolated from that hegemony due to its pronounced Koreanness, which is cost-efficient, squeaky-clean, and easily disposable in this era of fast-evolving, ephemeral postmodernity.

After renegotiating the terms of originality and mimicry in this book, I stress that the new Korean subjectivity in the global era is a racialized modality, just as alternating and powerful as is blackness, which has offset whiteness as the singular American hegemonic subject (see chapter 2). Throughout the past several decades, Koreans have been racially situated somewhere between white and black. Long before the media's attention was captivated by escalating tensions between Korean business owners and African Americans during the 1992 Los Angeles uprising—and, more recently, during the post–George Floyd protests—Koreans were awkwardly caught between the white and the African American populations dating back to the civil rights era. Before Korean American businesses became a visible buffer between white and black neighborhoods in urban areas across the United States, back in Korea throughout the past half century, local proprietors who ran the clubs and shops in US military camptowns around the peninsula had often found themselves thrust into the race war between white and black clients. As explained in the introduction, it was the duty of the Korean businesses to separate entertainers and sex workers servicing white soldiers from those servicing black soldiers. For white Americans, Koreans were not black, while black Americans did not see Koreans as white.

Building from their own racialized mistreatment and survival instincts within the militarized American cultural and economic sphere of the twentieth century, Koreans re-created an American-Korean nexus in the twenty-first century, one that asserted both a classic national identity from the Cold War Pax Americana period and a new ethnic entity in the post–

Cold War space that is being remapped by the increased power of social media, the rise of East Asia as an economic power, and new standards for entertainment that move beyond the politically correct color palette that tends to feature only black and white. In this era of social media symbolized by Facebook, Twitter, Netflix, and YouTube, music and images cross linguistic frontiers with much greater efficacy and facility than during any previous era. The popularity of Korean cultural content has proven that the new kind of globalization is, in reality, more excessively American than anything else. Just as black music became emblematic of American music throughout the twentieth century, in the twenty-first century, Korean music, film, and other global ethnic cultural content are now making their mark as yet another iteration and integral form of Pan-American mass culture in the new century. K-pop of the new millennium is the latest sensation in a Pan-American pop that started with the British Invasion of the 1960s.

This book both celebrates and critiques the Korean Wave of the past twenty years, a phenomenon that may mark the first time a postcolonial Asian society has become a critical voice in the makeup of a global pop culture, as Korea has successfully breached the linguistic and cultural walls that surround a minor culture — although this success came at the cost of rendering its ethnic background opaque.[6] This opacity of ethnicity, I argue, is precisely the reason the K-culture industry can be considered both racialized and nonracialized. It is probably not coincidental that Koreans entered the twenty-first century rich in soft power after enduring the traumas of a modern-day period of slavery during the colonial era and subsequently confronting spectacular forms of nationwide disruption and trauma during the Cold War (the Korean War, fervent anti-Communist campaigns, and military dictatorships).

These are the reasons why in this book I have attempted to analyze the roots of linguistic diversions in, for instance, rap music; genre transformations in cinema and television; and the prevalent reliance on captions in Korean variety shows. I have attempted not only to work the "surface" of many films, popular cultural texts, and even songs in order to decode the opaque racialization of Koreans therein but also to lay a foundation for a deeper understanding of the new racialized consciousness of Koreanness in the twenty-first century. The field of Korean popular culture studies has exploded in recent years, and yet serious theorizations based on historical and textual analysis have regrettably often been ignored. There are, admittedly, glaring omissions in this book. In a study that deals with Korean popular culture, conspicuously absent are discussions about K-drama and K-games. These phenomena were largely left out, but not because I deem them insignificant; in fact, they constitute topics of central importance in a volume on Korean popular culture that I previously coedited. However, such topics are not only notoriously difficult to teach but also resist academic theorization, insofar as many popular fan and consumer ratings sites already constitute informational hubs that are far more engrossing than anything an expert opinion can offer at this point. The topics in question also require endless hours of dedicated consumerist behavior in order to adequately address them. Probing deeply into Korean games and television dramas might have jeopardized my attempt to balance my life as a father of a young child, an academic, and a writer of creative fiction. From the very beginning of my career, I have learned that it is almost always better to remain mum about subject matters when one's knowledge and expertise are no more advanced than that of one's audience. Nonetheless, I have taught Korean popular culture courses over the years that have included these topics. Korean dramas, especially the *Reply* (*Ŭngtaphara*) series, which has thus far spawned three seasons (2012, 2013, and 2016), have stimulated my students' interest in Korean history, language, and society and have in many ways constituted teaching tools just as, if not more, efficacious than literary and cinematic subjects. However, these so-called miniseries are not exactly "mini" in length, and finding time both in and outside class to view ten-plus-hour-long dramas becomes a challenge that can overwhelm their potential for productive discussion, and asking students to watch hours of television and play games can also run the risk of undergraduates getting hooked on nonacademic addictions and social gatherings that potentially yield little to no intellectual effect as academic study topics. As a former game addict who knows all too well the dangers of playing video games into the wee hours of the morning, asking my students to play on Korean gaming platforms such as Lineage in order to subsequently engage in serious questions about Korean identity would have been plainly irresponsible. Despite these cautionary warnings, theoretical explorations into why and how certain television dramas and computer games manufactured in Korea continue to attract consumers outside the peninsula must continue to be wagered.

Furthermore, since we appear to be entering a prolonged era of remote learning, I accept that game platforms of artificial intelligence and role-playing could enhance the learning experience for students who must now productively engage their screens. I completed the first draft of this book's manuscript just as Korea was experiencing an unprecedented surge of COVID-19 cases stemming largely from the outbreak at the cult megachurch in Daegu. The manuscript's lengthy revision process coincided with the imposition of stay-at-home orders in my home state of California, the murder of George Floyd, and the rise of Black Lives Matter protests nationwide. It was disheartening—for instance—to once again hear, over and over, the name of Latasha Harlins, the fifteen-year-old black girl who was killed by a Korean business owner in Los Angeles in 1992, which led to thousands of Korean American businesses being damaged during the Rodney King uprising, but it served as a necessary reminder that Koreans are still deeply associated within the systematic racial injustices that are now truly global in scale.[7] It is therefore my hope that *Hegemonic Mimicry* will in a small way help further the discussion of race in Asian and Asian American studies.

While working on this book, I have been plagued with various nagging injuries and illnesses, and at the moment of this writing, I, like millions of Americans, am trying to recover from lung diseases associated with COVID-19. My symptoms have fortunately been mild but are nevertheless an ongoing reminder that the virus's impact on the body's organs is real and serious. I am grateful to Courtney Berger, my editor at Duke University Press, who gave me both the courage and the time to finish this book. She also made the entire editing and vetting process painless, responding to every one of my gripes and complaints with grace and composure. Hers was precisely the kind of response I needed from my editor as I struggled with medical appointments, tests, anxiety, and pain. This is the third book project that Courtney and I have worked on together, and she—along with her assistant, Sandra Korn—has impressed me each and every time. The two anonymous readers of this manuscript also made suggestions that far exceeded their pay scale and duty. Although disagreements did arise here and there, almost every one of the issues that they raised was expressed in a true spirit of collegiality. In an academic environment that has unfortunately grown more spiteful and mean over the years, partly due to the ugly sociopolitical climate and partly as a result of the incendiary communication modes of social media, these two readers exemplified the deep value and importance of academic debate guided by care and courtesy. Carl Good and Zury Lee also read earlier drafts and provided many copyediting suggestions that were incisive and insightful and made the manuscript infinitely more presentable. One of my graduate students, Sue Kim Asokan, helped me compile the bibliography.

I wrote my first book, also published by Duke University Press, *The Remasculinization of Korean Cinema*, in my twenties; my second, *Virtual Hallyu: The Korean Cinema of the Global Era*, in my thirties; and this one in my forties. A famous Korean proverb tells the story of how "even rivers and mountains undergo change every ten years." This has been all too true for the landscape of Korean popular culture in the United States and beyond as it grew from a negligent blip in global culture when I was a teenager adjusting to my new life in America to one of the most productive and attractive worldwide more recently. Korean studies and cultural studies disciplines in general were unable to keep up with the explosive demand by students virtually from all over the world who sought in-depth historical and theoretical analysis of Korean popular culture. Hopefully this book will ease some pressure off the academics who are anxious that some of the information compiled by students and popular internet sites simply outweigh their expert knowledge of the field of Korean popular culture. I know this all too well, since the motivation to write this book was to avoid this very shame I felt when teaching a course on Korean popular culture for the very first time. With each passing decade, I witnessed dialogue across transnational paradigms on the subject of Korean popular culture exponentially grow, but now I am wary that the impact of COVID-19 may have indefinitely foreclosed these cultural and intellectual flows. Despite the terrorizing power of this virus, hopefully soon we will be able to return to the movies, concerts, exhibits, and academic conferences where we can again fully appreciate the energy of youthful Korean popular culture.

The humanities dean's office at the University of California, Irvine, first headed by Georges Van Den Abbeele and then by Tyrus Miller, has supported this book by offering me generous support through the Humanities Center's publication subsidy grant. Andrzej Warminski, the associate dean, throughout the past decade also generously offered his time to respond to all my administrative queries as I crawled to the completion of this book. The Korea Foundation Field Research Fellowship also allowed me some time off from teaching to visit Korea and to concentrate on writing. Many of the staff members of the department and in the School of Humanities — including Mindy Han, Joo Hoon Shin, Erica Yun, Michelle Hu, Veronica Portal, Stephanie (W.) Wijetilleke, and Amanda Swain — helped me get through one crisis after another.

Many of my colleagues, graduate students, and staff members at UC Irvine and beyond also helped me shape, share, and publish earlier versions of this work. The past and present chairs of the East Asian Studies Department at UC Irvine—Martin Huang, Michael Fuller, and Hu Ying— shared with me the pains of having to go through caring for a small child while writing this book and sympathized with me greatly. Many of my past and present colleagues in the department—Will Bridges, Chungmoo Choi, Ted Fowler, Jim Fujii, Susan Klein, Mimi Long, Bert Scruggs, Serk-bae Suh and Elisabeth Tinsley—also provided productive conversations and feedback on a range of subjects discussed in this book. Colleagues outside the department—including Nahum Chandler, Chris Fan, Joseph Jeon, Adriana Johnson, Eleana Kim, Horacio Legras, Jerry Lee, Sei Lee, Jane Page, Jim Steintrager, and Michael Szalay—offered comfort and wisdom that I lacked while working on this book. I was blessed with intellectually sparkling graduate students who gave me opportunities over the past eight years to discuss the topics covered in the book in seminars; they are Benja-min Aaron, Sue Kim Asokan, Eun-ah Cho, Monica Cho, Jessica Conte, Zach Gottesman, Seok-kyeong Hong, Tiffany Hong, Kristina Horn, Yunjong Lee, Tian Li, Kiki Liu, Ying Liu, Adam Miller, Forest Muther, Hyunseon Park, Anat Schwartz-Meron, Eun Young Seong, and Jean Shon. Friends in academia—Jinsoo An, Chris Berry, Steven Choe, Youngmin Choe, Jinhee Choi, Karen Fang, Hoduk Hwang, Andrew Jackson, Marcia Landy, Im-manuel Kim, Jisoo Kim, Suk-Young Kim, Youna Kim, Aynne Kokas, Bodu-rae Kwon, Young-Jun Lee, John Lie, Ingyu Oh, Se-Mi Oh, Suk Koo Rhee, Youngju Ryu, CedarBough Saeji, Haerin Shin, Ji-young Shin, Sowon Park, Young-chae Seo, Victor Shmagin, Mi-seong Woo, and Hyon Joo Yoo— invited me to discuss portions of this book in classrooms, publications, and restaurants.

This work was supported by the Core University Program for Korean Studies through the Ministry of Education of the Republic of Korea and Korean Studies Promotion Service of the Academy of Korean Studies (AKS-2016-OLU-2250005). An earlier version of chapter 2 was published as "Becoming-Black: Exploring Korean Hip-Hop in the Age of Hallyu," *Situations* 12, no. 1 (2019): 23–46. Portions of chapter 4 appeared as "Running Man: The Korean Television Variety Program on the Transnational Affective Run," *Telos* 184 (Fall 2018): 163–84. Last but not least, I am indebted to Yourim Lee, my wife, and Sidd Kim, my daughter, who was born during the period when this project was conceptualized and then matured to be a per-ceptive young woman who now, when this book is going into production, teaches me everything there is to know about BTS and Blackpink. Yourim was working as a film producer at CJ Entertainment & Media (CJ E&M) in Seoul when the book was first incubated. She underwent an incredible career change to accommodate our life together in the United States while this book took shape. I cannot thank her enough for having made the changes necessary for us to be together. Her insights into Korean popular culture—from the business side to the aesthetic one—allowed me to stay current and focused. I dedicate this book to her.

Introduction

Of Mimicry and *Miguk*

Imagine a dystopian world where American cities have been devastated and turned into slums after a long decade of economic repression and total war. Large numbers of young people are dead, missing, or badly wounded. Survivors — mostly women, children, and the old — are forced to pull themselves together from ruins of concrete slabs, metal scraps, and war ashes. In the midst of starvation, despair, and family loss and separation, the foreign army that has defended these American cities is asked by the humiliated leader to remain and help restore order. Let's say that the foreign army that has been asked to save these American territories comes from a country across the Pacific: Korea. They speak only Korean, eat Korean food, and socialize among themselves. Because tens of thousands of Korean lives have been sacrificed to defend American soil, once the war has ended, their rest and recreation, or R&R, is given priority by the American leader. Koreans occupy the best hotels downtown and hold auditions for local singers, musicians, dancers, and vaudeville-type magic and freak shows. Because talented young American women and men desperately need work to survive the postwar devastation, they audition before panels of Korean military officers. Because the Korean soldiers prefer to watch female singers performing on stage, American girls frantically learn the musical scores and lyrics of Korean folk songs on the fly. Korean traditional melodies registering in the moody minor pentatonic scale sound foreign to young American ears and are almost impossible to learn because the lyrics are in a language that sounds nothing like any of the more familiar Indo-European languages they have heard before, let alone English. Yet, because the income generated from each week of work is easily three or four times the income earned from working at any local farm, you desperately audition for the Koreans, even though you have heard horror stories about the long bus rides on unpaved roads, about the sex-deprived soldiers who will grope you onstage and later try to whisk you away to Korea. Because your performance is evaluated by Korean military officers who serve as judges, you force yourself to learn new songs by transliterating the lyrics into the English alphabet, even though the Korean words make no sense to you. You may pass the first audition, but even when you succeed in touring onstage for a couple of months, you must continue to compete against newer and younger faces who try to take your place every change of season. Each audition requires you to learn the new hit songs on the radio. Mimicking the accent and intonation of each and every Korean word is almost painful—physically because you have to use different facial muscles to pronounce iotized vowels such as *yŏ* (yeo) or *yo* and the frequent syllabic assembly of phonemes with preceding consonants of *n* or *k*—and psychologically because Korean soldiers constantly mock you for each pidgin diction you make. Just when you think you have mastered standard Korean, a new wave of hit songs with beats sung in nonstandard Korean come in vogue. The new Korean songs are recorded in a regional dialect, which is much more difficult to learn than the songs sung in standard dialect. But you never lose hope. Soon, you tell yourself that you can fulfill your dream of singing in front of real Korean audiences back in Korea on a beautiful stage in the poshest, most exclusive neighborhood—Gangnam. You must learn each and every song with a sincere and positive attitude, or else you may not pass the constant tests, get kicked off the tour, and lose your livelihood.

I begin my book with this sketch of a scene from what looks like speculative fiction because not only does this hypothetical reversal of a hierarchical, hegemonic cultural imperialism sound horrifying for Americans, but this fictive representation also pointedly decenters regimes of representation prevalent throughout the twentieth century that have heavily prioritized an American-centric axis while devaluing the peripheries of any culture, nation, or history that is non-American. Flip the Korean with American in the preceding paragraph, and you get a snapshot of what actually took place during the postwar years in Korea before the heyday of *sho-dan* (Korean show troupes for the US Eighth Army) came to an end with the intensification of the Vietnam War by the late 1960s.[1] Most of the best-known South Korean popular music acts and composers throughout the first three decades of the postwar era, such as Korea's first diva crooner, Patti Kim, and the Godfather of Korean Rock, Shin Joong-hyun, started out their careers as sho-dan performers.[2] Although the United States of the twenty-first century now espouses more political sensitivity regarding issues of race, this was much less true of the United States of the mid-twentieth century. When the US military entered the Korean War, then remained there to defend South Korea (hereafter Korea, unless otherwise indicated) from further Communist aggression, America was still a racially segregated nation whose values, cultural identity, and historical determination to bring world peace were cultivated very much in the pallor of ideologies of white racial superiority. The treatment, in other parts of the world, of nonwhite races, along with their cultural identities and languages, as equal to that of white America was at the time unthinkable.

The elimination of racial inequality between black and white soldiers was only in the infancy of *discussion*, and still far from reality, during the Korean War (1950–53) and the subsequent decades. Although black-only platoons were phased out during the war by then president Harry Truman, racial discrimination and segregation remained entrenched in barracks, social life, and civilian life back home.[3] Well until the mid-1970s, camptown clubs for US military personnel in Korea were segregated — so much so that race riots broke out in several clubs near Camp Humphreys, motivated by black soldiers upset by the de facto policies of segregation enacted by these clubs and their proprietors, which separated entertainers and prostitutes who serviced white soldiers from those who serviced their black counterparts.[4] So intense and widespread were some of the racial tensions between black and white service members in Korea that during the 1970s several committees, such as Get It Together (GIT), formed by US military personnel, and Promote Equality Action Committee (PEACE), formed between military officials and Korean bar owners, had to be established in order to investigate and end racial segregation at off-base clubs.[5] Even after more than two decades of desegregation in the American military, so real were the racial tensions and disparities in US military bases that the music played in clubs had to be policed and the Korean club owners censured. As stated by Captain A. D. Malloy, who headed the US Army GIT, "We check on the variety of music played in the clubs. They must mix it up; some soul, some rock, some country and western. If they don't mix the music, you get . . . segregation."[6] Koreans were often awkwardly caught between the white and black races and were the frequent targets of African American anger. A bar owner in Itaewon interviewed for a 1971 article published in *Stars and Stripes*, which probed the racial war brewing in US military bases in Korea, stated, "If a black GI comes into a place frequented by white GIs, there'll be trouble. There'll be fights or the whites will just leave and not come back. The blacks don't spend as much money as the whites do."[7]

Korean bar owners' refusal to serve African American soldiers or play the music of their preference out of fear of retribution from white soldiers did not exactly help ease the tensions in these camptowns, but at the same time it would be unethical to find Korean bar girls and proprietors culpable for the escalation of American racial tensions that were being played out in Korea at the time. US military officials could have purchased these clubs and managed them on their own. However, the American military's acquiescence in the illegal prostitution arranged in these clubs largely steered it away from taking such measures. The Korean bar owners and entertainers were thus left with a problem too hot to handle on their own, thereby turning them into victims without agency in another country's race war. Korean proprietors, like the 2,200 Korean American business owners who suffered heavily from damages incurred during the Saigu event that took place twenty years later in Los Angeles when four white officers were acquitted for beating a black man, were beginning to find themselves awkwardly caught between white establishment power and black anger.[8]

As a country, Korea held a strategic geopolitical significance for US policy makers, but the Koreans themselves were merely a native people who happened to inhabit a location that did not and could not figure into this discussion for racial equality other than as victims sandwiched between the two races.[9] For US politicians, Korea has always had more importance as a territory serving as a bulwark against Communism than for the people who inhabit it. The Korean bars thus had very little agency beyond their reluctant control of jukeboxes that had to be played sensitively and equitably in order to reflect the musical genres that separated white and black customers. Koreans, considered sufficiently light by white Americans and simultaneously sufficiently dark by black Americans, managed to cross the strictly delineated color lines during this racially segregated era; yet sometimes this "crossing of the color lines" caused more trouble than necessary.[10]

By 2020, exactly seventy years after the war in Korea that desegregated black soldiers from white soldiers for the first time in American military history while making permanent the division of the Korean peninsula along the thirty-eighth parallel, much had changed. Music, figuratively speaking, has ceased to play on the jukebox and is instead listened to via social media–driven streaming apps. And some of the very talents featured on these new online jukeboxes such as YouTube, Spotify, and Apple Music apps popular among young generations of Americans are Korean idols whose music is composed and produced by pop artists influenced by a diverse selection of 1970s American music—including country, rock, funk, soul, disco, and even Latin beats. Korean *minjok* (national ethnic) identity, which has long been situated awkwardly between the two dominant American races, often as an anxious bystander, is fast emerging as an active global leader in health, tech innovation, and manufacturing and is claiming a strong stake in global popular culture as well. It took more than several generations for Korean identity to once again become fully engaged in amusement and pleasure through a buoyant cultural revival because refiguring a new subjectivity under a tightly administered capitalist expansion—under the auspices of the American-led order—inevitably took time. Koreans are no longer meekly forced to the sidelines to cautiously push the buttons for an American playlist preselected along color lines or learn songs whose meaning and historical background are foreign to them. Although it is difficult to compare such audition programs of local talents held in Seoul during the postwar period to the public slave auctions held in the United States in the eighteenth century, what I would like to propose in this book is that South Koreans had to undergo a kind of transformation that included a process of what Achille Mbembe describes as "exclusion, brutalization, and degradation" that despised and dishonored their own indigenous form and spirit in order to be given a manifestation of cultural rebirth as a "living crypt of capital" that has become the fungible norm of the twenty-first century that expanded into the "entire planet [as] the *Becoming Black of the world*."[11]

What Mbembe is here specifically arguing for is, in the Deleuzian spirit, the renewal of a worldwide blackness that removes itself from a conventional link with a race-specific category into an economic and cultural alliance of twenty-first-century subjectivities sought by the underprivileged class. This two-way deracialization and broadening of blackness is also being hatched specifically in the twenty-first-century Korean cultural sensibility, which no longer participates in the American racial war from the sidelines. Korea's expanding political, economic, and cultural responsibility now requires Koreans to participate in redefining their ethnic identity in relation to the categories of global racial subjectivity—including Mbembe's "becoming-Black." This renewed sense of Korean nation-ness or "becoming-minjok" no longer speaks to the essentialized anticolonial or antiforeign kind of nationalism that was first championed by Korean intellectuals and leaders during the twentieth century, such as Sin Ch'ae-ho, Yi Kwang-su, and even former president Park Chung-hee, who idealized and defined minjok as a pure, patriotic political idea that defined the people who shared the cultural, linguistic, and geographical space of the Korean peninsula. My sense of becoming-minjok, or becoming-Korean, in the global cultural scene of the twenty-first century—an era propelled by social media, "dividual" subjectivities demanded by internet surveillance, and a renewed importance of subcultures organized around hip-hop and eating—draws on the less essentialized notion of minjok that frees Korean culture, tradition, and language from the intractable and anticolonial struggle for a pure and patriotic assemblage of ethnocentrism.

I concur with Jin-kyung Lee, who declared that "Koreanness [has] begun to be delinked from its exclusive attachment to ethnicity."[12] But this process has taken place only after a lengthy period in the twentieth century during which Korean minjok was almost exclusively aligned with the ethnic differentiation of the Korean people under Japanese colonial rule and then over its reassertion over the subsequent decades. As Lee has also argued, "rather than [the Koreanness] that is defined by a modern *national* citizenship," the term *han-minjok* (the term *han* is derived from both *one* and *country*, *hanguk* having been used by South Korea to name itself after 1945) has always insisted on blurring the boundary between the common blood ethnicity and the national citizenship that represents Korea.[13] However, the continued currency of this term has been threatened by recent reconsideration of the non-ethnocentric designations that must be given to the terms of citizenship in order to include non-Korean ethnic migrant settlements and the country's expanding transnational cultural and economic activities. It has been the productive activity of K-pop and other Korean popular culture products in cinema, food, and television that has ushered in this new sense of "becoming-minjok" or "becoming-Korean" that has loosened the link between the notion of a common ethnic bloodline and Koreanness.

As an ethnic identity of the previous era, the Korean minjok has rarely been given any kind of notice in America, with the rare exception of the ever-present North Korean threat. The earlier sketch of foreign military–sponsored auditions for local entertainers directly showcases what Michel Foucault described as biopolitics, established through "a new mechanism of power" that exerted a control apparatus over a large population of local entertainers who could be replaced, dismissed, and disposed at whim.[14] Here, too, I am indebted to the work of Jin-kyung Lee, who has employed Foucault's concept of biopolitics, as well as that of Mbembe's necropolitics, in examining the precarious and disposable labor of Korean sex workers in US camptowns throughout the postwar years. Lee focuses on three working-class labor contexts (Korean military labor in Vietnam, Korean military prostitution for the United States, and Asian migrant labor in contemporary South Korea) in what she calls the "transnational proletarianization of race," arguing that these labors have constituted the "most disposable (labor) commodities."[15]

Missing from Lee's analysis, however, is the extensive entertainment labor produced by Korea throughout the latter part of the twentieth century. Because some of the entertainment labor devoted to the US military overlapped with employment in Korean broadcasting companies and clubs, it is difficult to estimate precisely how many sho-dan performers were needed at a given time in Korea. However, as early as the late 1950s, the demand for Korean performers in American military clubs was so high that several Korean talent agencies—each employing hundreds of singers and musicians—began operations to train for the auditions held in Yongsan.[16] Trained and auditioned before American military judges, these performers would soon come to constitute the critical labor base for the entire Korean popular music industry in the years to come. Many of these talented instrumentalists and vocalists, who included many composers and singers ranging from folk singer Cho Dong-jin to rock superstar Cho Yong-pil, could copy an American song within days of it hitting the charts in America. Many of these Korean male and female artists of sho-dan were treated as disposable and forced to work under dire conditions, much like the sex workers in the military camps. However, one significant distinction has to be made between these two conspicuous service labor sectors that emerged from the US military base camp areas in Korea: unlike female sex workers, whom Lee associates with "necropolitical labor" ("the extraction of labor from those 'condemned' to death, whereby the fostering of life, already premised on their death or the disposability of their lives, is limited to servicing the demands of the state or empire"), some of these musical performers were able to move forward in their lives and careers, preventing their own labor from becoming disposable by seeking out musical and artistic innovations that led to them becoming the biggest names in Korean showbiz after retiring from their American sho-dan careers.[17] Put another way, what could have potentially been disposed of as simple copycat machines comprising a mere footnote in world music history emerged from these postwar ashes to sow the seeds for authentic acts on some of the most prominent stages in the world, incubating an exciting hybrid form of twenty-first-century cultural identity. The demand for Koreans to produce an endless supply chain of disposable, off-white/blackish entertainment bodies regulated by American hegemony would, throughout the latter twentieth century, become remediated, re-ethnonationalized into a new, cool Koreanness, one that would prepare itself for the transnational, cosmopolitan sense of hallyu (the "Korean Wave") located between the essential and the disposable, between white and black, and between Korean and American. This was perhaps the entertainment version of what Joshua Neves has termed "underglobalization" to describe the "frictions and folds between an emergent China and prevailing hegemonic structures" that focus on the role of counterfeits and fakes that undergird China's relationship to global media technologies in the twenty-first century.[18]

Despite the Korean traditional experience that has overvalued austere erudition of Chinese poetry stemming from *sadaejuŭi* (revere the great) and has simultaneously underappreciated peasant performances rooted in oral art and mask dance due to their vulgarity and unpredictability, the postwar cultural development in Korea steeped in mimicry of the foreign was possible because popular culture in traditional Korea was one that was driven by the power of *sinmyŏng* (in Korean, the hallucinatory divine energy that drives up the Shamanistic spirits and excitement for communal fun and entertainment), as will be explained in chapter 7. Because sinmyŏng can only be enacted by participatory conditions of performances where the stage is arbitrarily set and the demarcation between performers and participants constantly breaks down, unlike that between *yangban* (aristocrats) and *kisaeng* (courtesans) whose separation is critical along the lines of class, gender, and performative roles, it can be argued that Korea is among many countries, such as Ireland, Poland, and elsewhere, where its mass culture always actively engaged in a postmodern culture long before the term *postmodernism* was even coined. As Namhee Lee points out in her analysis of *madanggŭk* (open-air theater) in the 1970s, when sinmyŏng had been recaptured for the purpose of transforming the traditional mask dance (*t'alch'um*) into a protest theater during the Park Chung-hee era, the "most potent aspect of folk drama was not only the breakdown of the traditional actor/spectator and self/other division, but also the transformative power of liminality, enabling the audience to move from observing a drama to participating in a transformative event."[19] Because the entertainment industry, whether in the West or in the East, has always been centrally engineered not by people from the class of nobility but by those from the class of daubers, crooners, shamans, and clowns, who almost always resided along the margins of the society, many Koreans, as long as they adopted the language, gestures, and styles of the foreign, could swiftly purchase an agency of cultural assets or capital that could be communicated in a shared, communal environment that moves beyond an individual, private enterprise that mythologizes the artist as a hermetic romantic genius.[20]

SHO-DAN 2.0

Through these uneven and erratic historical developments, Korean identity as a new postmodern and a new proto-ethnic enterprise is now creeping into the lives of American youth through its enormously seductive music videos and alluring television dramas, which draw enormous attention and numbers of likes in the global social media scene while dominating new culinary and fashion trends. The worldwide twentieth-century youth culture that grew up with the internet and social media and was no longer confined to the same national, mono-ethnic, or even monolingual identities found the hybrid identity retweeted from Korean YouTube channels fascinating and attractive. The previously intractable Korean identity of the twentieth century, steeped in an anticolonial, proto-ethnic minjok identity by the time it produced a new generation of post-sho-dan performers, had already undergone a huge facelift: call it a "Sho-dan 2.0" update. Many of the young talents in Korea who vied for a spot in K-pop idol groups during the early years of the twenty-first century were auditioning for management company executives who were either younger partners of original sho-dan performers (such as Lee Soo-man of SM Entertainment) or new clientele of American military R&R club culture in Korea (such as Yang Hyun-seok of YG Entertainment, who learned breakdancing by associating with young black soldiers in Itaewon and was the sidekick to Seo Taiji, who was once a bassist in the legendary heavy-metal band Sinawe led by guitarist Shin Dae-chul, the son of Shin Joong-hyun). Since the 1980s, these executives had begun to see how American soldiers and Korean entertainers had started to exchange their cultural capital and socialize in places like Itaewon without monetary compensation for their entertainment services. "Sho-dan 2.0" loosened and rendered opaque historical and ethnic specificity of minjok from Korean identity—a necessary step that broadened the Koreanness in order for its pop music, comedies, dramas, films, and food to flow into the everyday lives of young people living outside Korea. When Korean entertainers first picked up their electronic guitars and sang into the microphones in order to sell their talent to Americans, their ethnic cultural background had to be repressed; after seventy years, in the era of social media, Koreans have naturalized this cultural condition where their ethnic identity remains compromised.

The several-decade-old pursuit of a musical *mugukjŏk* (nonnational) identity, or a pseudo-American one, has manufactured success that is unprecedented elsewhere in the world. K-pop is one of the most successful popular music genres in the world today, not because of its accentuation of beats, melodies, and rhythms that distinguish themselves from those of American hegemonic sounds but because of its close proximity to these sounds. The ironic effect is quite evident when Korean entertainment companies hold auditions to select their new trainees—many young singers, dancers, and talents from all over the world, including the United States, make their pilgrimage to Seoul—or when former US president Donald Trump discusses a Korean film as a foreign cultural element that unsettles the purity and wholesomeness of American culture.[21] The young auditionees are sometimes asked to perform before their Korean judges only a few miles away from Yongsan, the very spot where the auditions were held for Koreans to entertain the occupying American military personnel. These days, despite the recent diplomatic and economic war brewing between South Korea and Japan, many young Japanese talents, some of them established stars in their own country, learn new songs in Korean to compete against the local Korean talents.[22] The putatively postethnic rendering of Korean language, customs, rhythm, beats, and themes has permitted these cultural products aestheticized, performed, and enacted by Koreans in the twenty-first century to reach a quasi-global and ambivalently hegemonic status.

Despite the ubiquity and popularity of K-pop, K-cinema, and K-drama that seemingly reached every corner of the world today, this cultural hegemony is ambivalent because it is built on cultural reappropriation crafted from mimicry. My usage of "mimicry" is derived from Homi K. Bhabha's seminal article, "Of Mimicry and Man: The Ambivalence of Colonial Discourse," where he argues that the colonial subject is a product of a "reformed, recognizable Other, *as a subject of a difference that is almost the same, but not quite.*"[23] Korea's globalization that took place during the post–World War II years had to do with a new form of mass culture constructed under the rubric of undeniably American identity. However, Korea's own version of its America, or *miguk* (the Korean term for the United States, which is derived from two Chinese characters—*mi*, beautiful, and *guk*, country), just like India's appropriation of Britishness, simulated and reinvented American cultural artifacts, styles, and pop products. Between the source (America) and its Korean quotation (miguk), a slippage and a misappropriation were undeniably interjected, despite the best efforts by Koreans to replicate the American performances. This simultaneous appropriation and misappropriation opened the door for innovation—an innovation that was fraught with an appreciation of imitation and fakery that framed the everyday life of many of the Korean artists who could not even understand the language and gestures of the American standard and model. The century-old repression of minjok identity—first under the colonial occupation of the Japanese empire and then under the military occupation by the United States—was lifted, but Korea's cultural renaissance during the first two decades of the twenty-first century had to satisfy the global commercial demand, on the part of a social media–driven youth culture, for a non-ethnocentric identification that evaded the continuing racial-cultural war between whiteness and blackness. In the newly negotiated cultural plenitude of the post–Pax Americana era, miguk-ified South Korea was the perfect "Murrica," celebrating the new post-ethnonationalist K-pop and K-cinema and also rejecting the category of both Donald Trumpian whiteness and the intense, urban subjecthood of blackness.[24] The blackish or off-white Korean subjectivity that emerged in the era of social media was a perfect assemblage of codes, styles, and memes that would self-correct the potential errors and insults that could risk damaging one's reputation around the issue of race.[25]

A new cultural post-minjok (or becoming-minjok) Korean popular sentiment was born out of these critical imitations that re-membered the foundation of the soul—of both Korean and black American. There was probably no other place in the era of Pax Americana outside the United States where the learning of the American—the aesthetics, styles, and language—was as intense and durable as it was in Korea over the past three-quarters of a century. During this time, relearning the foreign culture meant not only recalibrating the Korean soul and the wounds of being a Korean but also forgetting the origins of black resentment that were deeply rooted in many music genres, such as jazz, blues, soul, rock 'n' roll, R&B, and hip-hop. Koreans learned to enact a two-step, double gesture of mimicking and innovating—which immersed its own miguk in the

Korean movements, rhythm, and language. This process of miguk-ification both weakened and intensified the Korean emotions and soul, which for many decades ended up playing hide-and-seek with Korea's survival acts of mimicry. Thus, one can argue that South Korea has exploited a close sociopolitical alliance with the United States over the past several decades that produced a simulation of American conception of culture—one that rescrambled and rendered opaque the local Koreanness before it began circulating through global social media.

If Bhabha's postcolonial employment of the term *mimicry* sought to question the level of success of the cultural appropriation the colonial and postcolonial elites were forced to adapt by raising the impossibility of approximation in every act of simulation or imitation (he sarcastically transforms "almost the same, but not quite" into "almost the same but not white"), there are other instances of the use of mimicry that come to define the tradition of, for example, mask theater.[26] As will be discussed later, especially in the chapter on Korean comedies, mimicry can be a form of carnivalesque play where the hierarchical difference between adult and child, original and imitator, and the colonizer and the colonized breaks down. I am drawn not only to the postcolonial employment of the term *mimicry* but also to the theories of Roger Caillois, a postwar French theorist who has argued for the term *mimicry* as the defining tendency of human nature toward play.[27] In the following chapter's discussion of Korean reality comedy programs, I rely on Caillois's definition of mimicry. African American literary scholar Henry Louis Gates Jr.'s theory on the "Signifyin(g) monkey" is also one trope that references figures of tricksters and talking animals from black folk tales and verbal games of exchanging insults such as "Dozens" in order to foreground the importance of game and play in instances of black cultural production. Here, mimicry becomes a crucial tool to offset not just one form of power but all forms of power. Gates's theories valorize parody, mask theater, and the taunting that constantly seek to deconstruct power to the extent where much of the essences of power disintegrate. Gates's observation on "Signifyin(g)," which broadly includes imitations, jokes, and even travesty as a critical practice exhibits the pleasure of liberty that is at stake within the discourse of mimicry.

This book also pays attention to how the act of mimicry passed from an initial colonial simulation of the dominant colonizer to an ambivalent and ironic one before assuming a hegemony in an ambivalent form. When I examine the controversy of "kimchi imperialism" in China in a later chapter,

I question whether this charge against Korean imperialism in China is valid. Perhaps the biggest cultural paradox of the first two decades of the twenty-first century is that South Korea, a country that once had no identity to the rest of the world other than the nation ravaged by war and the threat of Communism, has not only survived the "audition" tests administered by US military officers but within a generation and a half has graduated from these acts of simply copying American hit songs to achieving its status as one of the most successful cultural content makers in the global arena. Auditions are still popular, but in the place of foreign military advisors trying to entertain their soldiers, local businessmen who grew up themselves listening to American songs serve as judges to select young performers who will together set the new global standard in world pop today. Young Korean talents do still fear getting kicked off the "tour bus," but even if they do get kicked off eventually, they will not face starvation and poverty. And once they are officially on the bus after years of hard training, the results may be much sweeter than sharing a stage in front of an audience of drunk soldiers.

Over the first two decades of the twenty-first century, a Korean's acceptance of Americanization and commercialization helped overcome their own deep internal contradictions between global and local, and effectively allowed them to transcribe cinematic language, music genres, and even ideology that originated in America into a powerful discourse that we now brush aside along with the coinage of hallyu. However, what needs to be recognized here is that this first step or act of appropriation-cum-double gesture that at least had to acknowledge and abandon its own minjok (ethnic nation-ness) was not just a national reenactment but a reconstitution of itself as a proto-ethnic identity within the Pan-American global order. The unraveling of the boundary between authenticity and quotation gestured through the Korean act of mimicry, in other words, proclaimed the birth of a new ethnic and national subjectivity that is both American and Korean and that is raciopolitically located somewhere between off-white (complicit) and blackish (resistant). I insist on this refusal of the essentialist bifurcation between "whiteness" as a form of complicity and "blackness" as a resistance because for a Korean throughout the days of Pax Americana to identify more with an African American than a Caucasian American would have still required one to subversively reinscribe the praxis of American hegemony. Throughout the book, I offer these two terms, *off-white* and *blackish*, as a discourse that tries to read these two colors as metonymic references to suggest the two-headed condition of hegemony that inseparably interarticulates the Gramscian tropes of coercion and subversion.[28] How this new identity trapped between neocolonial subjectivity and a postcolonial one became rearticulated into a dominant wave of culture—where its new act of the day (BTS, for instance) has totally subverted the dominant hierarchy between original and copy and can now rival even several of the top American music acts, such as Taylor Swift and Justin Bieber, in terms of album downloads, YouTube views, and concert ticket sales—is what forms my theoretical frame of *hegemonic mimicry*. In other words, what my book aims at is, first, to situate Korean popular culture of the past two decades as one of the most discernible and conspicuous examples of the blurred boundary between original and copy that has rendered a catalog of postmodern cultural contents par excellence. Second, this book explores the phenomena that made this K-pop fame possible, including not only the ingenuity and persistence of Korean artists and cultural innovators who notoriously spend countless hours in training but also the global culture dominated by social media, which over the past two decades has empowered users' parody, fandom, and remakes, and these, in return, have weakened the traditional borders between nations, languages, and the originality-copy divide. Third, what I would like to also insist in this process of Korea's act of creative mimicry, or as I call it, "hegemonic mimicry," is the recognition of Korean reclamation of both the proto- and post-minjok identity that has rendered opaque its national identity, for its very survival, and which has shadowed many of the Korean performances, experiences, and cultural utterances of the modern age. This book considers race, along with national identity, as one of the most important, if not the most significant, criteria through which the K-pop and other Korean culture waves of the twenty-first century have enacted a cultural renaissance.

Though the era of colonial rule more or less came to a halt with the conclusion of World War II, the cultural Koreanness that was developed in the latter part of the twentieth century and has attained a recognizable global awareness in the twenty-first century is one case that exemplifies an idea that Stuart Hall insisted on when he stated that the "notion of a national formation, of a national economy, that could be represented through a national-cultural identity is under considerable pressure."[29] Hall was then discussing the untenable nature of national-cultural identity formation for the UK and the decline of unitary British culture throughout the early part of the twentieth century. But this untenable trend has become more or less true also for Americanness, which replaced Britishness during the latter part of the twentieth century. Also valued is Hall's emphasis on the "de-centering of national-cultural identity," for this modern Koreanness is linked to an experience of opposition: colonial subjection and not subscription to major language blocs divided into English, Spanish, French, Chinese, and so forth that now signify the structure of world culture today.[30] The increased significance of the new "becoming-Korean" identity is less unitary and more transnational, and is the cultural consequence of the accelerated pace of expansion of American cultural imperialism of the twentieth century.

Koreans have nourished a system of popular culture that has rendered its own ethnic and nationalist flavors opaque in order for its survival in the face of global competition against American cultural content and media industries. So the ambitions of cultural power for the Koreans settle for a milder and tamer version of Koreanness that is as deeply fried as its own recipe of "yangnyeom chicken" that was once imported from the United States soon after the Korean War but, since then, has made great strides as a foreign-adopted Korean cultural product to achieve a flavor all its own. If just one short decade of severe cultural and ethnic eradication in the form of *naisen ittai* (squashing of the two national bodies, Japan and Korea, into one), ushered in during the Japanese colonial era between 1937 and 1945, produced an entire generation of Koreans who were later forced to relearn their own language and reacquire their own ethnic pride, by contrast the hallyu identity cultivated during the American military occupation, although making the ethnic identity of Koreans opaque, also clearly celebrated Korean as a unique language, thereby leading to the rise of global stars who were not necessarily fluent or even semi-fluent in English. Most BTS members, with the exception of RM, still refuse to speak any English on American television shows, and filmmaker Bong Joon-ho will not publicly appear on stage without the aid of a translator. Even after generations of close military, economic, and cultural alliance with the United States, can Koreans, who still insist on speaking a minor language that most Americans do not register as a distant cousin of English, such as Spanish or French, attain more than the status of "honorary" American partner? Can Koreans achieve the status of a "true" American friend with crossover sensibilities that diversify the very meaning of America or, in Korean terms, a miguk, a "beautiful country" that stretches even beyond the neoliberal idea of multiethnic diversity and a parochial sense of American exceptionalism?

After 1945, South Korea was politically and economically already well placed within the column of Pax Americana, but culturally a Korean had to chart a path forward between "two warring ideals"—the clash of these ideals being not between the Korean and the foreign but between one occupying foreign imperial power and another. Japanese music, language, and fashion had totally overwhelmed those of Korea during the era of naisen ittai (1937–45), and, despite the violence and the resentment that Koreans suffered during the Japanese colonial period, because of the proximity of race, geography, and shared cultural heritage between the two nations, Japanese-style songs and culture did not immediately vanish after 1945.[31] Furthermore, some historians argue that Japanese-style songs called *enka* are rooted in Korean folk tradition, which may further complicate the use of the term *Japanese-style*.[32] Ethnomusicologist Dohee Kwon writes that television and radio stations in South Korea often had to face a choice between American-style Korean pop music (AKPM) and Japanese-colored songs (JCS, which were composed in the Western-Japanese pentatonic scale), which had the fourth (Fa) and seventh (Ti) notes of the octave scale (Do-Re-Mi-Fa-Sol-Ra-Ti-Do) missing.[33] By the 1980s, the JCS-inspired trot ballad songs had declined rapidly against the increasing popularity of AKPM songs. The most dominant band of the 1980s, Tŭlgukhwa, for example, was heavily inspired by American rock bands such as the Eagles and Styx, and the popular songs they performed for the past four decades did not pay any homage to the trot ballads that were cousins to the JCS. Cho Yong-pil, who has remained a bona fide superstar in Korea for the past several decades and is better known as an American-style rock star, started his career as a trot ballad singer. As will be discussed in chapter 1, the hallyu idol at the turn of the millennium was incubated after Korean entertainment management company heads were inspired by J-pop idols; however, K-pop has developed a genre and style that is decisively AKPM. The thudding sounds of drums and low bass lines—accompanied by powerful dance choreography—distinguish K-pop from other music genres that are popular among young teens. Influenced in part by the Swedish songwriting phenom Max Martin, who produced for the Backstreet Boys and Britney Spears simple melody-driven hit songs laid over exaggerated bass instrumentation and drum tracks, some of the top songs of K-pop, such as BTS's recent "Icon" and EXO's "Growl," feature an addictive balladic chorus soaring over the distinguished bass lines and hard-hitting drum tracks. Though trot beats and melodies still resonate deep in the soul of most Koreans today, as sensationally popular audition programs *Mister Trot* and *Miss Trot* aired in 2020–21 on *TV Chosun* have proven, K-pop has effectively erased the specter of JCS-inspired trot music from its repertoire.

The tension between JCS and AKPM resulted in perhaps the biggest cultural battle during the second half of the twentieth century in Korea—without either of the two being the decisive winner for several decades. The Godfather of Korean rock, Shin Joong-hyun, wrote not only rock tracks but also ballads inspired by both AKPM and JCS influences, respectively blues and trot, such as a 1970 song, "Nim ŭn mon kot e" (Love so far away), crooned by female diva Kim Ch'u-ja. Sung in the key of E minor, "Nim" is quite possibly the most beloved song composed during the post–Korean War era.[34] Just like many of his other songs, such as "Mi-in," "Nim" is composed in a pentatonic scale, which has brought the charge that it falls neatly into the trot style. The song was revived again in 2014 in a music audition program called *Trot X*. However, the minor pentatonic scale alone does not a Japanese-style song make.[35] Many popular guitar riffs and solos, including Led Zeppelin's "Black Dog" and "Stairway to Heaven," rely on guitar play that derives from the same minor pentatonic scale, and yet hardly an ounce of what Koichi Iwabuchi has called "a cultural odor" can be sniffed on these classic hard-rock songs that would carry a fragrance of "Japan."[36] They rely on a minor pentatonic scale because Led Zeppelin and many rock bands during the 1970s were influenced by blues melodies that veer away from the octave scale.[37] Well-known rock 'n' roll ballads composed during the 1970s, including "Another Brick in the Wall (Part 2)" by Pink Floyd, used this scale, simply because it was then fashionable for white American and British rock bands to appropriate the minor pentatonic blues scale from African American music of the South. Since both enka and blues are built on a minor pentatonic scale, as is much of folk music from various traditions, one could argue that the fact that "Nim" is sung in an E-minor pentatonic scale does not define its sound as distinctively Korean, as opposed to distinctively Western or, more specifically, American. But still the question remains, which between the two constitutes a larger influence on the song "Nim"? Is it the Japanese, and therefore East Asian, enka icon Hibari Misora, or the African American blues icon Etta James singing "Swing Low, Sweet Chariot"? The truth is probably somewhere in the middle. Shin Joong-hyun was influenced by both classic Korean trot structures and African American blues melodies when he composed the song; in fact, "Nim" could be sung in the style of either Hibari Misora or

Etta James. There are many versions of the song available—in blues, trot, or even disco and rap.[38]

The battle between JCS and AKPM tilted heavily in favor of the latter as the sho-dan performers started to produce, compose, and sing for these Korean consumers who were increasingly embracing American trends and fads. Throughout the latter part of the twentieth century, blackness in South Korea was both a taboo subject and a cultural fascination. The Korean War was the first war engaged in that officially ended racial segregation within the US military, which resulted in the higher visibility of African American soldiers. During the Korean War, the all-black infantry that were in existence in the US military since 1869 were disbanded, officially ending the era of segregation in the US Army.[39] Six hundred thousand African Americans served in the Armed Forces during the Korean War, and millions more since have served their duty in Korea after the armistice was signed in 1953. Black soldiers have consistently represented a higher share of active-duty military personnel over the past several decades than their share of the US population.[40] Though it was illegal for the US military to racially identify their personnel in the 1950s and 1960s, black soldiers continued to occupy a central place in the popular imagination of Koreans who perceived black soldiers as a visible and integral part of the US military. Much of the popular fiction that depicts the Korean War, ranging from Ahn Junghyo's novel *Silver Stallion* (1990) to the more recent film *Swing Kids* (dir. Kang Hyong-chul, 2018), centrally foreground black military personnel in the US Army.[41] While the postwar Korean literary canon does not feature a writer such as Ōe Kenzaburo, who sought alliances between "Negro American Literature and Modern Japanese Literature" by creating, in the words of William H. Bridges IV, "an analogical link between his own works and black literature," the impact of "blackness" on Korean popular culture is profound and unerasable.[42] In a recent interview, Han Myung-sook, one of the most famous singers of her day and still known today for her megahit song "Noran shassŭ ŭi sanai" (The man with a yellow shirt) from 1961, was one of the performers who learned her trade while singing for the US military sho-dan. She was so popular among the American troops that she led several tours of her own in Vietnam during the 1960s and performed for the US troops there. Han recalls, "Every time an audition was held, we had to pull an all-nighter. New songs were sung, especially in black pronunciation, so it was even more difficult. But we still try to copy it . . . copy it all the way. . . . We could never leave behind a tape recorder. We would always carry it with us. Because if a new hit song came out, we had to study it on the spot."[43] The act of mimicry that singer Han Myung-sook is recollecting here is a specific kind of cultural appropriation located among the full variety of Americanness. It was the black variety of Americanness that needed to be copied by the Korean in order to survive as an entertainer during postwar poverty-ridden Korea.

As testified in numerous interviews given by Korean entertainers of the 1960s and 1970s, the essence or act of putting on Americanness was, in other words, authenticated by Asian, specifically Korean, musicians and artists by emulating and reproducing black voices, black bodily movements, and black styles.[44] If English colonialism in India, to borrow the words of Bhabha, was a tongue "that is forked, not false," the experience of American neocolonialism in Korea over the past seventy-five years was steeped in a tongue that occupied a territory definitively beyond simple dichotomies of black and white, somewhere between off-white and blackish.[45] This is true despite the fact that Koreans as subjects occupied by a dominant global-political power often constituted a position that fell lower than that of either black or white American, as reflected in both novels and films of the time. The Korean ethnic identity that was born out of a post-1945, neo-colonial experience with the United States was different from that of the postcolonial identity defined by Bhabha and Hall, whose scholarship was shaped by the English colonial experience in India and in Jamaica within the span of their or their parents' generation's lifetimes. The style of Bol-lywood filmmaking that began in postwar, postindependence India also reshaped global music, fashion, and food, and continues to impact con-temporary global culture today, while the reggae and Rastafarian fads from Jamaica that took the world by storm in the 1970s have sustained their popularity and global influence well into the twenty-first century. How-ever, these cultural phenomena initially served largely the Anglophone and global ethnic populations that motivated fandom across regions that shared common cultural heritage. Bollywood, for example, continues to enjoy popularity almost exclusively among English-speaking or Hindi and Hindustani-diasporic regions. The unique and ironic characteristic of Korean popular culture is that its cultural essence has been carved out by Korean, a minor language spoken by only seventy-five million people among a global population of seven and a half billion. This number makes Korean a minor language but certainly unique if one considers the fact that it is a language that stepped onto the global stage with its use among almost exclusively one single ethnic identity. This opaque, and yet linguis-tically unique, raciality that Koreans and Korean cultural production have staked helps establish an ambivalent cultural hegemony in other countries that do not feel as threatened by this Koreanness as by American cultural domination.

We must remember that merely a few decades earlier, cultural content made by and featuring Koreans was barely known outside Korea. In reality, this content was barely known *inside* Korea. The biggest hit films, hit dramas, and most conspicuous songs blaring in the streets and cafés of Seoul were products that bore stamps of the foreign. No nationalist campaigns, no foreign film quotas, and not even outright cultural bans against particular countries could help relieve the perception of Korean cultural content as poor entertainment consumerist products. Just about the only popular cultural products made in Korea that were popular among Koreans before the turn of the millennium were television dramas broadcast in the evening hours that catered largely to female audiences and ballad songs called *kayo* that sentimentally appealed to audiences of various age groups. Before the unique and unified linguistic system of *hangul* helped relaunch K-pop and other Korean cultural content in the twenty-first century, far more popular than the local variety in the Korean soil was the music by American and British rock groups. From the mid-1970s to the mid-1980s, the Korean music industry went into a deep recession. The biggest reason was, of course, the political censorship of the time that targeted popular culture in Korea, resulting in the blacklisting, imprisonment, or exile of many great musicians. But there were other reasons as well. Kim Young, the record company head executive who led the renaissance of Korean kayo throughout the late 1980s representing Korean blues singers Kim Hyun-sik and Kim Hyun-cheol alongside rock bands like Tŭlgukhwa, states, "At the time [from 1978 to 1982, when Kim Young was running a small record store], Western classical and pop constituted about 80 or 90 percent of total sales of LPs. Who would buy kayo those days? . . . In my store, I would play music all day long. Beatles, Bee Gees, and Simon and Garfunkel, and then I would play a Korean album . . . and it was embarrassing. Professional engineering was absent in Korean albums at the time. . . . Arrangement, production, and recording technology had to all change, and be updated."[46] South Korea's failure to technologically keep up with the recording and cinema industry of the rest of the advanced world could not satisfy the consumers who were beginning to have more choices as Korea was opening its cultural sector market to the West.

Throughout the 1980s and 1990s, Korean cinema also similarly slumped and could not recapture the glory days of the 1960s. Theaters were old, subject matters anachronistic, and the production value of films not up-to-date with the standards set by Hollywood. An average Korean during the 1990s only chose to watch one film per year (compared to more than four films annually now), and chances are he or she would choose to watch a Hollywood film rather than a local one.[47] As I have written elsewhere, against the firepower of Hollywood stars such as Arnold Schwarzenegger and Sylvester Stallone, Korean cinema could throw only naked bodies of women and erotic images to compete for just a sliver of domestic market share.[48] While Hollywood blockbusters dominated the local box offices, it was also foreign films featuring Kevin Costner and Sharon Stone and tele-vision drama and action series such as *The Incredible Hulk* and *MacGyver* that constituted the talk of the town as popular entertainment's center-piece. So popular were Hollywood series and films on television that Ko-rean voice actors cast to provide the voices of Hollywood stars such as Al Pacino and Sharon Stone were even busier than the local Korean stars.[49] Even for the toddler and youth audiences, Japanese animations such as *Doraemon, Candy, Sailor Moon,* and *Dragon Ball,* dubbed in Korean voices, filled the airtime on daytime television.[50]

So what happened? Well, leaving out miguk-ification from the equation for now, in two words, the internet. South Korea was one of the earliest adopters of internet technology. In Korea, cell phones, personal computers, and high-speed internet technology caught on very quickly — penetrating the majority of personal homes as early as the 1990s. If the military dicta-torship from the 1960s to the 1990s achieved one thing in Korea, it was the protection of the *chaebol* industrial conglomerates to become competitive in the global marketplace. Electronic companies in particular grew very fast in Korea. Many electronic companies, such as SKC, Samsung, and LG, rose to international power through their manufacturing efficiency and innova-tions in digital technology, and the smartphone market in South Korea proved fertile testing grounds.[51] Korea Telecommunication (KT) was one of the first companies in the world that allowed smartphones to leap beyond the hoops of 3G, LTE, and now 5G networks and equally fast-paced cable in-ternet speeds. This paralleled the upward swing of Korea's youth to become power players in online games, peer-to-peer technology-based streaming video channels, and K-pop music content distribution. Both the dazzling speed through which Koreans could type because of the unique alpha-bet system of hangul that allows for faster typing speeds and the Korean telecommunication companies that drive each other to compete for higher internet and mobile data network speeds allowed early online forums for young fans of K-pop and K-cinema to meet, socialize, and trade informa-tion at a clip faster than that of any other place in the world.[52] While enter-tainment industries in the rest of the world remained wary about possible copyright infringement and the illegal downloads that would result from actively posting official music videos of their artists online, when YouTube caught fire in the early years of the twenty-first century, K-pop manage-ment companies saw its potential as a partner for the future and began posting their content on the video-sharing website to create an immediate connection with their fans overseas.[53] Needless to say, this bold move paid off, as YouTube became as sensational and viral as K-pop over the past decade and a half. It is extremely difficult to imagine the global K-pop sensations of the 2010s — "Gangnam Style" in the early part of the decade and BTS, the boy idol group from Korea, in the latter part of the decade — without the aid of YouTube and other social media platforms to galvanize fans around the world.

It is tempting to say that the internet was the sole factor that changed the game for Korean pop culture and leave it at that. But, as the term *K-pop* has become ubiquitous and has boasted perhaps the most recognizable icons around the world over the past two decades, Korea's early adoption of "internet" culture and its quick embrace to spread K-pop content cannot alone explain the reasons behind K-pop's success. Korean popular culture did indeed suffer during the era of the military dictatorship, and the Ko-rean hallyu wave did benefit from the South Korean government's policy to promote cultural content initiated by the more liberal presidents that followed the long period of military dictatorship. But again, that alone does not suffice to explain the global success of K-pop or other Korean cultural content. Neither can South Korea's economic rise as one of the most sig-nificant financial global powers over the past half century offer on its own an adequate explanation for the rapid global success of Korean cultural content. If economic indexes were to serve as the most important criteria through which popular cultural values are set, then the United Arab Emir-ates and Norway, which boast two of the highest per capita GDPs in the world, should occupy a level of global dominance for their respective cul-tural content far beyond the level that these countries currently do. While all these factors — Korea's utilization of the internet as a tool to spread its cultural content, the government's active engagement to promote cultural content through its subsidy programs, and South Korea's meteoric rise to the top of the world's leading economies in the twentieth century — played a role in creating one of the most dynamic cultural industries in the world today, one crucial reason has remained unprobed in most discussions held on K-pop studies.

Over the past three-quarters of a century, Koreans have learned to gain attention in global popular culture by redubbing American hegemonic music, visual culture, and drama through a process of revaluing, reauthenticating, and, perhaps most importantly, reidentifying their ethnic subjects, aesthetics, and content. As well publicized through the compulsory visits to the demilitarized zone (DMZ) by almost every sitting US president since Dwight D. Eisenhower (John F. Kennedy and Richard Nixon, the only two presidents of the postwar years who were unable to complete their presidential terms, are notable exceptions), the American military presence in South Korea has remained strong ever since Korea was liberated from Japan in 1945. The military presence the United States has maintained in the peninsula not only influenced the politics and economics of South Korea that provided America its bulwark against Communism; it has also had a profound impact on South Korean culture. Shin Joong-hyun, the aforementioned guitarist-composer, after being inspired by black soul music and psychedelic rock in the 1960s, learned his trade growing up near the American military base.

> During the 1960s, the influence of the US 8th Army [stationed in Korea] was absolutely strong. I thought that they were not here to fight any war, but here to fight a war to defend their culture. If we were to go to war, I can't imagine that there would be any place for music. But for the Americans, it was different, it felt as if they were here [in Korea] to listen to their music. After their training hours, they would without fail come to one of the clubs to listen to music. Every base had at least three clubs — one for the officers, one for the sergeants, and one for the soldiers.[54]

Among soldiers, as had been mentioned previously, clubs were also segregated along color lines.

During the first several decades of the postwar years, the foreign cool that swept South Korea originated from the United States but also elsewhere. Alain Delon, for instance, a French film star who was little known in the United States, became a household name in Korea because his films were popular in the major cities, and stories about his personal life became magazine headlines. *Plein Soleil* (*T'aeyang kadŭkhi*, dir. Rene Clemont, 1960) was one of his most sensationally successful films in Korea, and the phrase *handsome like Alain Delon* became viral in Korea several decades before messenger apps were in vogue. Very few Koreans spoke French during the 1960s, and the war-ravaged country had no colonial vestige owed to the French, but one of the reasons attributed to the success of these European films in Korea, and other popular cultural items such as the *chansons* of Yves Montand like "Les Feuilles Mortes," was their popularity in Japan. Despite having very little to no direct exchange between Korea and France, Koreans accessed these European cultural fads by looking to Japan to satiate their intellectual hunger.[55] European stardom and pop icons, in other words, first spread to Japan before making their way to Korea through book vendors, publishing company heads, and cultural connoisseurs who still subscribed to large volumes of Japanese books, magazines, and other cultural merchandise.

The global cultural flow, before the advent of social media, had a major transit stop between Europe and Korea, and that was Tokyo, the former metropole for Koreans during the Japanese colonial period. Much of the popularity in Korea of European movie stars, songs, and even high-brow literary books by Franz Kafka, Jean-Paul Sartre, and Friedrich Nietzsche was owed to their popularity in Japan. Most films, magazine articles on European trends, and even literature were translated by Korean publishers and film distributors not from their original French or English but from existing Japanese subtitles or translations. In other words, even twenty or thirty years after Korea's liberation from Japan, and despite the ban on almost all cultural products of Japan, with the sole exception of Japanese television animation, Korea was in many ways reliant on this preexisting colonial flow of information, scholarship, and popular culture. Most Koreans working in the literary and cultural establishments during the 1960s and 1970s were fluent in Japanese, for they had attended school during the colonial era, when Korean schools prioritized learning Japanese for several decades.[56] Like the black Martinican in Frantz Fanon's *Black Skin, White Masks* who returns home from Paris, where he "can no longer understand Creole; he talks of the Opera House, which he has probably seen only from a distance," a member of the postcolonial cultural elite in Korea only wanted to talk in his "master's language," but his Japanese, unlike French, English, or Spanish, became not only frowned upon but downright forbidden, even at home.[57] Fanon writes, "When I meet a German or a Russian speaking bad French I try to indicate through gestures the information he is asking for, but in doing so I am careful not to forget that he has a language of his own, a country, and that perhaps he is a lawyer or an engineer back home."[58] Unfortunately for South Koreans, it's probably not an exaggeration to say that it would have been almost impossible to find an American officer working in Korea around the time when Fanon was writing this first book, in the 1950s, who shared similar sympathies that Fanon had toward the German with poor French-speaking skills. A Korean with poor English-speaking skills simply had no value for an American—no matter his profession or his mastery in other languages.

The linguistic conundrum that Korean elites entered during the postliberation era was far more complex than the one that Fanon or other postcolonial intellectuals found with their own humiliating experiences involving the mastery of a European language. Unlike the experience of Fanon, who spoke and wrote French better than the French themselves and found Paris, for better or for worse, his home away from home, where he could publish and help other anticolonial efforts after World War II in other Francophone countries such as Algeria, for Koreans the value of Japanese, the former colonial master's language, simply collapsed after 1945. For a Korean intellectual, the linguistic and cultural continuity between the new metropole (Washington, DC) and the old one (Tokyo) was simply nonexistent. As such, the cultural bridge between the new metropole (Washington, DC) and the occupied capital (Seoul) had to be built from scratch, while the one between the old metropole (Tokyo) and Seoul only existed in old records and photographs that were literally locked up in family chests.[59] The old metropole, now also occupied by the Americans, was a new land of exile, humiliation, and, perhaps most importantly, forced amnesia for Koreans.[60] Koreans had to overcome symptoms of aphasia in a triplicate of languages—the present native language of Korean, which was suppressed in formal education and had to be brought back from oblivion in 1945 with the end of Japanese rule; the old colonial language of Japanese, which became obsolete with the defeat of Imperial Japan in 1945; and the new colonial language of English, which was heavily censored during the latter part of the Japanese colonial era, for it was the language of the "enemy" and had to be completely suppressed, and therefore learned from scratch by Koreans under their new, American miltary occupiers. Pyongyang emerged as an intriguing socialist alternative but quickly became unattractive because of the spread of Stalinist terror and the violent war that permanently split Korea. Korea's purchase of European fads during the first two decades after the Korean War was not firsthand but one that was akin to a clandestine consignment store shopping stint in the dilapidated and haunted house of old colonial glory.

By the time the 1990s came around, with the American Forces Korea Network (AFKN) generation now coming of age, a cultural shift of seismic proportion had placed Korea totally within an American sphere of influence.[61] The dominance of secondhand cultural purchase in which Japan was the conspicuous gateway to cultural imports by what Iwabuchi calls "cultural odor" or what Jinsoo An refers to as "Japanese color" (*waesaek* in Korean) waned by the 1980s and came to a close ironically when the ban on cultural goods from Japan was lifted in the late 1990s.[62] All the major figures of the Korean entertainment industry of the first two decades of the twenty-first century—including Bong Joon-ho and Park Chan-wook, star directors in Korean cinema; as well as Yang Hyun-seok and Bang Si-hyok, two corporate heads of K-pop management companies (YG and the Big Hit); Lee Woo-jeong, head writer of top variety shows such as *Grandpa over Flowers* and the *Reply* (*Ŭngtaphara*) drama series; and Na Young-seok, the producer-director of these hit television programs—are from a generation that spoke little to no Japanese and instead grew up as AFKN-generation kids in the 1970s and 1980s, when South Korea could receive images and sounds from America on television and radio.[63] Though they also witnessed the anti-American sentiments that swept the college campuses during the 1980s and 1990s when South Korea went through intense democratization, the act of cultural mimicry that shadowed the Korean peninsula during this pre-hallyu period was one that ironically had to embrace a cultural consent to American culture—for the concept of America, especially the black and ethnic postwar entertainment flowing from it, was fun and diverting. America was inculcated and disseminated to many Korean youth of the time as not only a manifestation of cultural-political exploitation and coercion but one that earned the unintended consent of locals when the American television stations intended to entertain only the US troops stationed in Korea ended up affecting a far larger number of local people than ever imagined, simply because AFKN content was free and much more enjoyable than the local Korean broadcast channels that were heavily censored throughout the 1970s and 1980s.[64]

The American influence in South Korea was not restricted to just one part of the country. Unlike Germany or Japan, where US military forces were mostly concentrated in either Frankfurt or Okinawa during the post–World War II occupation, South Korea, partly because of its small size and mountainous geography and partly because of the heavy casualties suffered in the all-out war during the early 1950s, had American military bases established throughout the entire southern half of the peninsula. The central military headquarters was located in a 620-acre garrison in Yongsan—a district in central Seoul—while a handful more were in operation in almost every corner of South Korea. Operating a colossal-sized military base in the middle of Seoul, South Korea's capital and one of the most significant cosmopolitan cities of the past several decades, was rather unprecedented even for the American military. Yongsan and its neighboring district of Itae-won offered a visual testimony to the almost unscripted consequences of American cultural hegemony. Itaewon, which was originally known as a land of foreigners even as early as the Chosun Era (Yi-t'a-in 異他人, "people of the foreign land," after some of the Manchus and their bi-ethnic descendants had settled there in the seventeenth century and were eventually given the title "Yi-t'ae-won," which means "pavilion of the foreign land"), became rather infamous for its red-light district dubbed Hooker Hill since the relocation of the headquarters of the US Eighth Army in Yongsan in 1953, and for its clubs that offered opportunities for Koreans to mingle with Americans.[65] South Korean musicians of several postwar generations learned their trade through their consumption of radio and television and their interactions with American military personnel who needed to be entertained through live music performances. While the American television and radio stations in Germany and Japan were available to only a small segment of the local population concentrated in Frankfurt, Stuttgart, and Okinawa during a similar time frame, the AFKN was ubiquitous in South Korea because it broadcast signals from eight stations (Seoul, Hwaaksan, Paju, Gunsan, Busan, Daegu, Daejeon, and Gwangju) using the all-access VHF signal for four critical decades (from 1957 to 1996).[66] Until 1996, almost all Koreans with long-range TV antennae could easily access AFKN, a phenomenon that rendered it an inadvertent yet significant influencer of Korean modern culture. Even before the days of the internet, by tuning into this American channel, Koreans could advance their English learning, watch live American sports broadcasts such as the NFL and NBA that were not aired on Korean television, and even watch Hollywood films that were banned in Korea. Many Korean children, including myself, learned the alphabet and the English count of "one, two, three" through the *Electric Company* broadcast on the AFKN channel. The network circumvented the Korean censors, and rumors floated around that sexually explicit scenes were screened on AFKN during the wee hours of the night at a time when no scenes of nudity were permitted even in Korean movie theaters.[67]

This reauthentication and redialing of American culture were simultaneously unintended and yet intended for Koreans, since local Korean-language newspapers posted the daily TV guide for the AFKN right next to the listings for Korean-language channels. The American military presence in Korea chipped away at Korean political sovereignty but also helped retool the Korean cultural identity in preparation for the new challenges of the twenty-first century. The competitive audition system that the US military maintained throughout the 1950s and 1960s for the locals undoubtedly helped Koreans reinvent their music, culture, and identity throughout those decades in ways beyond simply aligning them with that of the Americans. The same club district in Itaewon that had local women prostitute for the American GIs also served as the incubation lab for K-pop where local b-boys learned how to dance to black music throughout the latter part of the century. All these ironic expressions of American cultural hegemony would help cultivate a substantial local innovation platform for Koreans during the twentieth century, which then helped Koreans launch a reverberated holler back to global audiences over the past two decades, including even American audiences. This ambivalent form of American hegemonic culture that loops through the act of Korean mimicry is what I propose as the core idea behind the concept of hegemonic mimicry.

Much of the previous work on K-pop studies has focused on the national production of K-pop, critically analyzing governmental involvement and branding it as "made in Korea." As a matter of fact, a recently published book on the subject of Korean popular music is titled *Made in Korea*.[68] In his book *K-Pop*, John Lie states, "From tax breaks to outright subsidies, the governmental policy of soft-power promotion would serve to propel the Korean Wave around the world. By 2013, the government's budget for promoting the popular-music industry was reportedly $300 million, roughly the same amount as total turnover in the industry a decade earlier."[69] It is difficult to get an exact figure on how much government spending is used to promote the popular music industry, but the Ministry of Culture, Sports, and Tourism quotes a budget in 2019 of roughly US$5.5 billion.[70] Of course, not all of this money subsidizes K-pop; much of this budget is earmarked to support national museums, arts and sports schools and academies, and promotion in tourism and national sports teams. However, through its subsidiaries, the Korea Creative Content Agency and the Korean Cultural Centers scattered around the world, along with local training programs, the Korean government's funds and initiatives to support and expand K-pop and other cultural content such as K-dramas, games, and even food overseas quite possibly constitute much more than a subsidy package that easily can be projected to be about US$1 billion per year. The Korean government has actively engaged in promotions of Korean cultural products overseas because it has calculated that for every $100 in cultural goods exported, it can generate a $412 increase in exports of other consumer goods, including food, clothes, cosmetics, and manufacturing products such as smartphones.[71] In other words, in the era of transnational capitalism, K-pop and other cultural content *made in Korea* cannot help but continue its association embedded in a form of ethnic identity despite their effective way of crossing borders as an export product that erases its national origins, just as Hyundai Motor's best-selling SUV model, the Santa Fe, is known to many people globally as a mugukjŏk brand in isolation from Korea, the company's nation of origin. Many consumers across the globe are clueless about the national origins of the apparel and cosmetics brands they consume, such as Zara, Uniqlo, or Estée Lauder, but it is unlikely that BTS, or any other boy or girl idol group from Korea, can be cleansed of its national origin, for music and other cultural production, no matter how commercialized and Westernized, must be rooted in the linguistic, aesthetic, and ethnic background of the performers and artists. However disposable each and every new K-pop act that emerges every two- or three-year-cycle, there is a soul embedded in every cultural product "made in Korea," even when it is appropriated from another nation, one that makes it distinct from, for example, the Samsung electronics goods that are also "made in Korea."

BEHIND THE HEGEMONIC MIMICRY

My use of the term *hegemonic mimicry* already acknowledges that the Korean popular culture that blossomed during the twenty-first century was incubated from a contested field of negotiation between two national identities—the hegemonic American culture and the local culture—and between, as discussed earlier, two racialized subjectivities, off-white and blackish. I argue that Korea continues to straddle what W. E. B. Du Bois terms *double consciousness*. Du Bois, one of the pioneering figures of African American studies, described the condition of black citizens in the United States in the earlier part of the century as "two-ness, an American, a Negro; two souls, two thoughts, two unreconciled strivings; two warring ideals in one dark body, whose dogged strength alone keeps it from being torn asunder."[72] Any Korean raised during the twentieth century probably knows what it would feel like being *torn asunder* between the two warring ideals in one body. The first half of the century was split between a Korean national identity and a Japanese one, replaced in the latter half by a split between a Korean identity and an American one. One could even argue that it wasn't just the double consciousness with which Koreans were attempting to reconcile but a triple consciousness, as the vestiges of Japanese consciousness did not recede completely into oblivion the moment Japan was defeated and retreated back to its archipelago in 1945. Also, the America that Korea experienced during the postwar years was not only a white America but a mottled one that was very much both white and black. Many Koreans were exposed to Americans in the military, in business, and in everyday life, and in so doing, they encountered two types of Americans as defined by American racial subjectivities—one white and the other black.

This book focuses on blackness and hip-hop alongside black humor and Korean comedy because hip-hop in Korea was perhaps the first Western music genre that paid little to no tribute to the vestiges of culture from the Japanese colonial era.[73] In Korea, hip-hop is a music genre that was introduced through a direct link with Korean hip-hop artists' interactions with the US cultural influence. Rapper Seo Taiji's "Nan Arayo" (1992) and his subsequent hit "Hayeoga" (1993) are regarded as two of the most significant songs in the history of Korean pop, not because they successfully erased any trace of enka-style emotional root that formed the backbone of Korean music aesthetics throughout the twentieth century but because they were made in direct cultural exchange with American rap. Korea was arguably the first non-US nation that came into regular contact with American rap, because many of the African American soldiers stationed in Korea wanted to listen to, dance to, and even perform this innovative music genre in clubs, particularly in Itaewon, as early as the 1980s. Many of the pioneering Korean rappers, including Yang Hyun-seok, were frequent visitors to this American hip-hop scene set in Itaewon. Also, Korean American rappers, such as Tiger JK, Yoon Mi-rae, and Epik High's Tablo, all returned from the United States to dominate the Korean rap scene during the new millennium after spending their youth in the United States exploring the relationships between Korean and English rhymes (figure I.1). These artists were the first to reconceptualize the meaning of hip-hop in the Korean sense, a move that allowed for the maturity of the Korean hip-hop music genre in the 2010s through both K-pop idol and independent solo artists.

Chapter 1 historicizes the emergence of hallyu, detailing how Korea, in the postcolonial and postwar years, broke with a historical narrative centered on the US military occupation and Korea's place as a piece of bulwark in the Cold War confrontation. With the recent thawing of relations between the United States and the Democratic People's Republic

I.1 Tiger JK (*right*) and Yoon Mi-rae during a concert, 2019. Photo by Kyung Hyun Kim.

of Korea (DPRK), this chapter explores how music, television programs, and films channeled South Koreans' fears and anxieties into a pleasurable and fluid cultural production throughout the latter part of the twentieth century and also prepared for the peace process of the Korean peninsula in the first two decades of the twenty-first century. The translation of music, for instance, that culminated into hallyu—an aesthetic form that both conforms to national boundaries while also resisting them—is this chapter's main consideration. The chapter also lays down the theoretical foundation of this book and engages in the discussion of how the act of mimicry passed from an initial colonial simulation of the dominant colonizer to an ambivalent and ironic one before assuming a hegemonic, and even a subempiric, form.

Chapter 2 analyzes the history and aesthetics of rap music in Korea from an ethnic studies perspective. If Koreans excelled in the "hegemonic mimicry" of the dominant American culture by equating it with whiteness projected in many of the girl and boy K-pop idol groups, how does the prominent placement of hip-hop in K-pop reformulate and complicate the question of race? With the rise of American hegemony in South Korea over the past seventy-five years, the centrality of blackness also becomes pronounced in the discourse of hallyu. One of the key questions I address in my book is about race and authenticity. Korean hip-hop artists—many of whom barely speak English—are forced to grapple with, for instance, this issue when their music is brushed back by illegitimacy because it does not actively engage with authentic claims of the ghetto and the street vernacular of African American English through which rap was born. What I am interested in examining further is how this particular accentuation of "blackness" complicates the binary through which the most dominant paradigm of national boundaries (US/Korea) or racial boundaries (whites/Asians) is drawn. Beyond the question "Can Koreans rap?" are the critical interventions in African American studies such as Du Bois's theory on race and culture, and recent hip-hop studies. This is all to perhaps creolize the hierarchies, the binary structures of sustained colonial forces, and the racialized hegemony that remain within the discourse of K-pop or hallyu.

Chapter 3 explores how digital-age surveillance, particularly pronounced in South Korea, has impacted the ways in which narratives, both film and television, are made. If the New Korean Cinema led by Lee Chang-dong and Bong Joon-ho had thematized temporality, the present age of data-ism—with its infinite capabilities of digitization and powerful algorithms—has enabled Korean cinema and television dramas to generate narratives that are no longer bound by specific metaphors and allegories. This chapter examines popular body-switch films such as *Masquerade* (*Gwanghae*, 2012) and *Miss Granny* (*Susanghan kŭ nyŏ*, 2014), and argues that Korea's entry into the overwired era has allowed these body-switch films to dominate on screen. This chapter also focuses on how Korea has successfully localized European "hero" models such as *Ivanhoe* and American Hollywood body-switch stories that have been delineated from the plotline of Mark Twain's "The Prince and the Pauper."

Chapter 4 asks why and how a Korean variety game show such as *Running Man* has achieved a smashing global success on the internet. It explores how the game show's "transmedia storytelling" taps into passing around a global kind of "affect." This chapter also explores how the on-screen captions, which are pervasive in Korean television, promote a sense of non-phonocentrism, which counters the primacy of phonocentrism that Jacques Derrida had once identified as the root of the problem behind Western ethnocentrism and Saussurian formalism in order to help realize what I call "affect Confucianism." The Chinese remakes of *Running Man* allow this chapter to foray into the transnational exchange of remakes between China and Korea. By comparing this East Asian cultural exchange to that of France and the United States, where French critics and filmmakers, as early as the days of André Bazin, condemned Hollywood's practice of the remake as a debasement of the French "original" and a form of vulgar American commercialism, it problematizes some of the charges made in China against "kimchi imperialism."

Chapter 5 deals with two very recent films about food—one perhaps well known only in Korea (*Extreme Job*) and the other well known world-wide (*Parasite*). At first glance, these two films seem worlds apart, and yet they share their commonalities in food. In both films, the predictable melodramatic codes usually reserved for blockbuster films are switched out for comedic conventions of wordplay, con-artist schemes, and food drama. These themes not only problematize the division between real and fake and a larger subject of the tension between haves and have-nots but also allow us to look at how food has lost its social or even cultural significance and has instead assumed a perverse, negative, and almost undesirable association with gluttony and psychological depression in the era of *mukbang* (*mŏkbang*; eatcast). Both *Extreme Job* and *Parasite* explore the theme of vicarious eating in South Korea. In the former film, a fried-chicken joint is used as a cover for the narcotics police squad whose mission to bust a drug lord turns sour when they find unexpected success in the rotisserie chicken business; in *Parasite*, writer-director Bong Joon-ho pays close attention to the preparation and serving of food, sickness and hysteria around fruit allergies, and the secret door in the kitchen pantry.

Chapter 6 pairs a study of Samsung with that of K-pop through the trope of what I call "meme-ification." This chapter discusses Samsung not simply because Samsung's products and K-pop are the best-known exports Korea had to offer over the past two decades but because the Korean electronics company's corporate system called chaebol in many ways reflects that of the K-pop industry. As argued throughout the book, the enactment of mimicry inscribes a hegemonic form through the everyday use of digital media and social media platforms, and nowhere is this more evident than in Samsung's "innovative" technology and products. I examine in this chapter how the ambiguity of distinction between original and counterfeit in both K-pop and Samsung is emblematic of the broader flows and tensions in the global economic and cultural structures in which Korean industrial and entertainment products have claimed a place as ironic inflections of both hegemony and mimicry.

This book's final chapter goes back in time—first to the madangguk tradition of the 1970s and then to Choe Sŭng-hŭi's dance piece "Eheya

Nohara" from the Japanese colonial period—in order to retrace the origins of satire in modern Korean performances and connect it to the comedy sketches and the double gestures of mimicry as well as the re-creation of global Korean phenomena in the "Muhan Sangsa" episode of *Muhan Dojeon* (*Infinite Challenge*) and "Gangnam Style" by Psy in the 2010s. This chapter returns to the basic cultural elements of *mŏt* (beauty), *hŭng* (joy), and *sinmyŏng* (exalting joy) and argues how they continue to reproduce the beats and souls of Korean popular culture. This chapter aims to affirm to the reemergence of the double consciousness of Koreans, even during the era of social media, via the detour of hegemonic mimicry rebuilt around the disavowal, indignation, and negativity through which Koreans have had to both accept and reject the fate of subjugation by foreign rule.

1   Short History of K-Pop, K-Cinema, and K-Television

K-POP

K-pop's global success was and continues to be as improbable as South Korea's miracle on the Han River; both are built on a precarious foundation, yet both continue to defy the odds by staying relevant despite the innumerable obstacles that the South Korean economy and the culture of K-pop have faced throughout their entwined histories.[1] K-pop is perhaps the only globally recognized music movement from the past several decades to focus less on the actual music and more on the online fandom that has largely ushered it to global fame. Innovations in visual style, including apparel, hair style, and makeup; spectacular synchronized choreographies; and an expanded use of social media to interact with fans have all contributed to building a nation-based, twenty-first-century idol empire. Live performances in clubs and cafés—which in the twentieth century often served as an entry-level platform whereby new musical acts secured recording contracts—have now been replaced with the use of the live audition as a new convergence point between record company executives and young talents. K-pop members dedicate their young lives training and preparing for their debuts under the guidance of systematic management companies, much like young athletes prepare for national competitions. As such, K-pop has proven to be a fertile training ground for global music acts in this fast-changing twenty-first century driven by neoliberal corporate values, export-driven desires, and a youth culture dominated by intense social media fandom activity and a continually evolving landscape for streaming music.

K-pop is a smooth, highly polished pop sound that evolved from a simple dance-oriented style associated with contemporary bubblegum pop and fuses rock 'n' roll, hip-hop, rhythm and blues (R&B), glam rock, and more recently electronic dance music (EDM). Almost all K-pop acts are also accomplished dancers, and each of their songs is accompanied by intricately choreographed dance performance. Many K-pop songs also feature quick key and beat changes, multiple bridges, and genre variations that better accommodate the taste of a young generation of music fans that have shorter attention spans partly because of the easy swipe function available on smartphone music apps. BIGBANG's 2015 hit song "Bae Bae," for instance, uses an unorthodox musical structure that quickly moves between hip-hop and ballad before all of the members land on a group chant of "ch'apsaltt'ŏk" (sticky rice cake) that creatively mimics the traditional folk sounds of rice cake vendors walking around in the middle of wintry nights in Korea (a sound as familiar to Koreans as ice cream truck music is to Americans) on a trap hip-hop beat. Unlike its antecedent musical genres that emerged during the post–World War II era, including jazz, rock 'n' roll, hip-hop, reggae, and samba rock, which were strongly associated with charismatic musical virtuosos such as Charlie Parker, Chuck Berry, Dr. Dre, Bob Marley, and Carlos Santana, all of whom changed the style and history of popular music, no K-pop band members are yet known as innovators in music, nor are any K-pop figures considered to be making their marks as musical composition geniuses.[2] K-pop is also a postnational music genre as many of the hits from K-pop are written by musicians who have very little to do with Korea itself. The first No. 1 song, "Dynamite," by BTS, the K-pop group known for its members' songwriting abilities, was written exclusively by two British songwriters, David Stewart and Jessica Agombar, whose affiliation with K-pop was virtually nonexistent prior to 2020. The overall genre of K-pop also does not associate itself with solo-act artists in the style of divas such as Adele or crooners such as Bruno Mars.

Yet K-pop is visible and ubiquitous worldwide today because it is built around an "idol" culture that parades mostly Korean performers. K-pop relies on creating values and identities that resonate far beyond just music. In other words, the music genre that emerged out of Korea over the past two decades is more about looks, style, dance, music video aesthetics, lifestyle, a unique talent training system, and an extraordinary fandom than the creation of unique music with new styles or properties of sound. In fact, one of K-pop's flagship events is not a concert, but rather a convention-oriented event called KCON that takes place in four or five venues around the world (typically in New York, Los Angeles, Tokyo, and Bangkok—though Mexico City and Abu Dhabi have also been venues in the past). Rather than focusing on performances, KCON heavily promotes fan engagement services through which fans can buy "Hi-Touch" passes for prices as high as $500 just so they can high-five or handshake their favorite artists, an experience lasting mere seconds. "Audience" passes and "red carpet" passes are also available for lower prices. It is this type of fan interaction—both online and offline—where K-pop has found its enormous appeal in the era of social media.

At no other time since perhaps Beatlemania has fandom been such a central factor in facilitating a new music genre. Just as much of the early fandom of the Beatles saw the consumption of paraphernalia centered around the idolization of the members of the band from Liverpool, UK, K-pop idols have generated a fan culture that involves merchandise collecting, penning of fantasy fiction, role-playing, and obsessive behavior toward the stars. Many K-pop fans buy and trade for multiple copies of the albums released by the groups they like—not because of the music contained therein (indeed, it would be highly redundant to own multiple copies of the same CD) but because of the fan meet invitation cards, books, and photos of the individual idols that are often included in the various iterations of the CD package. As such, these bonus merchandise items are, for many of these idol groups, not just supplementary but essential components that enfranchise K-pop.

Pop is of course shorthand for *popular*, and this means that there has to be a mass following or fanfare for any music to truly attain the status of "pop." Unlike many other art forms, such as literature, visual arts, theater, arthouse cinema, and classical music, whose audiences do not always rely on mass appeal, K-pop has always, from its inception, revolved around the creation and nurturing of a mass audience. However, not only is it a genre supported primarily by a maniacal fandom, but it is also a music that is born out of and driven by the interests of both the South Korean government through fiduciary subsidies and South Korean corporations through entertainment business arrangements. It is also a genre of music that has been forged by the American cultural influences that have dominated South Korea ever since its liberation from Japan in 1945 through the presence of the US military, which occupied the region and has remained ever since. Not only have the sociopolitical conditions of South Korea been conditioned by the US military occupation over the past seventy-five years, but this close alliance has also been critical to the development of South Korean popular culture. Struck by the sizable number of American military bases located in the nation's capital, many Koreans found employment serving the entertainment needs of US military personnel by supplying music and dance performances that catered to American tastes. In addition, the US military television and radio networks programmed American pop music in broadcasts that were widely available to the South Korean public. Most Koreans who grew up in the 1970s were familiar, for instance, with music from *Soul Train*, as this program featuring black people dancing to African American beats was publicly broadcast on the American Forces Korea Network (AFKN). These shows programmed largely to please the growing African American military audiences featured music that was far more entertaining than the programming offered by Korean television during the days of Park Chung-hee's military dictatorship. While Park's regime succeeded in censoring all Korean music deemed subversive to the public during the 1970s, thus suppressing any exciting domestic musical innovations, it—somewhat ironically—could not block out the Channel 2 American military forces network carried on VHF signal and FM radio, which unwittingly and openly broadcast American popular music to any South Korean with a TV set or an FM radio.

THE EARLY DAYS . . . AND SEO TAIJI

It is probably no coincidence that K-pop was founded while the entire nation was brooding amid the economically disastrous effects of the International Monetary Fund (IMF) crisis, Korea's most devastating recession since the war. The IMF crisis of the late 1990s marked Korea's first economic downturn since the end of the Korean War in the early 1950s. Partly due to the democratization that took place a decade earlier when the "June Uprising" gave way to direct presidential elections in 1987, and partly due to the loosening of the centralized economy as part of the IMF-bailout deal, by the late 1990s, the large-scale corporate monopolies known as the chaebol were forced to exit several of the entertainment markets. During the 1990s, three of the chaebols, SK, Daewoo, and Samsung, owned predominating stakes in the film and music industries and were preparing to establish an even bigger share in the entertainment businesses for the corporate empires they had built up through the manufacturing plants of VHS players, televisions, audiocassette tapes, and computer chips. However, after the IMF crisis hit Korea in 1997, the large chaebol players shut down their respective entertainment media subsidiaries. Once the chaebol packed up and left, the music industry itself reorganized under several ambitious singer-songwriters seeking to train a younger generation of musicians to create cultural content for both the domestic and export markets. Notable among these were Lee Soo-man, who started his career as a folk singer-songwriter in the 1970s and founded SM Entertainment in 1995; Yang Hyun-seok, one of the two boys in Seo Taiji & Boys, who began YG in 1996; and Park Jin-young, an R&B singer who modeled his career after Michael Jackson and launched his company, JYP Entertainment, in 1997. All three benefited from the policies of the Kim Young-sam and Kim Dae-jung governments of the 1990s, which recognized the importance of cultural development and legislated the government subsidy program to give the entertainment industry a facelift. Much of the financial subsidies intended to support the performing arts and arthouse ventures also flowed into the popular music industry, which claimed that the development of popular musicians could raise Korea's national brand image by manufacturing cultural content slated for international export. This was the so-called *Jurassic Park* theory—the argument that the sale of a single cultural property had the potential to duplicate the profit margin from the sale of 1.5 million Hyundai cars. This theory spurred government investment under the belief that cultural products could themselves prove to be viable, and valuable, national assets for export. More than any other cultural industry produced by South Korea, Korean popular music has excelled in raising the profile of a country once torn by foreign occupation, civil war, and rampant poverty. Despite the fact that it has taken twenty-five years, the recent success of BTS provides plausible evidence in support of the *Jurassic Park* theory.[3] Very recently, the Hyundai Research Institute (HRI) reported that BTS generates US$3.54 billion in economic value to South Korea per year and $1.26 billion as added value per year.[4]

K-pop's musical essence may be closer to that of American pop, but most of its creative formations were borrowed after peeping through the entertainment business of its neighboring country. All early idol group inspirations in K-pop were in fact taken from J-pop. The Johnny and Associates talent agency in Japan created a male idol group called Shonentai (Boy Platoon; pronounced Sonyŏndae in Korean, which may have influenced the naming of the world's biggest boy band today, Bangt'an sonyŏndan) in the 1980s and followed up its success with SMAP in the early 1990s. Using variety show platforms to debut, these male J-pop groups took the Japanese entertainment industry by storm. Indeed, the idol acts from Korea's neighbor, probably more than contemporaneous US acts such as New Kids on the Block or the Backstreet Boys, whose popularity rode more on the looks and entertainment skills they showcased on variety shows than on their musical talents and performances, were inspirations for SM chair Lee Soo-man, who trained and debuted the girl group S.E.S. (1997) and the male group SHINHWA (1998), which emerged to become the prototypes for future idol groups in Korea. Although during the first two decades of the twenty-first century, male idol groups have enjoyed far more success both domestically and abroad than their female counterparts, in the nascent stage of K-pop up until 2000, it was girl groups such as Fin.K.L., S.E.S., and Baby V.O.X that were far more popular than their male versions. At the time, it was common for teenage girls, the demographic that has been and still continues to be the driving force behind idol fandom, to root for performers representing their own gender. In recent decades, however, this tendency of the adolescent female fan base to support female performers has shifted to focus more on male performers and idol groups. In addition, with so many Korean teenage males filling their spare time with hobbies such as online games, the overall interest in girl groups has lagged further behind the popular interest in boy groups. These days, rather than amassing an adolescent fan base, girl groups are heavily followed by *ajŏssi* (middle-aged men) and preteen girls.

Although they were initially modeled after J-pop stars, K-pop idols were certainly different from J-pop idols such as SMAP, which were better known for their appearances in comedy variety programs. In Korea, despite the increasing popularity of illegal downloads during the new millennium precipitating the decline of music sales, ratings for popular music programs on television have remained very high over the past three decades. Several of the original members of formerly popular but now disbanded idol groups — such as Hyori of Fin.K.L. or Moon Hyo-joon of H.O.T. — eventually leveraged their stardom to become television personalities on variety shows, or, in the case of Yoon Kye-sang of g.o.d., to become an actor on the big screen. But almost all idol groups made their debuts on music programs such as KBS's *Music Bank* or MBC's *Show! Music Core*, both of which remained popular throughout the first two decades of the twenty-first century.

Despite the continued importance of television music programs for K-pop idols at the dawn of the new millennium, the rising significance of social media and the internet has since then transformed the hand-in-hand relationship between television broadcast networks and K-pop idol management companies. Until 2000 or so, just when the first wave of K-pop idols was beginning to crest, television and radio were the only venues through which popular music could be showcased to the public. The heavy censorship placed on popular culture throughout the latter part of the twentieth century had an adverse impact on the music industry. Much of Korea's burgeoning folk and rock music went into hiding on college campuses and in the underground mini-concert scene. The underground political folk movement formed during the 1970s and 1980s, however, dissipated when the *minjung* movement became compromised by the liberal democracy movement of the 1990s. Unlike the 1970s and 1980s, when the names of the folk song movements or underground rock stars such as Kim Min-gi, Kim Kwang-seok, or Jeon In-gwon could be etched onto the pantheon of the great popular musicians of all time, from the 1990s, only a select group of musicians could achieve fame without the powerful backing of the mainstream media.

Even so, during the 1990s, the power of the music industry, which had become concentrated among domestic television music program producers, began to reveal some cracks and fissures. This was when Seo Taiji began to emerge as the true superstar of the twentieth century.[5] Seo was probably the first K-pop star to successfully blend both hip-hop dance choreography and Euro-pop-inspired songs, and he was also the last K-pop star to work without a management company while writing and performing his own songs. Seo—who together with Yang Hyun-seok and Lee Juno formed Seo Taiji & Boys in 1992—set the trend of both Korean pop music and youth culture throughout the 1990s and beyond. Though Seo Taiji & Boys broke up precipitously and unexpectedly in 1996, many of the K-pop boy bands such as H.O.T. and SechsKies that followed in their wake in subsequent years were heavily influenced by them. Even BTS, despite the fact that some of its members were born after he retired from the music scene, pays homage to Seo Taiji. In Seo's 2017 comeback concert, every member of BTS joined him on stage, performing several of his signature songs from the 1990s, including "Class Ideology" and "Come Back Home."

Unencumbered by both the austere political activism of the 1980s and the postwar poverty that trailed the Korean War (1950–53), the new youth of the 1990s celebrated the freedom of consumerism enabled by the economic prosperity that had finally arrived in South Korea with the globalization launched by the Kim Young-sam government as its central policy. The young generation that arrived during the 1990s was also buoyed by its record-high population numbers. The South Korean birth rate peaked in 1971 before declining during subsequent years. The so-called post-386 generation (the Korean generation who were in their thirties in the 1990s [3], went to college in the tumultuous 1980s [8], and were born in the 1960s [6]) came of age in the 1990s. In addition, because of the education fever that swept Korea, there were also more college students in the 1990s than ever before. The substantial pocket money afforded to college students, combined with an increase in the leisure time enjoyed by a generation of youth yet to face the uncertainty of postgraduate employment thanks to the double-digit economic growth of the South Korean economy before the IMF crisis in 1997–98, and the lifting of many bans — including on international tourism, foreign film quotas, Japanese cultural contents, and so forth — led to a new wave of youth movements. Film festivals, music magazines, *noraebangs* (karaoke leisure rooms), and dance clubs that catered to the young generation began to germinate at that time. By pitching new trends in music, dance, and style, Seo Taiji was the king of this 1990s consumerist youth culture.

Seo Taiji & Boys were the first idols in a nation that later in the twenty-first century would become known worldwide as an idol republic in global pop music. For these idols to reach that status of idolhood, however, they needed to disentangle the power of a national media monopolized by television music program producers. Throughout the 1980s, South Korea had only two television stations, both of which were owned by the government: KBS and MBC. Only in the 1990s, through democratic reforms, did the government allow the only true commercial television station to open: Seoul Broadcasting System (SBS) started broadcasting in 1991 and, shortly thereafter, several more privately owned regional broadcasting companies followed. The power of television stations in the 1980s and much of the early 1990s was unprecedented. With newfound confidence in the nation's burgeoning economic prosperity, the government permitted television stations to increase their programming hours in the mid-1980s. Television stations that had broadcast only black and white for just several hours in the evenings until the early 1980s began to remain on air from morning until well beyond midnight in the 1990s. Music programs were a way to provide cheap entertainment and fill the dead hours during the day and into the night. Unlike producers, writers, and news reporters, music stars were not formal employees of the television stations. Nor were they, in contrast to actors and comedians, on union contracts. Musicians were cheap, willing to showcase their talent for very little pay or even no pay, and could boost the ratings the television stations needed in order to justify their *public* presence.

Many of the music stars of the late 1980s and early 1990s—such as Cho Yong-pil, Yi Yong, Jeon Young-rok, Lee Seung-chol, Na Mee, and early incantations of K-pop idols such as Park Nam-jeong, Lee Ji-eun, and Um Jung-hwa—could not openly protest against the television station's exploitation of their services since the only way they could become popular was through television appearances. Sales of LPs, CDs, video CDs, and concert tickets failed to pump up the revenue these early idols needed in order to stay afloat. To make ends meet, these early K-pop stars all found themselves performing short sets in innumerable nightclubs in Seoul and regional cities, and in order to strike a deal with these nightclubs, they had to stay relevant on television. During those days, television paid them only about twenty dollars for each appearance in the form of a voucher; yet because the producers of weekly music chart programs had so much influence on potential audiences, the musicians could not ignore the requests they received to appear on television almost on a daily basis. Any refusal to appear on television could lead to a ban on television, which, more importantly, could result in the idols losing their jobs on the nightclub circuits. The so-called PDs, or television producer-directors of the time, were kings during this golden age of Korean entertainment television that stretched from the 1980s well into the mid-1990s, while music stars were treated no better than pawns on their chess board.

Seo Taiji was perhaps the only nonpolitical entertainer of the 1990s who refused to remain acquiescent to this hierarchical social structure that privileged the inflated egos of television producers. Seo, recognizing his need to find alternate revenue streams, was able to locate the means to profit from his music without the aid of television (figure 1.1).[6] Due to the booming economic circumstances mentioned previously, young people were now in possession of pocket money doled out by their middle-class parents. This disposable allowance meant the new generation of youth could now afford to buy albums in mass numbers, attend arena concerts at the new Jamsil gymnasiums that had opened in 1988 for the Seoul Olympics, and access the internet and early forms of social media networks that allowed pop artists to communicate directly with fans. Seo Taiji was the first pop artist to become a popular subject of discussion of the nascent online clubs formed in the early 1990s. Early manifestations of what would later be coined *sasaeng* (literally meaning live-or-die, it refers to fans who are obsessive and whose behavior toward stars is sometimes akin to that of a stalker) would be found here. Many high school girls who projected themselves as docile and reticent in their offline personalities would often engage in vocal and sometimes aggressive actions online when engaging with other

새로운 청소년 문화를 창조한 서태지

"노래도 아니다"

1992년 어느 날, 이상한 아이들이 이상한 몸짓으로 이상한 노래를 부르기 시작했습니다. 어른들은 그게 무슨 노래냐고 혀를 찼습니다. 그렇습니다. 노래가 아닙니다. 그것은 새로운 세계입니다. 새로운 세계를 만들기 위해선 어른들의 너그러움이 필요합니다. 꿈과 아이디어와 용기로 새로운 세계를 만들어 갑시다.

꿈과 용기로
새로운 세계를 만들어 갑시다

1.1 "Not even a song," media once disparaged about
Seo Taiji's rap when he debuted in 1992. By 1996
this became a popular advertising copy of Sinsegye,
a department store that capitalized on the rising
currency of "sinsaedae" (new generation), which was
almost synonymous with Seo at the time.

members of the fandom. The power of these fans was not lost on Yang Hyun-seok, one of the members of Seo Taiji & Boys, who would later create his own K-pop idol empire, YG Entertainment, which, as recently as 2018, had contracts with some of the biggest K-pop acts including Psy, BIGBANG, 2NE1, and Blackpink.

THE DISINTEGRATION OF THE TELEVISION STUDIO AND THE PD KING

It was not only the increased spending power of an entire youth generation that allowed Seo Taiji to shun television and instead focus on releasing the best album possible during the prime of his career but also the burgeoning online service technologies that enabled him to offer online forums for his fans at cheap rates for efficient propagation of his image and updates on his music. Korea's early internet technology and its dissemination in many ways caught on much faster than equivalent technologies in the United States; this rapid pace was largely attributable to Korea's unique alphabet, hangul, that allowed for faster typing speeds, coupled with the availability of cheaper computers due to the manufacturing power of local electronic and computer companies such as SKC and Samsung that regarded adoption in domestic markets as critical to launching their products. For instance, Chollian and Hitel, the Korean equivalents of Compuserve and AOL, provided internet service through dial-up modems, quickly becoming online docking centers for many of Seo Taiji's young fans to connect and trade information. Discussion sites and trade forums formed on Hitel elevated the young generation's identification with Seo Taiji and helped increase Seo's sales of CDs, merchandise, and concert tickets. Seo could now directly communicate with his fans while easily bypassing the traditional media outlets of newspaper, television, and radio. Seo Taiji fan clubs on Korean dial-up services were perhaps the first community groups formed on online social media for a reigning pop act that would directly impact and influence the media coverage and activities of the star that they supported. Well before the BTS fandom, called the Army, began campaigning for millions of views, clicks, likes, votes, and purchases online in support of BTS's activities while vigilantly monitoring media coverage from Korea and abroad of their favorite boy band, Seo Taiji's fans were chastising journalists critical of Seo Taiji's albums and Seo's subversive stage behavior on broadcast media. Of course, the critical question remains to be answered. Why, or perhaps how, as early as 1992, did the maniacal activities of young fans come to occupy the central place of K-pop fandom that we now define as sasaeng?

In order to answer this question, perhaps we should return to the sociological elements of modern Korean society and the critical function of music as a cathartic outlet for many repressed teenagers. Music is consumed by people of all ages but especially by young people coming of age. Music is as therapeutic as it is educational. Modern Korean society, especially because of its adherence to neo-Confucian principles that regulate everyday relations and its embrace of neoliberal capitalism, has placed its focus on education to prepare its youth for the infamous college-entrance exams and employment exams of the Korean corporate world. Korea is one country where low school scores or high college dropout rates are not one of the government's worries. Instead, there are opposite concerns. The after-school private cram institution system called *hagwŏn* dominates the everyday lives of almost all school-aged children in Korea, leading to traumatic stress and high suicide rates among teenagers.[7] This intense competition among peers is actually encouraged, even by teachers. In this cut-throat environment, music often provides the only outlet teenagers have to take out their frustrations, angst, and vehement energy against the adult world that conspires against them. For the average Korean teenager, many prohibitions and taboos, including coed social interactions, drug and alcohol use, and even intense physical activities, limit outlets for relief of this stress. Just about the only activities permitted to them that might help them to release their pent-up feelings are occasional online games, listening to music, and infatuation with hypersexualized idols. If male teenagers are allowed to compete against each other through online games as their only permitted leisure activity, female teens are allowed to engage in fan activities with opposite- and same-sex idols. Just as online games in Korea have resulted in serious addiction problems among male teenagers, K-pop has also produced overidentification among female teenagers that has in turn led to the phenomenon of sasaeng fandom. For the past three decades, just as K-games and Korean e-sports players have achieved incredible success, K-pop male idol groups ranging from Seo Taiji, H.O.T., TVXQ, 2PM, BIGBANG, and EXO to today's BTS have stolen the hearts of generations of youngsters. Underpinning all the successes of these K-pop girl and boy groups are the intense obsessions of teenagers who are repressed in a neo-Confucian environment, and the emotional price tag resulting from the unrelentingly high-pressure overeducation that these teenagers are taxed with, all of which conspire to create a captive fan base for these idols (figure 1.2).[8]

1.2 The overwhelming majority of K-pop fans are women, as in this 2019 photo. Photo by Kyung Hyun Kim.

IS IT KOREAN?

Despite the fact that K-pop is an amalgamation of different foreign influences that range from African American hip-hop to J-pop idol bands, K-pop, much like the Kakao-talk (Korean messenger app) soundscape that has reimagined the modality of Korean communication, has reauthenticated the Korean language and reintroduced the unique and playful cadence of hangul. Seo Taiji was not immediately embraced by music critics and experts when he first burst onto the scene back in the early 1990s. It was not because he had become a bubblegum pop idol for the young teenagers, or even because he had disobeyed the rules of the day when appearing on television was a mandate for all musicians. It was because he had selected hip-hop as his genre of choice to express his music. Hip-hop, while slowly making its way in Korea throughout the 1980s through various musical acts such as Hyun Jin-young and Deux, was not a genre of music preferred by the older generation of musicians in Korea. No one created more controversy through this genre than Seo Taiji, who, before forming his own idol group when he was only seventeen, was touted as a genius bassist for a popular heavy metal band, Sinawi. Seo's first song, "Nan arayo" (I know), released in 1992, is probably the most memorable song in the entire history of Korean popular music. However, it stirred up controversy for reimagining and restructuring Korean rhyme in a song and, in so doing, reinvented perhaps the entire pronunciation of Korean language for the youth of that and succeeding generations.[9] In other words, "Nan arayo" became a seismic event not only for Korean popular music but also for the Korean language (see chapter 2).

Despite Seo's preference for a sometimes sentimental balladic hook, he left an important footprint for the rest of K-pop that followed. The intermixing of Korean and English became the signature move not only in Korean rap verses but in K-pop lyrics as well. Though not much advanced research has been conducted on K-pop's global impact on the Korean language, K-pop is arguably the only music genre after bossa nova in the 1960s to have achieved this kind of global-scale popularity while retaining its lyrical basis in a language other than English. However, the mixing of playful onomatopoeic words in the lyrics has produced new idioms and phrases in the Korean language and has also begun to impact English as well. Consider "Growl," the biggest hit song by EXO, the "king of K-pop" in the mid-2010s until BTS took the reins away from them over the past five years. Released in 2013, the title "Growl" is "Ŭrŭrŏng," an onomatopoeia in the original Korean, which renders futile any effort to properly translate it into English. It is the Korean vocalization assigned to a large wild mammal, usually the tiger, which until the 1920s roamed the mountains of the Korean peninsula; this choice reflects the male gender's willingness to beat the competition in order to monopolize the attention of the opposite sex. Though the lyrics are apparently aggressive, and repeat the onomatopoeic title, "ŭrŭrŏng," no fewer than nine times in the chorus, the song never feels as if it's R-rated because the Korean term avoids verbal offense or obscenity. The chants of "ŭrŭrŏng, ŭrŭrŏng, ŭrŭrŏng-dae. Mulrŏ-sŏji anŭmyŏn tach'ŏdo molra" (I growl, howl, and growl. If you don't back up, you might get hurt) by the boy idols sound in some way too cute and too indecipherable (even to Korean ears), and too tonally pleasant for these sounds to proximate any appetite for violence. These less-than-meaningful non-English sounds reverberated through a purely Korean cadence match the asignifying beats and chants that global pop currently craves. These days, the news, social media, and advertisement emails constantly beep and blare on our smartphones and screen monitors in an attempt to capture our attention with too many meaningful feeds and messages. K-pop, especially to audiences outside Korea, allows people to turn off their faculties of cognitive linguistic processing by providing human sounds that are devoid of clear signifiers, not too serious, and intended and received more or less just for fun. In Latin American countries, the K-pop phenomenon reaches an audience where the majority of the fans speak neither Korean nor English; language is mediated through a secondhand translation of incomplete, frustrating, and sometimes offensive fansubs on YouTube. Here, because Korean, unlike Spanish or English, is a minor language, K-pop's fansub is able to achieve a linguistic and cultural mediation that is indistinctly opaque, nonthreatening, and comical, thereby sidestepping supercilious Western values of hierarchy between stars and fans.[10]

EXPORT MUSIC AND THE THIRTEEN-YEARS-A-SLAVE CONTRACT

As early as the final couple of years of the twentieth century, K-pop's vibrant colors and heavy sounds were noticed by Korea's closest neighbors, Japan and China. However, over the past two decades, despite the sometimes turbulent political situation mired between Korea and these two larger and more powerful East Asian countries, K-pop's popularity in the region soared to sky-high levels. Though successful in each of these two countries, the reasons for its popularity remain radically different. K-pop reminds Japanese fans of their own J-pop, but in a form that produces heavier beats much more closely resembling American music. For Chinese fans, K-pop has presented looks, styles, and sounds that seem more fashionable than any of their own pop acts. Just as Hong Kong movie and music stars such as Chow Yun-Fat and Leslie Cheung presented trendier and more cosmopolitan foreign idol alternatives than their domestic versions for Korean youth during the 1980s, it is perhaps not surprising that the tide turned when Korean music acts such as Super Junior and Baby V.O.X were fronted by idols who, for many Chinese fans, were much more attractive than their own domestic counterparts.

Though K-pop was conceptually appropriated from J-pop, historically, it was heavily influenced by African American music. For instance, one of the most popular songs in the history of postwar Korean pop music is "Miin" (Beauty) from 1974 by legendary guitarist-composer Shin Joong-hyun, who was inspired by both *changt'aryŏng* (a Korean traditional beggar's song) and the African American guitarist Jimi Hendrix's "'Voodoo Chile," which together make up the song's famous opening guitar riff.[11] The hybrid of African American music and traditional Korean sentimentality has set off a rare but important surge of creative energy that has endured to this day. Hence, well before the nine members of Girls' Generation donned their bright-colored American-style cheerleading outfits and grabbed pom-poms and football helmets that completely fall outside the cultural context in Korea, well before Seo Taiji popularized "the snowboard look," and certainly before Psy picked out the Western props such as cowboy hats, boots, and whip for his music video, Koreans had mastered a negotiation with the African American brand of global pop music. Some of the best-known hybrid songs that continue this black-Korean partnership are Seo Taiji's "Hayeoga" (1993), which blended traditional Korean folk music instruments such as the *taepyŏngso* to play the melodic structure but also sprinkles in elements from Jamaican reggae, heavy metal, and hip-hop, and aforementioned BIGBANG's "Bae Bae," a fusion between Korean traditional *t'aryŏng* and African American R&B, among other influences. This was a cultural coproduction created unofficially and spontaneously because so many Korean musicians during the postwar years received their musical training while performing for and with African American soldiers stationed in Korea. Seo Taiji and Yang Hyeon-seok themselves had learned b-boy dancing moves and hip-hop rhyming structures through direct interactions with black soldiers who hung out at clubs in Itaewon—the district in Seoul still famous for its large foreign population due to its proximity to the American military base (see Introduction).

Soul, R&B, and hip-hop were the biggest and earliest musical influences for K-pop while the growing industry also looked to J-pop to borrow the structure of its idol trainee programs. Korean management companies were able to build their training academies for idol groups by casting teenagers at an early age because the Korean educational system allowed hagwŏns to substitute for compulsory schooling to provide critical learning for schoolboys and schoolgirls. Just as elite athletes are allowed to skip classes to pursue intensive training in their sport as early as elementary school, so do elite trainees enjoy extraordinary privileges that allow them to focus on their music and dancing apprenticeships in ways that are unimaginable even in Japan. Due to training them in highly competitive environments at a very early age through endless hours of sweat and tears, K-pop produces supersized idols who dance and sing from the age of adolescence and who are as chiseled as professionals in the Alvin Ailey American Dance Theater group. As attested by recent audition programs such as Korean Mnet's *Produce 48*, where the J-pop idol group AKB48 collaborated with Korean idol trainees, K-pop's group synchronization, athleticism, and crooning prowess simply overmatch those of neighboring J-pop brands. Many of the Japanese fans fall in love with the boys and girls from their smaller neighbor, for they recognize that K-pop groups are in many ways supersized J-pop—in both quantity and quality, and with as much hair gels as their compatriots. While J-pop's girl group AKB48 (99 active members as of February 2021, according to the group's official website), for instance, has had more members than any other pop music act in the world, this is more an anomaly than a rule. J-pop groups almost always have fewer than five members. Manufactured by the world's most unique trainee system, K-pop members, in general, are more youthful in their looks, more expressive as singers, and more agile as dancers than their Japanese counterparts. In order to maintain their youthful idol status, the average life span of these K-pop groups is typically no more than half a decade. If K-pop were to be known for its music rather than for its idols whom you want to high-five or with whom you want to take a selfie, perhaps this would have had a positive effect on the longevity of these groups.

Probably the most controversial element of K-pop is its unique trainee system, which often keeps the performers tied by "slave contracts" and subservient relationships to the management company heads. The thirteen-year contracts that trainees are required to sign at the time of audition, which was standard until 2010, is somewhat ironic, since most of them—even those who do make it—cannot retain their idol career beyond their midtwenties.[12] Some critics cynically pronounce K-pop bands to be yet another of Korea's disposable export commodities based on cheap human labor that underpins the chaebol system.[13] The K-pop industry is indeed a vertically integrated mogul system the likes of which the entertainment industry has not seen since the days of the classical Hollywood system when MGM, 20th Century Fox, and RKO ruled the day. Just like Samsung or Hyundai, which have co-opted neo-Confucian and patriarchal values in order to justify the corporate leadership of the founders' family for generations, many of the idol members of the K-pop industry are systematically programmed into docility and economic, practical, and emotional dependence on corporate heads despite the fact that in many cultures, most artists are by their very nature autonomous and nonconformist when it comes to hierarchical values. That the Korean state continues to play a major role in providing the K-pop industry with subsidies, tax breaks, and free promotion supports some of the theories that the K-pop industry is nothing more than a governmental outfit that makes and promotes music that remains nonpolitical and uncritical of South Korea's reigning neoliberal patriarchy and its values.

If the breakup of the Beatles during its creative prime is the most storied divorce in the history of pop, in K-pop history, it is the declaration of independence proclaimed by the three members (eventually reformed under the name JYJ) from the quintet idol group TVXQ (Tong Bang Shin Ki) in 2009 that is likely the most painful breakup in K-pop. The only difference here is that while the escalating tension between two individual members, John Lennon and Paul McCartney, served as the basis for the Beatles' dissolution in 1969–70, TVXQ's breakup was facilitated by acrimony not between the band members themselves, but between three of the core members of the band and the head of their management company, SM Entertainment's Lee Soo-man. The three members of TVXQ, who tried to split from the Korean agency SM Entertainment—Jaejoong, Yoochun, and Junsu—cited their thirteen-year contract with SM as an exemplary case of an unreasonable "slave contract."[14] However, their efforts to sever themselves from their contracts incited an emotional roller coaster both for them and for their fans. But although the Korean court eventually sided with the three members and released them from their contracts and since then has limited entertainment companies' terms of agreement with talent to seven years, the legal battle dragged on. Not only were the three exiles, who afterward formed their own idol group called JYJ, barred from using the group brand name owned by SM Entertainment and from performing onstage the songs they had sung as TVXQ, but Lee Soo-man requested a court injunction that prohibited JYJ from performing on television—while the three idols were still under his contract. Television stations had to honor Lee's request to treat JYJ as if the three were renegades from law, in fear of retribution from SM in the form of a blanket boycott of the televised music programs by all SM Entertainment acts. Within a mere decade or so of tilting the balance slightly in favor of performers vis-à-vis television producers when Seo sought self-induced exile from television during the 1990s, the star performers, when heavily fortified by giant management companies, could strike fear in the hearts of television producers.

Separation between SM Entertainment and JYJ was easier said than done. By 2010, TVXQ was not only the most famous music group in Korea but also one of the most famous in all of Asia. The group's affable smiles, powerful dance moves, and ability to sing songs in Korean, Japanese, and Chinese had won them popularity throughout East Asia and beyond. Their latest single, "Break Out," for instance, broke the record of most consecutive weeks by a foreign artist at the top of the Japanese charts, a record previously held by Elton John in the 1970s by holding the number 1 position for a stunning fourteen weeks. And so, Jaejoong, Yoochun, and Junsu's desire to leave SM and their pursuit of independence were widely reported by many international entertainment news outlets abroad—resulting in lawsuits and counter-lawsuits in territories outside Korea. When JYJ split from TVXQ, the fans also split. Many fans remained loyal to the now duo version of TVXQ, while some chose to follow the newly formed trio. A similar battle also took place several years later when Kris, Luhan, and Tao, three popular members of EXO-M (the second EXO performing almost exclusively in Chinese Mandarin), at the height of their career, split from SM Entertainment in 2014 and 2015, thereby igniting another round of legal and ethical controversy. This kind of pitting of performers against company that would lead to the breakup of a K-pop group in its prime once again illustrates that the K-pop industry was less about music and more about business.

K-pop's biggest difference from J-pop is that it was indeed birthed as an industry programmed for export to other countries. The K-pop bands often released their songs on YouTube several days before their CDs hit the stores domestically simply because YouTube guaranteed global access to their songs. The fact that YouTube typically did not pay much for views and that having YouTube stream your songs could lead to a decline in downloads and CD sales did not alter the release patterns of K-pop, which continue to rely heavily on social media. The global availability of K-pop was far more important for Korean management companies because this easily accessible global form of promotion could open up potential export markets overseas. After 2000, with the youth population in precipitous decline in Korea, domestic fan support was important but insufficient to guarantee financial viability of the management companies that were reportedly spending more than US$2 million on the development of each one of their talents. The population in China was younger and much larger than it was in Korea, and the concert and CD deals in Japan were much more lucrative than they would be in Korea. K-pop bands typically made more money overseas than from their proceeds in domestic markets.

PSY'S "GANGNAM STYLE" AND FINALLY AMERICA

Psy has always transcended accusations of being a copycat. Unlike some of the K-pop acts that always had a prototype elsewhere in the United States or in Japan, there was no previously existing act with which one could compare Psy's unique style, which combined a carnivalesque parade of his slightly overweight body in tight garments with flamboyant and satirical dance music tracks. Psy wrote, performed, and produced one of the biggest hit songs in the age of YouTube and rewrote the global meaning of "viral" when the song was released in the summer of 2012. It was probably the most ironic cultural sensation in the first two decades of the twenty-first century that a slightly chubby Asian performer singing a dance tune with Korean lyrics accompanied by horse-dance choreography in the middle of barren parking lots, a horse stable, and empty subway stations in Korea registered one of the most recognizable beats and movements of the global pop moment. Psy's horse-dance was quite possibly the most iconic dance since Michael Jackson's moonwalk debuted in 1983. While most K-pop performers are built on a base of screaming fans who strongly identify with or desire the good-looking bodies of their idols, Psy's rotund body and double-chinned face more closely resembled the physical appearance of a typical Korean comedian than a YG Entertainment star. As one of Korean popular music's rare singer-songwriter solo acts, Psy was an outlier within the system of K-pop. Psy's success with his inimitable "Gangnam Style" proved that the erasure of Korean identity is not a prerequisite for K-pop's success in the United States or overseas — paving the next generation of K-pop's arrival.

Featuring two members of the comedy program *Muhan Dojeon* (*Infinite Challenge*), No Hong-cheol and Yoo Jae-sok, the aesthetics of the "Gangnam Style" music video are steeped in satirical humor. The biggest selling points of "Gangnam Style" were the outrageous grotesque body humor and the simple burlesque slapstick act that allowed the song to transcend borders. That this humor actually has its roots in the Saturday TV program, *Muhan Dojeon* — a Korean equivalent of the United States' *Saturday Night Live* or the UK's *Monty Python's Flying Circus*, where Psy was a frequent guest — is perhaps not a coincidence. "Gangnam Style" is a product of both Psy's music and of *Muhan Dojeon*'s comedy skit formula, which has circled around *ajŏssi*, or Korean middle-aged male, self-deprecating jokes, for years. *Muhan* perfected its Korean brand of satirical humor, in which ordinary ajŏssis (middle-aged men) often find themselves outclassed and humbled by attractive women and wealthy and better-looking powerful men. Although Psy is himself originally from Gangnam, the persona he created for the "Gangnam Style" music video could only work because he severed himself from the glitzy trappings of the Gangnam district and created a mismatch between his on-screen persona and the pizzazz of Seoul's nouveau riche district.

The laughter produced by "Gangnam Style" among local domestic viewers, however, must be differentiated from that generated among, for instance, American viewers, who do not recognize the cultural specificity of the "Gangnam" district and the ajŏssi joke that surrounds the persona created by Psy and his proxy cast from MBC's hit comedy program. Many Americans laughed and snickered—not *with* the singer-cum-comedian who self-deprecatingly jokes around with the chubbiness of his body that can never truly belong to the elite class of Gangnam but *at* the performer, who they feel is a poor imitation of American pop references such as Westerns, fast cars, and race-car girls. Racism played no small factor in making his song one of the most recognizable tracks in the United States over the past several decades. The gap between the cultural hegemony of American popular culture and the imitation of the Korean pop star produces what I consider to be *cultural insufficiencies* that may signify the Korean singer's inability to strip his or her voice from the political predicament that represents a minor culture trapped between the globally perceived *advanced* culture of American pop and Hollywood and the presumed *backward* copycat that is K-pop. This creates an awkward humor that arises out of a form of insufficiency, which is both corporeal and linguistic. The repeated sounds of just the first syllable of "oppa" are not funny because of the pure cadence produced by "op-op-op" but because it sounds like something between a malfunctioning EDM electronic machine and a fart. With his body straddling the boundaries between an opulent American and a crazy rich Asian, and his song lyrics wavering between English and Korean, Psy appears not unlike an infant gazing into the mirror and recognizing no form or necessary existence of a coherent subjectivity. He becomes a harrowing object of nomadic and homeless identity of the new global cultural order, subject to both ridicule by the hegemonic racist gaze cast upon him and celebration as a cultural icon in an age of meme-ification (see chapter 7).

Psy's phenomenal run on the Billboard charts gave hope to many K-pop managers that their success in the Top 40 charts in the United States was waiting just around the corner. The increased attendance at KCON by fans, the sold-out US concerts by a handful of K-pop acts such as BIGBANG and 2NE1 during the mid-2010s, and the collaborative projects between mainstream American musicians and K-pop performers gave new hope that many more K-pop acts could follow Psy's breakout success. However, Girls' Generation and EXO could not break into the American market the way they had succeeded in Asian markets, CL's solo career launch in the United States did not catch fire, and the extended hiatus of BIGBANG due to its members' conscription into the South Korean military and then Seungri's trouble with the law all contributed to the systemwide failure of K-pop in the middle of the second decade of the new millennium. Just as one was losing hope of K-pop ever coming close to achieving its true global stardom in the United States, by the end of the decade, Bangt'an Sonyŏndan (better known as BTS) had seemingly come from nowhere to become a household name in North America and Europe. They were the first Asian music act to appear as musical guests on NBC's *Saturday Night Live*; their singles "Boy with Luv" and "Dynamite" became platinum hit songs in the United States; and their album *Love Yourself: Tear* was the first true non-English album to top the Billboard charts since Selena's album sung half in Spanish and half in English topped the charts immediately after she died in 1995.[15]

BTS DOMINATES THE WORLD STAGE

If Milli Vanilli had Frank Farian (a German producer who was also responsible for the disco-pop group Boney M), and Whitney Houston had veteran recording industry executive Clive Davis, BTS had Bang Si-Hyuk, composer–cum–talent management company CEO who has been the veteran mastermind behind the group. Bang was quite possibly the most important composer and producer in the JYP Entertainment group, which produced hits for early idol groups such as g.o.d and Wonder Girls, but when he left the company in the mid-2000s and formed his own outfit, Big Hit Entertainment, his hits dried up. Aside from Baek Ji-Young's 2009 "Feels Just like Being Shot" (Ch'ong majŭn kŏt ch'ŏrŏm), Bang had failed to produce a big single or effectively groom any rising music acts for about a decade—that is, until BTS rose to the top. The group had not been contracted by any of the Big Three entertainment companies (SM, JYP, and YG), each of which had branches in America and had been launching their domestic stars there for more than a decade without making the kind of splash BTS has made. While only one of the seven BTS members (RM) can speak English, and although the group was formed in 2013, they went largely unnoticed even in Korea for several years. They had no representation outside Korea, and yet, by 2019, BTS was selling out some of the world's biggest and best-known venues, such as Los Angeles's Rose Bowl and London's Wembley Stadium. So what happened?

BTS's rise on the world stage was facilitated by three changes during the 2010s—the expansion of online music fandom, the global explosion of music video programming and consumption on YouTube, and the advent of an idol empire involving nonmusical merchandising, games, and fantasy fiction. The transformation of music culture continued to benefit K-pop in general because by 2000 Korean pop itself was reliant on attractive performers and sharp dance choreographies that fit well into the medium of YouTube videos. Although radio DJs in the United States largely continued to shun the Korean lyrics of K-pop acts, music in the new millennium became far less reliant on radio airplay. Today, in light of the overwhelming emphasis on social media convergence—which involves ringtones, quick meme jingles, and Instagram photos—the popularity of K-pop music videos has proven that neither the visual nor the music can be considered secondary when it comes to the contemporary musical consumption experience: images and sound in music videos are in fact inseparable, evidencing what Michel Chion has called "audio-vision," which privileges neither element and warrants new theorization.[16]

Critic James A. Steintrager, with the aid of Rey Chow, has advanced the concept of audio-vision into what he calls "sound-objects" that "contemplate the place of sound."[17] The "sound-object" is perhaps useful for understanding K-pop, a music genre that is still heavily reliant on Korean language lyrics even though they are inaccessible to most American listeners. There are many sounds in the world that cannot be reduced to semantic meaning but are nevertheless considered beautiful. Many sounds from nature—the chirping of birds, the pelting sound of rainfall, or ocean waves breaking against cliffs—constitute soothing "sound objects" even though no meaning can be deduced from them. However, without a visual imaginary associated with these sounds, could they still be considered "beautiful"? To respond to this question, Steintrager discusses Kant's example of deceptive aural misidentification and compares it with *trompe l'oreille*, a term derived from *trompe-l'oeil*, the artistic technique of creating an effect of three-dimensionality using two-dimensional images. According to Steintrager, Kant speculated about "the effect on listeners who, thinking they are enjoying the 'bewitchingly beautiful song of the nightingale,' discover that the source is a 'mischievous lad' hiding in the bushes and imitating the bird with a pipe or reed."[18] Although the two sounds might be the same to the ear, the listener might feel disgusted if the source or even the motif behind the source turned out to be completely different from the one imagined. The importance that Kant placed on visual confirmation of the auditory source has remained relevant throughout the modern era, as seen in the hiring of "ghost singers" to perform behind the stage for Hollywood stars, as incorporated into the plotline of the classic movie *Singin' in the Rain* (1952) or in the models who posed as singers for the pop sensation group Milli Vanilli in the late 1980s and early 1990s. Milli Vanilli, a European rap/soul duo, even received a Grammy before it was revealed that neither of the two headliners, Fab Morvan and Rob Pilatus, had sung any of the vocals for their album. Frank Farian, Milli Vanilli's German producer, had almost cribbed his playbook from Kant, who argued that auditory sensation alone cannot please the listener, especially if visual confirmation shows that the source is completely different from the one imagined. By hiring two attractive young men with reggae hair and stylish moves to visually match the sound of Milli Vanilli, Farian wanted to ensure that the listeners of his songs would not be disappointed even as the real singers were a couple of middle-aged musicians well past their prime. Farian's desire to visually represent his new dance songs with two lanky, attractive models fulfilled the trompe l'oreille ruse, but when audiences discovered that the nightingale was just a mischievous lad playing a pipe, they did indeed become as upset as Kant had predicted. The Milli Vanilli models were forced to return their Grammy and pay fines to many concert promoters.

I have long wrestled with this decades-old controversy about Milli Vanilli, because K-pop acts, although they feature no ghost singing, are built around lip-sync performances, attractive looks that far outweigh vocal talents, dance choreography, and splashy videos that reduce music to sound-objects. K-pop in fact raises the question of whether *music* in pop music is even relevant today. More than any other K-pop idol group, BTS has built its career around writing and performing quality songs, which could be the real reason for its success despite the declining importance of music in global pop today. BTS has long showcased music written by its members rather than solely caring only about its stars' looks, despite the fact that the septet is still squarely situated within a K-pop platform that draws on dance energy and idol fandom.

BTS started out by claiming to be a hip-hop group. Although hip-hop has been an integral genre for K-pop over the past twenty years, no Korean boy group had ever actively embraced the African American music genre the way BTS did during its early years. The group took on hip-hop not only as a style or a dance choreography but as the spirit of "telling stories of underdog experience." All seven BTS members hailed from Korea's countryside, and nearly all came from working-class families. Their first couple of albums, although commercial duds domestically, helped to build a solid fan base outside Korea, where fans came to perceive BTS as the

K-pop boy group that told stories many young listeners could identify with. Early songs such as "No More Dream" and "N.O." (both 2013) were neither party songs nor assembly-line bubblegum tunes but expressions of rebellion against the establishment that tapped into Korean teenagers' frustrations with the country's educational system. This energy helped BTS build a solid fan base, particularly among young North Americans and Europeans. During this rather dark, formative period, BTS even recorded a cover of Kendrick Lamar's "Swimming Pool" with Korean lyrics, "Tears of School" (Hakgyŏ ŭi nunmul), replacing Lamar's original message about persistent alcoholism problems in black communities with a protest against violence in Korean schools. Telling their own stories meant that BTS members had to write their own songs. Although, ironically, BTS's first number 1 song in America, "Dynamite," was not written by any of the group members, many of their hit songs from 2017–18, such as "Spring Day" (Bom nal), "DNA," and "Fake Love," each of which featured memorable hooks and gritty rap bridges, were at least partly written by BTS members. RM and Suga, the group's two rappers, are accomplished singer-songwriters and producers who engineer songs both on stage and behind the scenes for BTS. The sophisticated songwriting and producing abilities of the group's members, which have matured over the years, have given BTS a musical edge that is not currently shared by any other K-pop groups.

Songwriting talent alone of course was not responsible for BTS's rise to global fame. The most surprising and ironic element in BTS's sudden rise is that it was virtually an unknown idol act for several years in Korea before becoming the most significant K-pop act in history. The actual significance of social media culture lies at the core of K-pop's influential power abroad. Specifically, with K-pop celebrity culture, the connection idols actively create with their fandoms is such that for some fans, there can be no distinction between a fan identity and their own personal identity. The obsessive fan behavior that first exploded in repressed Korean teenagers in the 1990s has found its match now even in North America and Europe, where increasing numbers of young fans see no separation between themselves and their idols. When their idols succeed, fans feel exalted, and when their idols fail, they feel as if they themselves have been kicked in the guts. In other words, the kind of intense infatuation young teenagers developed toward their idol groups in Korea that first steamed up the internet social media chatrooms of Chollian and Hitel as early as the days of Seo Taiji's heyday are emerging again overseas, and this time it is BTS that has become the subject of many so-called sasaeng fans' obsessions. Exactly twenty-five years after the Seo Taiji syndrome swept Korean cyberspace and produced a new idiom in the Korean language called *ppa-suni* (oppa-infatuated girls), and fifty years after Beatlemania died with the last rooftop concert given by the Beatles before their breakup in 1970, BTS, the seven-member Korean pop group, achieved a global conquest that seemed highly improbable from the outset.

Although BTS has no agency in the United States, or anywhere else in the world for that matter, it does have one true ambassador: the Army. The fan demographic being both overwhelmingly female and also young, some of the fans of BTS have quite possibly become more influential on social media than the band's managers themselves. In this era of social media, having influential fans on Twitter and YouTube turned out to be a much better way to "conquer the world" than making music that is innovative yet familiar to all ears. Browsing through the Army fan site reveals that they have publicly stated goals once new BTS singles are released on music-streaming sites and YouTube: 65 million views in twenty-four hours, 1 million streams on Spotify, 150 spins on radio on day 1, 350,000 downloads on Shazam, and so on (figure 1.3). The remarkable thing is that in actuality the Army achieved all this and more. There were, for instance, a record 78 million views compiled on YouTube in a twenty-four-hour period, exceeding the 65 million views for "Boy with Luv" that was set as a target number for the Army. Now, most music or sports fans, for example Chicago Cubs fans, no matter how much money or time they spend following their star musicians or athletes online and offline, do not end up achieving their dreams of making their chosen team or group champions. In most of these arenas, a clear division exists between the group's performance on the field and the fans' passion off the field. No matter how much energy gets expended by fans rooting for their star idols, the fans themselves cannot write the number 1 hit song for the star, nor can they step up to the plate to hit that home run for their idol shortstop. Yet the strange phenomenon with BTS's fandom is that its supporters, while not exactly sharing the stage at the Citi Field in New York, feel like they achieved what they set out to do through their campaign to drive the clicks, votes, and purchases in order to make BTS's latest single the top song in America. K-pop fandom in the twenty-first century found a way to maximize contact between individuals and stars, not by bypassing capitalist structures but by rebuilding them. Even the Army, for instance, had found ways to exploit the utopian potential of internet-generated peer-to-peer social relations that had given rise to nonprofit sites such as Wikipedia, Kickstarter, and Reddit. (Of course, Red-

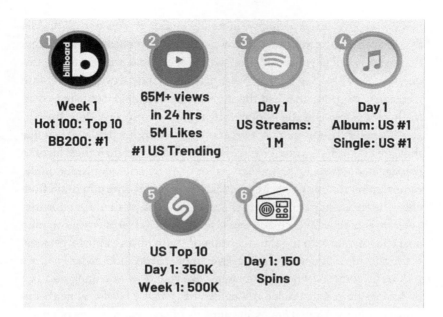

Week 1
Hot 100: Top 10
BB200: #1

65M+ views
in 24 hrs
5M Likes
#1 US Trending

Day 1
US Streams:
1 M

Day 1
Album: US #1
Single: US #1

US Top 10
Day 1: 350K
Week 1: 500K

Day 1: 150
Spins

1.3 Army, the most powerful fandom in the world, posts its mission for its members who anticipate the release of "Boy with Luv," a single from BTS. Screen capture from https://www.usbtsarmy.com, 2019.

dit is also where the motley crew of amateur day traders banded to rally around GameStop stock against Wall Street elites made up of hedge fund giants and short sellers that provided a miracle story in 2021 that is almost as improbable as the BTS's global rise to fame.) K-pop fans were eager to garner a minute of attention from their favorite group. Some of the online platforms gave these fans the power to build alliances and mobilize campaigns to enhance the stardom of their favorite idols as well as, in the process, increase their own chances of meeting those idols. Without the internet, it might never have been possible for K-pop to spread beyond its own national borders.

But this book is perhaps asking the wrong question right now. The question that should warrant our attention is this: Why did the Army—which includes hundreds of thousands of Americans and more to date—choose to root and campaign for BTS rather than for any other K-pop act? Of other possible groups, BIGBANG was more mature musically and had a longer career than BTS; members of Blackpink, the latest girl group sensation, speak better English and have the backing of a larger management company (YG Entertainment); and Got7 and EXO are just as charming as male idol groups that boast perhaps a more ubiquitous presence in all of Asia than does BTS. And yet they are nowhere close to replicating the success that BTS has had in North America and Europe. The precise answer to this question may never be known, but it may be because BTS, partly because it was never a group that had the sponsorship of a major company, could freely post videos and chats online when it was starting out. Here, the personal is political, and there is a greater degree of fun when fans feel like they are choosing to vote for their favorite idol rather than their favorite management company. Campaigning for one's favorite idol is not unlike campaigning for one's favorite politician or one's favorite corporate franchise. Internet chatroom activities and campaigns, at their fundamental core, are fun because each and every participant gets to share a common goal and interact with the stars they identify with on an intimate, personal level. This fun element encourages even more participation when you are rooting for someone whose dream is just like your own — an underdog. The underdogs from Korea called BTS, which had a major label deal neither in Korea nor in the United States, presumably offered many points of appeal with which many young online users around the world today identified and shared. Indeed, fans rooted for BTS because RM, V, Jin, Suga, J-Hope, Jimin, and Jungkook, all gleaned from the countryside, were like a plain-looking sidekick character in a K-drama that had no chance of winning the prize or a struggling company that had no chance of surviving in today's global corporate world, and for BTS to emerge as the winner made the fans themselves feel like they were the winners.

THE EMERGENCE OF ASIA'S HOLLYWOOD

Cinema, and Korean cinema in particular, has almost always functioned as a medium of entertainment that seeks reconciliation with traumatic events in modern history. An early Korean example is the silent film *Arirang* (1926), which responded to Japanese colonialism. The film's brash young director and lead actor, Na Un-gyu, was only in his midtwenties when he became the most recognizable Korean star of the colonial era during the 1920s and 1930s. *Arirang* has been routinely voted the best film in Korean history even though all copies were lost during the Korean War. Its plot involves Yŏng-jin (played by Na), a young mentally ill student who regains his senses when a farm supervisor attempts to rape his sister, stabbing the man with a sickle. The supervisor treats his tenants with violence but bows before the landlord, thereby allegorizing—and reflecting national anger about—the relation between the Japanese colonial occupiers and their Korean collaborators. During film screenings, at the moment when Yŏng-jin is taken away by the authorities, a small accordion band accompanying the *pyŏnsa* (*benshi*) orators would play the title song. Reportedly, no one in the audience would be spared from weeping in response to the sad fate of both the nation and the film's main character.

Even after Korea was liberated from the Japanese colonial occupation in 1945, the nation's film production continued to function, perhaps with equal consequence, as popular entertainment, political propaganda, artistic medium, and profit-making vehicle. At each of the three key junctures in modern Korean history, cinema played a distinct sociopolitical role: the melodramas of the Golden Age of the 1960s variously highlighted, intensified, and reconciled the family traumas of postcolonial and postwar Korea; the "New Korean Cinema" of the late 1980s and the 1990s coincided with the *minjung* democratizing movement of the era, pushing for socially conscious themes and realist styles; and during the last two decades, the unsettled accounts of hallyu have laid bare the insatiable demands of global capitalism. The Golden Age melodramas of the 1960s, the New Korean Cinema productions of the 1980s and 1990s, and present-day hallyu commercial films have all responded to socioeconomic problems perhaps more effectively than any other medium, and this is especially the case today, in the face of the Korean film industry's unprecedented profitability, its increasing critical recognition in domestic, regional, and international markets and film festivals, and the growing geopolitical importance of Korea itself.

Two particularly important films that permanently redirected the trajectory of Korean cinema were written and directed by a pair of filmmakers who would soon become the darlings of Asian as well as world cinema. More so than other films, *JSA: Joint Security Area* (dir. Park Chan-wook, 2000) and *The Host* (*Kwemul*, dir. Bong Joon-ho, 2007) were groundbreaking not because of their innovations but because they approximated the Hollywood style to near perfection, with budgets that were only a fraction of the American studio standard. *JSA*, which was the first South Korean film to favorably portray a North Korean soldier, successfully introduced the winning formula for Korean blockbusters of the next two decades.[19] The film follows the thriller genre and represents North Korea with a new empathy, with the North Korean soldier choosing, at the film's climax, to remain loyal to the North Korean state. The South Korean film industry produced about thirty feature-length films featuring North Korean subjects from 2000 to 2008, the so-called Sunshine Policy period in which the two liberal South Korean presidents, Kim Dae-jung and Roh Moo-hyun, pursued a reconciliation policy toward North Korea. The South Korean film industry churned out film after film during this engagement period, using North Koreans as a character bank. Of course, as will be discussed in chapters 3 and 5, *sagŭks* (period films) and gender-war comedies were two genres conspicuous in their box office appeal during the first two decades of the twenty-first century, yet the South Korean commercial interest in North Korean subject matter never faded after *Shiri* (dir. Kang Je-gyu, 1999) and *JSA*, two films that showcased charismatic and psychologically complex North Korean characters, thereby setting the tone for Korean-style blockbuster conventions at the turn of the century. The two films in question were phenomenally successful at a time when the multiplex moviegoing praxis was being established, and over the ensuing two decades they helped sustain public interest in North Korean subjects as a bankable high concept.

During the subsequent ten-year conservative rule of Lee Myung-bak and Park Geun-hye (2008–17), many Korean blockbusters refused to remain politically acquiescent. Although the music and television industries became largely dominated by conservative pundits and bureaucrats and nonpolitical content during this period, Korean cinema helped sow the seeds for the candlelight vigil protests that eventually led to the impeachment of Park Geun-hye in 2017. Some of the biggest hit films from this decade include *Masquerade* (*Kwanghae*, dir. Choo Chang-min, 2012), *Veteran* (*Bet'erang*, dir. Ryoo Seung-wan, 2015), *The Attorney* (*Pyŏnhoin*, dir. Yang Woo-suk, 2015), and *Train to Busan* (*Busanhaeng*, dir. Yeon Sang-ho, 2016), which decried ruthless neoliberal economic policies, mourned the victims sacrificed during the democratizing protests, and openly advocated for progressive reforms in South Korea. Because many of these films were made during the administration of Park Geun-hye (2013–17), she reportedly sought to force out CJ Entertainment's head mogul, Miky Lee (Lee Mi-kyung), from her corporate leadership role.[20] It was Korean cinema's refusal to compromise itself in the face of the conservative politics of the day that allowed it to eventually churn out landmark films such as *Parasite* (*Kisaengch'ung*, dir. Bong Joon-ho, 2019), which sarcastically depicts the polarizing gap between economic haves and have-nots in Korea.

Despite these politically themed films, when it came to stories about North Korea, the Sunshine Policy seemed to have little impact on Korean

1.4 Film still from *The Spy Gone North* (2018).

cinema throughout the 2010s. For example, Ryu Seung-wan's *Berlin File* (*Berŭllin*, 2013), the first true post–Sunshine Policy spy film, was much bolder in its criticism of North Korean leadership. In this film, the new North Korean leader Kim Jong-un is not only portrayed with his real name but also depicted as being at the center of an internal corruption that has led to Trotskyite assassinations of innocent diplomats in Berlin still loyal to the party. Although the South Korean film industry was still not producing such ideologically distasteful films as Hollywood's *Die Another Day* (2002) or *The Interview* (2014), which taunt North Koreans as irredeemable villains, the days when South Korea pursued the liberal aim of portraying North Korea as a different kind of "other" was no longer in vogue throughout much of the 2010s.[21] Although films depicting North Korea have become scarce over the past ten years, there are still big-budget films made about North Korea that have met with both critical and financial success. For instance, *The Spy Gone North* (*Kongjak*, dir. Yoon Jong-bin, 2018) was based on the real story of a South Korean spy who disguised himself as a businessman seeking to infiltrate the North Korean political elite in China in the 1990s (figure 1.4). In its re-creation of the character of then North Korean leader Kim Jong-il, the film scrupulously reproduced every small detail about the reclusive dictator who secretly developed nuclear weapons and fascinated both the Western world and South Korea. The success of *The Spy Gone North* was a reminder that the topic of North Korea, despite its waning popularity, continues to serve as a story bank for South Korean blockbusters. Other recent films, whether set during the Korean War or depicting North Koreans in a new light, have inscribed the North-South relationship with a new meaning, blurring the distinction between the two sides by rewriting war trauma (death, betrayal between family members, and separation of family), recharacterizing Korean gender roles (loss of traditional patriarchy, frank female sexuality depicted through US military prostitution, and phallic lack suffered by local men), and reauthoring national origin myths (villainization of aggressive, dogmatic, and selfish men, need to help aid wayward, anachronistic North Korea, South Korea's inauguration as the Republic of Korea built around the Korean War that became a landmark twentieth-century Cold War event).

Beyond their thematic updates, these films also pursued another ambition. Unlike the explicit agenda of rewriting Korean history, this more tactical ambition was that of constructing a national cinema that spoke a film language on par with European art cinema and, later, the productions of Hollywood. The impact of the Korean War on South Korean society was, and continues to be, far greater than the combined effects of World War II and the Vietnam War on the United States. It split families, produced countless civilian casualties and damage, and permanently divided the nation. Once South Korean censorship of interrogations into the origins of the war was lifted, the enormity of trauma and efforts toward its reconciliation could finally be translated into elements for domestic commercial cinema. The challenge, then, was to construct a popular national cinema out of the tragedies of the Korean War and cinematically emblematize that war as a familiar setting for consumers and moviegoers outside Korea. This objective raised the question: Could Korean cinema render a cinematic landscape that would both transmit the intensity of the historical tragedy, thereby whetting local melodramatic emotions, as well as make that tragedy legible as entertainment even for audiences unfamiliar with Korean history? The latter part of this question would become significant in Korean cinema's effort to globalize itself for the outside world.

Many in the Korean film industry wanted their own version of the Omaha Beach landing as depicted in *Saving Private Ryan* (dir. Steven Spielberg, 1998). *Taegukgi: The Brotherhood of War* (*Taegukgi Hwinallimyeo*, dir. Kang Je-gyu, 2004) was one of the resulting big-budget Korean War dramas, which portrayed the 1950 Battle of River Nakdong in a style that approximated Spielberg's and was also produced at a record cost for a Korean film at the time (US$12 million). Ultimately, however, due to a combination of budget constraints, political backlash from the discovery of the North's nuclear weapons program after the Sunshine Policy, and the political sensitivity that still surrounds any depictions of the Korean War, the Korean film industry was prevented from fulfilling its dream of forging a unique global cinema out of the traumatic national experience.

Although the representation of the Korean War in Korean cinema during the early to mid-1990s focused on historically epic yet introspective local stories that allegorized the particularities of national history, the genre films produced after 2000 have aesthetically reshaped these allegories into a more universal and familiar genre topography. Hence, the aforementioned *Shiri* by Kang Je-gyu and Park Chan-wook's *JSA* became significant trendsetters for Korean cinema, insofar as both films loosened the allegorical force of the local and emboldened the figuration of the global. These films were exemplary in breaking free of the local constraints of Cold War politics while simulating Hollywood's configuration of the spy genre and war films. Their genre codes not only engaged in an artificialization of character-based conflict but also featured the computer-generated simulation of space, props, and spectacles. In *Shiri*, the cityscape of Seoul suddenly looks like a nonspecific cosmopolitan city, as if produced by a Marvel Studios film, with settings in critical scenes taking place in generic places such as a Broadway musical theater (showing *Guys and Dolls*) and a World Cup soccer stadium that has erased realistic, local textures in favor of a depiction of Korea through an illusory materiality. In *JSA*, much of the story takes place around Panmunjom, the small, heavily guarded building site in the DMZ between North and South Korea that serves as both a real setting of Cold War confrontation and, as discussed earlier, a tourism destination for foreign visitors. By building a set that simulated this globally recognizable theme-park-like destination, Park Chan-wook delivered a Korean topographical formation that blurs the boundary between the painful history of the Korean War and the entertainment that the site has also afforded to international travelers and moviegoers who might only be tangentially interested in Korea.[22] The entire film has the feel of a National Geographic photo shoot rather than offering a realistic depiction of what is, in fact, the North-South war zone. During the epilogue sequence, images are no longer provided by cinematic frames but are instead broken into snapshot images that further heighten the touristic impression of space and architecture. The elaborate and lavish movie set that replicates, for instance, the North Korean leader's office in *The Spy Gone North* or the Panmunjom located inside the DMZ border in *JSA* that is co-patrolled by American, North Korean, and South Korean troops, reminds the viewers that no other film industry can better visually represent the modern and yet feudal kingdom that the DPRK has become than the one in South Korea (figure 1.5).

Almost every male Korean filmmaker who has earned the title of blockbuster film director has sought to depict a theme from modern Korea's

1.5 The replica of Kim Jong-Il's North Korean palace in *The Spy Gone North* (2018) is more lavish than the real one.

tumultuous history, and Yoon Je-kyoon is also no exception. After his box office smash hit *Tidalwave* (*Haeundae*, 2009), a disaster genre film about a typhoon and tsunami hitting the shores of Busan, the second-largest city in Korea, Yoon turned to the theme of the Korean War with *Ode to My Father* (*Kukje sijang*) in 2014. While *Ode* does not offer an alternate history of the nation or necessarily affirm a conservative South Korean political agenda (i.e., by valorizing South Korean dictatorship, poking fun at North Korean leadership, and so on), it does exploit, for commercial, melodramatic purposes, hidden layers of Confucian values that are deeply embedded in Korean society (figure 1.6). Linking Confucianism with the melodramatic genre against the backdrop of the Korean War and the subsequent national division is the sort of commercial maneuver that Korean cinema has excelled at. Korean War films predating *Ode* focus on either the reconciliation or the impossibility of agreement between the two ideological sides of the conflict. However, *Ode*'s disassociation from the ideological struggle during and after the Korean War prevented its viewers from exploring the historical origins of the war and instead offered them a remythologization of Korea's Confucian values. The insistence on the Confucian mantra of ancestor reverence, of course, is already made explicit in the film's English title, *Ode to My Father*, which has no relation to the original Korean title, *Kukje sijang*. The Korean title refers to an international market, one of the oldest in Busan. *Ode*'s plotline, which begins with ten-year-old Tŏk-su

1.6 A couple weeps when paying tribute to the Taegukgi (South Korean flag) in *Ode to My Father* (2014): Is this an act of right-leaning nationalism or one of left-leaning blasphemy?

(played by Hwang Chŏngmin) becoming separated from his father during the Korean War and ends with his acknowledgment of his father's death more than sixty years later after a lifetime without him, affirms the deep-seated Confucian values that dictate both the film's tempo and its central leitmotif. *Ode* is exemplary for the resuscitation of neo-Confucianism on contemporary television and film screens, as a virtual form of familial affect that most Koreans no longer experience.

One of the most interesting aspects of *Ode to My Father* is that it gives far greater thematic priority to the father than to his children. Although Tŏk-su's father has reared many offspring (in one scene, I counted eleven), none of them are more singularly important than the man who is conspicuous by his absence throughout the film. *Ode*, which is also a film about genocide, reverses the script of typical Holocaust films, which tend to focus on the protection of children from harm. For example, in *Life Is Beautiful* (dir. Roberto Benigni, 1998), a father in a Nazi concentration camp remains resilient and cheerful in the company of his son until the very end when he is taken away to die; *Schindler's List* (dir. Steven Spielberg, 1993) celebrates the lives of survivors and their offspring rather than mourning the dead; and *Sophie's Choice* (dir. Alan J. Pakula, 1982) focuses on a mother's tragic choice to save one of her children and give up the other. By contrast, Tŏk-su makes a life decision favoring the spirit of his father, thereby causing him to sacrifice his own aspiration to become a marine captain as well as, ultimately, his leg. The central question posed in the film is how to determine the right time to mourn a father who failed to escape North Korea during the war and who therefore cannot be presumed either alive or dead in the intervening six-plus decades.

Movies depicting the epic confrontation between North and South Korea through genre conventions such as spy thriller, action film, war combat film, and melodrama have been key box office draws for Korean cinema over the past twenty years. In the wake of the success of *Shiri* and *JSA* at the dawn of the new millennium (2001), Korean films drew a new record of 46 percent of all moviegoers, thereby demonstrating a renewed faith in local products unseen in South Korea since the 1960s. By comparison, in 2000 the local market share in Japan was 31.8 percent, 28.5 percent in France, 19.6 percent in Great Britain, and 12.5 percent in Germany. Throughout the first two decades of the twenty-first century, Korean box office receipts have grown even more. Korean cinema consistently outperformed Hollywood films in local box offices, while overall ticket sales tallied right before the pandemic increased threefold since 2000. Over the past seventy-five years, the Korean film industry is perhaps the only national cinema that has regained its domestic audience after losing it to Hollywood. By comparison, during much of the 1980s and 1990s, less than 20 percent of moviegoers watched Korean films. Every top ten film in 1993, for instance, was produced by Hollywood, with the exception of Im Kwon-Taek's *Sopyonje*.

Not only has Hollywood dominance waned in Korea, but the country's moviegoing culture has undergone colossal changes over the past two decades. *Sopyonje*, which held the previous box office record for a Korean film throughout the 1990s, was initially released on only one screen (Dansongsa) in Seoul, a city of more than ten million people, and perhaps on only a few more screens in regional cities. At the time, individual 35 mm release prints had to be struck in order for the film to be released on more than one screen. Today, the need for bulky 35 mm prints costing thousands of dollars apiece to strike and ship to theaters has ended. The rapid proliferation of shopping malls with multiplexes around the country and the conversion to digital projection helped transition the distribution of films from a system where every new film was released on only one screen per city to the practice of opening films on almost every available screen in neighborhood multiplexes. High-definition (HD) movie files permit multiscreen projections and are easily accessible in film theaters, thereby giving spectators their pick of screenings for the latest *Avengers* film at 7:10 p.m., 7:30 p.m., and 7:45 p.m. Blockbuster films in Korea typically open on more than two thousand screens across the nation—without this distribution increase costing distributors a single additional penny. Bong Joon-ho's Oscar winner, *Para-*

site, was released on 1,800 screens and reached the ten-million-ticket mark in about four weeks after its release. *Along with the Gods: The Last 49 Days* (dir. Kim Yong-hwa, 2018) holds the record for films released before 2020 at 2,235 screens. *Avengers: Endgame* hit a milestone in Korea by reaching 2,835 screens on its peak day of release. This is a country that has a little more than 3,000 screens in the entire country.[23]

The combined box office revenue of the Chinese and South Korean cinema markets, which totaled US$10.9 billion in 2019 ($9.3 billion for China and $1.6 billion for South Korea), still falls below the size of the cinema markets of the top four Anglophone countries (United States, Canada, United Kingdom, and Australia), which currently stands at around $14 billion.[24] However, the Sino-Korean alliance, should it manage to sustain itself after the escalating tension between China and South Korea that began in the late 2010s, could potentially represent a market size of homegrown movies respectable enough to compete against even English-language film productions. In both China and South Korea, the box office share of domestic films stands at more than 50 percent, and the two countries' combined cinema revenue currently comprises about 22 percent of the global film industry and is expected to grow exponentially over the next two decades. In a global film culture where the amount of capital investment—to finance the ever-rising cost of visual graphics and other film technology—determines the taste and the preference of moviegoers, the Chinese market's 1.4 billion population has not gone unnoticed by Korean producers. The enormous consumer base in China both attracts and strains the film industry in Korea, which shares a cultural and linguistic heritage with its western neighbor but also risks becoming subsumed by the Chinese market and losing its own identity. Because *A Wedding Invitation*, a 2013 Chinese-language Korean-Chinese coproduction (with an all-Korean film crew, including director Oh Ki-hwan), was so successful at the Chinese box office that South Korean film companies, headed by CJ Entertainment & Media (CJ E&M), have subsequently developed and rolled out continuous film projects in China and other Asian countries through the CJ E&M subsidiary CJ Global Studio. In 2017 the first local film made by CJ in Vietnam, *Girl from Yesterday* (dir. Phan Gia Nhat Linh), also became a hit film. That same year, CJ announced a plan to make more films abroad by 2020 (more than twenty films per year) than for the domestic Korean market (about fifteen films per year)—although uncertainty surrounding the THAAD deployment controversy as well as effects from the COVID-19 pandemic have thrown a wrench into this global strategy.[25]

The development of digital technologies has generated a sense of global culture that impacts the ways people interact with each other on a day-to-day basis. Currently more than 60 percent of the world's population — more than 4.8 billion people — uses the internet.[26] Korea is not the only country that boasts a very high percentage of its population using the internet, but it is probably the only country that has also seen its movie theater attendance rate soar since the onset of the internet revolution. Only India, China, the United States, and Mexico have higher movie ticket sales than Korea (see table 1.1), yet South Korea's population — fifty million — is only a fraction of these other countries.[27] Despite the challenges it confronts in exporting its products, Korean cinema has performed better than anyone could have predicted, particularly in the domestic market. Right before the pandemic hit, Korea boasted one of the highest movie-attendance rates in the world, at around 4.3 per capita; its domestic film market enjoyed local protection, with an overwhelming majority of Korean cinema audiences voluntarily choosing local films over those of Hollywood; and the Korean film industry became one of the largest film export markets in the world.[28] In less than a decade, Korean cinema overcame perilous conditions to become one of the sturdiest local film industries in the world, thereby impressing local fans as well as drawing the attention of Hollywood producers interested in remakes and global talent. In the face of the twenty-first-century challenge of digitization and globalization that has confronted all national cinemas operating outside Hollywood, Korean cinema has cleared the hurdle by developing and incorporating indigenous technology for computer-generated images and modifying and appropriating Hollywood genres such as thrillers, disaster films, courtroom dramas, Westerns, and comedies for its own blockbuster productions and releases. It has also adopted Hollywood's wide-release marketing strategies in the recent years. In other words, Korea has not shied away from experimenting with spectacles and vertical integration where distributors practice monopolistic behavior. Finally, the routine participation of Korean filmmakers such as Park Chan-wook, Kim Jee-woon, Lee Chang-dong, Bong Joon-ho, and Hong Sangsoo in major international film festivals is a strong confirmation that Korean cinema has enjoyed a masterful run during the first twenty years of the twenty-first century, and its efforts may stand the test of time.

One of the reasons for this success is that the heyday of Korean cinema has arrived at a time when the meaning of cinema has itself undergone a tremendous transformation. Action franchise blockbusters featuring climactic clichés and reboot imagery have come to dominate not only

TABLE 1.1 Largest Markets by Number of Box Office Admissions, 2017

Rank	Country	Number of admissions (millions of tickets)
1	India	1,981
2	China	1,620
3	United States	1,240
4	Mexico	338
5	South Korea	220
6	Russia	213
7	France	206
8	Brazil	181
9	Japan	174
10	United Kingdom	171

Source: UNESCO Institute for Statistics, "Feature Films: Exhibition—Admissions and Gross Box Office (GBO), accessed March 17, 2021, http://data.uis.unesco.org/index.aspx?queryid=59.

Hollywood but also the Korean film industry. Korean film technicians, including vfx (visual effects) supervisors and digital animators, are seeking to open doors in China. Bigger-budget blockbusters in China and Korea mean heavier reliance on digital characters and motion captures, which present favorable opportunities for the Korean film industry to find a niche market in Asian film industries. With Korean cinema vying for stories characterized by diminished appeal to the realist traditions and humanist ambitions of modernist sensibilities, its productions circulate within the world of hallyu fandom, undermining the local and national particularities of Korea's unique culture. Often lost is a bold commitment to aesthetic movements or cinematic expressions unfettered by commercial interests. Korean cinema is currently afloat, not simply thanks to the Hollywoodization of its business praxis but also due to the nationalization of its historical traumas.

On lists of the most commercially successful films in Korean cinematic history, it is difficult to find titles that do not deal with Korean history or social issues such as corporate corruption (*Veteran*) or class division derived from neoliberal capitalism (*Parasite*).

KOREAN TELEVISION IN THE POST-TELEVISION ERA

Around the turn of the twenty-first century, the national identity of cinema, pop music, and television was rather easy to determine. Cinema attendance records, physical CD and LP sales, and television ratings were tracked within national boundaries by the governing bodies of the national film, recording, and telecommunications industries; it was not difficult to monitor, evaluate, and write about each of these national media industries as separate entities. At the time, transnational cinema, pop, and television often only meant collaboration between artists and filmmakers from different national origins. However, the recent growth and expansion of global content companies—known as over-the-top (OTT) media providers—such as Netflix, Amazon Video, and Hulu TV, which stream over the internet and are played on smart TVs, smartphones, and other devices, are continuing to render national boundaries within these entertainment industries more or less obsolete. The internet blurs not only the borders between nations but also the boundaries between music, television, and cinema. Like it or not, OTT has replaced VHS tapes and CDs as well as movie theaters, home stereos, and television sets. Resulting changes in moviegoing patterns have also brought about transformations in content production itself. This phenomenon was foreseen by French theorist Gilles Deleuze, who, along with Félix Guattari, postulated that libidinalized capitalist desire-production would soon erode the traditional Marxist distinction between production, distribution, and consumption.[29] Netflix is perhaps the first global theater, but it may also be the first global television station. Currently any subscriber of Netflix can choose from more than twenty major languages available from the "profile management" menu, and programs feature subtitles in many of these select languages and more. Netflix services all of the major world languages, and its membership subscriptions in 190 countries simply create a universe that previous generations of Hollywood moguls could have only dreamed about building. The only significant market that Netflix has not yet penetrated is China, although of course Chinese is one of the languages that it services.

The rise of internet streaming services such as Netflix has impacted television stations more than movie theaters. For instance, although US movie ticket sales have declined following their 2002 peak, cinema is today not as threatened by OTT as many had feared, due in part to higher average ticket prices as well as exceptionally growing theater sales in Asian markets such as China and South Korea.[30] Yet in the 2010s, television stations were no longer as profitable as they once were. In Korea, the combined net income of the three major networks, KBS, MBC, and SBS, has remained stagnant at around $3.5 billion for the past ten years.[31] The earnings of Korean internet companies dwarf these amounts. In 2017 the net income of web portal giant Naver alone was about $4.3 billion, and Kakao, an internet company that runs a very popular instant messaging application, posted an annual income of $2 billion that same year.[32] Netflix is experiencing rapid growth in Korea, with a monthly subscriber increase of 274 percent in 2018 alone, although it is almost impossible to determine the net income and gross profit of OTT companies in Korea because their sales numbers are not transparent. Google Korea and Facebook Korea, which offer video streaming services through media channels such as YouTube and others, have recently come under heavy fire from South Korean National Assembly members because their CEOs have refused to disclose their sales and profits in Korea even under direct parliamentary questioning.[33] Many estimate that Google's advertising revenue and sales in Korea through OTT such as Google Play, YouTube, and Gmail exceed that of Naver, but as of 2018 Google has avoided paying domestic taxes. Because Google Korea is classified as a limited liability company and not a public company, it has no obligation to disclose any of its company information and instead reroutes all sales to Google's Singapore branch, even while industry insiders have reportedly claimed that Google's Korean earnings alone exceeded $2 billion in 2018.[34] These days, many Korean broadcasters, not unlike other YouTubers around the world, live and die by their YouTube channels and their associated advertising revenues, without relying on the traditional television format.

The decline of earnings for the television industry and the increase of earnings (reported or not) by global OTT and internet companies reveal three key points. First, the decrease in television viewing, which served as a mechanism for promoting modern domestic family values during the latter part of the twentieth century, was rather precipitous in Korea.[35] As we enter the 2020s, television content is increasingly based on private viewership (streaming, smartphone, and so on) rather than television sets. Korea, as one of the most wired countries in the world and boasting one of the fastest 5G networks, will be leading this process. There will be no more fights for the remote control, no more complaints about loud volumes, but also no more quality family time around television.

Second, declining domestic viewership and earnings could be supplanted by export sales of content. Successful cable companies such as Mnet and JTBC have realized that this export revenue is just as important as domestic advertisement revenue. As reported in several Korean media articles, the Japanese Ministry of Internal Affairs and Communications noted in 2017 that Korean television content exports trailed only those of the United States and the UK, at $350 million—which was about $100 million greater than Japan.[36] After the rise of the hallyu phenomenon with the release of *Winter Sonata* in 2003 in Japan and the production of the Korean television drama *Dae Jang Geum*, during what Dal Yong Jin describes as "Hallyu 1.0," many additional Korean television dramas, such as *My Love from the Star* (*Pyŏl esŏ on kŭdae*, SBS Drama Production, 2013) and *Descendants of the Sun* (2017), became international hits during the era of Hallyu 2.0.[37] Moving away from the austere romantic dramas that characterized the first decade of hallyu, these urban romantic comedies of the 2010s such as *My Love from the Star* were characterized by outrageous and absurd imaginary geographical spaces and time-travel settings but ultimately proved popular among young urban viewers in many Asian markets.

Third, the need for television networks to distinguish their offerings from OTT streaming content forced them to generate popular formats that rely on the reality-TV model. Television stations sustained their popularity through two types of reality shows: reality-based comedy variety shows and reality audition music programs. The success of YouTube and Netflix during the 2010s was built on highlight reels and the convenient, individual streaming of premade content, but traditional television networks still possessed the advantage of presenting "live" television. Perhaps not surprising, some of the highest-rated Korean television shows of the 2010s were live audition programs such as *Superstar K, Show Me the Money,* and *Produce 101,* which encouraged audience participation, and reality comedy variety shows that sought to incorporate an unscripted and improvised sense of liveness. Social media and OTTs have just started to venture into these live audition programs, although they will probably be able to take over traditional television by 2030. The reality variety show *Running Man* was one program that achieved phenomenal international success, although the reigning comedy of the first two decades of the twenty-first century was *Muhan Dojeon* (*Infinite Challenge*), which aired on MBC on Saturday evenings.

The use of farce and "mimicry" as the central driving force in carnivalesque theater is not only particular to the case of Korean comedy; it is also the case for almost all comedy traditions and game cultures. Particularly in the life of modern capitalism, where competition is not a rarity but a rule and everyone must take their chances, the play of simulation becomes more intensified. When Roger Caillois classified games into four categories—agô (competition), alea (chance), mimicry (simulation), and ilinx (vertigo)—in the 1960s, he was not motivated by the postcolonial articulation of mimicry as a politicized gesture in the separation between colonizers and the colonized.[38] His game categories are expressions of the fundamental human desire for play. In many contemporary game shows, particularly in Korean variety shows, these categories are dynamically employed to deliver pleasure to their audiences. Instead of an emphasis on narrative, ethics, or themes, mimicry and the other three categories in Caillois's grouping provide an overwhelming sense of enjoyment for the carnivalesque folk traditions prevalent in many play cultures. It is perhaps no surprise that the Korean reality-television shows with dominant ratings over the past decade, such as *Grandpa over Flowers* (*Kkotpoda halbae*), *Three Meals a Day* (*Samsi sekki*), or *Muhan Dojeon*, are not narrative-driven. If narratives are constituted by sequences of events that reveal themselves through a temporal structure that engages heroes, villains, and rewards, most of these reality-television shows do not observe the basic rules of narrative structure. The success of these comedy variety programs is instead inspired by Korea's own improvisational street theater tradition, which traces back to *t'alchum* (mask dance), *nongak* (farming music), and *p'ansori* (street opera for commoners), all of which emphasized interactive play between performers and audiences, unpredictable plotlines, and nonprofessional stages. Over the past two decades, Korean television (as will also be later argued in chapter 4) has learned to be interactive with its audiences through the innovative use of captions that constantly weave literary pleasure into viewing pleasure. Written texts in the form of captions dispense with the need for a traditional host, moderator, or omniscient commentator in Korean variety programs.

Over the past decade, mukbang (eatcasts) in Korea became sensations— domestically as well as overseas—with live broadcasts of video jockeys (usually petite female Koreans) eating enormous amounts of food while chatting and interacting with internet audiences and satisfying the vicarious pleasures of eating. The violence, sexuality, and political satire that commonly thematize Western comedy programs are repressed in Korean television humor, where pleasure is instead derived from the joys of watching people prepare food, seeking places to eat, and consuming food. Korean television promotes a virtual sense of neo-Confucian harmony that is often missing from people's lives. Just as Japan underwent a disintegration of family and its values during postwar industrialization, the social fabric of family networks and values in Korea has thinned over the past few decades. The critical concepts on which these eatcast television programs are built include the empathization of communal ethics and the restoration of filial piety, as part of an effort to address recent demographic-cultural shifts. South Korea is currently experiencing the world's lowest fertility rate, and despite governmental efforts to increase it—spending nearly $200 billion on this effort from 2006 to 2018—it continues to decline (figure 1.7).[39] The falling birth rate has not only significantly slowed the economy but has also changed the dynamics of the family structure in South Korea. The rejection of marriage among young people, in particular, has led to increased numbers of people living alone. Television programs, which formerly had a direct impact on family leisure activities, have had to shift their orientation in order to promote a cyber sense of family for viewers desiring to fulfill their ambitions and dreams of a life filled with domestic pleasures through family living. In other words, family values, though no longer sustainable in the form of true family viewing, are still very strongly felt in Korean programs. Since a family viewing television together is becoming less and less important, stations instead tend to focus on individual viewers who have yet to create a family of their own. Three examples of these programs are *The Return of Superman* (*Sup'ŏmaen i torawatta*), a hit program on KBS since 2013 focused on male celebrities raising babies; *Grandpa over Flowers* (*Kkotpoda halpae*), airing on TVN from 2013 to 2018, featuring septuagenarian actors going on backpacking tours; and *We Got Married* (*Uri kyŏlhon haetssŏyo*), airing from 2008 to 2017 on MBC, which paired up heterosexual single celebrities who pretended they were living as married couples. These programs sought to compensate for the absence of real-life family members (babies, grandfathers, and spouses, respectively) in the real lives of audiences. They are smash hits that have sold multiple remake rights in other countries.[40]

Insofar as the comedy shows *Muhan Dojeon* and *Running Man* have each aired more than five hundred episodes and created international fandom all around Asia over the past decade, one could liken them to some

1.7 South Korean government poster promoting the two-child policy, 1981.

of the most innovative comedy programs in the history of television, such as *Monty Python's Flying Circus*, which was associated with the popularity of Swinging London of the 1960s, or *Saturday Night Live*, which emerged as part of the counterculture landscape of 1970s New York. *Muhan Dojeon* found success in an era of multiple crises—political, economic (stemming from the IMF loan repayment in the late 1990s), and postfamilial—celebrating as well as criticizing the complacency of a Korea that still struggles with its identity in an age of sluggish growth, occupies an ambivalent position between the superpowers United States and China, and dreams of pairing neo-Confucian domestic harmony with the pleasures of singlehood.[41] This is not to suggest that shows like *Muhan Dojeon* are as innovative or as cinematically brilliant as the British or American comedies of the 1960s or 1970s. However, the continued success of *Running Man* in China and the surprisingly high ratings of *The Masked Singer*'s first season in the United States (in 2019, using a remake format after production rights were bought by the American company Fox from Korea's MBC) does pose the question as to whether Korea is now finally leaving behind its bruised, traumatic past as a colonial or neocolonial country trapped in its own *han* (suffering) in favor of exporting various innovative forms of television game culture to the rest of the world. This shift would strongly affirm Korea's status as a soft-power hegemonic nation that has successfully extricated itself from its status as a nation known only for its mimicry of Japanese and American popular cultural content. However, as long as South Korea's ambiguous identity persists as that of the only country still caught in a Cold War scenario in a post–Cold War world, and as long as it continues to be caught in the belligerent rhetorical crossfire between the United States, North Korea, and China, South Korea's ability to achieve a truly independent cultural tone beyond the gimmicky pastiche inspired by street comedy culture may not be possible, even as its television products become highly visible across many continents.

Since the smash success of *Superstar K* starting in 2009, audition survival reality-TV shows such as *K-Pop Star* and *Produce 101*, both of which feature a combination of professional judges and live internet and text voting participation by viewers have garnered high transnational ratings in markets all over Asia. The diminished importance of television and declining CD sales at the time led the two media industries, television and entertainment management companies, to seek a new alliance. In the wake of the global success of *American Idol*, two Korean music audition programs began with great fanfare around 2010. The station SBS started broadcasting *K-Pop Star* in 2011 after recruiting the three big entertainment companies (SM, YG, and JYP) to serve as judges of the program. *K-Pop Star* wasn't the first Korean music audition program on television, but it was certainly the most popular when it first aired. About two decades had elapsed since Seo Taiji began his personal coup d'état against broadcasting companies by boycotting television programs. The power reversal was now complete. There was no difficulty in identifying exactly who the people in control were. It was no longer the television producers, who had seized power away from the sho-dan performers during the politically acquiescent period of the 1970s and 1980s by providing off-white music programs during those two decades, but the former musicians who now chaired the entertainment companies. Programmed at the same time that Donald Trump was still appearing on NBC's *The Celebrity Apprentice*, this was one of the first programs in Korea to feature business owners directly engaged in selecting talent to hire in the interest of furthering their profits on broadcast television.

Although Lee Soo-man, the chair of SM, chose not to participate directly in the program, his deputy manager, Boa, served as the judge. The two other chairmen, Yang Hyun-seok of YG and Park Jin-young of JYP, came on the show to serve as judges — letting their acerbic tongues freely fly after each of the contestants' performances. The fact that Simon Cowell, the British television producer and talent agent who founded the global boy band One Direction, served as the star judge of *American Idol* made the setup of Korean audition programs palatable for audiences who may not have been prepared for such a crudely transparent display of the neoliberal capitalist structure on television. Up to this time, Korean audition shows had been dominated by song festivals such as MBC's annual Campus Song Festival (Taehak kayoje) and Beach Song Festival (Haebyŏn kayoje) that had promoted wholesome values and had showed little concern for "commercial viability" and "professional maturation."[42] The campus song festivals, which at one point produced many star bands such as Sanullim and Songgolmae and singers such as Lee Sun-hee and Lee Sang-eun throughout the final three decades of the twentieth-century, stopped broadcasting altogether after their ratings plummeted in the new century. Despite the intense public pressure to sign the audition winners and the public's next heartthrob, during the first two seasons that it participated, SM Entertainment chose not to contract any of the contestants from the program. After the first two seasons, SM dropped out of the program entirely, suggesting that its own audition process worked better in mysterious and nontransparent ways for its idol selection than the one showcased live before the public. The decision by SM to shun *K-Pop Star* represented an explicit rejection of participatory democracy and a reaffirmation of the mogul-structured system of K-pop. In the late 2010s, *Produce 101* became the highest rated audition programming show — only to have the government investigate it for violating ethical codes. It turned out that the program's winners were fixed by the producers, who had been bribed by entertainment company managers. The situation reconfirmed suspicions that there is very little room for democracy even in social-media-driven live television audition programs.

If *K-Pop Star* garnered popularity by directly connecting young contestants to the big entertainment companies, *Superstar K* was another audition program that focused on searching for singing talents and signing them to record deals. Starting in 2009 on the cable network Mnet, the program featured veteran singers headed by Lee Seung-cheol, who reemerged as a star thanks to the popularity of this program. Before *Show Me the Money* replaced *Superstar K* as the top-rated music program in

2015, *Superstar K*, after the dwindling popularity of *K-Pop Star*, was one of the most watched music programs on television. Perhaps the biggest highlight of *Superstar K* was when Busker Busker placed second in its third season. Busker Busker was the best nondance musician band discovered in the era of K-pop. Though the band, which is heavily reliant on acoustic guitar, chose to remain unsigned by any of the entertainment management companies, Busker Busker (named after the act of busking free music in public spaces) has produced hit after hit. Relying on no electronic dance beats and a visible lack of colorful apparel or synchronized dance movements, the trio, led by singer-songwriter Jang Beom-joon from Gwangju, has continued the folk-rock tradition that focuses on the theme of travel, nature, and coming-of-age love in Korea. Busker Busker's popular songs "Yeosu Night Sea" and "Cherry Blossom Ending" can still be heard in cafés and streets in Korea today, proving that music and mature lyrics can still move people from all walks of life in the age of K-pop.

CAN BTS MANIA EVER BE ACCURATELY COMPARED TO BEATLEMANIA?

> I agree that there have been more things to look at in Korean movies, but I can't shake the feeling that they are imitations of Hollywood. I wonder whether it is significant if the movies Koreans are making are the same as the ones made by Hollywood producers. . . . One thing to be learned from Hong Kong [film industry's demise] is that movies lacking criticism and creativity will suffer a fate that is no different [from Hong Kong's].
> —Tsai Ming-liang, 2001

Taiwan's Tsai Ming-liang, one of the most coveted Asian and queer film directors, criticized the Hollywoodization of Korean cinema as early as 2000, when Bong Joon-ho and Park Chan-wook's careers began to take off. After twenty years, Tsai has been proven both wrong and right about Korean cinema. Every indication was that Korean cinema over the past two decades was on a similar path to that of Hollywood industry. Aesthetically and industry-wise, Korean cinema did produce, distribute, and exhibit its commercial films as if it's a true competitor to Hollywood. However, it did not collapse the way that the Hong Kong film industry had in the 1990s. Why? While Korean cinema's increased spending on sci-fi, an editing style that focused on the fast-moving trend of the day, and an active engagement with sophisticated genre codes did make it resemble Hollywood's cinema, thematically, it was extracting themes and subjects from Korean history and local issues. While most countries throughout the past twenty years saw a decline in movie theater admissions, Korea witnessed an exponential rise in movie attendance. A comparison between 2008 and 2018 Korean theatrical box office receipts reveals that Korean movie attendance doubled within just a decade.[43] No wonder Korea has become a major stop for all major Hollywood film releases and media junkets with obligatory YouTube videos made by action hero stars eating street food from Korean vendors to earn affinities with Korean fans in recent years, and why pitches are made for collaborations with Korean film directors such as Bong Joon-ho and Park Chan-wook. It is no longer a surprise when actors such as Chris Evans or Jake Gyllenhaal, when visiting Korea to promote their Marvel Studios or DC Comics films, *Captain America* or *Spiderman*, discuss how they had to fly long hours to meet and audition with their favorite Korean directors. These young American talents do not have to audition in Korean, but getting coached in a few Korean words certainly would not hurt.

Korea became hegemonic in the new century by both broadening its minjok identity and actively pursuing playful, mimicked subjectivities that became commercially viable in the era of social media. Embedded in Korean history is an amazing ability to mimic and parody the dominant cultural practices by a cavalcade of Korean acts, whose history stretches back much further than the history of YouTube and Psy's sensational one-hit wonder. The success of BTS also amplifies the importance of global fandom in the age of social media where an aggressive campaign by fans can outweigh the musical quality of a song. However, the Beatles would have been no more than just a footnote in twentieth-century history if the only songs in their catalog were giddy bubblegum tunes, and the group was remembered mostly for their boyish looks and the sea mammal suits that only inspire YouTube imitations. The names of John, Paul, George, and Ringo are permanently printed on every wall of pop fame because of the mature melodies, discordant unity, and melancholic poetry displayed in many more songs that rival even the work of some of the best classical composers that Western civilization has ever produced. Thus far, despite the popularity of RM, Suga, J-Hope, Jin, Jungkook, V, and Jimin, Korean popular music has yet to produce one single progression of chords that has created a ripple effect of global critical response without the super aid of maniacal campaigns by their fans. Just as rabid fans cannot turn mediocre athletes into champions, fandom alone cannot make music last forever. History or herstory only has room for true performers, artists, and innovators even in the era of social media. Just as the Chicago Cubs cannot become world champions with only the support of their fans, whether any of these or future K-pop acts can etch their names onto the global Music Walk of Fame is a question that will continue to plague future scholarship on this subject.

2 The Souls of Korean Folk
in the Era of Hip-Hop

Eazy-E, who has yet to claim his status as the first gangsta rapper from Compton, walks into the recording studio booth for the first time in his life. His producer, Dr. Dre, and other cohorts, DJ Yella and Ice Cube, remain behind the sound controller as creators of what turns out to be the N.W.A's historical first album that announced to the public the arrival of West Coast rap power. Though a writer of many successful rap songs himself, Eazy-E is visibly anxious about rapping for the first time into a professional microphone. He keeps missing the entry point of his first line of chorus, "Cruisin' down the street in my six-four," from his classic song, "Boyz-n-the-Hood," and earns for himself a scornful laughter from Dre and others intently listening outside his booth. After several aborted tries, Eazy-E gets angry at the disrespectful chorus hanging outside and demands both DJ Yella and Ice Cube leave the room. When they are alone together, Dre stops from repeatedly laying down the beat from what now seems to be a familiar ring-tone-like, synthesizer-driven sample from a Whoodini song from the previous decade. Through the intercom, Dre starts instructing, "You've got to say it like you believe that shit." In the real story, Eazy-E's first rap song took two days to record. Here, in the film adaptation version of the real story, he gets it right—after putting on his sunglasses—delivering the line about the fictive Eazy-E character in the song cruising down Crenshaw Boulevard in his red convertible after killing a car-thief friend as if nothing has happened.

—*Straight Outta Compton*, 2015

Yubong, after being visibly drunk, returns to his lodging where his two teen-aged children are waiting. Earlier in the day, he was upset with Dongho, his son, a drummer of his p'ansori troupe, whose performance in the traditional Korean marketplace was subpar. After Songhwa closes the sliding door that separates their room from the courtyard, Yubong begins to demonstrate to Dongho the precise time and versatile rhythm his drum has to keep. His speech, almost as if he is performing an episode of p'ansori itself, starts very gently, "the drum beats must be kept in harmony with the song," and then as his tone becomes more animated, Yubong's drum playing becomes louder and more frequent—to a point where he demands: "As the road has been well paved for the automobile to run very smoothly, so does the drum and your supplemental sidekick cheer [ch'uimsae] in order for the road to be well paved for your sister's vocals!" As Yubong's chastisement reaches a new level of cre-scendo when he emphasizes how the dynamic evolvement of drum beats of "pushing [milko], hanging [talko], tying [maetgo], and undoing [p'ulko]" ought to imitate the specific characteristics in the four seasons of "spring, summer, fall, and winter," which are vital to the harvesting cycle, the complaint from next door's lodger, who is actually the head of the vaudeville show on the road to sell "pills that cure all diseases," also gets louder and louder. "What the hell! Hills peep over another hill!" yells the next-door proprietor. Yubong remains completely unconcerned, as the most important thing in life is for his children to understand the aesthetics of p'ansori. Indeed, there is no resolution in sight; Dongho never grasps the concept of hard work involved in matching his music to the natural environment that surrounds and informs his aesthetics. Not only are they banished from the medicine traveling show, but the son will also leave Yubong, the recalcitrant master of p'ansori, who will not give up his dream of pursuing art only because poverty threatens to pulverize his family.

—*Sopyonje*, 1993

These two scenes—one from a 2015 blockbuster American film about the rise and fall of N.W.A, a rap group from Compton, California, the other from *Sopyonje,* a 1993 film that is one of the most important in the history of Korean cinema—initially appear to be saying totally different things.[1] *Straight Outta Compton* (dir. F. Gary Gray) is based on a true story about a group of hustlers trying to innovate hip postindustrial music in an urban setting in Southern California using high-tech recording technology right before the Rodney King uprising, and *Sopyonje* is about a fictive group of itinerant musicians trying to save the dying art of premodern Korean music called p'ansori that features nonamplified voice and is accompanied by only a drum made of wood and cowhide. Despite the differences, however, there are several paramount elements that commonly bind them. Both clips insist on the act of authenticating a playbook of aesthetic form, which requires in-depth training—both physical and psychological. Eazy-E, the rapper in the booth, is right. Both Yella and Ice Cube need to be thrown out of the studio in order for him to dig deep into his own psyche and get his verses right. Just like any other aesthetic endeavor, the true spirit of aesthetic innovation, in this case alone in the recording studio, is possible only through an exercise of discipline, which includes his willingness to accept the words of his mentor, Dr. Dre, while pulling from a reservoir of self-esteem that mentally blocks out the scornful reaction of a chorus outside. In *Sopyonje*, we also witness the same kind of emphasis that focuses on the real condition of aesthetic spirit. A willingness to filter out the chorus of boos and complaints that loudly creep through the thinly divided spatial compartments and the determined mind of a musician who can self-reflexively tap into the realities of both hostile and beautiful natural conditions that surround you are prerequisites as these conditions allow your drum playing to transcend into the sublime beats of p'ansori. Again to return to *Straight Outta Compton*, the scene of p'ansori musicians being kicked out onto the road without much chance of securing any employment is not dissimilar to the experience of cruising down the street in your Chevy Impala "Six-Four" even though you have been constantly harassed by police brutality, poverty, and discrimination against your kind; ultimately, a will of an almost subconscious disavowing and resistant subjecthood turns your incantations and performances into an expressive art—no matter how low the odds of your survival are. Also, beyond such obvious descriptions of psychological dimensions of the details, both scenes insist that the authentication of aesthetic form can only be realized when you are able to, as Dr. Dre says, "believe in that 'shit'" for yourself. And "believing in that shit" means that not only do you have to intensify your feelings of "joy," "fear," "pain," and "harmony" at a moment when you are "driving down the street of Crenshaw," but you also have to incantate and reproduce them later—alone in your studio—which exactly simulates the experience of the open air of Compton in your Chevy six-four.[2]

The hollerin' exhortation in Eazy-E's "Cruisin' down the street" is obvious; in *Sopyonje*, with the teacher/father Yubong, it is perhaps less so. But the holler is actually right there in front of the audience. It is p'ansori rap that is being expressed through the immaculate delivery of Yubong played by accomplished p'ansori singer / theater actor Kim Myong-gon as he begins an improvised monologue performance. His frustrated words of chastising his son reproduce themselves in rhymes and rhythms of what he calls "pushing (spring), hanging (summer), tying (fall), and undoing (winter)" as if they themselves are part of an act of p'ansori. In other words, Yubong is already spitting verses that flow almost too perfectly within a musical groove of arrangement of Korean words that both intensify and versify emotions. Yubong, through this self-reflexive operatic mode, has already crossed the threshold that separates everyday speech and poetic form, which reauthenticate themselves in the spirit of, for the lack of a better word, rap.

Finally, neither scene reaffirms any kind of racialized essence as the musical foundation of the black tradition of rap and the Korean music of p'ansori. On the contrary, these two scenes help deconstruct the essences in question, reaffirming what I describe, borrowing from Achille Mbembe, as "becoming-black" or "becoming-Korean." Eazy-E, despite the fact that he is a "brother from the 'hood," has a very difficult time hitting the first note hard on the beat to execute the fundamentals of rappin'. He lacks the groove, and the only way he can achieve it is through intense self-cultivation and self-discipline.[3] In *Sopyonje*, the fact that Dongho is the prodigal son of a great master of p'ansori isn't even a factor. Talent, the film seems to insist, is not hereditary—automatically passed on from one generation to the next.[4] Dongho lacks the focus that he needs to carry on the family tradition. The Korean film seems to be saying that the only way you can reauthenticate an aesthetic form is through, again, cultivation of character, willingness to learn, and, to draw from the German philosophical tradition of negative dialectics, a recognition of the negation of the negativity of the present status quo as necessary steps in promoting enough destructive energy that can never reach a synthesis.[5] Dongho, the son, it turns out, lacks all three qualities. He laments the family has no money, and will soon run away from his father and his sister—an act that he will later come to regret.

The conclusions of both films are dramatically different. *Straight Outta Compton* paints a dark picture of the aftermath of N.W.A. (Eazy-E dies after battling AIDS, Shug Knight continues to exercise his thug terror in the Death Row Record company, Ice Cube splits from the group, the police harassment never ceases, and other white executives exploit the group's success.) However, as everyone who knows just a little about rap history would recall, two of the surviving members of N.W.A have become some of the most financially successful musicians on this planet. Ice Cube is still making hit records and holds a celebrity status in the American pop scene, and Dr. Dre continues to serve as a producer for many major hip-hop artists (50 Cent, Eminem, and Kendrick Lamar) and, after having sold his stake in the Beats company to Apple in one of the biggest merger deals in the history of the tech industry, he is one of the wealthiest men on the West Coast.[6] On the other hand, the path of Korean p'ansori has been on a precipitous downward spiral throughout the twentieth and twenty-first centuries—just as *Sopyonje* chronicles. Over the past one hundred years, p'ansori has struggled to find a wider audience, and despite the recent global success of K-pop, very few Korean musicians outside the small-knit group of p'ansori performers, whose incomes are subsidized by the government, perform it on a regular basis. The near impossibility of preventing the art of p'ansori from dying has partly contributed to the rise of hip-hop culture in Korea as the bona fide expression of autobiographical storytelling and aesthetic expression.[7] Hip-hop will renew a blackish and "becoming-minjok" sense of Korean spirituality and what French-Caribbean writer Édouard Glissant calls the opacity of language, which has also impacted the Korean language.[8]

ESTABLISHING LINGUISTIC AUTHENTICITY

In this chapter, I am not interested in reprising the several-decades-old argument about the authenticity of hip-hop that points only to an ethnic fixity or a hypercommodified essentialism about race and blackness. Now, almost every ethnic community around the globe is producing its own local rap culture, re-creating its own version of the "black man."[9] South Korea just happens to be one of them. As Dexter Thomas Jr. has suggested in his exploration of the Japanese hip-hop scene, even good intentions to embrace another culture can almost always backfire when the "blackness" of rap is essentialized and becomes less "hyper-visible."[10] Rock music, for example, has become less conscious about race over time. While acknowledging that such an idealistic projection of rap becoming a color-blind music genre may take some time, I am considering how the Korean Americans' and Koreans' participation in creating a global rap culture opens up to the Korean subject what Du Bois once suggested as a trapping of an African American that had to have a sense of always "look[ing] at one's self through the eyes of others."[11] In other words, rap music enables a Korean to visualize what Du Bois called *double consciousness* and more fully explore the meaning of a multiple consciousness in an ongoing mix. What I am at-tempting to probe, in an effort to move away from the question of whether Koreans who share no cultural heritage with African Americans have a right to rap or not, is the issue of whether the verses of Korean spiritual-ity can be paired with that of the African American. Here, I again insist that hip-hop offers another prime cultural example of twenty-first-century "becoming-Korean" that is less about essentialized fixity around the idea of ethnic purity and more about an expansion of the nation's cultural heritage that now overlaps its consciousness with an African American one. The blurred line between authenticity and copy in hip-hop helps amplify the ruptures in the conventional ways of drawing color lines between black and Korean as well as the ruptures between American national identity and the Korean minjok identity. I return to these questions on ethnic and national subjectivity after an analysis of Korean rap's linguistic and sonic qualities that may also refigure the aesthetic qualities of rap music itself.

As such, this chapter continues with the questions that engage them-selves as the central crux of my study on Korean popular culture. Just as much as an African American has felt what Du Bois defined as "two-ness, an American, a Negro; two souls, two thoughts, two unreconciled striv-ings; two warring ideals in one dark body," any Korean born in the twenti-eth century will know precisely what it means to move through the world with this kind of double consciousness.[12] In the first half of the twentieth century, a Korean had to chart a path forward by blending the "two warring ideals" of Japanese imperial subject and Korean minjok-ian body; in the second half of the century, this same Korean had to reconcile the irrecon-cilable ideals of the United States and Korea. Immediately following the Korean War, during the 1950s and early 1960s, Korean music performers had to learn various genres of American popular music on the fly and per-form for many of the American soldiers stationed in Korea, whose numbers reached as high as eighty thousand even after the United States had signed an armistice with North Korea in 1953.[13] It is well documented that many of the best Korean performers and composers of the day, including Patti Kim and Shin Joong-hyun, grew out of this new music tradition that began when American military services needed Koreans to perform their music. As discussed in the introduction, the main musical genre tension in Korea during much of the latter part of the twentieth century was not between the local music such as p'ansori and foreign music but between Japanese colored songs (jcs) that were composed in the Western-Japanese penta-tonic scale and the American-style Korean popular music (akpm).[14]

In both the culture of African American communities at the beginning of the twentieth century and that of the war-ridden, US-occupied region of the Korean peninsula about a half century later, the soul of a black folk and that of a Korean folk had to find themselves, as Du Bois suggested, not by resurrecting an essentialized ethnic or national identity but by "blend(ing) the original" that came from a nonessentialized elsewhere. In "The Sorrow Songs," which is included in his collection of essays *The Souls of Black Folk*, Du Bois discusses how the "elements of *both* Negro and Caucasian" had to be recovered in a song in order for "the slave [to speak] to the world."[15] After having been emancipated from the Japanese in 1945 and subsequently having to endure the era of American military occupation, Korean musicians found no well-trodden path of p'ansori or other *kugak* (traditional music) available. They had to learn to mimic the original American genre elements and then slowly cook the "Korean soul" into their Western music. The hope in the song breathed through the sorrow, and it took, for instance, an accomplished Korean blues musician and composer, Shin Joong-hyun, almost two decades, after cutting his teeth as a child prodigy guitarist playing in the US military clubs, before he perfected the Korean rock sound in "Miin" (Beauty, 1974).[16] Another four decades would pass before K-pop and Korean hip-hop artists regularly incorporated elements of kugak, ranging from G-Dragon's "Niliria" (2013) and BIGBANG's "Bae Bae" (2015) to rapper Deepflow's "Jakdu" (2015) and BTS's "Idol" (2018).

For rock music and ballad-driven pop, the effort to "blend" American music was a difficult but not impossible task for Koreans. However, because hip-hop culture is tattooed in the language of black vernacular from the 'hood, the assimilation process of rap for non-English-speaking regions such as South Korea proved to be even more difficult.[17] After all, style, food, or even musical beats can migrate from one society to another with relative ease. One could learn how to cut a style of garment from different cultures, experiment with new culinary recipes, and play foreign-sounding beats on an instrument within *hours* if one is already gifted as a designer, a cook, or a musician. Appropriations are most difficult, if not impossible, however, when it comes to language because language is deeply rooted in one's formative experiences of family and community. Even if you are a gifted linguist, foreign-language acquisition normally takes years to master a level of linguistic authentication. You may be the best rapper ever to have walked this planet, but could you be sure, after having taken just a few lessons, that you could spit immaculate verses that rhyme in a foreign language? Even a Dr. Dre can't help you there because, again, this is not only a difficult task but perhaps an altogether impossible one. Virtuosity in rap is determined by coming in hard on the first beat as well as by properly enunciating the aspirated consonant, such as the *krrr* sound in the word *cruise*, which opens N.W.A's famous anthem song, "Boyz-n-the-Hood," and rhymes with the *krrr* of "Crenshaw Boulevard," forcefully enough for the succeeding syllables to roll out with ease. As cool as this all sounds, it is difficult for anyone unfamiliar with the street vernacular form of Compton to get it precisely right.[18]

If hip hop has indeed created a benchmark of rhetorical innovations for the social minorities, in what sense has this cultural aesthetic, which is both emergent and hegemonic worldwide right now, helped fuse the disenfranchised Korean soul in the global popular culture industry. What I am gravitating toward is the idea that the waning of melody might be tied to the reauthenticating of Koreanness in the oral musical storytelling, in the form of either p'ansori or *mandam* (comedy stand-up), which were popular during the Japanese colonial era but withered during the years following liberation. Legendary Sin Pul-ch'ul attained his nationalist comedian/funny storyteller status during the colonial era, before he defected to North Korea following Korea's liberation. The years after the Korean War saw the rise of two superstar MCs who had begun their careers as mandam performers: Sŏ Yŏng-ch'un, who was quite possibly Korea's first rapper with the release of his popular *Cider Song* in the early 1970s; and Kwak Kyu-seok (Fry-boy Kwak). However, after the wild early 1980s popularity of Yi Chu-il (a member of what was likely the last generation of mandam-ga, or stand-up comedians), whose career was cut short because of a ban from television by the Chun Doo-hwan military government, a career change to politics, and a struggle with lung cancer, the tradition of the Korean stand-up satirist—a gig that played a critical role in modern Korean history, comprising a crossover between p'ansori, storytelling that embedded nationalist pride, and risqué humor—likewise disappeared. Just about the only stand-up comedian still remaining in Korea who continues the tradition of political humor is Kim Je-dong, who seems to have lost his edge after progressives won in two landslide elections in 2017 and 2020. This stands in contrast with contemporary African American stand-up satirists such as Michael Che and Dave Chappelle, who continue to extend the legacy left by Richard Pryor.

Hip-hop's resurgence in Korea over the past two decades is tied to the anticipation of mandam's rebirth. This amplification of the rapture experienced in the blending of Koreanness and blackness in the Korean hip-hop scene will hopefully lead to an aesthetic analysis that recalibrates Korean aesthetic identity for today's global era. I also focus on two factors that had to take place for hip-hop to be rooted in Korea as a form of "becoming-black-of-the-world" that I first raised in the introduction. First, the language barrier between Korean and English had to be compromised so as to facilitate the capacity to rap in the Korean language. Here, I am drawn to the concept of "opacity" proposed by Glissant, who discussed the beauty of a new opaque language, such as a plural *francophonie* opening up "in a symphony of languages" rather than "in some reduced universal monolingualism."[19] As the minjok identity of Koreans became less essentialist in the twenty-first century, the Korean language—which initially acquired its form and identity through centuries of collision between native Korean and Chinese, and subsequently through several rounds of renegotiation with Japanese and English loanwords and hybridization during the twentieth century—underwent yet another transformation during a new era of online and text communications that brought back the use of ideograms and new slangs. The ways in which hip-hop, from Seo Taiji and Tiger JK to, more recently, Woo Won-jae and Vinxen, participates in reflecting this poetic and opaque condition of new Korean will be a critical topic in this chapter. Second, Koreans had to undo their ingrained linguistic tendencies and reconstruct a Korean musical sensibility through the rhymes and flows of a melody in Korean kayo (pop song) by constantly hitting the beat hard on the first syllable of a line or a flow of a rhyme.[20] This accentuation of the first syllable of a word in the opening of a rap not only reconciles the blackness and Koreanness of the hip-hop rhyme but also draws attention to the gap between Korean, a syllable-timed language, and English, a stress-timed language. Furthermore, as demonstrated in my later lyrical analysis of young rappers Woo Won-jae and Vinxen, syllables that were perfectly in tune with African American vernacular but regarded as somewhat coarse in polite Korean language had to be ventured in a rap song in order to evoke the cynical urban American style of language that became popular among the Korean youth as early as the 1990s.

SEO TAIJI'S FIRST

Seo Taiji and Boys' single "Nan arayo" (I know), released in 1992, may not have been the first rap song recorded in Korea, but it is still remembered by many Koreans, close to three decades since its release, as the first Korean rap song they have ever heard. Though Seo Taiji was undoubtedly an icon of the youth culture in the Korean popular music scene of the 1990s, "Nan arayo" was a song trapped in a balladic melody rather than within the domain of the hard-hitting, storytelling style of true hip-hop.[21] The first verse of Seo's landmark song begins after some raw shrieks and record-scratching sounds mixed in with dance beats reminiscent of the hip-hop scene in the United States in the 1980s; the opening words are an almost self-bravado announcement of *Nan arayo* (I know). Like Eazy-E, who is coached by Dr. Dre to "hit the first beat hard" with the rolling of his *krrr* of *cruisin'*, Seo Taiji, the young heavy metal bassist-cum-rapper, makes a dramatic entrance with the first syllable from *arayo* and rolls out his *arrr*. This short, sudden blurt of the informal polite style of the present-tense declarative of *I know* (난 알아요) (or its homonym *I am sick* [난 앓아요]) in Korean is deconstructed in two parts: first, the pronunciation of the syllable *nan* (impolite form of *I*) that precedes *arayo* (informal polite form of *know* more commonly used by women and younger people) is deliberately dragged; and second, it is followed by a very sudden dropping of a hard-hitting *arayo*. *Nan* takes up almost three beats in a four-beat measure, while *arrrr-a-yo!* occupies the other single beat. This helps the familiar *arayo*, which shares the same word stem as the popular Korean folk song *arirang*, especially if it is read as "I am sick" instead of "I know," to become unfamiliarized before rehashing it as a new rhythmic speech in African Americanized Korean diction. The accentuation of the first syllable of the word *arayo* produces an extraordinary cadence in the Korean language or Korean music to feel the powerful declarative: *arrrr-a-yo*, which stresses the braggart version of "to know" as either "don't take me for a fool" or "it's something I already knew all along." This rhyme is able to vocally transcribe an ordinary Korean verbal suffix of *-yo* into the so-called African American vernacular of the hip-hop genre from which Seo was borrowing. In other words, Seo Taiji's pronunciation forced what would be the feminine- or juvenile-voice dangle of the *-yo* into an English urban exclamation of "yo!" Seo had completed his first cool rap phrasing in Korean with a single blackish stroke that would grip an entire generation of schoolkids for years to come.

However, despite this dramatic entrance, which constitutes a new metric structure of rap using a hybrid form of Korean rap that mediates between the African American vernacular, a slice of Korean folk diction, and Korean teenage protest, the rest of the song sinks into a tear-jerking production about a failed love affair. As Sarah Morelli intuitively remarks, "In 'Nan arayo' Seo Taiji employs rap only during the verses, singing choruses in a pop style. . . . The lyrics of Seo Taiji and the Boys' first rap song are rather innocuous."[22] Koreans fell in love with this new dancing music trio throughout the 1990s, but it remains uncertain whether they were infatuated with the songs about innocent puppy love accompanied by early hip-hop dance moves or Seo's edgy rap slotted between these ballads.

Posturing is perhaps the most underlining poetic and signifying element in the storytelling technique of a rap song. One popular slang among youngsters in Korea, "swag," which effectively replaced "cool" or "sexy," is of course an idiom that was first populated in American hip-hop culture where posturing became an integral part of the rapper's dress code and attitude. If hip-hop, as previously mentioned, was centrally characterized by autobiographical storytelling of the performer, the *I* of the rapper had to be elevated almost to a level of subjectification that moves beyond the rapper and is disseminated to the experience of the listener, who has to offer a sympathy or an identification against the putative *you* that the rapper has constructed as the force against him or her. Many American rappers, including The Notorious B.I.G. and Eminem, have exploited this technique of "posturing" by telling autobiographical stories about themselves that draw on their experiences from their respective 'hoods. The authenticity of this posturing can only be circumstantial, however, because of the performative aspects of "truth-telling." As Katja Lee argues, "It is important to recognize that Eminem's autobiographical impulses and postures do not represent a new trend in rap so much as a return to an older one with new innovations for posturing the complexity of the postmodern self."[23] In other words, the "real" self in contemporary hip-hop culture, as almost continually acknowledged by rappers like Eminem himself, is actually fictional and hyperbolical in order to appeal to the fan base that increasingly has to market the underdog myth the rapper has been engulfed in by his or her verses.

In the absence of a "ghetto" and the diminished relevance of the live club scene (changes exacerbated by the corporatization of music, via heavy regulation exerted by entertainment moguls and social media throughout the past two decades), where performers could formerly exercise their autobiographical swagger and authenticate their hustling image, Korean rappers—those savvy enough to understand that rap is about sublimating personal experiences with traumas and social injustices—quickly learned that their own ghettos were childhood classrooms where an excessive number of kids had to be jammed into an educational hell and where long school hours (usually from dawn to nighttime) and grade-based hierarchies ruled the day.[24] By the third album, released in 1995, Seo Taiji used metaphors like "how far do you think you can fly with the broken wing of yours" ("Sidae yugam" [Regret of the times]) or "every morning at 7:30, we are forced to walk into our tiny classrooms" ("Kyoshil idea" [Classroom ideology]) to protest against the tyranny and violence in Korean society and its educational system. Since 1995, when Seo rapped about "dark, closed classrooms" where precious young lives are wasted, various K-pop acts such as Epic High ("Lesson 2," 2004) and BTS ("School of Tears," 2014) have highlighted the issue of injustice in Korean classrooms that has propelled the engine behind Koreans' education fever and postwar economic success.

While the critique of education fever and classroom prison supplied a small measure of compensation for the absence of ghetto that fueled the rise of rap in the United States, much of the authentication of language that seeks a compromise between English and Korean in Korean rap songs has been misguided. For instance, the misappropriation of the "N" words that sometimes pop up in a Korean rap song best illustrates the difficulty of translating English-language rap slangs into Korean. The word *you* in Korean, which can be pronounced as *ni-ga*, for example, would often occupy an unorthodox place of a last word of a sentence or a verse of a rap track. One of the most popular love songs for rapper G-Dragon is "Ni-ga Mwŏnde" (You who?), which builds crescendo in various moments in his song by chanting the word *ni-ga* in a lengthy, affectionate croon. Who really is the subject here for G-Dragon, the leader of the K-pop group BIGBANG? Is he really singing about an anonymous female lover who is tormenting him or is he intending ironically a fictive black subject who he so desires to emulate as a rapper? That the birth of rap and its continued success around the world for the past forty years owes itself to the recognition of brilliance of creative African American vernacular is perhaps not all that surprising. At the same time, however, rap music's reliance on the particular kind of vernacular street English implies that the poetic nuances of American street culture often get lost in translation while only hard-core slangs uncritically get locally manifested.[25] Though largely avoided by rappers in their official lyrics, the continued circulation of urban slang language in American rap music that has misogynous and racist origins, such as the "bitch" or the "nigga," imperil many Korean rappers and K-pop stars who irresponsibly spit out those words in social media and in concerts, which then propel some of their fans to protest.[26] Eithne Quinn, in her study of gangsta rap, writes that rap groups like N.W.A embraced "the term *nigga* as a badge of honor [because] many young black men are still so often treated unjustly—the traditional racist hierarchies enshrined in the term are still all too pervasive."[27] Neither Korean rappers' employment of bad language like *ni-ga* in their lines as a wordplay or a rhyming tool nor the accidental blurting out of such terms in a concert or a tweet qualify themselves as an act of solidarity or an uplifting self-representation against the racism, police brutality, or economic discrimination that African Americans have persistently faced in the United States.

ARRIVAL OF A KOREAN AMERICAN RAPPER: TIGER JK

In a short skit that begins one of the most critically acclaimed hip-hop albums released in Korea, *The Great Birth*, the two members of Drunken Tiger, DJ Shine and Tiger JK (Seo Jeong-kwon), are asked a question by a radio commentator: "What is hip-hop?" Both DJ Shine, a Korean American raised in New York, and Tiger JK, who spent formative years of his youth in Los Angeles and Miami, burst out laughing. Without a verbal response, the short skit then continues with the two young rappers laughing before it fades to their next song. Why produce this laughter at the beginning of an album released in 2000 that is now certainly hailed as a masterpiece album in hip-hop? By posing a question in Korean that perhaps has no answer to a couple of hip-hop artists from America, the album is making a bold statement that the meaning of hip-hop can only be found in the form of music. Tiger JK's meaningless laughter denies its replacement with any signifier with a solid meaning associated with it and actually helps us better conceptualize the kind of impact rap has made in Korea. Tiger JK and his partner are perhaps claiming that the genre of hip-hop ultimately succeeds in delivering significations that exceed the boundary of, for that matter, any national or ethnic identity. The rise of hip-hop is a sign of US cultural dominance, but one where the white hegemonic domination reveals its cracks since it recognizes, for instance, a feat for poor migrants from Jamaica who sample beats without proper authorizations and make money off their so-called plagiarist art. It is an ingenious art but also a simulacrum that can appeal to cash-strapped migrant societies that find neither expensive music equipment nor professional studio rentals within their reach. Tiger JK, who as a teenager personally witnessed the 1992 Rodney King uprising—which targeted the Korean American community in Los Angeles—and was deeply impacted by the black-Korean conflict in the urban neighborhood, could perhaps easily find a verbal answer to the question "What is hip hop?" that closely identifies with the musical inspirations from the 'hood that was close to his heart. He is both legitimate and illegitimate. He is born a minority, both in Korea and in the United States, but lacks a black body rooted in hip-hop. Tiger JK's decision to first laugh and then simply respond with their music rather than uttering any verbal explanation to the term *hip-hop* may speak to Drunken Tiger's identity as both Asian Americans in a global hip-hop scene, which was and still is rare, and Korean American rappers in the Korean music scene, which was also just as rare since it was heavily dominated by dance music, in which rap had only a remedial function.

Though they were not the first Korean Americans to rap on the Korean pop scene, Tiger JK, who debuted in the Korean pop scene four years after Seo Taiji shocked the nation by announcing his band's retirement after just four years of activity, has become the most respected member of the Korean rap community today. Tiger JK's longevity over the past two decades is a testament not only to his classic rap style, which relied on neither dance beats nor grungy metal, but also to his productive troping of elements from his autobiographical experience that laid a foundation to his vernacular rap in Korean that created a niche between his multiethnic American identity and Korean identity. Though his main partner during the first decade of the twenty-first century was DJ Shine, he also partnered with an African American rapper who spoke very little Korean during the earlier incantation of Drunken Tiger, and since his second album, his albums and concerts have featured guest collaborations with his then girlfriend (and now his wife) Yoon Mirae (born Natasha Shanta Reid and raised in Texas), another Korean American with a black father and a Korean mother.[28]

That Drunken Tiger enjoyed success with its first album was perhaps not surprising; the fact that it took several more years for him to come out with his second album was. His Korean American identity was groomed in the Southern California scene, with N.W.A, Ice Cube, and Dr. Dre making a deep impression on him. Tiger JK, after making his musical debut in Korea, was often challenged by Korean television and radio producers who questioned him about his musical direction and demanded that he conform to the dance beats and choreography that dominated the television stations of the day. YouTube or other social media outlets were not available then to help his music kick into larger circulation. Rap culture was slowly being mobilized in the underground through both the Hongdae club scene and the dial-in internet service Hitel chatrooms. It would take at least several years before the so-called Movement, a rappers' collective that Tiger JK galvanized, would take root in Korea. As rap continued to descend deep into clubs and YouTube channels with low circulation in the late 1990s and early years of the twenty-first century, it is perhaps not surprising that the laughter of self-ridicule and self-disdain appears as the first track of their second album, *The Great Rebirth*.

"The Great Rebirth" (Widaehan T'ansaeng) was the first single off the album and received airplay and television spots for Drunken Tiger. As a matter of fact, it would also be the last single for them because Tiger JK would be incarcerated for a charge of possession of marijuana, which is a serious offense in Korea. In a critical moment in Korean hip-hop history, just days before his arrest, Drunken Tiger performed the title single from *The Great Rebirth* on the television stage for the first time.[29] Following the heels of their enormously successful first album, their stage presence is impressive even by the standards of South Korean music television, which was well known for the extravagance shown by dance music acts at the time. The two rappers, dressed respectively in gimmicky sushi chef attire and a colorful baggy suit, were backed by a small army of b-boy dancers clad in kung-fu uniforms and waving enormous military flags, a DJ spinner, and a *kugak* (Korean traditional music) section featuring a ten-piece group of string players of Chinese zithers and Korean kayagum and a gong player. The articulation of Asianness is reinforced by the melodic structure that abandons the Western octave scale. The simple melody hook in "The Great Rebirth" distinguishes itself in a pentatonic scale that is missing the fourth and seventh notes from the octave.

"The Great Rebirth" is a blend between reggae and hard-core free-associative rap—which became vogue in the East Coast rap scene in the 1990s through the emergence of the hip-hop group Wu-Tang Clan—laid over a simple traditional Asian melody. As Amy Abugo Ongiri argues, "From Wu-Tang Clan's 'Shaolin Shadow Boxing' to NBA basketball player Marcus Camby's prominent Chinese character tattoos and the kung-fu signifying movement styles of 'vogue' innovator Willie 'Ninja' and various hip hop artists, African American culture is replete with images drawn from popular cultural representations of Asian and American culture, particularly images drawn from early martial arts films."[30] Though such popular reception of martial arts films in the African American culture does not often dispel simplistic cultural stereotyping that could lead to negative repercussions between African Americans and Asian Americans, this type of cultural circulation between black and Asian artists also produces, in my mind, alternate kinds of mimicry and appropriations that expose fissures in the conventional colonial or postcolonial praxis that are bifurcated almost exclusively along the traditional color lines of black and white or between colonizers and the colonized. Direct exchanges between African Americans and Asian Americans promote cultural flows that form possible bonds outside the hegemonic relationships between white people and racial minorities. This exchange also acknowledges different kinds of masks black people don while imitating Asian kung-fu screen masters and Asians wear when imitating black rap heroes that escape the white-black performative relations that typify the instrument of hegemonic sociocultural hierarchy. This mask-wearing allows for an opportunity for the complex bodily transactions and performances that might even lead to what Stuart Hall has mentioned as "the double movement of containment and resistance" that ought to be the departure point in any analysis for popular culture.[31]

Pop music, perhaps more so than any other artistic sensation, is capable of producing a powerful affect that conjures up and identifies one's linguistic origin and place. At this juncture, I think about Korean rap's capability to produce an explosive Korean street vernacular in the vein of the hip-hop culture African Americans have created in the United States. The experimentation of music by Tiger JK had to take place both in the form of musical aesthetics and also with Korean language through rap music (figure 2.1). This means that he had to take sometimes complicated English words and mix them up in Korean. Many young rappers today confess that they would phonetically write down Drunken Tiger's rap chant of their name in English *in-to-ssi-kae-i-ti-ed*—replete with aspirated and double consonants of *t*, *k*, and *ss*—and practice them at noraebangs (karaokes) without necessarily understanding the meaning behind it. Drunken Tiger, in a similar vein that had Seo Taiji recalibrate the Korean word *arayo* (know) into a hip-hop vernacular of *arrr-a-yo!*, tries to find a rhyme in the first syllable for every line of the first stanza. Every first syllable that the two rappers chant together scrupulously follows the order of the Korean alphabet's consonants that children in Korea tend to sing when they first learn to read and write in kindergarten. By shouting each of the Korean consonants—the nine plain ones (*ka*, *na*, *da*, *ra* . . .) and the four aspirated consonants (*ka*, *ta*, *pa*, *ha*)—Tiger JK, with the beat composed on a simple pentatonic scale, was seeking to reclaim his native root language skill of Korean that diminished while growing up as a Korean American in the United States.

가위 (Gawi) 눌리는 현실에서 깨어나고 싶어
나는 (Nanun) 나 너는 너 그들을 따라가기 싫어 모두

2.1 JK Tiger (*back left*) and Bizzy (*back right*) talk about the history of rap in Korea while Kurtis Blow (*foreground*) listens, 2019. Photo by Kyung Hyun Kim.

다 (Da) 의지를 버리지 말고 앞으로 밀고 나가봐
라일락 (Railrac) 향기보다 달콤한 독을 알아봐
마구 (Magu) 입을 놀리는 내 주먹의 맛을 봐
바람과 (Baram) 함께 사라지는 우리 인생들
사슬에 (Saseul) 묶여 함께 끌려가는 인생들
아무리 (Amuri) 외쳐봐도 듣지않는 그 이들
자신의 (Jasin eui) 노예 속박에서 뛰어나와서
차가워진 (Chagaweojin) 마음 녹여 모두다 다가와 더
타오르는 (Taoreuneun) 열망으로 깨달음으로
카마카마카마카마 (K'ama . . .) make a million
파란 (Paran) 하늘 향해 겨뤄 babylon
하늘을 (Haneul) 향해 주먹을 질러봐

I like to wake up from the reality that is depressing
I am me; you are you; and I hate following them all
Do not give up your determination and seek a way forward
Get a taste of poison that is sweeter than the fragrance of lilac
Get a taste of my fist rap punch that flows out of my mouth
Our lives are going to disappear as if it's gone with the wind
Our lives are being dragged away as if our feet are shackled
No one pays attention though we yell at the top of our lungs
Try to be released from the self-imposed slave mentality
Warm up the frozen hard by coming closer
With the burning passion and recognition

Kama kama kama kama . . . make a million
Aim for the blue sky . . . that's babylon
Try to punch straight at the sky

As one — even those with just basic knowledge of the Korean alphabet —
can readily notice, each line of this verse in "The Great Rebirth" begins with
the fourteen consonants of the Korean alphabet (hangul) in a sequence
that exactly resembles the order of reading the chart of consonants after
those consonants are coupled with a vowel of A (ㅏ) sound. Forming the
rhyme not through the ending of a word vowel but through the hitting of
the first consonant hard in the *ga na da ra* sequence, Tiger JK is proclaim-
ing that the rhyme in a rap song can newly be achieved in Korean through
the accentuation of the first consonants. Also, when those accentuations
are made, the mood of the song shifts from a sorrowful or melodic one to
one that is playful and childlike. After all, repeating the *ga na da ra* in a
song in Korean would be the equivalent of having a rap song composed
with rhymes that fall in line with the rhythms adapted from the children's
"ABC Song." Also, rather than speaking in the voice of one single Korean
vernacular, Drunken Tiger proposes to expand the vernacular of Korean
by focusing on the aspirated sounds of *k'ama*, which is a Koreanized word
from *karma*, the English Buddhist word. The repetition of *k'amak'ama* (not
k'arrrma) toward the end of the first stanza becomes heavily emphasized
since this indecipherable, gibberish word is followed by an English phrase,
make a million. The emphasis of the aspirated consonant of *k'a* (카) into a
childlike, gibberish sound is appropriate because this *k* sound is the closest
Western phonetic sound a Korean alphabet (*k'a* 카) has to offer, but certainly it's a sound that in Korean is only available as an onomatopoeic and
childish sound. (Since my young daughter routinely refuses to brush her
teeth, I use a Korean word, *ch'ik'a ch'ik'a*, as many as twenty times a day.
This word is not formal Korean but an onomatopoeic phrase that matches
the imaginative sound of toothbrushing.) In other words, aspirated consonants such as *ch, t, k,* and *p* are normally avoided in the palette of proper
standard Korean, for they sound too foreign or too childish. The Korean
government officially discourages the use of double consonants because
they are too often associated with sound of obscenities. Tiger JK, who had
to face the challenge of having to relearn Korean after having left the country when he was ten, deliberately exploited these aspirated sounds, rather
than the plain one, to redraw the soundscape of rap that was composed
between two sonic canvases of Korean and English.

There are quite possibly many reasons why *American Idol* became such a phenomenally successful television platform in the United States and abroad. The diminished popularity of the sitcom in primetime television; the emergence of cable television such as MTV, which provided cheap and shocking reality-TV content; and the interactive internet social media culture that craved more user participation in selecting finalists all played a part in making the audition television show a landmark cultural phenomenon. However, a less visible but highly charged impetus came from the US recording industry, the profits of which kept declining every year in the twenty-first century, as each and every technological advance increased internet speed and enabled the transfer and download of free music. Clive Davis, one of the world's most prolific pop music producers, was persuaded to enter into a partnership with *American Idol*, during the early seasons when Kelly Clarkson and Jennifer Hudson became stars, simply because "pop music was diminishing in impact."[32] The man who was responsible for the signing of superstars of the final three decades of the twentieth century such as Billy Joel, Neil Diamond, Barry Manilow, Chicago, and Whitney Houston was now too old-fashioned to embrace hip-hop, which quickly grew to become the most financially profitable genre since the 1990s. Television, which Davis shunned during the early days of his producing career, now made sense for him as it spoke directly to the American heartland in the form of a reality-television audition program. *American Idol* gave a much-needed lifeline to ballad-driven pop music. Davis's role as the head of BMG Music Publishing was essential to *American Idol* because most of the songs that the contestants sang were licensed from his company.

If audition programs in America sprang up, in part, out of the music industry's effort to appeal to a provincial America that still savored the crooning style of pop singing, and as a strategy for regaining market share lost to urban hip-hop music and club beats, it would seem an irony that the resurgence of hip-hop in Korea between 2012 and 2021 owes itself to the launching of a television rap audition program. The Korean hip-hop club scene was not as vibrant as it was elsewhere around the globe. Only a single club called Master Plan in Sinch'on (where Yonsei, Ewha Women's, and Hongik Universities are located) operated legitimately from 1997 to 2001, as an unofficial hip-hop venue that sowed the seeds for many rappers, including Deepflow, MC Meta, and Naachal.[33] During the first decade of the twenty-first century, hip-hop in Korea was mostly shared and incubated not through actual club venues but through online clubs (PC *tonghohoe*) that arranged for mixtape album releases, concerts, parties, and festivals. Producer Han Dong-chul, who became the Mnet channel's programming executive, was an enthusiast of these online hip-hop chatroom fan clubs during his youth. He would cautiously approach the idea for a hip-hop-only music program in 2012. Han, who would later also produce *Produce 101* (he would leave the show after only the first season and before it was embroiled in the corruption scandal), a K-pop idol reality-television show that is equally popular among young viewers in Korea, has stated that his goal in creating *Show Me the Money* (*SMTM*) "was to let people know that there is more than just idol dance music in Korea."[34] Once it debuted, *SMTM* quickly galvanized the hip-hop performers and fans, though it first began airing with only a hard-core base. However, after its first winner, Loco, became a star, *SMTM* quickly became one of the most popular audition programs in Korea. *Show Me the Money* and other affiliate hip-hop programs such as *Unpretty Rapstar* (running for three seasons, beginning in 2015) and *High School Rapper* (four seasons, beginning in 2017) quickly seized on the commercial potential of the expressive medium of hip-hop. The already weakened club and underground hip-hop scene began to show its disintegration when massive corporate cash and recording deals enticed young artists eager to perform before primetime television audiences.

By the time *SMTM* began seasons 4 and 5 (2015–16), it scored the highest viewer ratings ever recorded for a music program on cable television. For example, ten thousand participants signed up to audition in Seoul for *SMTM 4*, which attracted some of the biggest names in television, such as comedian Jeong Joon-ha (of *Muhan Dojeon* fame). It created enough of a sensation to feature surprise judges such as American rapper Snoop Dogg.[35] If K-pop was built on bubblegum pop and the immaculate, sexually suggestive dancing choreography of young idols and essentially rejecting the vestige of the Romantic ideals predicated on "an independent musician-artist," *SMTM* and its spin-off *High School Rapper* intuitively understood that the role of a rapper or an MC in contemporary South Korea was to restore the storytelling tradition of mandam. As discussed earlier, both traditions of satire in traditional performances of p'ansori and mandam had all but disappeared in Korea due to the draconian political censorship during the years of military rule and the dominance of American culture. But they would return — slowly but discernibly — through the rap audition program where youngsters created poetry and performances by protesting against and ridiculing their own ghetto of education hell.[36]

The storyteller-performer who creates a pose by drawing on real auto-biographical material such as his or her name, ethnic identity, past illnesses, bodily art, and other life experiences cuts a common figure in many of the *American Idol*–style audition programs that have thrived in Korea. Since the smash success of *Superstar K* starting in 2009, audition survival reality-TV shows such as *K-Pop Star* and *Produce 101*, which feature a combination of professional judges, live broadcast, and text-voting participation from viewers, have garnered high ratings in markets all over Asia. *Show Me the Money*, a rap-only audition program, is distinguishable from other programs not only by featuring interviews with contestants who talk about early struggles in life but also by encouraging them to transcend their hardships through their self-composed songs to allow the audiences to enjoy a cathartic viewing experience.[37] This self-reflexive blurring of the boundary between the autobiographical *I* of the anonymous contestant and the posturing *I* of the rapper-performer became the perfect television medium material in the era of smartphones where real-life stories trending on the internet are often considered to be sometimes far more engaging than the fictive and one-dimensional stories that unfold on the traditional screens of television and movies.

Given the expectations that rappers are expected to write their own music and lyrics, it is perhaps not surprising that some of the most poetically minded performers get quite far in the competition. Among the record number of twelve thousand contestants who gathered to audition for *SMTM* season 6 (2017), it was Woo Won-jae, then an unknown twenty-two-year-old college student, who became a star. Woo reached the final three, and his single, "Sich'a" (Time difference; English title, "We Are"), written and released during the show, became the only number 1 track that *SMTM* released in 2017. Because of a format change starting in 2018 that eliminated first-round auditions held in large auditoriums and making the selections from audition videos, season 6 still holds a record for in-person auditions. "Sich'a" also became an anthem song on college campuses.[38] Making a run to the top three on the final day of competition against veteran rappers—and gaining acclaim as one of only a handful of amateur rappers to have made it that far in the history of the contest—Woo became an overnight sensation. The success of Woo Won-jae, a student who had to overcome serious mental illness to even get into college, merits attention; he not only fully embraces the autobiographical "posturing" of rap culture, but his techniques also make impressive use of internal rhymes and unorthodox word breaks which elevate his songs to the virtuosity of great Korean poetry.

Woo Won-jae rescues Korean rap from the domain of dance and club music by syncing it with the genre of autobiographical storytelling. Fully exploiting the essence of swag by retaining the subjectivity of the *I*, he rapped about his struggles with antidepressant pills and his repeated hospitalizations. After the successful run to the final three at *SMTM*, Woo Won-jae was immediately signed by star and new entertainment mogul Jay Park. Woo's alliance with Park can be viewed as both natural and ironic since, to pursue his own solo career, Park had to seek a controversial divorce from his own group, 2PM, controlled by JYP Entertainment, at around the same time that JYJ was seeking separation from SM Entertainment's TVXQ (see chapter 1).

Twenty-three years have elapsed since the legendary Korean star Seo Taiji rapped about the misguided zeal for education in Korea in his song "Classroom Ideology." Unsurprisingly, the theme of educational tyranny in the classroom has become a motif for many rap songs in Korea. The classroom is the one place that almost every Korean would identify as a ghetto-like experience, being trapped for endless hours to prepare for high school and college entrance exams. The opening lines of "Sich'a" are as follows:

밤새 모니터에 튀긴 침이   Pamsae monit'ŏ e t'wigin ch'im-i
마르기도 전에 / 강의실로   Marŭlkito chŏn e / kangŭisil-ro
(#1)
Even before the spit smudged on the monitor of an all-night session
    dries up /
(I head) To the lecture hall

아 참 교수님이 문신 땜에   A ch'am kyosunim i munsin ttaem-e
긴 팔 입고 오래 ~~   Kin p'al ipko orae~~
(#2)
oh yeah (I forgot), cuz of my tattoos,
the prof told me to wear long sleeves

난 시작도 전에 눈을 감았지   Nan sijakdo chŏn-e nun-ŭl kamat ji
(#3)
I close my eyes before the lecture even begins

날 한심하게 볼 게 뻔하니,   Nal hansimhake pol-ke ppŏnhani
이게 더 편해   Ike tŏ p'yŏnhae
(#4)

He's gonna think I'm a loser anyway,
so it's just better this way

Despite the similar focus placed on the stifling repressive conditions of the classroom, the differences between the song rapped by Seo Taiji in 1995 and the one by Woo Won-jae in 2017 are stark. Even though Seo wrote lyrics about the "ghetto-like experiences" that many teenagers in Korea have to go through because of the education fever of their parents and because of the grade-based social hierarchies, he never rapped about his *own* experience of dropping out of middle school in order to pursue a career in music. Hesitant to use the almost too-obvious elements from his autobiographic life, only hyperbolic metaphors and mediocre figures such as "we are sold off to package centers" are employed to convey the anger in Seo's rap song "Classroom Ideology." Though a pioneer in music and dance, Seo's forte was never lyrics.

In contrast, Woo achieves a fluent command of Korean rap vernacular by setting his story within the realm of his own experience as both a rapper and a college student. (figure 2.2). The first two lines of "Sich'a" set the tone of the song by physically moving between two different spaces—the computer workspace where the narrator has spent all night working out his rap verses and the "lecture hall" he needs to hustle to in order to get to class on time: "Even before the spit smudged on the monitor of an all-night session dries up, (I head) to the lecture hall / Oh yeah (I forgot), cuz of my tattoos, the prof told me to wear long sleeves." Temporally too, these two different spaces are divided between day and night. The class, of course, takes place during the daytime, during which Woo Won-jae, who has forgotten to wear his long-sleeved shirt to cover his tattoos, will soon fall asleep since he feels as if the professor has already given up on him anyway. As evidenced by his spit that has left a smudge on the computer monitor, which is a metonymic figuration of his rap verses that have yet to be edited, it is his nocturnal hobby rather than his daytime class that draws his attention far more. Spitting is not a traditional metaphor that can be traded for an equivalent value as a symbol of something else; it is a metonymic stand-in for rapping, which retires the grand ideology (or as Seo Taiji would say, "yi-de-a") that was pervasive among the previous generation of rappers, including Tiger JK. The posturing self of the *I* in the song rushes to his college classroom, where, despite having graduated high school and having reached an age of adulthood, he lives in a world still vigilantly regulated by dress codes that ban his bodily art. Woo Won-jae has taken the theme of "classroom tyranny"

2.2 Woo Won-jae guest stars at Vinxen's Aquarium vol. 2 concert, Samsung Blue Square iHall, Seoul, October 2018. Photo by Kyung Hyun Kim.

into both the space of the private and the signification of a postmetaphoric, metonymic vernacular that realign his rap with the cultural mood that is just as innovative and self-reflexive as that which produced some of the best rap stars, such as The Notorious B.I.G. or Eminem, who have graced the American pop scene over the past thirty years.

As local cultural critic Yoon Kwang-ŭn states, the track "Sich'a" features Woo's hustle about "protests against *not* the poverty and police of the [American] ghetto, but against the lifelong standardized-test driven system of Korea that tries to set the clock to one single standard that dictate the tempo and manners of everyone's daily lives."[39] The revolt against homogenization and uniformity in the classroom is carried forward not only through the theme of *sich'a*, which literally means *time difference* in Korean, but also through a rhyme structure that uses internal rhymes, simultaneous lining of rhyme schemes, bar lines that do not enclose full sentences, and the assemblage of aspirated consonants. In the first line, *t'ŏ-e* 터에 is broken off from the Korean loanword of *monitor* and pairs with *chŏn-e* in the second line, but it is also usurped by another flow of rhyme that begins with the first word of the second line, *ki-to* 기도, which triangulates the first word of the third line, *sil-ro* 실로, and the second word of the fourth line, *ipko* 입고. None of these word-ending rhymes are regulated by the syntactical rules governing the ends of sentences. They are motivated by rhythmic structures that constantly cross bar lines in order to assemble a smoother flow for the rap.

The search for the smooth rap flow is not just about hitting the first note hard (such as Eazy-E's *krrrr* of *cruisin'* or Seo Taiji's *arrr* of *arayo*) but also about lining up the aspirated consonants such as *t*, *k*, and *p* that actually mobilize a vulgar group of sounds in standard Korean that, as a matter of fact, better accompanies ring-tone high-pitched beats used today. What is impressive about the quality of cadence that mediates the seemingly chaotic rhymes of Woo's rap lines is the manner in which his carefully chosen Korean words build a sound template of almost-Western phonetic cacophony. In English, accents on aspirated consonants and tense consonants such as the *s* of *Sam* are frequent and popular, but these same sounds are rare and even shunned in the standard and plain Korean lexicon that tend to avoid confrontation and intensity. The *s* of *Sam*, for instance, produces a double consonant of an *s-* sound (*ssang-siot*) that Koreans usually equate literally with the sound of obscenities. Aspirated sounds or tense sounds in Korean are frequently associated with slovenly, or animalistic, or barbaric behaviors.[40]

The accenting of the first syllables in rap tends to lay down the foundation of each song's rhymes with aspirated or tense consonants, since the English language does not necessarily discriminate between the *k*, *p*, *t*, and *ch* sounds. These sounds often make up the foundations of effective and efficacious *spits* of rap verses. Korean rappers, in order to reach a poetic sophistication that best matches up with the beats of rap that come in with metallic cymbals or high-pitched drum sounds, have to abandon their humble plain consonants and find sounds that are deliberately impolite. Woo Won-jae, rather than dipping into English phrases or resorting to loanwords, chooses three words that build the flow of the first line — the *t'ŏ* is accentuated by separating it from the word *monitor* (*monit'ŏ*). By so doing, he instead creates with *t'ŏ* (터), a sound that closely resembles an onomatopoeic sound of the spit pitched out of the mouth (*t'wae* 퇴), and triples it with *spit* (*ch'im* 침) and the verb action of *smudged* or *splat* (*t'wigin* 튀긴). All three words triangulate the same action of a *spit* that uses the aspirated consonants *t'ŏ* 터, *t'wi* 튀, and *ch'i* 치, suggesting that his song is already more vulgar and disobedient than one that might be expected from a humble college student who is stressed from having to wear long-sleeved shirts to cover up his tattoos. The *t'ŏ*, the *t'wi*, and the *ch'im* in the first line driven by fluid (*ch'im*) spitted out (*t'wi-gin*) localize the flow of Woo by defamiliarizing standard Korean usage. It effectively triangulates the rhyming flow of the provocative opening line of the song, innovating within the Korean language by defamiliarizing it.

| 밤새 모니터에 튀긴 침이 | Pamsae monitŏ e t'wigin ch'im-i |
| 마르기도 전에 / 대기실로 | Marŭlkito chŏn e daekisil-ro |

(#1)

Even before the spit smudged on the monitor of an all-night session
    dries up /
(I head) to the dressing room (of a television studio)

| 아 참 (피디님이) 문신 땜에 | A ch'am munsin ttaem-e |
| 긴 팔 입고 오래 | Kin p'al ipko orae |

(#2)

Oh yeah (I forgot), cuz of my tattoos
(Producer) told to me to wear long sleeves

Storytelling is an art form that must take passage of time into consideration. After the guest rapper of the song "Sich'a" and the winner of the first edition of SMTM, Loco, raps the second verse, and Gray sings the hook, Woo returns to the microphone and sings the final verse of the song.[41] All words in the first two lines of the last verse are identical to the words in the opening of the song, with two exceptions: Woo has deleted *Kyosunim* (professor) from the final verse and has replaced *Lecture Hall* with *Dressing Room* (of the television studio). This repetition with one small word replacement creates a powerful shift that catapults the narrating rapper-student from a *private* citizen going to class to a *public* media star waiting to perform on camera for millions of people. This repetition and difference best serve a Deleuzian affect or a James Joycean eternal recurrence that is inherently transgressive—both formally and thematically—which allows Woo to both proudly swag about his maturity as a musician that has earned him a national reputation and sadly lament Korea's social condition that symbolically imprisons the rapper in a system of surveillance. So much has changed, and yet nothing has changed. He cannot but humbly acknowledge the power of the regimented culture and the state apparatus that still censors him and his bodily art. In the music video for "Sich'a," released by CJ's Mnet, Woo Won-jae does not showcase his tattoos and is instead seen wearing a long-sleeved shirt.[42] It is unfortunately an irony that must remain understated. Day and night have been reversed, as he is able to spit his rap verses no longer just at night but during the day as well, but the true revolution has yet to take place. Woo Won-jae pushes the thematic power of *negation of negative present status quo* as far as he can by committing to neither an affirmative change in the future nor a rejection of it in the present.

The most famous epistolary pop song ever written might possibly be one of the early songs of the Beatles, "P.S. I Love You." But if you were to ask anyone under the age of forty-five today, you would find that that distinction probably belongs to rapper Eminem's "Stan," a song released in 2000. The song is structured around verses that read as if they were fan letters written to Slim Shady, Eminem's alter ego. The haunting first two verses begin with "Dear Slim," with the third verse followed up with "Dear Mister 'I'm Too Good to Call Or Write My Fans.'" The tension escalates as the crazy fan Stan begins to show signs of being obsessed and furious, threatening to commit violence against his pregnant girlfriend and himself. In the last verse, Eminem finally raps, as himself and breaking his code of silence, with "Dear Stan." The song has hit a nerve with people all around the world and far beyond just the hard-core rap fans because of the affective and somewhat rare dramatic pop-song storytelling. However, even in this song, what is important to note is that between the verse breaks, the distinction between Stan, the fictive fan, and the target of his adoration, obsession, and later hate, Eminem, remains clear.

Not only does the Korean language often obfuscate the use of the singular first person (*na*, 나) and plural first person (*uri*, 우리) in both oral and written communication, but it also strongly avoids, along with Japanese and Thai, the use of the pronoun *you*.[43] These obfuscations and omissions of subjects and addressees create confusion for translators trying to render Korean literature into English and help make it virtually impossible for foreign readers or listeners to establish who is speaking and who is being addressed in Korean poems and songs.[44] The recent surge of the use of KakaoTalk chatrooms by Koreans with their smartphones makes the already opaque condition of distinguishing between the speaking subjects and the addressees in a conversation even more difficult. The rise of "Kakao talkscape," commented upon by media scholar Dal Yong Jin, represents a blending of a creative individualized lifestyle with a participatory and public mode of subjectivity for almost all Koreans today where new fun idioms, emoticons, and other expressive forms of communications are invented and circulate, but it is also a realm where a variety of societal stresses, such as peer bullying, the pressures of a Confucian hierarchical order, and never-ending work hours also become heightened—so much so that the government recently had to issue guidelines to discourage employees from sending out "talk" messages to each other after work hours.[45]

New Korean rap verses help capture the essence of a "Kakao talkscape" milieu where the new form of language and communication as well as peer and family pressures emerge, as evoked in the first verse of the hit single "Not at All" by Vinxen (Lee Byung-woo): "For I'm 100 percent certain that I suffer from the victim complex of a pessimist [비관론자의 마인드 피해망상 백 프로 찍고] / It's again time to blame myself [이제 다시 날 탓 할 차례] / But that's why my present address basement room is both cold and beautiful [현주소 지하방이 가장 춥고 아름다워] / I am both grateful and sick and to my father I am sorry [고맙고 또 아프고 아빠에게는 너무 미안해]." In this song, which became his final song during the second successful season of *High School Rapper* in 2017, the listener recognizes that the enmity and negation that reverberate through the repetitive holler of *chŏnhyŏ*, which literally means "not at all," also finds its assonant rhyme with *chŏnnyŏk*, which means "evening." Both words are dark, but through this darkness the rap exhibits a strong sense of defiance. Vinxen, then a seventeen-year-old high school rapper, is sliding away from the bifurcated condition that pits him against the socioeconomic system. It really is he who is to blame for not being happy and for also being stuck in a basement room (*jihabang*), a synecdoche for the condition of Hell Chosun and also a metaphor used in the 2019 film *Parasite*, which evokes a South Korea stuck with a high youth unemployment and suicide rate, a low fertility rate, and a deepening crisis of the middle class that has led to a widening divide between rich and poor.[46] Rather than blaming the system that has pushed him to the edge of suicide and his mother into long hours of servitude at a convenience store, Vinxen creates an interior monologue between his alienated self and the putative form of the other who must stand in as his snickering friends in a Kakao chat room. However, as he continues his struggles with his deep fear of suicide, his anxiety and fear deepen.

Along with peer bullying and economic deprivation, family pressures make Vinxen feel guilty. And here, it is the Confucian filial piety that plays a big part in creating a psychological ghetto that reminds us of the simple truth that ghettos are created not only physically and geographically but also psychologically and within family relations. Though there has been some suggestion that the abundance of risqué wardrobes and sexually suggestive dance moves in the contemporary Korean pop-music scene is a signal that Confucianism is on the wane in Korea, neo-Confucianism is still alive and kicking in K-pop, certainly if we consider the emphasis on collective values among the K-pop idol groups or the lyrics of some of the contemporary music acts.[47] Here, even in the rap song, the sentiment that pours out from Vinxen, a young man who has left his home physically but cannot leave it psychologically, is Confucian shame or guilt. The line "I am both grateful and sick and to my father I am sorry" is then followed a little later by the following:

> I'm gonna make money so that my mom won't need to work at a 7–11
>   no more
> So that she could retire in the countryside that she loves
> It's a promise I gotta keep
> But I ain't sure that I can keep that promise
> It's a promise I gotta keep
> But I ain't sure that I can keep that promise.

The repeated lines of a promise to his mother that he "needs to keep" but he "ain't sure that [he] can keep" intensify the guilt the teenaged rapper feels toward his mother, who spends day and night working at a convenience store. When he performed the song live for the first time in front of an audience, during the final episode of *High School Rapper*, the producers of the show chose to exploit this melodramatic tension that exists between the rebellious son who has chosen to drop out of high school and run away from home and his working-class parents who have been the object of both his frustration and his remorse.[48] Several times the camera cuts to a reaction shot of Vinxen's parents, who cannot hold back their tears while Vinxen sings his song. Especially the lines where Vinxen raps about his promise of an early retirement for his struggling mother that he may or may not be able to keep create one of the rare perfect moments in television that sentimentalize the mind of a tough young Korean rapper through the conventions of an enduringly strong filial piety.

Although the Korean rap here reinvokes Confucian filial piety, Vinxen also simultaneously helps raise the Korean underdog spirit that had always strongly identified with the socially disenfranchised through wordplay that amplifies the tension between foreign loanwords and native Korean words. Such creative wordplay in a rap is not novel. Sin Pul-ch'ul, who was born in 1905 and died in North Korea, after choosing to support the Communists during the Korean War, is perhaps the most famous Korean mandam-ga of the twentieth century.[49] One of his popular lines on stage during the colonial era, which had led to many of his arrests, was "men are faced with the problem of replacing the question of asking 'why' [*wae*, 왜] we live, with one that asks 'how we are supposed to live.' This means that we should eliminate the letter 'wae' [倭, which also means 'Japanese barbarians'] altogether from the dictionary."[50] Here, Sin Pul-ch'ul creates a classic wordplay that operates on the basic level of linking two words that sound the same and allowing his subversions to erupt through the homonymic soundscape. Of course, his wordplay undeniably evokes the Korean "slave" who snickers behind the Japanese "master." Could Sin's branding of a Japanese as a barbarian ever be accused as a racist projection? What if Sin's comment is well aligned within a 'slave's trope' that simply pokes fun at the 'master'? Sin's joke recalls the "Signifyin(g)" practice of taunting the master through tropes during a period when direct criticism of the master was banned. I borrow this literary trope from Gates, who has argued that "Signifyin(g)" is the double-voiced African American tradition of wordplay that rearticulates Du Bois's double consciousness. Taking his cue from the tale of the Signifying Monkey, which originates in the days of slavery, Gates argues that Signifyin(g) is a "slave's trope," a trope-reversing trope that is pervasive in black culture, ranging across its music, art, folklore, and literature.[51] Evading the tyranny of metaphor and instead adopting what he calls the rules of metalepsis anchored by the play of the chain of signifiers, he emphasizes the importance of wordplay based on "phonic similarity" as one of the Signifyin' "slave's tropes."[52] Vinxen and Sin Pul-ch'ul both display their specific kind of Korean defiance through the linguistic tension that Korean words can engender through the coding and decoding of subversive "Signifyin(g).'"

Despite the fact that we have reached a postcolonial, postpoetic, and even postepistolary epoch, the phonic similarity based on such Signifyin(g)' also reaches a new level of sophistication in Vinxen's Kakao talkscape rap song "Not at All," which interrogates and questions both the linguistic privilege of English and Vinxen's street credibility: "Hey you've worked hard, but since you are now popular and could make money on your own, you must now be happy, but [I am] not at all, sheeet." Vinxen suddenly shifts from the perspective of his friend/fan probably snickering over a chat and reauthenticates his own personal perspective with an insistence of "not at all, sheeet." Vinxen creatively mixes up the onomatopoeic sound of the *sheeet* in Korean that refers to *shush* and the vulgar profanity of *shit* in English, which refers to *rubbish*. Between the sound of Korean *shush* and the sound of English *shit*, Vinxen is able to find a new voice that both mediates between the two languages and undermines the fixed, rigid meaning of the two that both signify condescension. The clash between these two forms of *sheeet* (English *shit* and Korean *shush*) creates an opening that allows the opposite meaning of silence to emerge (figure 2.3). During Vinxen's live concert, the young teenage crowd breaks out by yelling "kaekkul" (fucking

2.3 Vinxen at his Aquarium vol. 2 concert, Samsung Blue Square iHall, Seoul, October 2018. Photo by Kyung Hyun Kim.

good—also a Kakao talkscape idiom) that overwhelms and even silences Vinxen's rap of *sheeet* in an act of defiance that strongly identifies with Vinxen's street and blackish dirt spoon (Hŭksujŏ 흙수저) identity.[53] Vinxen's simple dexterous usage of *sheeet* helps him reach beyond the ordinary fixtures of a singular language or meaning. This is a rare joyous occasion where an offline public celebration of an online subculture based on communal sharing of wordplay and rap can be documented.

TWO TURNTABLES AND A MICROPHONE

Often cited in the history of hip-hop is the emphasis on the phrase "two turntables and a microphone" when describing the birth of rap music. Overlooked is the truth that hip-hop grew out of a change in the tastes of a public that no longer wanted music driven by melodies. If previous eras of pop music dominated by the Beatles, the Eagles, and Billy Joel saw as mandatory the figure of the singer-songwriter whose inspirations came through vivid melodies, by the late 1980s, the beats and the language of the street had come to headline the music scene. Melody-driven music was relegated to the background as DJs needed more intensified loops of repetitive beats that could get the crowds to dance in the clubs. Techno beats and funky repetitive rhythms began to dominate the 1970s and soon, under glitzy discotheque lights, melody-driven music by human voices grew cumbersome and quaint. Through the microphone, one would need from the human voice not a song but a thumping rap that matched the rhythm of raw shrieks, scratches on the records, and powerful bars from guitars and instrumental beats sampled together simply to *not* distract it from dance.

Hip-hop was born at a time when the distinction between the "authentic" and the "copy" had begun to fade and made a praxis out of a postmodern theoretical discourse that blurred the gap between consumption and creation and, consequently, between the original and its simulacrum. Is Korean hip-hop—imported from the United States—a translation, a plagiarized text, or an act of mimicry? It is probably all of the above; that is, it is no more of a translation, a plagiarism, or an act of mimicry than the ones produced in Compton or in the Bronx. Rap also categorically declares itself as an aesthetic supplement to the "becoming-black-of-the-world." What is essential in achieving an original text in the era of hip-hop is that an act of authenticity must be added through the rearticulation of the swaggering or posturing *I* of the performer in his or her own linguistic vernacular. The *I* here in Korea has to be derived from a subject that posits himself or herself as a Korean rapper. In a later scene in *Sopyonje*, Yubong yells, "Just you wait! The entire world will someday be on their knees rapping to our beats of p'ansori!" Was this tragic Korean musician, who ended up blinding his own daughter in a desperate attempt to compel her to achieve perfection in the art of p'ansori before dying in the poverty of starvation, singularly and absolutely wrong to blurt out these words about the glorious future of Korean traditional beats? He turned out to be wrong. But should we—right here and right now—borrow a line from Du Bois in "The Souls of White Folk," to exercise the right to join the jeering chorus to "deny [his] right to live and be" and to "call [him] misbirth"?[54]

Every innovation in art, music, and literature requires an update that begins with disavowal, misbehaving, and even misbirth that negate the old establishment. *Sopyonje*, almost thirty years after its release, still booms its bass drum beat that echoes beyond its two-hour run time. Dongho, right before he runs away from his father, Yubong, asks, "What's the point of committing your life to play that *vulgar* music that everyone hates?"[55] Or was Yubong actually "singularly clairvoyant" in predicting that his words (and music) would exceed and transcend the boundaries of bitterness? Was he actually right in believing that his musical soul would reach beyond the pessimism of the "world around him"? That it would allow Koreans to successfully morph into a "becoming-black-of-the-world"? Dongho—in this venerable film from 1993, when both *Sopyonje* and Seo Taiji's "Hayeoga," a rock song that blended influences from both hip-hop and p'ansori, became the cultural keywords of the decade—does not grow up to be a musician.

With Dongho's disavowal to carry on the tradition of his father, and his talented sister becoming blinded at the expense of Yubong's greed, Im Kwon-Taek's film suggests that traditional p'ansori of his time may have indeed died, but a piece of Yubong's music, his ideals, and his resilience continue to reverberate, touch, and uplift—in being enmeshed with the true spirit of hip-hop—many of those who create both uniquely Korean and transcendentally global hip-hop. Song-hwa, the blinded daughter of Yubong, who survives the onslaught of both Westernization and the Korean patriarchy by becoming an itinerant, past-the-prime musician at the end of the film and wandering the snowy conditions of rural Korea, may have found her home in twenty-first century Korean hip-hop.

In the second-to-last line of "Sich'a," Woo Won-jae proudly swags, "The *noise from the Orient* that everyone used to sneer at is now echoing throughout the entire nation."[56] This proclamation of glory, however fleeting and ephemeral in the span of a quickly delivered rap verse, overcomes the vulgar misbirth of Koreanness and thematically triangulates the personal, the national, and the global. First, Woo is a survivor of several mental breakdowns that resulted in several stays in hospitals in order to keep him from inflicting self-harm. His depression forced him to constantly hide behind his beanie pulled over his eyelids, along with his tattoos and rap verses, and yet somehow he became an overnight media star. Second, he is a progenitor of a great national oral storytelling tradition that reclaims the meaning and form of p'ansori by flowing in and out of multiple subject positions (the rapper as *I*, the composer, the student, the dreamer, and even the audience) and ruling over multiple temporalities of day and night. Finally, he aims to fulfill a global ambition—staving off the insults, despisings, and hatreds of those who formerly called him a mimic or a "mini mic" of the hegemonic American pop culture. Whether or not Woo (or, for that matter, Korean hip-hop) could torch the *lamplight of the Orient* for a Korean folk—once envisioned by the Indian poet Rabindranath Tagore in 1929—as a revived p'ansori singer or mandam-ga rapping to the hip-hop beat remains to be seen. In a way, the Korean may have already achieved just that by the time this book is finished.

3   Dividuated Cinema

Temporality and Body in the Overwired Age

Photographs play essential, if not central, roles in two of the best-known Korean films of the New Korean Cinema movement of the past fin de siècle. In *Peppermint Candy* (*Pakha sat'ang*, dir. Yi Chang-dong, 1999), protagonist Yŏng-ho, barely twenty, reveals to Sun-im, the woman he had been fancying at work, while on a picnic that his dream is to photograph "nameless wildflowers." When this picnic episode takes place, in 1979, Yŏng-ho's dream of capturing nature's beauty with a camera could only be just that: a dream — for the prohibitive cost of ownership of a camera is too great for it to become a reality for Yŏng-ho, who is only a menial worker in a factory in a country that has yet to be freed from the shackles of a Third World dictatorship. If ownership of a camera is an explicit emblem of a First World hobby that is totally out of reach for the working class during this period still mired in postwar poverty and intense industrialization, it is the psychological trauma that disallows Yŏng-ho from accepting a gift of a camera twenty years later. Contemplating suicide, in the episode that is set in 1999, Yŏng-ho no longer wishes to leave a trace of himself, as he not only sells the camera at a pawnshop but also trashes the film that was kept in the camera without having it developed (figure 3.1). The hobby of photography will not help a young man advance his career, nor will it avert the traumatized middle-aged man from committing suicide.

The act of refusal of capturing and reproducing photography often depicted in Korean cinema during this time period, despite its association

3.1 Cameras and taking photographs are important metaphors in *Peppermint Candy* (1999).

with bourgeois leisure activity, signifies Korean cinema's grappling with the truth through time lag or temporality. Photographs also make their crucial entries in perhaps one of the most important Korean films made over the past seventy years: *Memories of Murder* (*Salin ŭi ch'uŏk*, dir. Bong Joon-ho, 2003). In this crime mystery set in the 1980s, when the first-ever appearance of a serial killer in Korea coincided with the coming of an end of military dictatorship, taking photos and showing them as pieces of evidence is what consumes the daily activity of Park Du-man (played by Song Kang-ho). Park's task is to crack the serial murder case that has consumed his small rural town of Hwasŏng. As Joseph Jonghyun Jeon has pointed out, *Memories of Murder* is a film about remembering, but the remembrance recalled here is a "missed . . . and even unmemorable" one.[1] None of the archived photographs can help solve the case, nor do the random shots of footprints, dead body parts, and misidentified suspects' mug shots translate into memorable images that help us reconstruct temporality, gallery, and ultimately history. Failures as a piece of evidence or a piece of truth, they are reduced to physical data tinged with uselessness and waste, especially because they are all photochemical images that have taken up costs—both financial and environmental.[2]

Both *Peppermint Candy* and *Memories of Murder* were shot on celluloid and physically depict predigital cameras, and both are built around the theme of remembrance and photography. However, the present era of data-ism—with its infinite capabilities of digitization, data storage, and powerful algorithms—has enabled Korean cinema to generate narratives that are no longer bound by specific metaphors and allegories that thematize the nation's distinctive recollection of its own wars, postcolonial histories, and dictatorships. Instead, the prevailing themes are those that cohere the crippling effects of late capitalist technology and discipline control through internet avatar-inspired body-switch narratives.[3] The proliferation of body-switch narratives offers demonstrations of Korean cinema as the product of a new kind of cinema that attempts to maneuver a newly articulated dystopian vision of neoliberal capitalism. Though Korean cinema of the past two decades (2000–2019) occupies a different time zone than the American cinema of the 1980s, this new brand of popular "body-switch" narratives from South Korea is not too dissimilar from what Fredric Jameson once declared about David Cronenberg's masterpiece *Videodrome*, the "post-contemporary spin given to . . . traditional heroic narrative."[4]

The criminal investigation or even daily act (like capturing the beauty of "wild flowers") rendered not simply through analog production and reproduction of photographs but through the infinite processing of data accumulated from closed-circuit television (CCTV) monitors or traces left on the internet withdraws from the conventional conflict between individuals and masses, and instead introduces, among other things, codes, avatars, and impostors that both reflect and mold the self. I take up the Deleuzian term *dividuals*, which regulates and modulates the new system of the digital in the control societies, to better illuminate the latest trend of Korean cinema's fascination with the body-switch genre. Body switch is perhaps just another way of depicting today's anxiety as the phenomenon of "disappearance of the body," as Kieron O'Hara and Nigel Shadbolt claim, spreads in the new state of global hypersurveillance.[5] The current popularity of body-switch genres in Korean cinema illustrates Korean society's full subscription to the new module of digital societies and reflects on its passion for the theme of ambiguity between the original and the counterfeit. The ambiguous relation between less-than-original enactments and iterations of course remains one of the central themes of this book as I attempt to understand the power embedded in mimicry, remakes, and fakes. The popularity of the themes of these body-switch films that pivot on the difference between originals and fakes as indistinguishable and reversable is not only a well-versed postmodern dictum but also a nostalgic aspiration of a previous underdeveloped country that has rebuilt its economy around imitations and counterfeits.

In movies like *Peppermint Candy* and *Memories of Murder*, the main conflict is not simply between the forgetting and the remembrance of history; it is also between the masses and the individuals. *Peppermint Candy* asks continually whether the fate of an individual could be severed from the destiny of the nation that underwent an era marred by dictatorship and massacre. *Memories of Murder* is no different. One of the most crucial scenes in the film unfolds before the audience when Detective Park and others attempt to identify a suspect who has made his run and is now lost in a crowd composed of night-shift workers who are wearing the same blue-collar uniforms. The hypersurveillanced society like today's Seoul would not face such problems of visual documentation or lost suspect in a crowd, as many of the busy intersections of workplace and public spaces are constantly monitored by CCTV. However, in the pre-internet era, such scientific systems of data inspection did not exist, so instead of relying on the machine to solve the crime, it is still Detective Park's accomplished individual skills that the system has to rely on to catch the suspect who has disappeared into the crowd. The investigation technique has moved beyond a contest between individuals and the masses, and a new era of data-ism has emerged that redirects cinema to engender a new subjecthood. This new subject ends up refashioning more flexible and dividuated identities that terminate the previous era's fascination with disciplinary societies and its struggle against the Panopticon.

Though Deleuze was deeply impressed with Foucault's concept of the Panopticon, which is, according to Foucault, an "instrument of permanent, exhaustive, omnipresent surveillance, capable of making all visible, as long as it could itself remain invisible . . . a faceless gaze that transformed the whole social body into a field of perception," he declared that the Panopticon was an emblem of a disciplinary society that was associated more "with the eighteenth and nineteenth centuries."[6] What Deleuze instead wanted to seek was a distinction between control societies of the late twentieth century and disciplinary societies with which the Panopticon was associated. Deleuze writes,

> Disciplinary societies have two poles: signatures standing for *individuals*, and numbers or places in a register standing for their position in a *mass*. Disciplines see no incompatibility at all between these two aspects, and their power both amasses and individuates, that is, it fashions those over whom it's exerted into a body of people and molds the individuality of each member of that body. . . . In control societies, on

the other hand, the key thing is no longer a signature or number but a code: codes are *passwords*. . . . We're no longer dealing with a duality of mass and individual. Individuals become "dividuals," and masses become samples, data, markets, or "banks."[7]

Deleuze was already able to determine as early as 1990 that in the digital age, capitalism produces energy and functions less in traditional dual structures composed of individuals and masses but more in terms of dividuals who often have to register their codes in the system of data that simply have replaced the term *masses*. Data or the system that collects data self-manages and assigns the individual as a man in debt, with a poor number of "likes" on Facebook or a low credit score. This process, which self-regulates and algorithmically computes the infinite mountain of data, succeeds in separating the *in-* from the *individual*, producing the *dividual*, which is likely to multiply the subject rather than consolidating rationality within the domain of a single subject.

The present postmodern, post-dictatorship, and post-traumatic turn toward the dividual is not only intimately tied with the age of post-photography but also intertwined with an updated trope of body switch. This genre renews the ontological question that imprints the dividual with multiple fantasy-inspired character provocations and a blurred boundary between authenticity and simulations. The popularity of the body-switch films in Korea during the 2010s, including *Masquerade* (*Kwanghae*, dir. Choo Chang-min, 2012), *Miss Granny* (*Susanghan kŭ nyŏ*, dir. Hwang Dong-hyuk, 2014), *Beauty Inside* (dir. Baek Jong-yeol, 2015), *Luck-key* (dir. Lee Gae-byok, 2016), and *The Dude in Me* (*Nae an ŭi kŭ nom*, dir. Kang Hyo-jin, 2019) to name just a few, illuminates the arrival of a new generation who grew up with both massively multiplayer online role-playing games (MMORPG) like Lineage and Starcraft and the surveillance system that is typical of a hyperurbanized society like Korea. In this era of data-mined network, the narratological models that previously provoked regimes of temporality to associate the past with trauma and spaces where the battle between the inevitability of death and the defiance against it gives the baseline of the heroic plotline also go through an evolution. Surely in the crime mystery films that employ surveillance technology to crack cases or exploit CCTV to mastermind a crime, the narratological models generically move toward what Peter Brooks explains as the "death that writes *finis* to the life and therefore confers on it its meaning."[8] Korean crime films that employ CCTV as the main device in cracking criminal cases, such as *Hide* and Seek (*Sumpakkokjil*, dir. Huh Jung, 2013) and *Cold Eyes* (*Kamsijadŭl*, dir. Jo Ŭi-seok and Kim Byung-seo, 2013), typically will not fundamentally change the ways in which conventional narratives are framed.

Crime films in Korea and elsewhere will continue to be structuring an end where the death drive is tightly interwoven with the termination of a plotline. However, there are more films that are driven by a sense of visual surveillance that identifies less with the Foucauldian sense of disciplinary societies and instead merely employs the surveillance-based network as a playful phantasm that inspires narratives that directly invoke the Deleuzian power-of-the-false, a theoretical maneuver that upsets the binary structure between truth and falsehood. Through this maneuver, an emergent critique of disciplinary societies and even neoliberal capitalism emerges. These stories, though their basic tenets are borrowed, plagiarized, and mimicked after commercial American comedies of the 1980s, cast Koreans as late capitalist subjects who become *dividuated* or multiplied into impostors, castaways, and social outcasts who are forced to internalize the gaze and then empower themselves through the power-of-the-false. These multiplications of the self through either swapped bodies or ever-changing bodies redirect the story of the classical struggle between the small individuals matched up against the masses into one that is now between the self and the data that mold, codify, and diverge into various forms of doppelgängers.

CALL ME KING

Masquerade, a *sagŭk* (historical premodern drama), best illustrates the dividuated cinema. In this film, which tells a story about an early Chosun-era king, Kwanghae, who ruled Korea from 1608 to 1623, the plot of a body switch perfectly allegorizes the themes of "dividual" in the internet-era surveillance that often ignores the physical body and instead privileges one's informational codes, traces, and data. My interest in focusing on the genre of sagŭk is two-fold. First, how does the spectacle that chronicles Korean history during the Chosun Dynasty reinscribe the impossibility of revolutionary ideals to be carried out but also increase our option to pursue a realist text with a progressive agenda? Here, I invoke the defense that Communist literary critic Georg Lukács had summoned for Sir Walter Scott's novels as a harbinger of revolutionary heroes at a time of relative social stability. Following Lukács, this chapter examines how the new sagŭks address the social issues that tend to upset and protest the status quo in-stilled by neoliberal politics. Second, I am also finding, in a series of strik-ing, enigmatic formulations, the relevance of postmodernism—especially its incredulity toward any instance of authenticity—which amplifies "the power of the false" and reregisters an interesting set of icons that rechannel the idea of what American semiotician Charles S. Peirce calls "indexical-ity."[9] In many ways, the idealization of the body switch in recent Korean blockbuster films, especially the recent *Beauty Inside*, expands the extraor-dinary power-of-the-false to the point where the multiplication of the self becomes so infinite that the truth of the face, the exterior, and even the visual signification can never be properly decoded.

The revisionist sagŭks in Korea, which arguably began with the suc-cess of *King and the Clown* (*Wang ŭi namja*, dir. Lee Joon-ik, 2005), dis-tinguish themselves from those of the early decades by portraying heroes of historical novels rather than those of the epics. Like the eponymous protagonist in Walter Scott's *Ivanhoe* (1820), these protagonists have both virtues and weaknesses, good and bad qualities, rather than characteristics that are eminent and all-embracing. This focus on minor characters (more like Shakespearean Mercutio or Horatio) rather than major characters (like Romeo or Hamlet) not only allows these dramas to translate great histori-cal collisions such as foreign invasions, tyrannical rule, and peasant rebel-lions into personal and intimate human terms but also brings them into a very complex and dynamic relationship with the age in which we live. To illuminate the transition from the epic to the historical novel, a brief comment on Lukács's work is perhaps necessary. While suggesting that the "'hero' of a Scott novel is always a more or less mediocre, average English gentleman," Lukács in *The Historical Novel* famously argued against the prevailing criticism that Sir Walter Scott is only a mediocre artist.[10] Though Scott was himself a petty aristocratic-conservative man, he, Lukács argued, had exceptional and revolutionary epic gifts that renunciated the Romanti-cist tradition of the day. The hero of a Scott novel, Lukács notes, "generally possesses a certain, though never outstanding, degree of practical intelli-gence, a certain moral fortitude and decency which even rises to a capacity for self-sacrifice, but which never grows into a sweeping human passion, is never the enraptured devotion to a great cause."[11]

Needless to say, the heroes of the new sagŭks possess similar qualities that have made Scott's historical novels such as *Ivanhoe* an ideal para-digm to imbue the Hegelian ideas such as "history of the spirit" (Geistesge-schichte). England of the early nineteenth century in which Scott had been active as a writer—unlike France during the similar era—is noted for its relative stability during a stormy period elsewhere in Europe. Scott, Lukács reports, belonged neither with the "ardent enthusiasts of this development [in which industrial revolution and the rapid growth of capitalism are threatening the old aristocracy] nor with its pathetic, passionate indicters."[12] This "middle way" is what makes Scott's novels so brilliant, by the standards of Lukács: by deeply sympathizing with the unending misery— brought about by the collapse of old England—of the people, who are yet unable to muster a violent opposition to the new emergent capitalist power. The socioeconomic climate of early nineteenth-century England seems to share common characteristics with those that surround Korean cinema today as more historical films continue to be made. South Korea, unlike the stormy situation in other capitalist countries such as the United States and the European Union that suffered severely from the housing bubble of 2008–9, was spared from financial or political ruins and enjoyed instead a moderate rise in average income during the first decade and a half of the twenty-first century.[13] Also in 2020, when the global pandemic and race riots ripped through the United States, Korea emerged from the rubble of COVID-19 by setting the gold standard in mitigating the virus with abundant testing and a highly regarded contact tracing system.

In *Masquerade*, finding a substitute for the ailing king is mandatory because the king, unlike a democratically elected figure, is an absolute monarch who can ill afford a break. Since even the king's most private matters, such as copulation, defecation, and consumption of food, are actually functions that are of grave state importance, every enactment by the stand-in must be vigilantly copied and coded. In other words, already in the premodern era, the detailed documentation and the deep analysis of everyday activities of the king serve as important data that generate handling and managing as an institution of data. Here, the gap between surveillance of the king's everyday and the data-ism of today's internet subjecthood becomes collapsed to a point where the reproduction of a doppelgänger or the clown becomes a naturalized process in both the premodern story and the realities of living in the postmodern era. The enormous amount of data available on the king and the tautological activities that he is engaged do not require him to be physically present in the palace and in the meetings even when he is perfectly capable of performing everyday duties.

Once the look-alike doppelgänger is found for the role of the king, he, the clown impostor, is given a crash course by Hŏ Kyun, the chief royal secretary (*tosŭngji*). And when Kwanghae does become poisoned by his rival faction, the chief royal secretary and the highest order of eunuch ask the clown to become the king's stand-in on a full-time basis. In this convention of impersonation and imitation rises yet another signification that Peirce called "indexical" that complicates the gap between signifier (clown impostor) and signified (royal majesty) and subsequently blurs the class barrier between the king and the clown, serving as a pivot point for progressive reforms. In other words, the indexical relationship between two signifiers (the impostor and the real king) initiates and anticipates the inevitable progress toward the Utopian elimination of all classes.

The climactic moment in the film occurs when the identity of the king is questioned by the group of incredulous conservative ministers. It is this nocturnal scene that crosscuts the private dialogue between the impostor and Hŏ Kyun and the public gathering of the group of ministers who demand that the king disrobe in order to visually confirm whether the childhood scar imprinted on his left upper torso is there. "Why don't you become then the real king?" the chief royal secretary asks the fake double before continuing: "If you want to truly seek revenge for the death of slain Sawol, if you want to nary exonerate those who suck the blood out of the people, and if you want to become a king who holds his subjects above him . . . if that is the king that you dream of becoming, then I will realize that dream for you." At this point, tensions rise, because the fake double, who has, over the past fifteen days, successfully learned the craft of kingship, begins to answer affirmatively, "I would like to become the king." Yet here the camera pauses the dialogue by turning to the disrobing scene, which involves the same actor playing the king. When his upper body is revealed, the scar becomes visible — confirming the real king's return to the palace from his sick bed just in time to quell any suspicion that his identity had been forged.

When the camera then returns to the earlier conversation between the royal secretary and the fake king, the impostor explains the reason behind why he cannot continue playing his royal role: "I would like to be the king, but if someone has to die for me to live, and someone also has to kill for that to happen, if that is what the meaning of the king is, then my dream belongs to me and me only." It is interesting here that the double enunciation of "me" and "me only" in regard to the "dream of being the king" not only denies the two characters (the king and the clown) a friendship, unlike the one in Hollywood comedies like *Trading Places* (1983) or *Dave* (1993) where a friendship is forged between the golden spoon and dirt spoon, but also affirms the sense of restoration of individual autonomy insisted upon by this very phrasing of "nobody else can dream that dream but me." The dividuated dream here comes to a close, and with it the possibility of a revolution rendered unimaginable. The clown, like Lukács's description of Scott's historical novel, never grows into a sweeping human passion and never shows the enraptured devotion to a great cause. The impostor's refusal to either strike a friendship with the king or permanently replace the real king displays both the discontent at the political status quo that levies no new tax against the aristocrats (as well as respecting Chosun's flunky relationship with Ming China even after its collapse against the Manchus) and the rejection of the revolutionary dedication to fully disclaim the king.

At the end of the film, the total collapse between the signifier (abject clown) and the signified (royal majesty) does not take place when the clown announces that he is not interested in taking over the throne for good and will only dream about being the king. If he were to dream the "dream of being the king" for the sake of the nation, then would he not be in a position to expose the Lacanian Real—in which a revolutionary change could indeed be materialized? The clown's failure to dream beyond himself instead achieves a measured sense of realism. The film settles for a complacent ending where each element of history (the king and the clown) is returned to the pre-drama order of things when the clown chooses to abort a real revolution by abdicating from his throne.

When *Masquerade* was released in Korea in 2012, there was much debate, especially by netizens, about whether the film's reliance on the story of an impostor was too close to that of a critically acclaimed Japanese film directed by Akira Kurosawa, *Kagemusha* (1980), made thirty years earlier. In *Kagemusha*, a thief is asked to serve as a body double for the ailing Lord Shingen. When the samurai lord is shot to death during a battle, the thief emerges as the film's protagonist by defeating the enemy, unifying the clan, and serving as a better lord than the original one himself. Though similarities exist between the Kurosawa film and the Korean commercial film, any kind of probing of a Japanese *jidaigeki*, I think, must begin with a study of Kabuki. Though Kurosawa is known to be one of the directors who tried to modernize jidaigeki by limiting the influences of Kabuki on Japanese cinema, viewing *Kagemusha* now reminds us how Noel Burch's thesis on Japanese cinema remains quite valid. He argued in his book *To the Distant Observer* that it is the flatness of the stage, and not the depth of illusion, that has made Japanese cinema unique in world cinema. As Mitsuhiro Yoshimoto has also noted, unlike Western cinema that has attempted "to erase the materiality of the signifier to create the illusion of the signifier," Burch emphasized that the materiality of the signifier in Japanese cinema is retained in a move of what he calls presentationalism, in which the separation between the stage (illusion) and the auditorium (reality) is not clearly demarcated. Burch argues that this historical background that stems from Kabuki was the real reason behind the lengthy tenure of "the *benshi*, the live 'narrator' of all silent films in Japan, who was to play such a vital role in the preservational character of Japanese cinema."[14] This presentationalism achieved through the benshi would make cinema's self-reflexivity more profound.[15] This anti-illusionist principle of presentationalism is at work in both Kabuki-inspired tradition of benshi (*pyŏnsa* in Korean) and the Korean tradition of p'ansori that draws my interest to the medium of sagŭk and the effective deployment of what Deleuze has called "the power of the false," which encapsulates the thirdness that is beyond the bifurcated boundary between the truth and the false, which is ironically taken up in these sagŭks' postmodern turn. This tradition in the cinemas of both countries that accentuates and even exaggerates the materiality of signifier between the stage and the auditorium or between drama and viewers has sown seeds for television of East Asia to cultivate a culture of onscreen captions (see chapter 4).

As can be imagined about the origin of the audience pleasure derived in a film that is primarily about the twist of fate between the king and the pauper, it is the voice that manifests a central kind of unconscious. After all, how well can the clown impersonate the voice of the king? As Michel Chion reminds us, the voice is bodiless and actually lies outside the core divisions of the Cartesian subject: the body and the mind.[16] Though the face is obviously a part of the signifying system in the visual medium of cinema, *Masquerade* neutralizes faciality by employing the same actor to play both the real king and his impostor, for they must look alike (figure 3.2). With the minimal difference of either face or body (with the exception of scar) registered, it is the voice that leaves the body, and yet emanates fully from it, that distinguishes the king from the rest of the subjects in the film. The clown also has to attain the voice of the king in order to pass the test to be the king.

The king's routines, mandates, and authority emerge from his tautological functions. When the clown is first given instructions as to how to behave during the ceremonious meeting between the king and the ministers, he is told by the chief royal secretary to repeat the same three phrases

3.2 The real king examines the fake king in *Masquerade* (2012).

throughout: "Please do as you please," "next," and "let him in, I say," which most likely conceal any real meaning. They are fillers since they do not have any substance beyond the emphatic nature of these phrases. Style rules over content. Even on the level of rhetoric, there is a convergence already between the premodern system of rule and the postmodern model of representation that is also dictated by when the signifieds vanish or wane under the weight of a continual sliding of the signifiers. The voice that carries these messages here is a perfect instance of a break from the body, but also, as Mladen Dolar notes in his wonderful book *A Voice and Nothing More*, it is the voice that "holds the bodies and languages together."[17] The importance of the voice is just as significant in the postmodern era as it is in the premodern one since it is a meeting point where the tensions between the presymbolic and the symbolic and between the signifying and the nonsignifying arise. "Low and majestically!" orders the chief royal secretary when he is training the clown for the next day's meetings with the ministers. For the clown, who first is better known for his gawkish slapstick gestures that rib at the aristocrats and his nonsignifying, inarticulate bodily sounds such as burps, farts, and coughs, a signifying voice begins to develop. Later this symbolic voice allows him to bolt from the tautological and performative rhetoric that simply straps the king to the status quo. When the fake king becomes upset with his conservative ministers and protests that aim to change the tax policies and diplomatic relations of Chosun, his voice no longer remains an empty premodern signifier such as "please do as you please" that has no meaning beyond it; it actually becomes tied to a modern subject that restores his mind's capability to articulate the positions of "historical determination."

Unlike most body-swap movies made in the United States or Korea, which tend to portray the main character switching bodies with one other single character or a younger self through the realization of a magical wish to become young, *Beauty Inside* (dir. Baek Jong-yul, 2015) features Woo-jin, a man who, since the age of eighteen, started to wake up every morning as a different person. He could be old or young, male or female, or even a non-Korean. *Beauty Inside* thus had to cast twenty-one actors to play Woo-jin, which leads to a dividualized screen time where the actors playing the lead have no more than on average five or six minutes of screen time. Though this concept of "same-inside-but-different-outside" was taken from the long American commercial sponsored by Intel and Toshiba and directed by Drake Doremus, the Korean film version is a standard feature film that best exploits the melodramatic impulse that is quite possibly prevalent in all body-swap genre films and asks, "Is it only the exterior with which one could fall in love and not the interior underneath the same skin?"

Without necessarily invoking Jean Baudrillard's famous claim that simulations and different forms of mediations that the media have proliferated during the postwar years have blurred the boundary between the real and the simulacrum, and between the authentic and the inauthentic, we can recognize that the multiple-faced protagonist and the articulation of infinite faciality that *Beauty Inside* embraces complicate the process of singular, authentic identity formation that individualizes the self from the masses.[18] Though there is one single authentic Woo-jin who exists inside, because each and every day he looks completely different than he was the previous day, he must live a life whose identity cannot be veiled beyond his mother and his best friend. In other words, his dividuated self limits his role in the surveillance society. He cannot maintain a social media ID nor even assuredly take a photo with his girlfriend for fear that their visual identification as a couple might mislead others in suspecting that she is having dates with a different person each day. In the latter half of *Beauty Inside*, Woo-jin's mother does reveal to her son a family secret, that his father suffered from the same disease, but beyond that, *Beauty Inside* does not provide a medical reason as to why he must undergo the kind of changes he suffers from. Also, Woo-jin does not make an attempt to voluntarily seek a physician's help to cure his ailment. If this were a typical Hollywood film, the most natural question embedded in the narrative would be: Wouldn't Woo-jin be tempted to commit a crime, like robbing a bank, since no one would be able to identify him once the day of the crime passes? Also, would not this be the best way to get back at the world that has given him the undesired face-off each and every day? However, the film follows the spirit of *Groundhog Day* (dir. Harold Ramis, 1993), an American film that is notably different from *Beauty Inside* because it's not the body change that is repeated but the same day (Groundhog Day, February 2), since it promotes the same value that tomorrow will always come, whether or not we like it, and for which Woo-jin's sincerity and good intentions are rarely tested. He uses his reluctant asylum from the surveillance culture and "soft cage" (he does leave a video diary on his computer every day, but putatively these are images that will never leave his own hard disk and therefore cannot be part of the data-scape that constructs the internet surveillance) to better master the carpentry of furniture making in an isolated environment.[19]

The reduction of the self to the ever-changing exterior (rather than the soul or the inside) that is symptomatic of the postmodern condition here also engineers the unconscious psychological fears and anxieties that limit the protagonist. The discrepancy between the inside (now a twenty-nine-year-old Korean man) and the outside (almost always someone else) wedges a monkey wrench into any long-term relationship. As expected, Woo-jin's affair with Yi-soo, a beautiful and affable furniture store salesperson, inevitably escalates into a nuptial possibility. Despite the fact that Yi-soo reciprocates his love, she cannot bring up the fact to any of her family members that she is considering marrying a person who is undergoing facial and bodily change every day. Her sister begins to suspect whether Yi-soo is secretly promiscuous, based on the pictures on her phone taken with Woo-jin. While Yŏng-ho in *Peppermint Candy* cannot access photography for an economic reason and then for traumatic reasons, for Woo-jin, the threat of cinematography originates from a totally different place. It is the infinite sprawl of instantaneous data-ization of images that could threaten his very identity and prevent him from being in the circuit of selfie culture. Knowing that he has become a burden to Yi-soo, Woo-jin decides that he needs to break up his relationship with her and moves his workshop to Prague. The film at this point races toward an end, unlike the conclusion of *Masquerade*, which privileges the social agenda over the romantic one and attempts to fulfill the fantasy quest.[20] Yi-soo, in the most frequently rehearsed motifs of the romantic narratives, now regrets the premature break-up with Woo-jin and recognizes that the domain of true love belongs exclusively with two individuals, and cannot be shared between extended family and friends. She decides to pack her bags and joins Woo-jin in the capital of the Czech Republic. During the climax of the film, when the two love birds finally meet in the East European city, actor Yoo Yeon-seok, who is widely known as one of the pretty-boy actors in Korea, appears to play the opposite role of Yi-soo, played by Han Hyo-ju, an actress considered to be one of the most beautiful in Korean cinema today. Having Yoo, the finest-looking among the twenty-one actors, cast for the "final" role of Woo-jin, play the decisive climactic episode in the film, in addition to having cast Han Hyo-joo to play his romantic counterpart Yi-soo, derails the legitimacy of the film's central theme, which putatively suggests that it is the beauty inside that matters, not the outside. Throughout the entire film, Yi-soo rarely shares a romantic moment with an actor or an actress who does not fill the bill of vintage star image, and the actors who are old or unimpressive in terms of looks tend to become Woo-jin only on a day when romance is not needed (figures 3.3–3.7).

Despite the film's shortcomings that in some sense discredit the very message of the film, *Beauty Inside* purports and projects an indelible feeling of *beauty outside,* and the film successfully speculates and debates an old philosophical question about authenticity and tempts us to think that visual faces in some ways may have lost their autonomy because of the social culturalization and data-ization of everyday life, where the gap between the self and the internet-driven doppelgänger or one between reality and the data-driven one has grown over the past couple of decades. The endlessly evolving faces of Woo-jin dispute any of the authenticity claims one could perhaps make with the value of a face. The original image of Woo-jin does not precede the fake or the impostor because there is nothing left in the original that can be claimed—seeing that each face is as fleeting and elusive as the one that has followed it and preceded it. There can be no logic, no erraticism, no value associated with any of the faces since it is as close to an empty signifier as an individuality can assume. Woo-jin is the perfect dividuated character, not only because the split between the inside and the outside is permanent but because the outside is hollow, unaccountable, and completely fallen off.

FROM TIME TRAVEL TO BODY TRAVEL

As David Martin-Jones argues, time-travel films consumed much of the production of South Korean cinema during the last fin de siècle. He cites three films—*Calla* (*Kara*, dir. Song Hae-sŏng, 1999), *Ditto* (*Tonggam*, dir.

3.3–3.7 By increasing the role of the actors who are young and handsome, *Beauty Inside* (2015) actually exhibits the theme of beauty outside.

Kim Chŏng-gwon, 2000), and *2009: Lost Memories* (dir. Lee Si-myung, 2002)—as productions that are part of time-travel melodramas that create a collective sense of mourning for "South Korea's experience of compressed modernity."[21] *Peppermint Candy* and *Memories of Murder*, which were respectively made in 1999 and 2003, in many ways could be classified as films that drift in time because *Peppermint Candy* adopts a "reverse chronological narrative structure that 'begins' in spring 1999 and 'ends' in autumn 1979."[22] *Memories of Murder* similarly invokes time travel by framing a story from 1987 from the perspective of 2003.

If time travel was one of the most popular trends of South Korean films in the late 1990s and the first decade of 2000s, it is clear that body travel is now one of the most palatable fantasies that top the Korean producers' list over the past decade. Over the last generation that has just come of age, this is largely due to the faltering of the grand ideologies that have impacted South Korea. A declining interest in history has resulted in a drop in film productions that simply say more about temporality, but the turn from temporality toward the body does not necessarily disaffect the turn toward the postmodern condition, which still attempts to recode and modulate control societies. Though dismissed largely by critics for being amnesiac and apathetic, one of the films that first flirted with the body-switch genre, which supplements the dividuated sensibility that refigures a new cinematic imperative, was *My Sassy Girl* (*Yŏpgi jŏk in kŭ nyŏ*, dir. Kwak Jae-yong, 2001). It was one of the trendsetters and the very first film adapted from an internet serial novel. This popular comedy about a college student who continues to place herself in fantasy movie roles was a loud pronouncement of the coming of age for a new generation that no longer felt burdened by the traumas and brutality etched in Korea's twentieth-century history. In this comedy that was released in the same period when post-trauma films were in vogue, neither undeveloped film (*Peppermint Candy*) nor evidence of DNA match (*Memories of Murder*) provoke metaphors of youthful remembrance or tearful injustice. And yet the depictions of bodily sensations of vomit, dance, and finally the act of morphing into fantasy genre heroes of either martial arts or sci-fi action flicks simulate the feeling of acute awareness that we are living in the era of the soft cage, where most of us cannot but leave records and data that are retrievable. These amalgamated data help set the stage for the new subjects that no longer value unique individuals but encourage dividuated beings that could help recode a form of becoming that helps us both move toward and move away from various kinds of either government or commercial surveillances that are only interested in crafting consumerist and conformist subjects.

The films *200-Pound Beauty* (*Minyŏ nŭn kwerowŏ*, dir. Kim Yong-hwa, 2006) and *Miss Granny* (2014) were sensational hits in Korea. Despite the popular success these two films have generated and the potential of these body-change films to re-create the post-traumatic subject through the Deleuzian dividual, their gender politics do not budge much beyond the conservative theme of heterosexual romance as a true fulfillment wish of a feminine ideal that restores the condition of some lost Eden hailed during the classical era. In *200-Pound Beauty*, Han-na, the overweight ghost singer standing in for an enormously popular singer, undergoes plastic surgery and becomes unbelievably slender and strikingly beautiful. So dramatic is the transformation, not even her best friend can recognize her. With this new identity acquired, Han-na rises to stardom and is even able to attract the music producer she had once fancied as a ghost singer. In this film, it is not wishing-well magic that creates a body swap but a real plastic surgery. But the secret behind Han-na's slender look threatens to drown her new rise to the top when her rival singer discloses it to the public. By coming clean to the public at a concert where her anti-fans are ready to disseminate waves of hate messages against her, Han-na becomes redemptive and her love with the baffled producer becomes restored. The message here is not only the acceptance of heterosexual love fulfillment but also the problem of never properly disgracing the "beauty outside" motto that the film putatively intends. Both fandom and spectacular boyfriend are purchased not by "beauty inside / ugly outside" presurgery Han-na but by the "beauty inside / beauty outside" postsurgery singer. Such a radical turnaround in her career would not have been possible had it not been for the plastic surgery, and instead of amplifying the power-of-the-false where the truth becomes undermined, the film essentializes the good-looks-will-prevail theory.

If time-travel films' reverse chronology, and as Todd McGowan claims in his analysis of *Peppermint Candy*, "disrupts the spectator's relationship to chronological time in order to call into question the nation as an entity that evolves through history," a body-swap film such as *200-Pound Beauty* or *Miss Granny* that is totally immersed in commercial enterprise never aims to disrupt the temporal orientation.[23] If a commercial film like *Miss Granny* simply tried to restrict the pain of history to the personal realm, *Peppermint Candy* makes explicit the disruption of the spectator's relationship to national historical development, as that itself remains the motif for the crucial inquiry into the evolution of the nation marred by repressive military dictatorship. In *Peppermint Candy*, the setting of both the beginning of the film and the ending of the film remains the same. The audience is led to the brook above which the bridge of the train tracks runs in the setting of both 1979 and 1999. All people who gathered for the picnic remain the same twenty years later. The film presents them as the same characters, but different—if one considers both their looks and their characters. Though their names have remained the same, they look ugly outside—reflecting the ugliness inside. The people gathered for the reunion are just as corrupt as protagonist Yŏng-ho, who after decades of co-opting with the authorities he had once loathed has turned, like them, ugly both inside and out. It is only the landscape of Korea that has remained the same—forcing the audience to question whether these people could have turned out to be different had Korea ensured them evolution—free from both violence and trauma.

One of the most interesting aspects of *Miss Granny* is that it attempts to turn back the clock while also swapping the two bodies between an aging grandmother and her younger version of the self. But unlike *Peppermint Candy*, people, despite the years elapsed, have remained the same inside. Neither corrupt nor malicious, *Miss Granny*'s characters are not beyond redemption. *Miss Granny* features a seventy-something granny, Oh Malsoon, who miraculously turns back the clock when she is given the body of a twenty-year-old, but this turning-back-the-clock act—explicitly made during the climax of her difficult youth as a newlywed who loses her husband and then struggles to raise her son alone—never calls into question the nation's illegitimate history. And, unlike all the films that are analyzed here, such as *Beauty Inside* or *Masquerade*, which fully exploit the phenomenon of the "disappearance of the body," *Miss Granny* remains realistic about the evolution of the body rather than one that fully encapsulates its disappearance. In order to forestall the complete "disappearance of the body," the film, not unlike *Peppermint Candy* or *Memories of Murder*, is reliant on predigital photography and a traditional photo studio. It is inside a magic photo studio where the septuagenarian halmŏni (granny) Oh decides to take a photo possibly to be used for her funeral that enables her to turn back her clock (figure 3.8). She transforms into a body and face that is not unfamiliar to her but completely familiar; Oh is no longer a *halmŏni* Oh but a *ch'ŏnyŏ* (young woman) Oh. Also, at a crucial moment in the film, when Oh's son, a sociologist tenured at one of the finest uni-

3.8 No longer able to find her own identity in today's selfie culture, Oh Mal-soon magically recovers her youth in an old-fashioned photo studio that still employs a celluloid camera (*Miss Granny*, 2014).

versities in Korea, tries to solve the riddle of his aging mother's absence, he flips through the photographs of her younger days. It is inside those stacks of celluloid photographs where he locates the truth of her whereabouts (figures 3.9 and 3.10). The lost object then ultimately becomes not his aging mother but his inability to adapt to the true essence of his mother, who was once young and talented.

In a well-known book of essays devoted to the study of photography, Roland Barthes begins with an essay that exclaims his amazement at looking at the photograph of Napoleon's youngest brother from 1852 and adds the caption "I am looking at eyes that looked at the Emperor."[24] This exclamation leads Barthes to cultivate a widespread theoretical concept called *punctum* that arises from great personal "sympathy, almost a kind of tenderness" that a photograph as a medium can muster.[25] Though the internet continues to push out the analog environment from which photography has initially developed, the ontological threat made to the body as a continually dividuated process is putatively terminated when the son identifies his younger mother posing in the photograph. The son's remorseful punctum is quite literally the reason behind the ceasing of the mother's corporeal multiplication or the hideout behind her younger self. Once the son acknowledges the mother, she can no longer continue to camouflage in a younger body. She decides to return to her *real* body and return home.

3.9–3.10 Through an old photograph, Oh Mal-soon's son uncovers the truth about his missing mother's whereabouts in *Miss Granny*.

Unlike Barthes, who always felt there was power to authenticity that rested with photography, Deleuze's central premise of his work on cinema is the revelation that the power-of-the-false inherently rests with the cinematographic image. Cinema's capability of manipulating time produces movements, Deleuze claims, that are "necessarily 'abnormal,' essentially 'false.'"[26] But this essential falsity does not delegitimate cinema; rather, it empowers it by blurring the boundary between true and false. Perhaps the body-swapping narratives affirm the missing object of cinema that now stands at the crossroads between analog photography and postphotographic culture. Korea is a nation that is both overwired and cinephilic; it is perhaps not coincidental that an updated body-switch genre—which absolutely heightens Deleuze's theories of both dividual subject and power-of-the-false—has gained popularity over the past several years.[27] The ascending popularity of body-travel genre films enables us to conceptualize a recurrent ontological fantasy that, in response to these surveillances and controls, helps decode, mold, and dividuate the individual.

4   *Running Man*

The Korean Television Variety Program
and Affect Confucianism

Anyone who has visited Korea in recent years has likely discovered, even before taking a step outside Incheon International Airport, that variety shows are very popular there. Rather than a one-on-one talk-show format, these shows feature a pack of male performers standing in a semicircle in a quasi-public space, such as a parking lot, a playground, a city park, or a large convention hall. They talk, giggle, and lightly push each other in a juvenile manner before dispersing to play silly playground games such as hide-and-seek, capture-the-flag, jump rope, wordplay, and pass-the-cell-phone—games that often involve interacting with area residents and other park visitors. Most of these variety shows are accompanied by endless on-screen captions and beeping sound effects, which can seem foreign to untutored eyes. Compared to comedy shows in the United States, background laughter (by either a laugh track or a live audience) and behind-the-scenes commentating by MCs are kept to a minimum or eliminated entirely. As a matter of a fact, no division exists between an MC and a participant, and the losers of these silly games are punished in a juvenile, humiliating way.

Running Man (RM) has been one of the most celebrated television variety shows not just in Korea but throughout Asia in recent years. The show has generated a few significant tropes related to Korean transnational popular culture today: reality television, affectivity, and remake politics. First broadcast on July 11, 2010, on Seoul Broadcasting System (SBS), as part of its Sunday evening lineup, RM initially received disappointing ratings, even though its main MC, Yoo Jae-suk (also an MC for *Muhan Dojeon* on another network), was already one of the most popular comedians in Korea at the time. However, after about a year, during which audiences became acclimated to the show's game patterns, RM overcame its initial low ratings and witnessed a dramatic turnaround. During the roughly three-year period from 2011 to 2013, RM was one of the most popular evening prime-time shows not only in Korea but also in many Asian territories.[1] Though its domestic ratings have declined over the past five years, in 2020 it celebrated its tenth year of broadcast with very little change made to the original cast members. After the cancellation of *Muhan Dojeon* (*Infinite Challenge*) in early 2018, *Running Man* is the longest-running variety show on weekend prime-time television in Korea. Against the threat of a "post-television era," which was experienced in Korea during the internet boom, the revival of local cinema, and the gaming fever among youth during the first two decades of the twenty-first century, the introduction of *Running Man*, a largely unscripted game show with middle-aged comedians competing with young idols or sports stars, exemplified the global trend in which reality TV became one of the dominant genres of the new television marketplace, as it offered a "relatively low-cost, high-rating, and internationally marketable alternative to more traditional prime-time series."[2]

Despite its low-brow association with tabloid culture, the popularity of RM, in both Korea and Asia, demonstrates the degree to which interactive self-reflexivity carves out not only a new postmodern Korean identity but also a platform of hallyu that serves as a facilitator between a young cosmopolitan Asian audience and what Aaron Gerow calls an "aesthetic of density" to describe the superfluous layering of information through texts, multiple windows, and multiple commentaries in the context of Japanese entertainment television.[3] The *Running Man* phenomenon that unfolded in Asia over the past decade provides a window to think about the shifting meanings in television, East Asian affectivity, and remake politics.

Running Man was originally characterized as an "urban action variety" show, a format coined in order to distinguish RM from the format of the KBS competitor *One Night, Two Days* (*Ilbak iil*), which was built around a weekly road trip the celebrity MCs and their guests would take from the city to the countryside. The emphasis on the *urban* distinguished RM from the concept of *One Night, Two Days*, which had a socially responsible agenda to recommend various rural places as travel destinations to urban viewers. By assigning Yoo Jae-suk, who was already an MC on *Muhan Dojeon*, quite possibly the first popular reality variety television program in Korea, it presented the viewers with a familiar premise, pitting a regular cast of MCs against guests in a largely unscripted format (see chapter 7). The show became popular for its mixture of genres, combining elements of talk shows, sketch comedy, *batsu* (Japanese-style punishment game), and sporting competitions. *Running Man* certainly was not the only successful mixed-genre reality-television program in Korea over the past twenty years, but it has arguably been the most successful in the transnational Asian market because it was able to effectively capitalize on its media convergence with the internet, which spawned innumerable parodies of games featured on RM.

After *Running Man's* online popularity exploded among young viewers in China, where cumulative hits for RM on YouTube reached over a billion and the fan tours of RM members in Hong Kong, Shanghai, and Beijing in 2013 caused mayhem, the format of *Running Man* was bought by a Chinese network for one million yuan (US$3.5 million), a record fee paid for the licensing agreement of Korean variety television content. Based on *Running Man*, Chinese game variety show *Hurry Up, Brother* (Chinese: 奔跑吧兄弟; pinyin: *Bēnpǎo Ba Xiōngdì*) first aired on October 10, 2014, and resumed its broadcast every Friday night at 9:10 p.m., a popular prime-time slot on Zhejiang Television Network, which services all of China through cable.[4] *Hurry Up, Brother*, featuring some of the biggest names in Chinese entertainment television as its main cast, became the most successful remake of Korean-originated entertainment programs, registering more than four-point viewership in a country where one-point viewership is considered a ratings hit.[5] Indeed, the show was so successful that it was adapted into a feature film, *Benpao Ba! Xiongdi* (2015). The motion-picture version was also a hit at the Chinese box office during the lunar New Year period, one of the biggest seasons for theatrical sales of the year.

Within the process of transcultural and transnational collaborative remakes of Korean entertainment TV programs, the shared values of Confucianism are what drive the theme of affect that commonly binds the many Korean and Chinese audiences that watch RM. Departing from the loosely termed "right chord of Asian sentiments" that have characterized hallyu's popular appeal across Asia, in the words of several sociologists, I call the kind of transnational affect that eases the border crossing of media products such as RM throughout Asian countries in the twenty-first century affect Confucianism.[6] In so doing, I rethink the role of Confucianism in Korean popular culture not as an essentialist cultural tradition or mandate adopted by the Chosun Dynasty during the premodern period and then hijacked by corporate chaebols to legitimate the collective exploitation of workers during the twentieth century but as one that has been renewed to induce a new communal viewing sensibility across Asia.

The collective identity that hesitates in separating the winner from the loser in the neo-Confucian ethics but requires everyone to excel in their own roles has even reformulated the narrative drives of many Korean game-show structures, and *RM* is no exception. Instead of Western capitalist values, the underlying principle of *RM* is the spirit of an *affect Confucianism*, a noncapitalist value system that motivates a hierarchical social structure but does not necessarily define the world as those with success and those without. Almost all American television game shows promote capitalism—with cash prizes often awarded to contestants. From golden-age television programs such as *The Price Is Right* (1972–present), to reality-television shows such as *The Apprentice* (2004–17), cash prizes and big contracts have been integral components.[7] Even daytime talk shows such as *The Oprah Winfrey Show* and *Ellen* are famous for giving out surprise cash and other prizes to audiences to boost ratings and promote capitalist values. If it weren't for the intimate relationship forged between television game shows and vulgar capitalism in recent decades, we might have had a very different kind of political landscape in the latter half of the 2010s.

The motivation behind every television game show surely is to "win," and many of *Running Man*'s game formats do indeed divide the group into teams, with each team member competing against the others until the last man or woman standing, usually the one whose name tag has not yet been ripped off from the back, is declared a winner. However, despite displays of intense desire to win by the cast members, it would be a great exaggeration to state that winning provides the kind of exhilarating drive that American television tends to motivate. When the popular name-tag game is played on *RM*, the contestant who has his or her name tag removed by the opposing team member (or by the co-team members who are sometimes designated as spies by the writers) is declared "out." However, even when the contestants are "out," they do not disappear from the game. Instead, from inside the waiting room, they are responsible for providing funny commentaries on the game or displaying all-too-important visual reactions after each advance of the game is announced. The losers, in other words, serve just as important a function in the game as the contestants who are still competing. Therefore, in this Confucian scenario, certain egalitarian principles are mobilized to find a subtle sense of self even when one fails to go far. While the Western capitalist enterprise of success and failure harshly evaluates the economic performance of an individual or neatly divides winners from losers in a contest, *RM*'s format seeks to redefine the nuanced sense of the self in a group environment that self-deprecatingly critiques modern Asia's fast-paced adoption of the capitalist value system.

Running Man disseminates a viewing pleasure that aligns itself with a kind of peer-to-peer social relationality over the internet, of the same type that has generated Wiki knowledge, memes, TikTok videos, and hashtag movements, and which enables an empathetic, noncoercive, and collaborative sharing culture that points to a potential future for a "new type of commons-centric capitalism."[8] Although—unlike Wikipedia— YouTube, Twitter, Instagram, Kakao-Talk, and TikTok are all giant corporations, many of today's media productions, file sharing, and distribution of community-building hashtags and memes on the internet are based on a free production and distribution system that relies on peer-to-peer protocols and their inherent ethical values. Most K-pop, K-drama, and K-comedy fandom activities, which include reaction and parody videos on YouTube and other platforms, build communal frameworks and incur very little, if any, financial incentive. Although Western critical discourse has coined this social media–driven collectivity as *affectivity* in recent years, there is a deeper embeddedness of communal values in Korea and China that cannot be easily overlooked, one that produces a particular kind of empathetic viewing praxis that I call affect Confucianism. As I discuss in chapter 2, a new linguistic identity has emerged out of the alliance between youth Kakao talkscape and hip-hop, which has helped articulate an opaque sense of Korean language; in this chapter, I probe the underlying reason why Korean comedy variety shows, such as *RM*, have relied heavily on on-screen captions.

The accelerated process of industrialization and modernization that has deeply penetrated into the everyday life of Koreans and Chinese over the past several decades has weakened Confucian values in society to a point that some critics, such as John Lie, have claimed that the recent "K-pop violates almost all the Confucian precepts."[9] Though I agree with Lie that the influence of Confucianism in contemporary Korea is sometimes overstated by conservative sociologists in order to explain every phenomenon, from education fever to family-oriented chaebol economy, it is difficult not to valorize its salient presence even in Korean comedy. When, for instance, the news reports of the Ch'oe Sun-sil scandal surfaced in the fall of 2016, *Muhan Dojeon* programmed a two-episode special, "Hip Hop and History Special" (November 12 and 19, 2016), which refrained from parodying the political scandal and instead focused on comedians and rappers learning about serious historical material, such as the Japanese colonial era, from historians and public intellectuals. While Western countries such as the United States would surely have capitalized on the absurd nature of a political scandal involving the inappropriate relationship between a political leader and the daughter of a phony cult religious figure, Korean comedies such as *Muhan Dojeon* and *Running Man* were cautious not to provide direct criticism through SNL-like parody sketches about the now-impeached president Park Geun-hye and her confidant Ch'oe. The little to no parody created on the subject of political scandal on all of the major networks and cable television then illustrates the impossibility of recultivating the *mandam* in comedy programs (see chapter 2). Koreans, partly out of respect for their leaders—even the ones who have failed and are fallen—and partly because of decades of political censorship, could not openly mock officials on broadcast networks.

George A. De Vos, a scholar of Confucianism, argues, "The sense of propriety in role [in Confucian societies] delivers to the individual certain forms of pleasure in accomplishment and a realization of self that is hard to understand for people imbued with a [Western] egalitarian philosophy that says that those beneath are failures."[10] Many of the traditional patterns and values of Confucianism have evaporated over the past one hundred years or so in Korea and elsewhere in Asia. Still, the idealized Confucian collective sense of a group that finds pleasures of accomplishment within a constrained role rather than an unconstrained individual heroic role holds the ideological makeup that allows RM to use the spirit of humility that devalues the triumph of winners and pities the downfall of losers, even in a program that features childlike game formats.

One of the greatest pleasures of *Running Man* is its ability to loosen the bond between the place where the game is played—such as a department store, a train station, or a museum—and the status that these places hold. The same could also be said about the celebrities who appear on these shows, as they often exhibit what Baudrillard would call a "hallucinatory resemblance" with themselves.[11] By getting adult celebrities to play children's games that often require a combination of hide-and-seek, floor-is-lava, wrestling, and freeze tag, usually in a real location outside the studio such as shopping malls, train stations, and museums, the primary functions normally associated with these places, such as shopping, commuting, and historical education, are loosened from them, thereby producing what Melissa Gregg and Gregory J. Seigworth call an "affective bloom-space of an ever-processual materiality."[12] According to Gregg and Seigworth, the affect is most powerful when perceived less as a guarantee and more as a transient bloom-space of hope. This process is vital because part of the reason why many viewers tune in to RM is to mimic the games they play in their own workplace or in schools. Thus, the intensification of traversing of the terrain between the visual medium of television and consumers leads to the bloom-spaces of imaginations that recast their workplace, schools, or street corners into a simulated game space. This bloom-space is a cornerstone of affect Confucianism in *Running Man*. The blurring boundary between the private and the public raises the specter of transnational visibility and voyeurism that best appropriates, first, the multimedia interactive landscape of television, one that feasts on internet spreadability, multiple medium convergences, and transnational appetites that continually reproduce the affective value of an object that attributes happiness; and, second, the hallyu that appropriates pioneering aesthetic forms—such as Japanese television or American hip-hop—and then localizes, palliates, or simulates them for pan-Asian consumption.[13] In this vein, I propose that *Running Man*, while hardly an innovative form, is also a "happy object," a term put forth by Sara Ahmed, where the traditional binaries between modernity and tradition, between production and consumption, and between celebrity and the public continually erode, to a point where each signifier anchored by these terms cannot be confined to their own definitions. Herein lie the possibilities for the affect Confucian comedy sketches and episodes to bloom into memes, parodies, and happy objects.

In her essay "Happy Objects," Ahmed explains that the most appropriate analogy of a *happy object* can be found in the concept of the family as it could be described as "shar[ing] an orientation toward those objects as being good."[14] It is not because the family affects us in a good way, Ahmed explains, "but because we share an orientation toward the family as being good, as being what promises happiness in *return for loyalty*."[15] Could the broadcasting of *Running Man* not only at a specific family prime-time frame on Sunday evening in Korea but also on YouTube almost immediately after its original broadcast with English, Chinese, Vietnamese, Thai, and Bahasa fansubs provide what Ahmed calls "a shared horizon in which objects circulate, accumulating positive affective value"?[16] How does this program that provides jokes, comic gestures, and dialogue almost exclusively in Korean travel across national boundaries that confirm a posturing of a happy object as a shared global phenomenon and as a pan-Asian franchise? Also, what "return for loyalty" does RM, like the family, promise—

other than a new episode every week with the same regular-cast MCs—for both domestic and overseas audiences? An attempt to respond to this question, I think, would help us rearticulate *Running Man*'s place within the regional, the national, and the global. Also, if global shows like *American Idol* are not free from the criticism that they promote American ideals, values, and prosperity even when the TV format has already enjoyed a global success, would any of the nine territories in Asia where RM has been sold find the Korean national or nationalist values sometimes raised in RM to be problematic?[17]

Jameson once described "American postmodern culture as the internal and superstructural expression of a new wave of American military and economic domination throughout the world."[18] It is difficult to claim that South Korea exhibits a military or even economic might in the Asian region that would parallel American dominance in the world. Some theorists dealing with nationalism in East Asia, such as Kuan-Hsing Chen, have argued for a new world structure that calls our attention to a more complicated system of imperialist discourses and maneuvers in the form of a subempire, which might be more appropriate for examining Korea's cultural dominance in Asia today.[19] However, the controversy that began when the United States decided to deploy an advance missile system against the potential North Korean nuclear threat called Terminal High Altitude Area Defense (THAAD) in South Korea in 2016—which has angered China and provoked a reaction that includes widespread restrictions in almost every cultural sector, including the cancellation of Chinese package tours to Korea, a ban on imports of Korean cosmetics, the cancellation of K-pop concerts, and protests against the South Korean shopping mall chain Lotte Marts in China—reminds us how fragile cultural power can be without the military or political power to protect it. Despite the recent and dramatic thawing of the US–North Korean relationship, which reached a new height with the continued meetings between Donald Trump and Kim Jong-un, the THAAD controversy again questions South Korea's hegemony as a subempire in the region and actually affirms the fragile status of its cultural and economic strength in the region, which is highly sensitive to the new Cold War brewing between China and the United States (figures 4.1 and 4.2). South Korea's inability to impose a travel restriction on visitors from China in January 2020 as a response to the outbreak of COVID-19 that originated in the region of Wuhan further confirms its weak political status in East Asia. Will Korean hallyu's success in Asia be ephemeral since it is only a case of soft superstructural power, lacking the deeper forms

4.1 Panmunjom seen from South Korea, 2011. Photo by Kyung Hyun Kim.

4.2 Panmunjom seen from North Korea, 2011. Photo by Kyung Hyun Kim.

of dominance associated with military and political power? *Running Man* presents a model of affective neutrality that defuses power and valorizes failure in the context of Confucianism rather than promoting the value of glory that allows itself to be circulated without the patriotic or nationalistic values that might be significant in our understanding of the discourse of hallyu.

REALITY TV AND USER-GENERATED ONLINE CONTENT

In one of the short segments in *The Korean Popular Culture Reader*, I attributed the success of Psy's "Gangnam Style" to silliness and idiocy because in the age of YouTube, K-pop music videos are enjoyed less for their musical authenticity than for their theatricality, which encourages endless imitations, memes, and reaction videos from amateur users.[20] As described in my first two chapters here, this is the very anchor of enactments of hegemonic mimicry. *Running Man's* charm is equally shared by its fans, who are interested in interacting with the show's silly format, which itself continually undergoes a perpetual evolution, with the introduction of new ideas for missions, races, and hunts in almost every show. The fact that most international viewers of RM access the content through YouTube or other sites featuring user-generated content helps transform passive viewers into active viewers.

Many of RM's original missions divide the participants into teams wearing tracksuits and require them to be physically active; running, jumping through obstacles, gulping down food, wrestling, spraying each other with fake paints, and splashing water are commonplace occurrences on the show. The most popular game played on RM is the "name-tag-ripping race," where the objective is to tear the name tags from the backs of others' tracksuits while playing hide-and-seek in an enclosed urban space like a school or a museum. With each show, even the rules of the same game undergo slight modulations. Like amateur parodies of "Gangnam Style," which quite possibly outnumber any of the parodies and memes generated by a single song in the history of pop music on the user-generated content sites, the enormous number of amateur parodies of RM available on YouTube may have already broken the record for imitations of any variety show in the history of global television. Posted by RM fans from almost every corner of the world, these countless YouTube parodies and internet memes have solidly established RM's status as a dominant format in the age of what Henry

Jenkins has called "transmedia storytelling" or what Youngmin Choe has called "affective *economy*" of hallyu.[21] *Running Man* is a format that inspires reenactments and mimicry: by amateurs on home video, by professional comedians in other nations (both licensed and unlicensed), and by the members of RM themselves, who stage them live whenever they tour other countries to greet their fans.

Though some recent American sports entertainment programs, such as *American Ninja Warrior* or *Wipeout*, are spin-offs of Japanese television shows that also rely on similar silly sports competitions, *Running Man* can easily be distinguished from these. First, *Running Man* makes no distinction between the guests and the host MCs. In the American or Japanese sports entertainment shows, contestants are clearly differentiated from the hosts, who remain largely invisible when contestants are in a race or a competition. Their function is to report or comment on the action, not to change into a tracksuit and compete against the participants. In *Running Man*, Yoo Jae-sok, its main MC, and the other six cohosts all change into tracksuits after greeting the show's guest stars.[22] Most of these guests are young Korean idols in either television or music, but sometimes the show welcomes international sports stars like Ji-sung Park or global film stars like Jackie Chan. By assembling teams that mix the guest stars and the main MCs, *Running Man* destabilizes the conventional distinctions between the contestant, the hosts, the producers, and the crew. The breakdown of these traditional roles makes RM seem amateurish at times but, in so doing, builds a more demystified and intimate bond with them. Disrupting the traditional boundary between appearing on camera and working behind the scenes, the show also sometimes features competitions between the guest hosts and the agents of celebrities, the crew, or the producers.

Second, taking the camera directly onto the streets and showcasing the interactions between RM's casts, its guests, and the public is not unlike a tactic the now-retired talk-show host David Letterman employed for decades. Rupert Jee, the proprietor of a deli located just around the corner from the Ed Sullivan Theater in Manhattan, where *Late Show with David Letterman* was taped, even emerged as a celebrity because of the frequent visits paid to his store by Letterman's crew. This routine, which Letterman first began using in the 1980s, has of course been widely adopted by several more reality-television programs, but RM is notoriously transnational in the ways in which it becomes interactive because of its attempt to locate many of its episodes abroad. The potential for mob scenes, disruptions by fans, and even threats to cast members and guests has translated into assorted mayhem and even instances when the taping of RM had to be canceled. But the way that these disruptions are depicted on the program actually helps the show achieve the sense of failure or punishment that is typically championed in the program rather than the glory or cash prizes that many game shows normally emphasize.

Third, and perhaps most important, replacing the voice-over commentary of the hosts or the commentators are the on-screen captions that Korean variety shows normally provide for almost every variety entertainment program. These captions seldom function to supplement the dialogue, which is difficult for viewers to understand since the contestants are constantly talking while in motion or disrupting each other's conversations. Added by the program's producers and writers during postproduction, these on-screen captions are an essential form for punch lines and sarcastic commentary on the action. Putatively made popular through other variety shows that began in the mid-2000s, on-screen captions are ubiquitous in *Running Man*. Japanese television first pioneered the use of the on-screen captions long before the Koreans began employing them. The popularity of the captions on Korean entertainment programs—which began to make their significant mark when MBC's star producer Kim Young-hee in 2004 spent his sabbatical doing research at Fuji TV before making his comeback with the enormously successful *Muhan Dojeon* in 2005—blurs the line that separates the real from the unreal. Though criticisms were levied against the use of on-screen captions in Korea, I find them to be intriguing, for many of the utilities of these on-screen captions explicitly or implicitly dwell on the theme of disseminating non-phonocentrism.[23]

Ever since the addition of captions to an intimate romantic scene between Woody Allen and Diane Keaton in Allen's *Annie Hall* (1977) left a big impression on both critics and moviegoers, captions or subtitles have been deliberately used by filmmakers or television producers to add comic subtext that often satirizes the spoken dialogue. *Running Man*, like almost all comedy shows in Korea, seeks a similar impact of resuscitating the role of *pyŏnsa* from the silent cinema era and then situating it, in the form of on-screen captions, somewhere between the drama and the audiences (see chapter 3). The intentional double entendre that is often the aim of the sarcastic captions that compete against the spoken words creates not only sophisticated wordplay but also an almost self-acknowledged disavowal of the untranslatability of many of the jokes that cannot be made intelligible in languages other than Korean. The double entendre and the wordplay suggested through the captions tend to confuse the viewers who do not understand Korean. Many of the fansubs of *RM* or other variety shows reliant on captions therefore omit the jokes that pivot around wordplay. Too many windows are already in operation on a busy screen. While the use of the on-screen captions succeeds in exaggerating the wordplay or the comic subtext of the action and the dialogue of the performers, the inundation of captions also self-reflexively acknowledges the failure or the disappointment of fulfilling the promise of a laughter only through dialogue and gags delivered by the cast members and the guests. Sometimes, the captions self-consciously announce to the viewers that the producers found the initial jokes not to be funny, and therefore required them to add punch through the written words.

MAKING JACKIE CHAN "KI-CH'AN HYŎNG-NIM" (BIG BROTHER KI-CH'AN)

With the ubiquity of the captions or subtitles that supplement the speech and gestures of the cast of Korean game shows, one is tempted to characterize *RM*'s doubling of both speech and writing as the very moment where Derrida's critique of phonocentrism is laid bare. As is widely known, Derrida's central critical concept of *différance* is mobilized through his opposition to phonocentrism, which values speech over writing as the more natural form of communication. After invoking Ferdinand de Saussure's protest against the multiple modifications of the name Lefèvre, now spelled both as Lefèvre and Lefèbvre, which has degenerated into the pronunciation of the name as Lefèbure (requiring the pronouncing of a *b* and a *u* that never once existed), Derrida asks: "Why should the mother tongue be protected from the operation of writing? Why determine that operation as a violence, and why should the transformation be only a deformation?"[24] Derrida points out that Saussure's phonocentrism is an exemplary case of Western ethnocentrism that wishes to privilege a hierarchical order of signifiers where writing inherently threatens the purity of the speech. The destabilization of the relationship between writing and speech is what is inherent in Saussure that Derrida sought to problematize. Derrida notes that "after all Lefèbure is not a bad name and we can love this play." This reminds us that Derrida does not empathize with Saussure's warning of a crisis between the orthographic and pronouncing divergences the name Lefèvre has taken over the years as Lefèvre, Lefèbvre, and even Lefèbure.

4.3 Jackie Chan (*front row, second from left*) with *Running Man* cast members, 2013.

Departing from Saussure's rigid formalism, Derrida calls this "deformation" of name a charming "play."

In perhaps the most famous episode of *RM* (episode 135, originally aired on March 3, 2013), the comedy pursued by *RM*'s main cast revolves around the charming "play" of renaming the show's guest, Jackie Chan (figure 4.3). Though many Koreans recognize Jackie Chan by his Western stage name, more Korean viewers are likely to refer to him by the name Sŏng Ryong, the Korean pronunciation of his Chinese stage name, Cheng Long (成龍), or his Cantonese name, Sing Lung. However, after one of the cast members, Haha, begins to address him as "Ki-ch'an hyŏng-nim (big brother Ki-ch'an)," Jackie Chan's name gets stuck as "Ki-ch'an" throughout the episode. "Ki-ch'an" even appears as the official nickname assigned to Chan after it is embraced by Chan himself. To the tutored ear of Korean, the renaming of Jackie Chan or Sing Lung as "Ki-ch'an" sounds as if it were based not on an unintentional mispronunciation of his name, which would have been the simple insistence of phonocentrism at the basis of this reinvestiture, but on the intentional reordering of the three syllables that constitute the making of Sing Lung as "Jae Ki-ch'an" so that it now follows the East Asian rule of placing the surname first and the given name last.[25] As most Korean names are structured according to a three-syllable neo-Confucian rule, with the surname dropped when being addressed as a form of endearment, the global "Jae-ki Chan" drops the "Jae" and is remade into a "Ki-chan," which earns the local affectivity that immediately gets passed around by other Korean members of the show as a showcase of *affect Confucianism*. What the Korean comedians have done, in other words, is to imprudently make audible the usually invisible writing of the Western ordering of the name of Jackie Chan by forcing the first syllable of that Westernized name into a local name. They then drop the pretend surname (Jae) in order to rearticulate the remaining fragment of the two syllables into a unique but charming Korean name, "Ki-ch'an," which also happens to be Korean slang for "amazing." This renaming of "Ki-ch'an" destabilizes not only the arbitrariness of the difference in naming rules between the East (surname first) and the West (surname last) but also the difference between writing and speech in the East, which heavily favors writing as the dominant signifier over speech, especially among scholars and the erudite. One must always think about the Chinese etymological roots of any names of places, people, and terms, and be able to imagine the idiographic *hanzi* rather than the pronunciation of these words.

Both Japan and Korea's political struggle against sinocentrism and hanzi (*kanji* in Japanese, *hanja* in Korean) contained within it a modern movement to unify the speech and the written. The pull toward phonocentrism, therefore, as both Karatani Kojin and Wang Hui have argued against Derrida's critique of Saussure, is not just a "Western" issue; it is all over East Asia.[26] The *ŏnmun ilch'i* (in Japanese: *genbun itchi*) was indispensable for the birth of modern nationalism in both Korea and Japan, since the phonetic writing system (hangul in the case of Korean and kana in the case of Japanese) presented an egalitarian and economic way of prioritizing voice and phonetic speech. However, despite one hundred years of Westernization that promoted phonocentricism and, along with it, the economy of the phonetic writing system, writing never really lost its privilege in East Asia.[27] The privileging of writing is still ubiquitous in Korea— in classrooms, where teachers and lecturers almost always rely on the use of chalk and markers far more than their counterparts in the West; in smartphone communication culture with its heavy preference for Kakao-texting over talking or voice-messaging; in traditional landscape paintings, where calligraphy and writing are equally dominant with the painting itself; and on television screens, where humor must be located between voice and writing in the form of online captions. This ubiquity of writing in East Asia, even during the era of social media, again demonstrates that even after one hundred years of ŏnmun ilch'i, the residual tension between speech and writing continues to generate everyday philological affect, which goes so far as to push a new form of communication system that now includes animation and ideographic emoticons along with traditional letters and romanizations. Korea has been an early adopter of social media communication language that includes graphic art, memes, and emoticons because it never abandoned the potential of a hybrid writing system that embraced Chinese calligraphy, the local phonetic system, and a combination of ideogram and alphabets. I hope it is not an essentialist claim to state that the philosophical origins of internet-era memes can be traced back to the landscape paintings of Jeong Sun from the eighteenth century, where the dynamics and pleasures of a drawing were incomplete without written texts.

There is a distinctive relationship between East Asia's resistance to the Western-style phonocentric universe and the ubiquity of online captions that provide an intertextual content that adds supplementarity to the dialogue of comedy cast members featured on television shows in Korea. Despite Kojin's protest that "Chinese characters are not simply ideographic, but also contain a phonetic element, and the Japanese writing system (kana) has transformed Chinese characters into phonetic signs," it is East Asian writing's accentuation of the ideographic over the phonetic that allows for the renaming of "Jackie Chan" into "Ki-ch'an," in my mind, to be possible.[28] "Ki-ch'an" briefly suspends the logocentrism that rests with the phonetic emphasis of "Jackie" or "Jackie-chan" and temporally allows us to speculate on the historical telos of East Asian entertainment and its shared cultural values by extending the legacy of Jackie Chan over the past five decades and the immediate localizing of his name into "Ki-ch'an." The inundation of screen captions, particularly in Japanese, Korean, Taiwanese, and now Chinese television, may even be the result of frequent usage of idiographic hanzi (yes, I do understand that hanzi is never purely idiographic and therefore at least partly phonetic) that similarly binds the affect Confucian signifying system in East Asia rather than the phonocentric system prevalent in Western cultures. As filmmaker Bong Joon-ho recently suggested during one of his award ceremony speeches for *Parasite*, "once you overcome the one-inch-tall barrier of subtitles," so many more amazing films and, subsequently, a broader vision of world culture might be accessible.[29] Bong's words come as no surprise to many of us who are already well familiar with Asian moviegoing culture, since reading subtitles still remains the predominant mode of watching foreign movies in East Asia. On the other hand, even in Europe, where subtitled films are more commonplace than they are in the United States, the privileging of dubbed versions of Hollywood films has largely made reading visual texts cumbersome.

Mitsuyo Wada-Marciano argues that when Japanese anime TV series such as *Astro Boy* were first released in the United States in the 1960s, "most viewers did not even realize that they were from Japan." Likewise, when an entire generation of South Korean audiences grew up in the 1970s watching Japanese anime dubbed in Korean, such as *Mazinger Z* or *Yokai Ningen Bem* (Korean title: *Yogwe inkan bem*), very few realized that these shows were from Japan, South Korea's sworn enemy because of the then recent memory of colonial violence. Wada-Marciano claims that Japanese animations had success overseas because they focused on the denationalized image: "with relatively easy dubbing and reediting . . . anime could be accepted without cultural resistance."[30] Though I am inclined to agree with Wada-Marciano's argument that these Japanese animations from the 1960s and 1970s do not necessarily accentuate Japanese nationality, they are neither a-national nor post-national entities since it is the traits of European whiteness that are emphasized in much of the anime and manga content that dominated Asia and other territories throughout the postwar years. Many of the Japanese anime characters were Caucasian Europeans with titles like count and baron that could only exist in the imaginary of a European setting. These characters would also be woven into plotlines steeped in mad scientist schemes, lost civilizations, and fallen European aristocracies—not exactly staples among East Asian stories. Along with the following generation's animation hit *Candy Candy*, which completely shed Asia and outright joined Europe, manga and anime helped Japanese cultural content achieve a "de-Asianized image." While this notion of "shedding Asia and joining Europe" in Japanese anime can be traced all the way back to 1885 when Fukuzawa Yukichi, the leading Japanese intellectual at the time, published an article titled "On Shedding Asia" in the Tokyo newspaper *Jiji shinpo*, the case of Korea or the recent hallyu tells an entirely different story.[31] Because until recently Korea has been unable to articulate a national discourse beyond economic and political declarations of independence and postcolonial autonomy from foreign domination, hallyu's cultural content can hardly be considered products that even remotely engage in the ideological discourse of "shedding Asia and joining Europe." Whereas it is not rare to find Japanese manga and anime that still portray central characters in a highly Westernized manner, with big blue eyes, bright colors, and white skins, the hallyu scene, though influenced by American pop culture, still centrally foregrounds slant-eyed, skinny-framed idols such as *Running Man*'s front man, Yoo Jae-sok, or G-Dragon or CL.

If Japanese cultural products had powerful historical roots that had a predilection for whiteness and sought to distinguish themselves from Asian values and traits, the defining thematic and visual signifiers in RM do not associate themselves with Caucasian features. None of RM's seven main cast members—Yoo Jae-sok, Gary, Haha, Ji Suk-jin, Kim Jong-kook, Lee Kwang-soo, and Song Ji-hyo—are known for possessing fair hair, large eyes, or Western physique. Yoo Jae-sok, Gary, Haha, Ji Suk-jin, and Kim Jong-kook are better known for their narrow eyes, and though Lee Kwang-soo, a former model, is tall and has large eyes, his body frame is thin and the rest of his features are closely aligned with being Asian rather than white. Song Ji-hyo, the only woman among the regular cast, is also not known for her Western features, unlike Angela-baby, her Chinese counterpart in *Hurry Up, Brother*, who is of Eurasian descent. Song is also average in height and skin complexion.

As is well known, American comedy shows, talk shows, or game shows are about individual personalities and their ability to perform comedy. Stand-up routines, individual gags, and single hosts who greet guests are talents that can make or break comedy shows. However, talk shows and game variety shows in Korea are almost always moderated by a group of comedians, and monologues are rarely featured on comedy programs. Yoo Jae-sok, probably the most popular comedian of the past twenty years in Korea, has never done a stand-up monologue as part of his comic routine. As the *kukmin* (national) MC of post-mandam era in the new millennium, Yoo's strength is based neither on a scripted act nor a political satire, but on an improvised sense of humor that reacts to others' comments or suspense-ful situations in real-life challenges. His ability to blend in with others is far more important than one that rises above everyone else as a comic god or a satirist. Instead of emphasizing greatness or ingenuity, Korean comedy dwells in real-life mediocrity or stupidity; instead of spectacles of violence, explosions, and sexual lewdness, the Korean extolls empathy, humanity, and humility; and, most importantly, instead of individual subjectivity that pits one against the political system that produces satire, the Korean tries to achieve a collective sense of viewers' empathy (*kamdong*) that has to compound a sense of excitement (*hŭng*). As discussed in the introduction and chapter 2, the Korean satirical tradition that was performed and individual-ized through both p'ansori and mandam in the early part of the twenti-eth century had to undergo a transformation—partly because of political censorship and partly because of the collective spirit of sinmyŏng, raised in chapter 7, that can be traced back to the mask dance tradition as well as to the recent pattern among idol group performances.

Running Man evenly distributes its power among its seven members. No division exists between the weakest member, who usually is eliminated first, and the strongest member, who usually wins the race. Contestants normally accept their roles, either finding themselves as cheerleaders on the sidelines or remaining in the game until the moment when the winner is declared. This aspect of the game is also recognized by the many fans across Asia who post their version of *RM*'s games online. They are there to share the affect and not to cheer for the heroes. For example, Ji Suk-jin, the oldest member of *RM* at an age now well past fifty, is also the weakest member in physical competitions, and he is frequently eliminated first. But his popularity has not dwindled in Korea—on the contrary, *RM* has revived his career. Ji Suk-jin saw his popularity rise not because he was a winner but because he was a perennial loser, whose role was relegated to background airtime. Cast member Kim Jong-kook is physically the strongest man, but even when he wins the race, there is no true glory awaiting him that would categorize him separately from the rest of the cast. Failure, though not exactly valorized, is never the impetus that propels its opposite, success, even in a competitive game. Perhaps this undercutting of the very format of competition is what allows *Running Man* to achieve its affect Confucianism.

EMPATHETIC REMAKE?

Defining how any given cultural codes or representations are communicated to a specific ethnic or regional group of spectators will fall into some form of general speculation that ends up in some way reinscribing essentialist ideas about a particular ethnocentrist position. I also acknowledge that the insistence on *RM*'s invocation of a theme of failure or its emphasis on group enjoyment rather than individual glory as a register of pan-Asian or what I have been calling affect Confucianism may be perceived as a projection of such gross essentialization. However, following film scholar Lisa Cartwright, I propose that an affective politics of spectatorship be expanded into an identification, even in a transnational exchange between China and Korea that takes into account an intersubjective empathy. Cartwright, in her study on postwar films about disabled children, introduces a model of *empathetic identification*. She claims that while conventional "identification" is equated with "*I see as you see, from your position*," which relies heavily on vision and psychic displacement to organize its terms, "empathy" works differently because it is "*I know how you feel*," which relies on knowledge and perception as structuring categories.[32] Cartwright's renewed sense of "empathetic identification" is an interanimation that calls less attention to "I know how you feel" but derives from the affective energy that comes from knowing the "force of the object ('you,' the image, the representation)." Thus, applying this line of empathetic identification thought to the non-Korean viewership of RM, while it is almost impossible to know entirely the nature and experience of "I know how a Chinese viewer feels," the empathetic identification would recognize the feeling I perceive in the expression of the "Chinese viewers" when they are motivated to empathize with the same visual object a Korean may also be watching, despite the fact that the Chinese are engaging it through the filter fansubs and through a different medium (the internet). This affect projects both a part fantasy and a part object reality that help construct a sense of affect Confucianism around the active viewer engagement of RM.

Existence of an empathetic identification that commonly binds China and Korea does not necessarily diffuse the deep-seated anxiety that had been worrisome for many Chinese who have seen the rise of Korean cultural content and hallyu as a threat to their national identity. Of course the general public's support of the hallyu ban, reported among Chinese during the recent THAAD protests, is an exemplary showcase of this anxiety. Remakes, whether in television or film, have never escaped media criticism, for they cannot bypass the scrutiny of the critic whose job is to assess how remakes hold up against the original. When Martin Scorsese's *The Departed*, a remake of Hong Kong action flick *Infernal Affairs*, opened in theaters in 2006, Manohla Dargis wrote in the *New York Times*: "Fine as Mr. DiCaprio and Mr. Damon are, neither is strong enough to usurp memories of the actors who played the same roles in the original—Tony Leung as the good guy, Andy Lau as the bad—both of whom register with more adult assurance."[33] Such wholesale critical condemnation unequivocally highlights the adult valiance of the source film (*Infernal Affairs*), while the remake (*The Departed*) is belittled as an infantile distraction.

While mentioned in the debate over international remakes, it was the critics of the source film who made the accusation of "cultural imperialism" against countries like the United States, which is notorious for its remakes, partly because of Americans' refusal to "overcome the one-inch" hurdle imposed by the subtitles.[34] In the case of Chinese remakes of original

Korean content, however, the most vociferous protesters against trans-national adaptation are not from Korea, whose original material is being appropriated and whose authorship is decentered, but from China, the country that is responsible for the remake. While China's official remake *Hurry Up, Brother* obscures its status as an import by featuring Chinese celebrities and transporting viewers to places and situations that are famil-iar to Chinese viewers, which even keeps many Chinese audiences from noticing that they are watching a remake, controversies among Chinese audiences and experts have nonetheless arisen. Well before the US THAAD deployment on Korean soil that took place in 2017 the Chinese periodical *Economic Observer* on April 17, 2017 tweeted a passage from *Beijing Daily* on Weibo regarding the Chinese audience response to the series remakes of Korean shows: "Nearly half of the entertainment shows in China now have Korean DNA. . . . A huge wave of entertainment TV shows pour out to TV screens this week, and each of the shows carries Korean DNA with-out exceptions — either adapted from original Korean version, or collabora-tively produced by Korea and China. Audiences sarcastically comment that the smell of kimchi is increasingly getting stronger."[35] Other similar tweets by prominent Chinese filmmakers and media producers also appeared at the time, harshly criticizing this "smell of kimchi" and its popularity among Chinese audiences.[36] In the context of globalization, this transcultural process of cross-national and cross-industrial collaborative remake used in *Running Man* and other shows of Korean origin has incited questions around the crisis of national identity in China. Though no one has explic-itly mentioned "cultural imperialism" in these criticisms, it is difficult not to acknowledge them as instances of decrying cultural imperialism against Korea, the source country whose origin is being stripped away by the coun-try that is much larger.

The transnational exchange of remakes between China and Korea is substantially different compared to, for instance, France and the United States, where French critics and filmmakers have, as early as the days of André Bazin, condemned Hollywood's practice of remaking films as a de-basement of the French original and as a form of vulgar American com-mercialism. In this prevailing argument, the "one-way trajectory from a valuable French 'original' to a debased American 'copy'" is often deeply rooted in the binary distinction between French high culture and crass American popular culture.[37] In the case of Chinese remakes of Korean cul-tural content, the potential degradation of Korean culture by the wealthier Chinese media entrepreneurs who are appropriating and purchasing shows like RM as remake properties is seldom brought up as a threat by either Korean or Chinese critics. On the contrary, the opposite has been argued. Indeed, it is the Chinese critics who suggest the stench of "Korean kimchi" permanently staining the psyche of Chinese audiences or the authentic Chinese identity, while Korean critics, for the most part, have steered clear from this debate. If the "one-way trajectory" from the high-brow French original to the vulgar American adaptation was held up as an exemplary practice of American imperialism, the trajectory from the creative Korean original to the debased Chinese remakes is ironically found culpable for a repugnant exercise, not of Chinese imperialism but of Korean imperialism. Of course, Korea, unlike the United States or China, has never been accused of economic or military imperialism in the past. On the contrary, Korea was once widely perceived as a suzerain or a vessel state of China during the premodern era. Once the dawning of the modern era came, it quickly became Japan's colony and then even after its independence from Japan, it reeled under the American military occupation over the past seventy years. Is it simply the economic reversal that has South Korea rise in the economic ranks and now boast an annual income per capita at a figure of about $40,000, which is about two-and-a-half times more than the figure in China, that must be held up as the reason for the accusations against Korean cultural imperialism? Also, the fact that South Korea continues to irritate the Chinese psyche by politically aligning itself with the United States even though it trades with China at a much bigger volume than it does with the United States may come into play here. If all these arguments hold some authority, is Korea's success with its cultural content overseas while still unable to shake loose the criticism that it is a perpetrator rather than a fair-game player another instance that it continues to get caught between China and the United States despite the fact that the Korean War (also fought between Chinese and Americans) concluded about seventy years ago?

The controversy surrounding the Chinese objections to the "kimchi smell" of Korean influence not only reverses the conventional ways in which the accusation of cultural imperialism has been used against another country but also raises the complicated dynamics of cross-fertilization and hybrid identity in East Asia. Despite the centuries of hegemonic Chinese influence on the entire surrounding region—including Korea, where its writing system, moral codes, and system of governance rendered its cultural identity—the popularity of RM to many critics in China reflects too much US-centered globalization (despite its stink of kimchi) and therefore constitutes a threat that needs to be opposed, as the US-inspired hallyu could potentially squeeze out the local identity of China. The "kimchi smell" controversy, in addition to the aforementioned THAAD ban of Korean culture, again reaffirms the inability of Korea to shore up its reputation as a true hegemonic power, despite its cultural and economic influence in the region, without necessarily succumbing to an inferior military and political position vis-à-vis that of both Chinese and Americans. Hallyu's hegemonic mimicry is at best an ambivalent hegemony.

Despite these complicated national issues around Korean cultural content in China, however, the success of *Hurry Up, Brother* is for both China and Korea a sign of how global and local interests have operated in a manner of highly fused tension and yet in a collaborative fashion. The valorization of the theme of failure in both Korean *Running Man* and Chinese *Hurry Up, Brother*, the deconstruction of phonocentrism, and the role of affective online spectatorship have demonstrated not a neat but a schizophrenic and discursive transnational merger between the values of internet-era cosmopolitanism and precapitalist Confucianism that have wormed their way into an affect Confucianism. After producing the first five episodes of *Hurry Up, Brother*, with the aid of seven other Korean crew and staff including writers, assistant producers, and camera crew, the original producer of *Running Man*, Cho Hyo-jin, observed that "there were similarities that Chinese and we [Koreans] shared when we looked at the same game culture, but there were also nuanced differences. As we were exchanging ideas about these differences with the Chinese team, I was able to learn quite a bit. Rather than veiling our differences, sharing them with the Chinese would help us also improve."[38] Despite such candid confessions by Koreans that tout the need for collaboration with the Chinese as true partners, a power imbalance persists between the two countries. While much of the Korean entertainment and film industry is financially dependent on the Chinese market, Koreans have yet to reciprocate by taking Chinese film and cultural content seriously in recent years. For instance, all Korean cast members of RM made guest appearances during the early episodes of *Hurry Up, Brother* (episodes 3–5 in season 1) that were shot entirely in Korea. With all Korean stars appearing equally with the Chinese stars, and the program inevitably being broadcast bilingually because the Koreans spoke in Korean, one would have expected these three episodes to be reaired on Korean television. Although the ratings for these episodes of *Hurry Up, Brother* were very high in China, as they featured Korean stars such as Yoo, Gary, and Lee Kwang-su, who are popular in both countries, these

Chinese-Korean coproductions were never broadcast in Korea. Even internet searches of the Korean fansubs of these episodes produce no results. This leaves those who hope for a different form of Chinese-Korean collaboration, one that does not tilt the balance of power toward one particular nation, continuing to be suspicious of the current climate of globalization, where one-way trajectory expansions, violence, and updated versions of imperialism rather than more equal exchanges have ruled the day thus far.

The THAAD controversy has taught us one thing: no cultural exchange during the twenty-first century can be severed from the political and national security interests. Even if hallyu were to take its roots in North Korea, without active governmental involvement from both North and South Korea, the flow of culture from South Korea to the North would be an extremely difficult one. Only with the Moon Jae-in government of South Korea's active engagement with the North, as well as the welcoming gestures of Kim Jong-un that began a new chapter in the North and South Korean relationship beginning with the Pyeongchang Olympics in 2018, could cultural content, albeit in limited forms of music performances, be exchanged between the two Koreas, which share the same language and cultural customs. Transnational culture that aspires to be apolitical, neutral, and independent of the past Cold War, driven by political differences, and of the present one, driven by the economic trade war between China and the United States, shows its fragility and will suffer from the growing impact of nuclear threats, war, and military concerns. I again propose, as a Korean critic, that we must better understand the empathetic affect of "I know how a Chinese viewer feels," which projects far beyond the putative "apolitical and neutral" position that many K-dramas and television shows have adapted in recent times. The affect Confucianism among Asian viewers formulated around the active viewer engagement of *RM* in the era of social media—and a renewed paradigm of remake politics and transnational exchange between China and Korea—will hopefully find a future that expands the "bloom-space" rather than one that squeezes it out.

5   The Virtual Feast

Mukbang, Con-Man Comedy, and the

Post-Traumatic Family in *Extreme Job* (2019)

and *Parasite* (2019)

The spectacular box office success of *Extreme Job* (*Kŭkhan chikŏp*, dir. Lee Byung-heon) in the spring of 2019 came as a surprise to many. Record-breaking films of the past decade such as *The Admiral: Roaring Currents* (*Myŏngryang*, dir. Kim Han-min 2014) and *Ode to My Father* (*Kukje sijang*, dir. Yoon Je-kyoon, 2014) had either stoked Korean nationalist sentiment or relied on melodramatic conventions. *Extreme Job*, an action comedy about a team of undercover cops who find unlikely success running a fried-chicken business, generated a stunning sixteen-million-plus admission tickets in a nation of just fifty million people.[1] The remake rights to the film were also sold to Universal Pictures, with Kevin Hart, perhaps the most popular African American comedian working today, set to star in the American version.[2] It is perhaps unsurprising that *Extreme Job* is slated to be made into an African American–themed comedy, given the triadic relationship it establishes between fried chicken (cheap neighborhood restaurants), a double social consciousness (whereby a warring ideology between the state and the downtrodden must be reconciled), and employment issues (the loss of lifetime employment jobs and their replacement by self-employment in small shops that have come to symbolize the nation's extreme class polarization and the high unemployment of its slum neighborhoods). Furthermore, the massive narcotics distribution ring set up by the fried-chicken franchises depicted in the film might become even more believable when the setting shifts from the streets of Korea to the American inner city.

The popularity of *Extreme Job* signifies that the melodramatic sentimentalities and nationalist themes long prevalent in commercially successful Korean films over the past several decades are now giving way to a code-switching comedic genre that explores the economic divide between the haves and have-nots as comic gag. This chapter pairs *Extreme Job*, a crass comedy film, with *Parasite* (*Kisaengch'ung*), an arthouse film directed by Bong Joon-ho that rode the wave of its best picture prize (Palme d'Or) at the Cannes Film Festival to gain domestic blockbuster success before winning Academy Awards in 2020. At first glance, the two films seem completely disparate, and yet they share commonalities. Both achieved great box office success (as of the time of this writing, *Extreme Job* had achieved second place in the history of Korean ticket sales and *Parasite* nineteenth) without taking recourse to the prominent national historical events exploited by other recent Korean blockbusters (such as the colonial-era occupation featured in *Assassination* [*Amsal*, dir. Choi Dong-hoon, 2015]; the foreign invasion theme of *The Admiral: Roaring Currents* and *The Fortress* [*Namhansanseong*, Hwang Dong-hyuk, 2017]; the creation of the hangul writing system portrayed in *The King's Letters* [*Naramalssami*, dir. Jo Chul-hyun, 2019]; or the focus on modern-day political massacre in *Taxi Driver* [*Taeksi Unjŏnsa*, dir. Jang Hoon, 2017]). Other proven box office ingredients, such as romantic narrative arcs, are also absent from the two films. In both cases, melodramatic genre codes are switched out for comedic conventions of wordplay, con-artist schemes, and what I refer to as food drama. In an era of mukbang (eatcast, short for "eating broadcast"), which is popular on YouTube and other livestream channels, food has lost its social significance as nutritional substance and necessity and has instead assumed a perverse, vicarious, negative, and almost undesirable association with gluttony and psychological depression, which are in turn linked with anorexia and bulimia. By contrast, both *Extreme Job* and *Parasite* revisit the pleasure and importance of eating in South Korea. In the former film, a narcotics squad opens a fried-chicken joint in order to bust a drug lord and finds unexpected success in the popularity of its product; in *Parasite*, which is loosely based on Kim Ki-young's classic 1960 film *The Housemaid*, writer-director Bong Joon-ho pays close attention to domestic affairs, including the preparation and serving of food, sickness and hysteria around fruit allergies, and the centrality of the kitchen (where a secret pantry tunnel leading to an underground bunker emerges as one of the story's main settings).[3] The cinematic representation of eating in both films enacts a *virtual* form of meal that shuffles between real and healthy consumption of food and one fraught with fakery, perversion, and class division.[4]

EXTREME JOB

Food is ubiquitous on almost every screen one is forced to look at in Korea—not just on television and electronic devices but also on giant billboard screens on the streets, and even on small screens installed inside building elevators. Although food commercials and food-themed programs are of course common in the United States, food is even more omnipresent in Korea, where fast-food franchises, children's snacks, and sports drinks are heavily advertised and visual media are dominated by comedy programs featuring celebrities doing nothing but preparing food and offering recipes. If Shin Ramen, the spicy noodles in flaming-red plastic packages, has set the standard for the instant-food business in Korea since its 1990 debut, fried chicken, it could be argued, has likewise set the standard for the nation's fast-food industry. According to Chŏng Ŭn-jŏng, author of *The Tale of Chicken in the* ROK (*Taehanminguk ch'ik'in chŏn*), fried chicken has never once fallen to second place in the rankings of Korean fast-food preferences over the past two decades.[5] No pizza parlors, *kimbap* (Korean sushi) joints, or even hamburger franchises can rival the popularity of fried chicken in Korea since 1997, the year of the IMF crisis that forced many middle-aged men out of work.

Although fried chicken comes from many diverse culinary traditions around the world, the kind of chicken parlors popular in Korea first came into existence during the 1960s and 1970s in districts near US military bases, where Southern-style fried-chicken joints were common even before Kentucky Fried Chicken opened its first Korean franchise store in 1984.[6] Although fried-chicken parlors did eventually spread to other domestic commercial districts, their numbers exploded in the late 1990s and early 2000s, for three reasons. First, fried chicken, which until the 1990s was considered a luxury food item only affordable on special days such as Christmas, birthday parties, and school picnics (once-a-year *sop'ung* outings), was slowly transformed into an everyday consumable food item for the working and middle classes. Second, many male employees fired from jobs that prior to the IMF crisis of 1997 were considered lifetime employment ended up using their pensions to open small convenience stores and fried-chicken delivery parlors. At the time, opening a restaurant required a small down payment of only $30–40,000 for purchasing ovens and culinary equipment and paying franchise licensing fees, rental payments, and other miscellaneous insurance premiums and permits. Third, during the 2002 World Cup fever when the South Korean national soccer team made a miraculous run to the semifinals after beating European powerhouses Portugal, Italy, and Spain, the entire nation became hypnotized by soccer while snacking on *chi-maek* (a portmanteau meaning "chicken and beer," derived from *chi*kin, "chicken," and *mae*kju, "beer"). The chi-maek phenomenon was therefore born less than twenty years ago, when many family livelihoods became dependent on small businesses. Over the past two decades, the number of small fried-chicken restaurants and delivery parlors quadrupled from about ten thousand stores to about forty thousand.[7]

Walmart, Amazon, and Chick-fil-A have virtually eliminated mom-and-pop stores across the United States and elsewhere, and Korea is no exception to this trend, given the dominance of the nation's chaebol system, which has generated an increase in the number of superstores such as E-mart and Homeplus in almost every urban and suburban district in the country. Jameson once noted that "the secret of [Walmart's] success is not profit but pricing, the shaving off of the final pennies, so fatal to any number of its suppliers."[8] The kind of "always low prices" campaign that these superstores have achieved by shaving off the last won (Korean currency) has also restored a capitalist faith in obsessive frugality, which has razed small neighborhood stores and markets. However, in Korea, small restaurant businesses continue to operate, in part because of proprietors' personal devotion to their family enterprises and in part because there is an inherent utopian alternative embedded in a *siksa* (meal) that cynically welcomes a sense of shared collectivity and temporarily shuns atomized and individualistic social values. Eating continues to be important in Korea even after the sweeping effects of neoliberal capitalism. Koreans still greet each other with the word *siksa* ("Have you had a siksa yet?") and often end meetings with the same word ("It's time for siksa").

I call the Korean emphasis on food and siksa—as portrayed not just in films but also in television variety shows and livestream shows such as mukbang—a cynical embrace of collective value because, again, so many broadcast images of home cooking, festive preparations in the kitchen, and family food-sharing gatherings suggest not a positively imagined utopia but an ideal that is unimaginable and inconceivable in real life. As discussed in chapter 1, mukbang, which feature live YouTubers (usually petite Korean women) eating enormous amounts of food, have become popular because they deliver vicarious pleasures of eating. I am drawn to the idea of mukbang as a site of familial disunity, as it presents overeating as a cynical, excessive, and even grotesque discourse as previously depicted in two classic European films from the 1970s and 1980s: Luis Buñuel's *The Discreet Charm of the Bourgeoisie* (1972), where every effort on the part of bourgeois society members to gather for dinner is continually thwarted, to the point where eating discreetly takes place in the bathroom; and Monty Python's *The Meaning of Life* (1983), an epic British film where the violently obese Mr. Creosote wines and feasts at a French restaurant only to vomit streams of undigested food into a bucket. If these European films are examples of a Marxist critique of the bourgeoise, the young razor-thin female YouTubers eating the entire menu of a Chinese restaurant in mukbang can be understood as a synecdoche for a post-Marxist negation of the negative condition of Korea's present that has continually witnessed a precipitous fall in family values, middle-class ideals, and job security for youth. As reported in the *Korea Times*, the number of single-person households has more than doubled in the last two decades, rising from 2.22 million in 2000 to 5.62 million (28.6 percent of all households) in 2018.[9] Disbelief in middle-class family values is what has given rise to these single-person households as well as to the lowest fertility rate the world has ever seen, as Korea continues to break its own record every year—no matter which political party is brought in to rule. This fundamental sort of skepticism exemplifies what contemporary German theorist Peter Sloterdijk has called "cynical reason," a way of tactical thinking, misspeaking, and forgery that inverts everything that is wrong with society.[10] There is of course a laundry list of things that are not right with Korea today: it is a country deeply mired in middle-class crisis, cut-throat capitalist competition, and a collapse of neo-Confucian family values that has resulted in a low fertility rate, a rise of suicides, and endless accusations of power abuse that point to the structural toxicities of the political system regardless of which political party seizes power. Despite this systemic failure, which is not unlike that of other capitalist societies, it is easier to imagine the end of Korea than the end of capitalism in Korea. Both *Extreme Job* and *Parasite*, in response to the negativity and grotesque social culture associated with mukbang, attempt to set the tone for new family values even when such traumatic failures—which now include the fear of virus transmission—continue to tear communities apart across Korea.

Those who have sat through a film screening in Korea understand that Koreans do not laugh much in movie theaters. Although laughter is of course conditioned by social factors that differ between cultures, Koreans tend to fare rather poorly on measures of enjoyment, registering low scores in Gallup's "World Emotional Temperature" poll. Of course, any polls measuring emotional temperature around the globe will be based on questions that cannot possibly quantify a universal system that might fairly compare one country's negative or positive experience to another's. Yet despite the problems of cultural bias that are embedded in these polls, just one glance into the Gallup figures would infer that South Korea fares rather poorly in the poll's categories of "Experienced Enjoyment" and "Smile or Laugh." According to the 2018 Gallup figures, only 68 percent of Koreans answered positively to the question, "Did you smile or laugh a lot yesterday?" Although South Korea is certainly not one of the bottom countries on this list, its response scores came in well below those of Nigeria, El Salvador, and Indonesia, which comprised the top three countries, polling at 90 percent or higher. And in their responses to the question, "Did you experience the feeling of enjoyment a lot yesterday?" Koreans scored only slightly better or about the same—at 60 percent—as countries in far worse economic situations.[11] Many of the developed nations registered metrics far above those of Korea. Sweden, Norway, the UK, Canada, and the United States all had positive response rates at above 80 percent. Korea's neighbor, China, registered among the highest of all countries polled, at 86 percent. Although economic welfare was clearly not the most important factor in these "enjoyment" metrics or their cultural expression (the top three "happiest" countries, Paraguay, Mexico, and China, are not exactly the wealthiest nations on the planet), financial well-being must have played an important role, since almost all countries that ranked lower than South Korea in the category of "enjoyment yesterday" were extremely poor countries undergoing severe economic and political crises.

There are many factors that have led Koreans to lose their appetite for laughter and enjoyment, and the reasons why Korean spectators are less likely to laugh in theaters than Americans include social norms stemming from a sense of neo-Confucian decorum, which has traditionally devalued emotional outbursts; an austere public spectatorship culture; and a national cinematic tradition that has always valued melodrama far more than comedy. Furthermore, this dismissal or repression of laughter partly explains why Korean comedians rarely find success as screen actors in their own country. Comedy is often considered a crass entertainment genre, and those who perform it are not considered true thespians. Great film actors in Korea known for their roles in comedy films, such as Ryoo Seung-ryong and

Song Kang-ho, the two popular actors who star respectively in *Extreme Job* and *Parasite*, are not known solely for their comic roles.

The success of *Extreme Job* and *Parasite* perhaps suggests that Korean cinema has moved beyond a post-traumatic phase mired in sentimentality and grief for the loss and devastation of the twentieth century. The use of laughter to depict the life of present-day Korea hardly means that its current economic recession has suddenly vanished. In *Extreme Job*, laughter becomes what Brandon J. Manning has described in his analysis of *Friday* (a post–Rodney King black urban comedy featuring Ice Cube and Chris Tucker) as "juice of survival" that "helped to fortify black existence against the pernicious effects of deindustrialization, Ronald Reagan's war on drugs, and the evolution of American racism that created an image of black urban decay in the 1980s and '90s."[12] In 2019 South Koreans do not necessarily face racism on an everyday basis, but they are certainly dealing constantly with a discrimination against Korean minjok (a term meaning "people-hood," signifying ethnic bonding more than cosmopolitan citizenship) that finds them humiliatingly squeezed between nations of titanic proportions. The United States and North Korea often bypass consultations with South Koreans while directly engaging each other to discuss a nuclear deal. The Chinese government whimsically and inexplicably bans the sale of Korean cultural products whenever political winds blow unfavorably against South Korea, often due to Korea's need to appease US pressure stemming from the military partnership between the two nations. Such bans sometimes lead to the cancellation of coproduction projects on music, film, and television shows that feed tens of thousands of Korean artists and entertainers. And finally, whenever there is a court ruling in South Korea that favors the victims of Japanese forced labor camps or comfort women exploited during World War II, the Japanese government retaliates vehemently, straining economic relations between the two countries. Such scenarios have led to the devaluation of the Korean currency and sent shockwaves through the Korean stock market. In addition to its waning optimism in the capitalist system and its diminished hopes for radical change in the future, the Korean minjok, who share an ignominious history of twentieth-century hardships, including generations of forced labor under colonialism, war, and military dictatorships, still tend to ask whether they are the one Asian nation that has been singled out for eternal damnation. In my mind, this question reflects a cynical reason aestheticized as humor—one that serves as a form of self-care at a time when the Korean middle class is diminishing, intense competition compels self-abasement, and families are being torn asunder. Koreans may be the outlier nation in East Asia most likely to grow accustomed to the feeling of schadenfreude as a way to overcome bitterness.

The perfect human sought in many Korean blockbuster films dealing with events of the twentieth century is a figure who signals a new post-traumatic subjecthood through the proper mourning of the dead (*Taegukgi*, dir. Kang Je-gyu, 2004), reauthorizes the writing of modern history from the perspective of victims (*Taxi Driver*), and celebrates survival throughout the course of a century marred by intense agony and pain (*An Ode to My Father* and *Assassination*). These films feature discernible plotlines that pay unequivocal respect to those suffering historical pains and traumas and yet seek to maintain the integrity of these individuals by projecting a unified vision of minjok. In some respects, it can be argued that Bong Joon-ho's two transnational films (with an international cast), *Snowpiercer* (2013) and *Okja* (2017), resurrected a great modernist vision of the past and envisioned a new global future where Koreans could find a cynical and yet empathetic key. Despite their thematic critique of a neoliberalism that punishes children and animals, these films retain a strong sense of optimism for the future. For instance, at the end of *Snowpiercer*, a female Korean child and a male black child are left as the lone survivors on Earth to carry on the mission of procreating humankind, and in *Okja*, a gentle giant pig is saved by the Korean girl who has raised her and returns with her to the Korean countryside.

Extreme Job and *Parasite*, however, depart from these mildly cynical yet festive story modes that celebrate a revitalized hope for humanity. *Extreme Job* demonstrates that there is no idyllic narrative past or utopian future left to salvage even though the evil drug lord in the story is finally captured, order is restored, and each member of the undercover narcotics detective team receives a promotion. When an army of gangsters loaded with guns and sharp metal weapons is easily defeated by the five-member detective team in the film's final action scene, the youngest of the undercover cops, Jae-hoon (played by Gong Myung), tries to hug Chief Go (played by Ryoo Seung-ryong), who is now seriously injured lying on an ambulance stretcher and unable to move, while a Cantonese song in the background intensifies the tone of the already unbelievable setup. "Can I call you Dad from now on?" asks Jae-hoon, overwhelmed by the sentimental overtures and after his leader has been forced to sacrifice his own body in order to pull off a miraculous victory. In pain, the heavily bruised Chief Go is only able to respond with a few mumbles. Misrecognizing the latter's gesture as an affirmation, Jae-hoon tightly embraces him. Rich capitalists (drug lords who drive expensive cars, possess beautiful women, and live in mansions) have been punished, hard labor has been properly rewarded, and family values have been restored, all of which has unfurled in the most unreal, painful, and hyperbolic fashion possible. When the team members are given decoration medals at the end of the film, even the police superintendent deliriously exclaims, "Can you actually believe what is happening here?" Such a colossal fantasy forces viewers to become aware of false consciousness, where cynical reason becomes both lucid and limpid. The film understands that its own ending—where labor is properly compensated; evil, greed-blinded capitalists vanish; and the state (in the person of the police superintendent) seeks justice—is way too perfect. With the 1980s Hong Kong soundtrack playing in the background, we all recognize that these ambitions can only be realized in the imaginary space of fantasy cinema.

The plotline of *Extreme Job* is simple. A team of five detectives is forced to undergo seemingly never-ending undercover duty in order to capture a drug lord called Lee Moo-bae (Shin Ha-kyun), who shuttles between Hong Kong and Seoul. After drawing unnecessary attention from the neighbors and even from the gangsters themselves, the detectives, led by Chief Go, decide to rent a dilapidated fried-chicken parlor adjacent to the gangsters' hideout. Problems compound for the inept detectives when customers keep visiting the parlor to try their delicious fried chicken. One of the detectives, Detective Ma, turns out to be an accomplished cook with exquisite taste, and a recipe he has acquired from his parents, "Suwon King Kalbi," works exceptionally well on chicken. So successful is the business that the doubling of the detectives' duties precipitates an identity crisis: they are unsure whether they are undercover cops trying to bust the bad guys or restaurant workers desperately trying to stay afloat in the chicken business (figure 5.1). The final straw comes when the enterprise is bought in a franchise deal by none other than the business consulting partner of the drug lord, Lee Moo-bae, who needs a better cover for disseminating drugs to his clients. What until this point has been a tightrope walk of quasi-realistic narrative undergoes a complete freefall into an underwhelming sequence of unbelievable situations. The cops-cum-restaurant workers are no longer interested in capturing Lee Moo-bae. Instead, they begin to investigate the real reason why many of their chicken delivery routes are infested with drug addicts. Little do they realize that their business investigation has led them to the same drug lord who was targeted by an earlier police undercover investigation from which they had taken a hiatus. A couple of

Suwon rib marinade chicken.

5.1 A struggling narcotics cop finds success in the fried-chicken business while working undercover in *Extreme Job* (2019).

busted covers and chase scenes deliver us to the final climax, where the five cops confront an army of gangsters who are protecting their bosses. Lee Moo-bae escapes on a boat, only to be pursued and captured by Chief Go. Successful as a restaurant owner but inept as a narcotics cop or reliable husband throughout the film, Go atones for his former mistakes by defeating Lee in a battle at sea.

During the final action scene, when Chief Go butts heads with chief villain Lee, the latter, still ignorant of the restaurant owner's true identity, perplexingly asks: "You are only a chicken restaurant owner, why are you trying to risk your life to catch me?" Still unwilling to reveal his identity to the villain, Go replies, "You, bastard, don't know what you are talking about. Every small business owner has to stick out his neck to keep his business open." Go's response conflates the damage to his personal reputation as chicken restaurant owner with his pursuit of public justice as a cop relieved of his duty, thereby setting up a classic conflict between a villain who embodies the golden-spoon global capitalist and a middle-aged dirt-spoon hero. Go also symbolizes an aging man stuck in a crisis between two jobs: one in the large company where he has hit the glass ceiling, and one in a small private business that may prove to suck all the money from his nest egg.[13]

Not only is the film's plotline deeply flawed and unreal, but the characters are also intentionally flat, lacking psychological depth. Admittedly, these characteristics are perhaps a point of attraction for the film — much like that flatness John Woo preferred for his Hong Kong films of the 1980s. Too many Korean films have created characters out of the struggle against posttraumatic syndrome generated by war, poverty, and colonial subjugation.[14]

I hail the evocation of Hong Kong's cinema heyday here, not as a sign that Lee Moo-bae is attempting to escape to Hong Kong but because the conflict between Lee and Go is hyperbolized to a point where cynicism overwhelms the sincerity with which the battle between capital and labor is waged. Yes, the film does end on a happy note where labor defeats the rich capitalist, but is the battle really over? The song played in the critical final scene is not rock- or hip-hop-driven contemporary pop music, which would suit the mood of an action film. Without any musical updates, the song played — almost in its entirety — is "In the Sentimental Past" (Dang nian ching 當年情), sung by the late singer-actor Leslie Cheung and featured on the soundtrack of John Woo's classic 1983 film *A Better Tomorrow*. This sentimental song, seemingly out of place in 2019, momentarily takes the viewers back to an exciting and almost innocent time in the 1980s prior to the internet era's unleashing of schadenfreude, that cruel form of delight in other people's failures. In the 1980s, good prevailing over evil was a choice of necessity, because the Korean dictatorship was decisively bad and those fighting against it were irrevocably good. Furthermore, the economic recession of the late 1990s was still more than a decade away, and the middle class was expanding. Much like the 1960s had a positive sociopolitical impact on the United States, the 1980s in Korea struck a chord of "better tomorrow" for Korean youth determined to make their march into the future. However, thirty years later, for the "386-generation" represented by Chief Go, the song "In the Sentimental Past" has been reduced to a reminder of the lost hopes of a bygone era, dampening optimism for the future and emphasizing the cynical present that the once-dreamed-of future has become. The seeds sown by progressive movements during the "spring of democracy" in 1987 has turned out to be a mere illusion or facade, the 1997 IMF bailout has effectively ended the lifelong employment system in the Korean corporate structure, intense competition and high spending through credit card debt have squeezed out the middle class, and the years of conservative rule (2008 to 2017) have eliminated the possibility of corporate and legal reforms in Korea.[15] Even the reenergized left that seized power after the 2016–17 candlelight vigil protest over the Choi Sun-sil scandal was showing signs of political and economic ineptitude by the end of the decade. Real estate prices have skyrocketed, creating a larger gap between haves and have-nots, political corruption scandals have intensified even among liberal leaders, and peace on the Korean peninsula is seemingly unattainable even after years of engaging the North. Cynicism and resignation therefore reverberate through the 1980s pop song played at the end of *Extreme Job*—again reminding viewers of a dream from the 1980s that three decades later could be no more than that: a nostalgic dream quashed by a foreclosed future.

As the borderline melancholic leader of the undercover team, Chief Go fits perfectly into the prototype of the modern-day cynic, that post-Enlightenment agent described by Sloterdijk. Go inhabits neither the top nor the bottom of the economic echelons of society. As Sloterdijk explains, cynics "lose their individual sting and refrain from the risk of letting themselves be put on display. They have long ceased to expose themselves as eccentrics to the attention and mockery of others."[16] They no longer stand out, and they are well integrated into the masses—on social media platforms, in workplaces, and especially on movie screens. Sloterdijk quotes Gottfried Benn, a German poet during the Weimar Republic, who formulated the idea of cynicism in the twentieth century: "To be dumb and have a job, that's happiness."[17] Chief Go has to wear a symbolic mask every day in order to veil his unhappiness as well as his intelligence in the face of his peers, his superintendents, and his family members. Played by Ryoo Seung-ryong, one of the best actors in contemporary Korean cinema, Go wears a wry smile that makes him a little bit sarcastic and extremely moody. He calls his friend, the captain of another detective squad, "big brother" despite the fact that his colleague is younger than he is. He bluffs his own young teenage daughter, telling her that the reason he can't give her more than thirty dollars for pocket money is because he has to obey "the Kim Young-ran Law," which prohibits Korean civil servants from accepting or giving gifts exceeding that value. He is caught in a Deleuzian schizoid condition; he lies by telling the truth. He maintains his existence by flipping between cop and chicken restaurant proprietor, between captain and subordinate, and between real being and fictive illusion—to a point where both the audience and the character lose sight of the truth. When he answers each and every phone call with the machine-like greeting, "There has never been a taste of chicken like this," he is no longer a man of deception but a genuine postenlightened being who must perfect the art of deception in order to stake out his false happiness as a cynic. He is beyond both trauma and its recovery. He is a schizo but, as Deleuze has explained, one who does need an armchair. Happiness would elude him if he worked only as a career cop or only as a chicken parlor restaurant owner, because otherwise he would be stuck in just one place. He can happily keep repeating the same line, "Chicken never tasted this good. Is this really chicken?" because he knows he is using it as a deception to cover for his real job as a cop. Otherwise, it's a dull job. If he were genuinely subordinated by the rules and conventions of capitalism, the fun of "taking phone orders" would be un-juiced. Only when his true identity keeps shifting between the two masks can he reveal some joy in the world of profit and utilitarianism—weathering the pressures of an unhappy job in the mundane world of capitalism.

One of the most delightful scenes from *Extreme Job* comes earlier in the film when Go and his police squad attempt to purchase the fried-chicken parlor from its original proprietor in order to use it as an undercover bunker. Go desperately tries to convince the proprietor that he and the gang are actually all members of a big family; he puts his arms around the only female member of the squad, Detective Jang, who murmurs, "Yes, I am her husband." The only problem here is that, when Go had been away to get the cash needed for the down payment, the squad, unbeknownst to him, had already informed the proprietor that Jang was married to Detective Ma. The proprietor displays a look of confusion and Go, realizing his blunder, quickly makes up another lie, telling the proprietor, "Actually, her former husband." Such a code-switch requires alertness in the art of deception but also an intervention in language. The surprised proprietor exclaims in English, "[You mean like] American style? Like in Hollywood movies?" Go glibly responds, as if acting in an American movie, "Uh-huh, yes." Shortly thereafter, when his deceptive act has succeeded and the proprietor leaves the restaurant, he adds, in almost perfect English, "See you later!" The switch into a "master's language" (not to mention into a master's film industry convention) to pass as a credible man reminds us of the black con artist's fake use of "white man's English" in order to elevate his social position as a staple gag in Hollywood comedies such as *Beverly Hills Cop*. In the Korean comedy, it is just plain English that replaces "white-man's English." Code-switching, deception, or what Gates called the "Signifyin(g) monkey" is a common trajectory of many comic film narratives starring African American actors, perhaps because the body of the black man is already steeped in criminality or negativity.[18] In *Trading Places* (dir. John Landis, 1983), for instance, Eddie Murphy's character undergoes a topsy-turvy flip from penniless pauper to Wall Street millionaire. One of the most successful recent films on the subject of code-switching is *Get Out* (dir. Jordan Peele, 2017), which uncovers the very cynical meaning behind the double consciousness that African Americans have been forced to assume throughout the history of the United States, where a persisting racial hierarchy has yet to free African Americans from systemic racial biases and discrimination that have extended the expiration date of black cynicism.

The notion of the postenlightenment cynic can also be found in the theories of Fanon, whose writings predate Sloterdijk and, for that matter, Deleuze, by at least several decades. Fanon writes, "It will be understood that the first impulse of the black man is to say *no* to those who attempt to build a definition of him."[19] Fanon also wrote in another passage that the "consciousness of the body is solely a negating activity."[20] Although Korea does not share the United States' history of annihilation of native peoples and black enslavement, few other modern nations have experienced such a combination of recent historical crises and challenges: a prolonged Cold War; the legacy of Japanese colonialism, during which Koreans were subject to forced military conscription, wartime labor, and sexual slavery; and the present-day American military occupation. Koreans' false consciousness (which also includes schadenfreude), their cynical art of deception, and their disillusionment vis-à-vis emancipation are all deeply rooted in these circumstances, with the Korean people still being assigned the role of political bulwarks and agents in the Cold War scheme and serving as an economic testing ground for US-led capitalism. Donald Trump often commented on the "awesome economic potential" of the North Korea of his "friend" Kim Jong-un, after realizing that South Koreans have become just as good capitalists, if not better, than Americans.[21]

Just as a language division between standard speech and pidgin distinguishes the master from the slave, Koreans' deviation from English has produced anxiety and humor around the proper use of this language and has also raised the stress level of almost every Korean who has undergone formal education after the Korean War. The proliferation of English in many comedic situations creates a double entendre that perceives English almost as a "devil's tongue." In *Writing in the Devil's Tongue: A History of English Composition in China*, Xiaoye You argues that English writing instruction in China has been similarly perceived in that country dating back to 1862, when the Anglo-American teaching of English coincided with the colonial ambitions of many Europeans to overwhelm the Chinese Confucian spirit. In Korea, this binary opposition between English and Korean is not as neatly organized as a "devil's tongue" scenario. Patricia Bizzell argues that the nonapplication of the "devil's tongue" argument in the Korean context is due in part to the fact that "the country was never colonized by an English-speaking power."[22] But perhaps this position also requires a more nuanced understanding of Korea's history. Bizzell is correct in pointing out that English was one of the languages used in the early twentieth century by Korean patriots such as Seo Jae-pil and Syngman Rhee who sought to appeal to the international community with regard to the horrors of Japanese colonialism. However, after the US military occupation, English became both a "master's language" and a language of practical necessity due to the ascendance of English as a hegemonic language not only in Korea but also throughout the rest of the world over the past three-quarters of a century.

Despite the difficulty of simply putting English under the column of *master's language* and Korean under *slave's language*, the trends in Korean cinema over the past fifteen years or so confirm the fact that English reigns supreme in Korea as a dominant language that commands respect, with one caveat: it must coexist with its Korean masterpiece counterpart, the hangul writing system. Unlike other minor languages that are constantly threatened with extinction and dishonored by major languages, hangul garners a vote of local confidence as a source of minjok pride. It is also the preferred writing system of K-pop in an era where languages other than English and Spanish are disappearing from the global pop scene. Therefore, the jokes and comedy situations that surround the misuse of English in Korea are not necessarily compounded by the fear of losing the local language but instead express, almost with an air of superiority, that hangul is not only irreplaceable but is actually a superior writing system. Whereas Fanon openly discussed the anxiety and indignation of postcolonial elites who feared losing their native tongue when acquiring linguistic facility in a European language, Koreans, despite briefly experiencing the threat of losing hangul during the latter part of the Japanese colonial era, have become comfortable with bilingualism as their modus operandi in the twenty-first century. This accommodation has allowed jokes about the misuse and misreading of English to circulate freely and shamelessly.

The first joke in English that became memorable since the turn of the previous century was one that is featured in the blockbuster film *Welcome to Dongmakgol* (dir. Park Kwang-hyun, 2003), which is set during the Korean War. A US bomber plane crashes near a remote Korean village. The white American pilot, Captain Smith, who does not speak a word of Korean, is rescued by a group of villagers. His leg is badly injured, but after he wakes up from a long slumber, his cognitive capacities are perfectly functional. He finds himself surrounded by a group of Koreans who still wear traditional clothes and are not even aware that a global war is upon them. One member of the group wears spectacles and has a neat Western haircut. Slowly, in broken English, the Korean man begins to speak: "Ha-ooh aa yoooo?" In an enraged fit, Smith yells back at the man, who is later revealed to be

5.2 An American pilot—injured and trapped in a remote Korean village during the Korean War—asks one of the questions most feared by Koreans in *Welcome to Dongmakgol* (2003).

a schoolteacher: "I mean, look at me. How do you think I am? I'm tied up with sticks . . . You know I feel like shit. . . . Shit!" Realizing that something is wrong, the elderly village chief asks the schoolteacher, in Korean, "Is it not going well?" The schoolteacher responds by pointing to a line in his English lesson book: "If I say, 'Ha-ooh aah yooo?' then he is supposed to say, 'Pa-een andew yooo?' That's what an American should say, so that I can say, 'Aiii aem pa-een.'" As the conversation between the village chief and the schoolteacher goes deeper into the pool of knowledge surrounding American social courtesy, Smith begins to lose hope (figure 5.2). Yet unlike the African American pilot portrayed in Oe Kenzaburo's award-winning novella "Prize Stock," who is taken captive in rural Japan during World War II and treated like an animal, Smith is handled with decency. As he recovers, he learns to socialize with the villagers and even helps them avoid a carpet-bombing attack from the US Air Force. What is funny in the film is the difference between how English is taught to be spoken in Korea and how English is really spoken. Such a divergence evokes the gap between the pedagogical imposed by the colonizers and the performative enacted by the colonized, as theorized by Homi K. Bhabha in his essay "DissemiNation."[23] Furthermore, it could also be a moment where discomfort, double talk, and nonsensical rhyming strip away the intended meaning behind the speech, which, in the words of Deleuze and Guattari, allows for a "minor literaturization" of English "where a minority constructs within a major language."[24] African American, Hispanic, and Asian American literature and cinema have all found ways to chip away at the framework of standard English, thereby configuring essential examples of the minor utilization of a major language. It could be argued that Korean cinema's utilization of English, even outside the Anglophone country context, could likewise become such a minor utilization of English in a space of US-occupied territory. In other words, when the tables are turned in the interaction between the American captive and the Korean villagers, the scenario shows Koreans attempting to strip away the meaning behind a hegemonic English by poking fun at the gap between the pedagogical and the performative.[25]

PARASITE

The role of English as a "master's language" likewise structures the spatial domain of *Parasite*, a film that is clearly focused on a distinction between haves and have-nots, contrasting the "stinky rich" who reside in picture-perfect mansions and those who are just literally "stinky" and work in and around the house. Interestingly, however, although English is sometimes used by the employers, the employees, especially the younger ones, speak the "master's language" better than their employers do. Bong Joon-ho's seventh feature film was a landmark not only because it won the best film prize at the Cannes International Film festival in 2019 (the first for a Korean film at the so-called Big Three international film festivals that also include Venice and Berlin) and the Best Picture prize at the Academy Awards in 2020 (the first ever for a foreign-language film) but also because it is among twenty Korean films that have surpassed the coveted level of selling ten million movie tickets in the country. It is also a film that effectively avoids a happy ending. As explained earlier, many Korean blockbuster films tend to depict historical events, even though Korean history is filled with inglorious and inauspicious drama for Koreans. Despite the fact that massacres, wartime defeats, and colonial subjugations have punctured a hole in the Korean soul over the past several centuries, Koreans have found a way to positively spin filmic narratives where heroism is cast as the sacrifice of individuals in a collective society.[26]

As both director Bong and his executive producer, Miky Lee, repeatedly mentioned during the 2020 Academy Awards ceremony, Korean moviegoers have made possible the success of Korean cinema.[27] Korean cinema was able to articulate its local and national particularities of Korea's unique culture while making its bold commitment to aesthetic movements or cinematic expressions because of its loyal local fans. Gritty-themed films by

Bong and Park Chan-wook, for instance, have been welcomed into South Korea's movie theaters while illegal pirating is also largely frowned upon by internet users. Despite boasting the world's fastest internet speed and the world's highest smartphone user rate, South Koreans still prefer the "big screen." As explained in chapter 1, currently only Iceland boasts a better moviegoing rate per capita than South Korea. During the late 2010s, South Korea recorded a per capita moviegoing rate of around 4.3, while that of the United States had dipped to a rate below 4.0.

Even among the films of Bong Joon-ho, *Parasite* is a rarity in that it intentionally fails to offer a satisfying resolution in its dramatic arc, in which a family of four living in a slum trying to improve their lives do not end up achieving their dreams. In the end, we instead see the family members' lives totally broken, with the father imprisoned, the daughter dead, and the mother and son trying to piece together their shattered lives. Although the film successfully critiques the failures of the meritocratic system, the neoliberal agenda to remobilize the middle class into a temporary gig workforce, and the increasing gap between the rich and the poor, unlike some of Bong Joon-ho's most beloved films, such as *The Host* (*Kwemul*, 2007), *Snowpiercer*, and *Okja*, *Parasite* leaves a bitter taste at the end when the father and the son fail to reunite and the daughter's death fails to be compensated for by a pledge of renewal among the surviving family members, who must now learn to live with each other beyond the trauma.

Ever since his first film, *Barking Dogs Never Bite* (*P'ŭrandasŭ ŭi kae*, 2000), Bong Joon-ho has been fascinated by the vacant spaces left behind by the frenzied pace of Korean modernization. In his films, the countryside is beyond repair, cities exhibit the monstrous destruction of ecological harmony, and dark secrets often lurk in basements and rooftop spaces. Not even a moment of lamentation for vanishing traditions is possible. The spaces of the ruined landscape are filled with contaminated, slimy water (*The Host*); lines of black ants cover the decayed body of a woman who is found in a golden harvest field (*Memories of Murder*); the lush green of a golf course is unbelievably artificial (*Mother*); and gigantic slaughterhouses exhibit rows of artificially created monster pigs lined up to be made into bacon (*Okja*). The depth of Bong's cinema is created not through the realistic portrayal of the landscape but through its perversion.[28] Unlike many American dystopian genre films — including Jordan Peele's *Us* (2018) — that only permit viewers to cinematically imagine today's growing job insecurity worldwide through fantasy genre or historical drama, *Parasite* depicts the growing fear of the poor and the parasitic unfiltered. Among nine films

5.3 Rich people often cover their noses and mouths in *Parasite* (2019).

nominated for the Academy Awards' Best Picture category in 2020, *Parasite* was one of only two films (the very personal *Marriage Story* being the other) that was not set in the historical past.

In *Parasite*, Bong continues to explore his mission to create Korean landscapes filled with waste, human excrement, and foul odors. Smell is extremely difficult to portray in cinema because it is neither visual nor auditory; changes in scent cannot be reproduced in theaters. However, not only is smell a topic of several conversations that take place in *Parasite*, but it is one of the central metaphors used in the film (figure 5.3). The insult that crucially arises from a putatively intolerable body odor might also be the very reason why chauffeur and head of the parasitic family Kim Ki-taek (Song Kang-ho) ends up stabbing his employer Chairman Park (Lee Sun-kyun). Sprawling urbanization in Korea has produced suburban areas and new urban developments that have triggered hygienic and health sensitivities. Because odors, as directly raised in the film, are unseen and undetectable before they brush right up against your nose, they can be invasive of other people's private spaces in ways that no other sensory elements, including auditory, visual, and oral ones, can. Mr. Park, a successful entrepreneur in his prime, who has a beautiful, light-skinned wife, a lovely mansion, and two children, one in high school and another in grade school, cautiously maintains an emotional distance from his employees. Despite his efforts, however, the boundary between the public and the private cannot be properly guarded when it comes to the offensive smell that supposedly arises from Kim Ki-taek. Park wants to keep this parasitic odor from reaching him, but he cannot.

Recent zombie movies or streaming dramas set in Korea, such as *Train to Busan* (dir. Yeon Sang-ho, 2016) or the Netflix drama *Kingdom*, have achieved popularity by formulating a metaphor of stench along with a sense of the visual grotesque that communicates fear and insecurity over disposable lives that must be excluded and therefore unseen in order for capitalism to continue its mission. Capitalism's hygienic sensitivity is extremely high; one cannot expect to sell products very well in filthy or stinky conditions. In the case of *Parasite*, the expression of fear against the poor and the parasitic does not take on an allegorical function; it is simply there on the surface for all to see. Not unlike zombies, the Kim family is not quite dead yet, but they also cannot confidently present their true identities to others. The CVs of both parents and children will not impress any future employers. The family has already fallen from the middle class after several of their private enterprises, such as a fried-chicken restaurant and a Taiwanese castella bakery shop, have failed to materialize. In order to climb back up from the cellars and basements where they crawl, they must rely on the resourcefulness of the son, Ki-woo, and the daughter, Ki-jung, who are both between high school and college and yet brilliant at exploiting their skills as cynics. Unlike entrepreneur Mr. Park's two children, who have mild psychic issues (the older daughter suffers from affection deficiency and sibling jealousy; the son has been "diagnosed" with schizophrenia), the two children from a lower echelon of society reveal no symptoms of physical or psychological ailments. Yet they live in a world of lies, employing deceit and forging counterfeit documents to get ahead. Since society has left them behind, they feel that they can keep their morality in check when working to extract a little bit of cash from those who are making obscene amounts of money. Despite his good English skills, Ki-woo has yet to go to college, because he has failed his entrance exams several times. Ki-jung has excellent computer graphics skills but cannot put them to good use other than for forging official documents. They use deceitful mimicry in order to put themselves in employable situations because their earlier hopes of finding honest work have crumbled.

From the film's opening scene, poverty is depicted as being predicated not necessarily on an economic divide between the haves and the have-nots but on digital inequalities determined by Wi-Fi access. They are not only poor, but dirt-spoon, digital poor. The family's inability to pay for monthly smartphone fees and internet data use affirms what Dal Yong Jin characterizes as the digital divide in the smartphone era, which has become "a new form of digital exclusion and is further marginalizing already oppressed and disenfranchised individuals."[29] The Kims live in a half-basement unit that demarcates their residential home from others but also creates interdependency with other units and nearby small businesses. They mooch off an unprotected Wi-Fi signal from a nearby café and beg for more part-time work from a local pizzeria that is trying desperately to grow into a franchise. The emphasis placed in the opening scene on the family's desperation for Wi-Fi (which produces an unintended rhyme with *choco-pie*, a popular snack in Korea) allows writer-director Bong Joon-ho to create his black humor even though his film is a stark statement on the dark reality of Korea that has squeezed out the middle class and widened the gap between rich and poor. Even though Kim's family fills the bill for the middle-class-cum-urban proletariat, the scramble for a free Wi-Fi signal allows Bong to express sarcasm not just for the rich but also for the poor. Digital signal, unlike food, shelter, clothing, or job, is a derivative of social necessity, not a necessity in itself. The family could easily walk to a public Wi-Fi area sponsored by the district office if they were truly desperate for it. Their fuss over the loss of signal gives the film a mood more insouciant than that of postwar neorealist films such as Vittorio De Sica's *Bicycle Thief* (1949), whose protagonist must find his stolen bike in order to keep his job in poverty-stricken Rome. Rather than learning skills that produce skillful or productive labor, the *Parasite* family's work constitutes mooching off others—including cracking the code of a password-protected Wi-Fi signal, producing forged documents, and finally concocting schemes to produce counterfeit identities and ghost companies.

It is first Ki-woo who is hired by Mrs. Park with his forged certificate showing his enrollment at prestigious Yonsei University—Bong Joon-ho's alma mater. He begins to teach English to Park's high school daughter, Da-hye, who soon finds herself romantically attracted to him. Exploiting the trust formed between himself and Mrs. Park, Ki-woo recommends his unemployed sister to teach art classes to Park's first grader, Da-song. Ki-woo deceives Mrs. Park into believing that his sister, introduced as a recent graduate of a studio art program at Illinois State University, although she has never set foot in the United States, is only a vague acquaintance. Once the two conniving siblings have befriended the "young and simple" Mrs. Park, they are able to find the rest of their family jobs with the Parks as well. The father is hired as Mr. Park's driver and the mother as a domestic helper. Although the Kim family has concocted a plan to force the termination of the Parks' previous driver and housekeeper in order supplant them, no criticism of their actions is drawn. Their trickery is "illegitimately legitimate," for it has merely helped them gain a small advantage in the highly brutal and competitive society that Korea has become. If neoliberalism has exercised no mercy in forcing them out of work, they will likewise show no clemency toward the previous driver and Moon-gwang, the former housekeeper, in stealing their places. Good jobs have become scarce, and the Kims must productively use their cynicism rather than become disillusioned by it. They will use their skills in deception, forgery, and mimicry to make up for their deficiencies in certificates, experience, and excellent recommendation letters, all so that their powerful employers will be forced to give them work. As Sloterdijk observes, hegemonic powers "do not come voluntarily to the negotiating table with their opponents, whom they would prefer to have behind bars."[30] *Parasite* recognizes that the era of Enlightenment has come to an end with the rise of neoliberal capitalism, and the poor can no longer reason with the rich. The only way the rich will come to the same table with the parasites is through violent terror or the mask of theatrical deception.

Instead of totally negating the status quo, the Kim family plans to affirmatively subvert the rules of neoliberalism in order to secure jobs, and their effort does initially succeed. The Parks remain clueless about the family they have let into their home and become entirely dependent on the Kims for transportation, grocery shopping, domestic chores, kitchen work, and their children's education. Their absolute reliance on the Kims has been acquired through the latter's outwitting of the Parks through a system of cynical reason. However, as the Kims gather in the living room of the empty Park mansion one night when their masters have taken a camping trip to the countryside, their true adversaries are awaiting them to unmask their real identities as family members and counterfeits. Stepping back inside the mansion that has become a theater is the former housekeeper Moon-gwang, along with her husband, a fugitive from the law who has been secretly residing in the basement cellar for the past four years. The real "parasites" have been residing in the house long before the Kims had arrived.

The Kims are soon introduced to that hidden cellar, a bunker accessed through a secret passage behind the pantry cabinets, of whose existence even the homeowners are unaware. Inside resides Geun-se, Moon-gwang's middle-aged husband, who has been without food for at least several days due to his wife's abrupt dismissal from her job. Despite the fact that every major character in *Parasite* is ethnically Korean, Geun-se is the darkest-skinned character in the film—highly unrealistic given that he rarely sees the sun. The lightest-skinned character is Mrs. Park, while the Kims have skin tones somewhere in the middle. Bong Joon-ho cynically declares that class positions are beginning to determine constituents' skin colors (or vice versa) even among the same-race people in Korea. The pair, Geun-se and Moon-gwang, just like the Bauhaus-inspired house that they occupy, may be genuine 386-generation political activists disillusioned with the former revolutionary ideals. Plastered on the bunker walls are images of dissident heroes from years past, including Kim Dae-jung. If political dissenters were formerly chased by riot police and Korean CIA agents, bad debtors are now being chased by loan sharks and hired thugs. After several business failures, including that of the Taiwanese cake franchise with which Kim Ki-taek had also been involved, he had no choice but to live in the basement as a parasite. In many ways, Geun-se is no different from Kim Ki-taek, as a middle-aged man who spent his youth during the 1980s, when the Korean economic and political landscape was filled with optimism, but has now been forced into a basement home without any substantial income. The only difference is that Geun-se lacks resourceful grown-up children who can cynically put a positive spin on the present-day negativity. He and his wife have chosen to exercise their cynicism only within a hidden space that remains unseen and unheard. Morse code signal is the only way to communicate to the outside world from the basement, with the secret code transmitted by the flipping of a lobby light switch by Moon-gwang's husband, and later by Kim Ki-taek. At one point, Moon-gwang begins to sound like a North Korean, pretending to read the propaganda news like North Korean anchorwoman Ri Chun-hee, who announces every news item from the centralized Communist country in a highly melodramatic tone — usually peppered with stern warnings against the American imperialists and their South Korean puppets. Moon-gwang's sarcastic mimicry of the North Korean newscaster once again propels the film out of Enlightenment discourse, where the possibility of reasonable optimism for utopian hopes and social change are all but rendered pastiche. The pair's ability to recognize the false illusion of capitalism and instead to usher the negation of the negativity of the present-day status quo has earned them, just like North Korea, only a parasitic and negligible worth in today's world order determined by capitalist output. Once young dreamers with visions perhaps similar to those of the socialist North Korean state in the 1940s and 1950s, Moon-gwang and her husband now constitute a class even below the Kims that can only dramatize their experience through puppet-show mockeries and the delivery of signals with no recipient but themselves.

The Kim family party is busted when Moon-gwang finds out that they are all in fact members of one family who have lied about their true identities

5.4 Preparation and consumption of food occupies a central significance in *Parasite* (2019).

to gain employment with the Parks. When Moon-gwang threatens to send Mrs. Park a cell phone video of them calling each other "mother," "father," "son," and "daughter," the Kims crumble to pieces. Yet although dispirited, they still outnumber the former housekeeper's team four to two and are therefore soon able to carry out a comeback coup d'état in the spacious living room of the Parks' mansion. As a battle ensues over Moon-gwang's cell phone containing the video footage, the house phone begins to ring. Mrs. Park has called to inform Mrs. Kim that a heavy rainstorm has canceled their camping trip. They will be arriving home in exactly eight minutes and will require a special late-night ramen snack prepared upon their arrival (figure 5.4). The battle between the two parasitic families must therefore be postponed. They hurry back to work. Order must be restored to the messy house and Moon-gwang and her husband, finally reined in, must be tied up and gagged in their basement. During the rush to prepare the house for the returning masters, Moon-gwang is pushed down the cellar stairs, where she falls and hits her head hard against a wall, incurring a fatal injury.

Space designed in *Parasite* is tragic in multiple ways. First, the Parks' mansion, the architecture of an exhausted modernist dream, grabs viewers' attention. The utopian aim of Bauhaus, an influential German school of design and architecture founded by Walter Gropius in the early part of the twentieth century to radically alter residential space and to merge art and technology for mass production, is invoked in *Parasite* not as a left-wing agenda but as the opposite: a legacy of a bourgeois dream that has been inherited by the young Parks. The simple and minimalist design of architect Namgoong Hyunja is an elegant brand of German socialism that is now cynically and ironically reduced to effect its opposite: a symbol of class division and capitalist wealth. Second, *Jane Eyre*'s "madwoman in the attic," whose psychic and physical impairment is caused by social mistreatment and neglect, is mimicked in *Parasite*'s "madman in the basement," who is a product of the neoliberal conditions that have ruled Korea for the past twenty years, since the massive restructuring of Korean corporations in the late 1990s.[31] Third, the "basement" depicted here, which was built as a secret haven for the rich in the case of another North Korean attack, is an allegory of both past and present. If it was the dark seedy underbelly of the colony that had embodied the anxiety identified by Victorian Gothic literature, in Korea, it is the division and the Cold War that continue to motivate the dark secrets in the bunker of a Korean film. Korea still occupies the world's center stage as the last remaining relic of the Cold War—which is anachronistic by the world's standard and yet still very vivid by the local standard, for the nuclear threat imposed by North Korea is real.

After four years in captivity, and now with his wife and main caretaker deceased, Geun-se's madness can no longer be restrained. The following day, Mrs. Park wants to make up for the canceled camping trip by throwing a birthday party for her son, who still suffers from the haunting effects of seeing a ghost in the dark when he turned seven. She believes her son was simply spooked by darkness, but what he actually saw that night was not an apparition but a real person: Geun-se, who emerged from the basement "attic" and was unexpectedly discovered by the young child retrieving a nighttime snack from the kitchen refrigerator. Much like the enormous gathering to celebrate Jane Eyre's and Mr. Rochester's wedding, where the identity of the madwoman in the attic is dramatically revealed, Mrs. Park's big birthday party for her son sets the stage for Geun-se to finally emerge from the basement. He is not satisfied with merely revealing himself but seeks to take revenge, although not against the Parks, not against the loan sharks, and certainly not against the world that has turned against him. He is only interested in getting back at the Kims, who have killed his wife. To that end, he will wield two weapons: a large mineral stone he has taken from Ki-woo and the sharp German kitchen knife.

Just like Franz Kafka, who, according to Deleuze and Guattari, "killed all symbolism, all signification, no less than all designation," Bong Joon-ho transforms his cinematic objects such as naval admiral Yi Sun-shin, the large mineral stone, or the German kitchen knife into deterritorialized imageries that cannot be translated into metaphors.[32] The apparent real-life madman from the basement unleashes his havoc just as the lunchtime birthday party designed to cure the childhood trauma of the Parks' young son is reaching its finale. The party is complete with singing sopranos, grown-up men dressed as Indians with fake axes, and tables arranged in a perfect semicircle ring in the "shape of a crane spreading his wings" that resembles the Sea Battle of Hansan where Admiral Yi Sun-shin defeated the Japanese naval fleet during the Toyotomi Hideyoshi invasion of Korea in 1592 from the position of the weak. As the cake is being served, Geun-se paralyzes Ki-woo by striking his head with the mineral stone. As a pool of blood rapidly forms on the kitchen floor, Geun-se then proceeds to stab Ki-jung with the kitchen knife. Ki-woo's life will later be saved in the hospital, but Ki-jung's wound will prove fatal, just as in *The Host*, where the daughter is fatally wounded by the attacking monster. The death of the female Ki-jung and the survival of the male Ki-woo could be said to decode the conventional gender relationship into a more intricate Deleuzian one, by suggesting the survival of the body of the proletariat that only has the brain left to function, with no heart to sense love, affection, and other sentimental feelings. Now lacking the central organ of the heart, Ki-woo is de-*organ*-ized, thereby potentially becoming a "body-without-organs," which can be both a productive and unproductive locus between the human and the android in this capitalist world.

Geun-se's serial attack will be stopped by none other than Mrs. Kim, the new housekeeper, who ends up piercing his midsection with a metal-tipped barbeque fork. Mr. Park makes a frantic effort to grab the key to his Mercedes-Benz from Mr. Kim as well as his son celebrating his birthday, who has lost consciousness. In the process, however, he pinches his own nose with his thumb and index finger to avoid the stench of Geun-se's body. The nose-pinching gesture prompts Kim Ki-taek to recall the insults and humiliations he has endured from his employer and therefore triggers a violent reaction from him. His response is not premeditated, which we know because he earlier revealed that he never makes plans for the future because "any plan can end up in a failure." (By contrast, his son, Ki-woo, has a plan for everything, which indeed does fail [figure 5.5].) His family's falsehoods and fabrications now having greatly exceeded the level of simple acts of mendacity and small lies, Kim Ki-taek can put an end to the situation only through murder, which, unlike the small crimes committed by his children, cannot be falsified, exaggerated, or reversed. Grabbing the very knife that has pierced his daughter's heart, Kim Ki-taek kills the employer who had earlier provided his family with some kind of optimism.

One of the most stunning moments in cinema is delivered by Chantal Akerman's *Jeanne Dielman, 23, quai du Commerce, 1080 Bruxelles* (1975)

5.5 "You actually have a plan, don't you, son?" replies the poor father when the son proudly waves his forged diploma in *Parasite* (2019).

when Jeanne, the titular character and the dull female subject for over three hours of running time, suddenly reveals herself in the final scene as a prostitute and then attacks her client with a pair of scissors. Left intentionally unanswered is the question of the motive behind Jeanne's violent murder of a man she did not seem to know very well. The film gives no explicit lead-in, motive, or explanation. Yet this shocking finale is widely regarded as a perfect existentialist cinematic moment that executes a feminist rage against a patriarchal world that contains and regulates the tragedy of a woman. In a similar vein, *Parasite*'s shocking ending, in which Kim Ki-taek pushes a sharp German kitchen knife into the heart of Chairman Park, denies us a discernible reason for the motive behind the murder. The accusation of his stink is simply a trigger—nothing more, nothing less. However, in this moment of madness initiated by Geun-se, his parasite-in-arms, the impulse of resistance that had been restrained by the formalities and materiality of capitalism seems to have been given a temporary respite, thereby reenacting a brief moment where the Lacanian Real gets its rare exposure. Torched here is the Hegelian "history of the spirit" (Geistesgeschichte) that produces an almost-unscripted drama that might not have been necessary as far as the cause and effect of the plotline is concerned but that is required in abstracting a system of class antagonism where the blackish dirt-spoon chauffeur must cease its business partnership with the light-skinned golden-spoon chairman. Kim follows in the footsteps of his fellow dirt-spoon character, Geun-se, by earning himself an invitation to the party through the use of a sharp weapon, an act born out of the necessity of negating the negativity of the present status quo. Like Yŏng-jin in Na Un-gyu's *Arirang* made almost a century earlier (see chapter 1), who had struck the pro-Japanese collaborator with a sickle before being taken away by the authorities, Kim Ki-taek has made a declaration: he will no longer have to watch an American YouTuber folding pizza boxes in order to mimic her, submit false documents and recommendations to gain himself a lousy job, or be subject to an endless taunting by his employers as a stinker. He has a right to work, just as he has a right to be seated at an occasional feast. Yet this form of lethal, destructive, and negative energy can only be a fleeting fire that must soon be extinguished. Once order is quickly restored, capitalism and its governing false consciousness once again will prevail — with the house vacated and the hunt for the accidental rebel commenced.

Kim Ki-taek's pushing the knife hard into his employer's heart is the first moment in Korean cinematic history that valorizes the killing of a capitalist for no apparent reason other than the fact that he is a capitalist. Unlike *Veteran* (dir. Ryoo Seung-wan, 2015), which revolves around a third-generation young chaebol whose boundless selfishness, his capitalist greed, and ultimately his own penchant for violence lead to his demise, or the classic *Sympathy for Mr. Vengeance* (*Poksu nŭn na ŭi kŏt*, dir. Park Chan-wook, 2002), where the factory owner protagonist played by Song Kang-ho meets his own death after successfully concluding his mission to avenge the death of his daughter by killing the factory worker and his girlfriend who were responsible for her kidnapping, in Bong Joon-ho's film, Park's death is almost unexpected and unjustified by the narrative causality, which never blamed him for the self-incarceration of the failed cynic nor for the unfair system that has led to the growing gap between the haves and the have-nots. Chairman Kim is guilty only of complaining about the foul body odor of residents from a scum neighborhood. In this ending, a modern and a postmodern subjectivity therefore swap places. The postmodern impulse to deliver the narrative pleasure and lightness of the blockbuster thriller or action film, which in *Parasite* initially poses the question, "Will the counterfeit family get away with their forgeries and lies against the unsuspecting and naive capitalist?," is replaced with the gravity of the film's thematic center of cynical reason, which protests against the radical polarization of classes that positions the rich as masters of the house and the poor as its parasites. As much as the death of the male client in *Jeanne Dielman* served an ideological function that critiqued patriarchal society, the death of a capitalist in *Parasite* can only be justified when one steps outside the narrative structure. After killing his employer, Kim Ki-taek becomes a fugitive from the law. As the main suspect for the murder, he will now assume the place of the secret occupant of the basement cellar, a site that will remain undisclosed to anyone other than his own family members. The film's narrative concludes at the very point where the story began, when the unaffordable price of Wi-Fi data forced the Kim family to seek an unprotected router signal to communicate with the outside world and to live pathetically as data parasites. Now, at the end of the film, not only has Kim Ki-taek replaced Geun-se as the house parasite, but the problem of communicating with the outside world also remains unchanged.

As was the case with the metaphor of the train in *Snowpiercer*, which reflects Bong Joon-ho's fascination with early modern power and its lingering modernist aura, in *Parasite* it is the expiring technology of Morse code, widely used during the telegraph era, that gets flashed on screen even as hopes dim for the father's liberation from the basement cellar. The only way the self-imprisoned fugitive Kim Ki-taek can communicate with the outside world is by transmitting messages in Korean Morse code through the light controlled by the basement switch. After seeing the message of illuminated dots and dashes, Ki-woo, in his final narration, proceeds to transcribe the letter his father has just sent him. Kim Ki-taek has recounted that the entire day when the murders took place is now like a dream to him. After those murders, his only escape was to go back inside the Parks' home and take refuge in the bunker where no one could tail him. He explains that after Mrs. Park sold the house, and following a brief period of vacancy, a German family has moved in. He informs his son not to worry about him because Germans do consume food items other than beer and sausage. He is unsure how long he can go on surviving like a parasite but also does not seem to have lost hope, since he tries to send a message to his son every now and then as a way of maintaining some form of communication with the outside world. After reading his father's letter, Ki-woo begins his own narration. He intends to forgo all other dreams he has and will instead make money, lots of it, in order to buy back the mansion and allow his family—sans Ki-jung—to reunite. However, once his narration and the corresponding images end, the film finds Ki-woo waking up from this reverie of reunion. There is little chance that he, the son of a *dirt-spoon* and now a body-without-organs, will ever be able to make enough money to buy the dream mansion. Without his dream fulfilled, the father will always remain a parasite and an apparition to the rich people who inhabit the house. *Parasite* therefore ends where it began—with no evident route of escape for the parasitic being who remains trapped in the basement cellar of a wealthy mansion. Kim Ki-taek and Geun-se are both fugitives from the law and parasites to the capitalist system, albeit the one big difference separating the two: Kim Ki-taek has stabbed a capitalist to death, while Geun-se has only made a small dent on the capitalist system by running away from the collection agency.

Twice Kim Ki-taek asks his employer Chairman Park whether "he loves his wife." The second time he does so is right before Geun-se makes his dramatic entrance at the birthday party for his son, and Mr. Park responds by getting visibly upset. Rather than answering this simple question from his chauffeur, he tells Ki-taek that he should focus on his job. A simple interrogation into his personal relationship with his wife has produced an unexpected neurotic reaction from Park, perhaps because "love" in bourgeois social relations can never be pure and innocent and instead becomes the "dirty little secret" of a repugnant private theater. As Deleuze and Guattari acknowledge in their reading of D. H. Lawrence, "psychoanalysis was shutting sexuality up in a bizarre sort of box painted with bourgeois motifs."[33] The minds of both Park and his wife are heavily regimented through the tools of psychoanalysis. They must seek treatment for their child diagnosed with schizophrenia after his nocturnal encounter with the apparition from the cellar. They must perform a "little theater" of charade in order to help cure him from this "imagined" encounter. And the only form of "love" manifested by the couple is depicted through kinky sex on the sofa, where their dirty talk brings up the subject of the "stinky women's panties" found (planted there by the Kims) in the back seat of Chairman Park's car and the drugs putatively inhaled before the imagined sex party of his former chauffeur. These episodes, in addition to the secret love affair being conducted by Park's high school daughter, have translated the true meaning of love into a box shrouded in secrecy, perversions, and psychological diseases that must be kept heavily guarded against any kind of probing or inquiry from the members of the lower class. The madness in the Park family, evident in the latent paranoias they suffer from, ends up having actual consequences for them all.

With the film's bitter ending, which is much darker than all his other films, Bong Joon-ho distinguishes *Parasite* from comedies like *Extreme Job*. However sarcastic and hyperbolic director Lee Byeong-heon's attitude may be toward the latter film's happy ending where good triumphs over evil, one cannot deny that *Extreme Job* reaches a narrative closure by offering family unification and a sanguine promotion for the members of the cop squad. With an ending where the capitalist is defeated and punished, *Extreme Job* does fulfill its mission by promoting capitalism's false consciousness that prohibits commoners from recognizing the true nature of their economic condition. By contrast, *Parasite*'s ending strikes against that conservative ideology only to return the two main characters to a condition far worse than the one they started out in. With the daughter dead, capitalism thriving, and the secret cellar now serving as a perhaps lifelong confinement for the father, neoliberal capitalism in Korea will not wane. This ending is much more bitter than that of international arthouse hits such as *Like Father, Like Son* (2013) or *Shoplifters* (2018) by Japanese filmmaker Hirokazu Kore-eda, which also depict a widening class gap in a contemporary Asian capitalist society but offer the warmth of family values restoration. In Bong's latest film, Kim Ki-taek can only be an invisible parasite, whose status will change into that of an apparition should he become visible to anyone residing in the house. Although his cognitive faculties seem perfectly fine, judging by the letter he sends by Morse code to his son and narrates via voice-over, it is only a matter of time before he will become a madman in the basement—an attestation that the era of Enlightenment has labored in vain. Falsities, sarcastic humor, and mendacity are all associations of cynical reason and still a confirmation that the individual desires to move beyond the negativity of the *stinky* class and to restore a middle-class life. Work is not opposed but embraced in both films. However, at Ki-woo's sentencing hearing, he is found guilty of two counts of breaking and entering and falsification of official documents, and his rights are suspended. These are light penalties, considering that his sister has died and his father has succeeded his predecessor in the role of the parasite. However, he is now a nonproductive worm and anonymous captive in the bottomless pit of the capitalist hierarchy. The Kim family's effort to aggressively and deceptively use their resources to find and keep work has led to their becoming even more shunned and alienated. Not even a double switch or an embrace, in this cynical instance, can yield a happy ending.

6   Korean Meme-icry

Samsung and K-Pop

Getting to the Samsung Innovation Museum (SIM) located in the heart of the corporation's main campus in Suwon, a city about twenty miles south of downtown Seoul, is extremely complicated. First, unlike most other public spaces in Korea, the museum is not easily accessible by public transportation. Traveling to Samsung Electronics Digital City (SEDC)—the largest company complex in Korea, to which thirty-four thousand Samsung employees commute—requires taking an extra bus ride from the Suwon subway station, which can double the commute time from Seoul. Buses also run infrequently from the subway station to the SEDC. Public transportation access to the SEDC is deliberately complicated because the company has chosen to make its campus into a fortress. The SEDC, which occupies about 450 acres of private land, lacks an easy access path for the public. Unlike other major corporate headquarters in Korea, which are typically surrounded by great restaurants, shops, and bars, the complex where Samsung's signature Galaxy phones are designed, tested, and marketed also lacks a real downtown. This absence of nearby commerce is not only due to the campus's relative inaccessibility from the enjoining neighborhood but also results from the fact that Samsung serves free food in its cafeteria and boasts its own discount malls, a spacious workout gym, and even doctors' offices. The adjacent neighborhood commercial area has therefore become a ghost town. Instead of a bustling downtown, Samsung's Digital City is surrounded by enormous parking structures and wide, uncongested roads and highways featuring on and off ramps built mainly for Samsung commuters. Samsung employees are encouraged to either use their own private cars or hop on free Samsung commuter shuttles instead of taking public transportation.[1] Second, the Samsung Innovation Museum strictly enforces a reservation-only visitation rule and permits walk-in admissions only on two or three days of the month.

The unusual, off-putting inaccessibility of SIM is even more surprising given the fact that the museum, with its impressive three-story halls, is the only publicly accessible area in what is already a heavily guarded complex. Unlike the Googleplex campus in San Jose, California, which allows curious visitors to wander around the entire complex, the SEDC is a heavily fortified castle with airport security cameras and scanning machines at all entrance checkpoints. However, access issues pale against the Samsung museum's real problems. Despite the prominence of the word *innovation* in its name, SIM ignores the Samsung company's actual innovations over the span of its fifty-year history. Samsung's history is showcased only through its past television and video products, largely erasing the technological breakthroughs of the corporation's own employees and researchers. Although the museum celebrates key moments in technological revolutions from electricity to radio and from telecommunication devices to computer science, it displays mostly Western technological history. Not only does the museum completely neglect the history of Suwon—the city where Samsung Electronics headquarters was born, and where founder Lee Byung-chul took his first step toward building a corporate empire by setting up a small electronics factory next to his textile mills in the late 1960s—but it also largely elides Korea's own place in global technological history, omitting any reference, for example, to the place and time of the founding of Korea's first electric and telephone companies (figure 6.1).

However, this failure to celebrate its own innovations does not imply that Samsung still identifies itself with what Laikwan Pang has termed "shanzai culture": that is, the culture of "copycat" companies, built on illicit and fake practices that parasitically siphon others' creative work.[2] Samsung might have been characterized as a "shanzai" up until the early 1990s, when it dabbled with the manufacture of cheap television and VHS components, but over the past several decades it has remobilized itself as a creative IT company. Both the Samsung name, which literally means "three stars," as well as its original logo were blatantly copied from the Japanese

6.1 "Forbes Company 100" reads the sign on a corner section of a bookstore in Korea, 2019. However Samsung is the only company Koreans care to read about. Photo by Kyung Hyun Kim.

company Mitsubishi (whose name literally means "Three Diamonds"), but the Korean company is no longer associated with copycat video and television products that were modeled after Mitsubishi and Sanyo products in the 1980s and 1990s.[3] Although other Korean conglomerates—chaebols— that ruled the Korean economy during the postwar years, such as Hyundai and Daewoo, were unable to withstand the pressure for structural reforms demanded by the IMF during the financial crisis of the late 1990s, Samsung has continued to defy the odds thanks to tight family control and has grown exponentially larger over the past two decades. Throughout the 2010s, Samsung Electronics' share of Korea's total exports rose to a whopping 30 percent, the largest single company share of national exports in the modern global era. Samsung's dominance of the nation-state economy is perhaps unparalleled since the age of imperialism.[4]

Globally, Samsung is widely seen as the only company with enough muscle to force Apple into legitimate competition in the high-end smartphone market, which is now largely considered a global duopoly.[5] A patent war waged between Samsung and Apple in US courts has now concluded. In 2018 Samsung was ordered to pay $539 million in damages and subsequently settled privately with Apple, although it appears that the company's financial portfolio has suffered few repercussions from its loss.[6] In 2019 Samsung's top rank in the share of worldwide smartphone sales rose even higher, climbing from the previous year's 18.8 percent to 23 percent. It easily beat Chinese tech company Huawei's market share (18.9 percent), while Apple was a distant third at 11.8 percent. The US Department of Commerce's blacklisting of Huawei in 2019 has also helped Samsung further expand its business in IT equipment sale in the United States. For instance, Samsung's sale contracts of 5G bases with American telecommunication networks such as Verizon, Sprint, and T-Mobile are reportedly now increasing because of the restrictions placed on Chinese products due to US national security concerns.[7] Samsung even emerged largely unscathed from a 2017 political scandal in Korea, which rocked the entire nation when Samsung's heir apparent Lee Jae-yong, grandson of founder Lee Byung-chul, was incarcerated for offering bribes to Choi Sun-sil, the secret confidante of the now-impeached Korean president Park Geun-hye. Lee Jae-yong was quickly pardoned and was subsequently tasked with leading Samsung to global dominance in semiconductors (memory chips), smartphones, and electronic appliances. After a January 2021 retrial, Lee was sentenced to thirty months in prison, though he will spend only eighteen months in jail because he has already spent a year in detention. Despite his legal troubles, the likelihood of Samsung becoming either another Daewoo, which underwent bankruptcy during the 1997 IMF crisis, or even another Nokia, which fell from global prowess in recent decades, is no longer within the purview of reality.

This chapter engages in a discussion of Samsung because the historical cultivation of its corporate system in many ways mirrors both the production and consumption praxis of K-pop, which heavily reinscribes the everyday lives of consumers of digital media and social media platforms. As Korean studies scholar Ross King points out in a brief discussion of the similarity between K-pop and Samsung on their shared associations with mimicry, "Where Apple is seen as the great innovator and the world's number one company by value, pro tempore, Samsung presents as the brilliant strategist, albeit largely an imitator, and the largest technology company by sale." King proceeds to assert that Samsung's phones "were mimicked after the iconic Apple's iPhones and its television sets followed the technology borrowed from Mitsubishi sets while K-pop also similarly was built on the models of Japanese and American pop."[8] Despite Samsung's enormous progress in the twenty-first century, this skepticism shows that the company is still vulnerable, much like K-pop, to accusations that it is lacking in innovation. Samsung poses an interesting comparison with K-pop, insofar as a litany of ethical questions have likewise surrounded the legitimacy of the latter, with the latter's attempt to promote an amnesiac culture and asignifying skin tone between black and white that disengages from and devalues the historical density embodied in the music genres of rock 'n' roll, R&B, and hip-hop.[9] As I argued in chapter 1 and elsewhere, K-pop is known as a music genre, not for its innovation but for its links to the viral reproductions and affective economies that have become vital to contemporary social media. Human gestures and bonding between fans and K-pop stars at concerts and other events such as KCON; memes and hashtags inspired by the mimicries of dance choreography; and the immaculate reproduction of newly coined terms, emoticons, and internet symbols in its lyrics help K-pop rethink the meaning of music in the age of simulacrum. Samsung's ascendance likewise reinforces the idea that the meaning of innovation or creativity, which Pang has debunked as a concrete property that services "today's global capitalism," has undergone a tremendous transformation.[10] As with the US Supreme Court hearing in the Apple versus Samsung case, even the most outstanding legal minds in the United States can no longer provide clarity with regard to determining the moral standards for assessing the value of damages that a fake product can incur on an original. In my reading of K-pop through Samsung and vice versa, I consider how the meaning of creativity is embedded in these two prominent keywords that South Korea has to offer today. Samsung and K-pop are entangled in the dynamism and tension between industrialist forces and postindustrial identity, between intensive human labor and user-driven Information and Communications Technology (ICT) algorithm engines, and finally between reproductive innovation and reproductive counterfeit. This last of these conflict pairings leads to a condition fraught with what I would like to call a *meme*-etic impulse in Korea that is still caught up in both the gratifications and discontents of being a late bloomer in global capitalism.

Thanks to both right-wing president Donald Trump's tweets protesting Apple's manufacturing plants in Shenzhen, China and the reminder by left-wing pundits of the suicide-prevention nets installed at Foxconn, Apple's own technological innovation no longer carefully distances us from the precarity of the outsourcing economy and its unfair labor practices.[11] However, the geographical distance between Northern California and Shenzhen assures us that the journey of iPhone products will continue to require a global value chain involving players and actions in many countries, languages, and cultures. The global production scenario has itself traveled a long way from its industrial beginnings. As Finbarr Livesey writes, the Ford Motor factory at Dearborn, Michigan, which opened the world's first modern production lines in 1928, "did practically everything for itself. In a classic case of 'vertical integration,' metal, rubber and other raw materials were pushed in at one end of the factory complex and complete motor cars came out at the other. That is very far from how the world of manufacturing works now."[12] Samsung, however, continues to cultivate a dream that resembles the one concocted in the early twentieth century by Henry Ford. It imagines the return of a single campus where both Apple's high-tech Cupertino offices and Shenzhen's Foxconn factory can share the same space. Samsung continues to have an enormous presence in the Korean economy as an IT company as well as a manufacturing company. This dual identity, which is increasingly difficult to maintain due to the global offshoring of manufacturing jobs, nonetheless continues to shape the company's vision. Despite various forms of offshoring that led Samsung to open plants around the world, Samsung's SEDC is largely a plant where Ford's "vertical integration" is still being realized, where raw material from semiconductor production (from wafers to computer chips) is pushed in on one side and completed Galaxy phones come out the other.[13]

The promise of housing innovation engineering offices at the same location as manufacturing production assembly lines might have been the single most popular fantasy concocted by early-day capitalist moguls, but in the United States the model has largely lost its utility ever since the Iron Belt became the Rust Belt in the 1970s. The same is true of the entertainment industry. At movie studios of the past, such as RKO, Columbia Pictures, and MGM, moguls, writers, actors, and film crews once shared the same workspace—as well as the same ethnic and linguistic background. Samsung's Digital City also houses its famous semiconductor plant and is practically adjacent to a facility in Kiheung that is only about a fifteen-minute drive from Suwon and only about a half hour by helicopter from Gumi, where the largest Samsung Electronics manufacturing plant in Korea is located. Digital City features a workforce of both creative and manufacturing labor whose members generally share the same national, ethnic, and geographical origin. As the traditional film and media companies have rapidly lost power over the past two decades, the success of HBO and Netflix has accelerated the disassembly of the Fordist vertical integration model. Because of the worldwide COVID-19 pandemic of 2020–21, this decline of traditional twentieth-century moguls in theatrical business will be even more precipitous than earlier speculated. Just as Apple outsources its labor to Foxconn, Netflix and other online movie studios no longer pay directly for the production costs of their content. In this global corporate climate where the innovators are separated from "factory" labor, only Samsung, among the IT giants, continues to operate within the twentieth-century mogul fantasy of limiting the outsourcing of manufacturing labor.

There are many reasons why Samsung continues to believe in the Fordist dream. First, the Korean company is both a private and a national public company, with 10 percent of its shares controlled by the Korean government's social security fund, a percentage exceeding that of any single private ownership share in the company.[14] George W. Bush's failed attempt to partially privatize the US Social Security system in 2005 has already been realized in Korea, with Samsung reaping the greatest benefit. Fearing government retribution, Samsung must continue to sustain a healthy growth in employment numbers and is therefore prevented from adopting the capricious and irresponsible corporate praxis of massive layoffs in exchange for cheap offshore labor.[15] Samsung, in other words, must ensure that it remains committed to a healthy national economy in both the blue-collar and the white-collar sector. It cannot opt for offshoring even though hourly compensation for manufacturing workers in South Korea is, for instance, twenty times higher than that of Vietnam.[16] Second, Samsung was not necessarily a company built on technological innovation as it rose to global ascendance; instead, the major factors behind its rise were manufacturing power and perfection. Third, the mogul system, where power is still held by the heir apparent, is ingrained in Confucian principles that seek harmony through hierarchical order. Confucianism's hierarchical structure in the chaebol model aligned naturally well with Fordist vertical integration where design and production, marketing, retail distribution, and financing and after-purchase service were all handled by the same company. If the outsourcing and management of hundreds of companies linked by supply chains has made companies like Apple great, the opposite is true for Samsung, which has built its success by shielding its vertical integration structure and being accountable at every step of the process from concept to consumer product and after-sales service.

It may be true that Samsung, and particularly its Korean semiconductor production line, continues to produce ever smaller computer memory chips at an ever faster pace and maintains a lower deficiency rate than any of its competitors thanks to innovations in its wafer technology engineering

6.2 Most of the dead victims of workplace accidents in Samsung Electronics are women. Screen capture from *Factory Complex* (2014).

(which has allowed it to double its capacity to store and manufacture computer memory chips, for example).[17] Less well known, however, is the fact that Samsung has relied on cheap, non-union, and particularly female labor still available in Korea and that it has for years disregarded environmental safety laws and used union-busting labor tactics that the Korean government has deliberately overlooked. In *Factory Complex* (*Wiro kongdan*, dir. Im Heung-soon, 2014), a documentary film focused on the lives of female workers who shouldered the burden of South Korea's rise to postwar industrialization success, a scene from an anti-Samsung rally protesting the company's refusal to acknowledge its responsibility for the deaths of workers reveals photos of young workers who have died prematurely from cancer and leukemia or suffered miscarriages due to toxic chemical exposure (figure 6.2). Of the ten faces featured, nine are women.[18] One wonders whether the lengthy period of Samsung's refusal to negotiate with the families of its deceased and injured workers would have been possible if the gender imbalance of the victims was tilted the other way. In other words, would Samsung and the previous conservative Korean government have been so complicit in the cover-up of these work-related illnesses and deaths if more of the young deceased had been male rather than female? Only after Moon Jae-in, the liberal president, was inaugurated in 2017 did Samsung offer a public apology and agree to accept the terms of compensation for its former factory workers.[19] Most of the 320 employees at Samsung who contracted lethal diseases were female, because electronics companies, unlike automobile, steel, and shipbuilding industries, have traditionally relied on a female workforce.

In explaining how the Samsung company, which began as a trader and distributor of products such as vegetables and dried seafood in the southeastern city of Daegu, came to build its empire over the course of three generations, Jaeyong Song and Kyungmook Lee, two business school professors at Korean universities, focus on Samsung's "innovative" management style.[20] Company chair Lee Kun-hee, who succeeded his father, Lee Byong-chul, in the late 1980s, announced his new idea for management (*sin kyŏngyŏng*) with the following words: "The old Samsung came to an end in 1987. . . . Now is a time to do better or die. Our products are still far from catching up with those from advanced countries. We must get rid of a second-place mindset. If we are not the world's number one, we will not survive."[21] The late 1980s and early 1990s marked the pivotal period when Samsung made its push to discard its *shanzai* image and seek a first-place ranking for every product it manufactured. As a curious teenager, Lee Kun-hee had been a self-taught mechanic with a penchant for breaking open and disassembling electronics products.[22] The young magnate reportedly used his own skill to open the cases of his competitor's products, such as Toshiba VHS recorders, and compare them to Samsung's in order to humiliate Samsung engineers and executives during meetings. The strategy of embarrassing his own employees by pointing out the inferior features of the company's own products seemed to have worked. Although Lee was a competent self-taught engineer who loved to tinker with electronics and even cars, he was never a truly innovative engineer like Apple's Steve Jobs, Sony's Akio Morita, or Facebook's Mark Zuckerberg, whose technological innovations in the field of consumer electronics and software engineering led to the creation of landmark products and services that would generate many billions of dollars of profits. Although under Lee Kun-hee's leadership Samsung did increase its budget on R&D, especially for memory chips, there were other factors to its success that go beyond the official rationale insisted upon by Song and Lee, who wrote their book on a grant funded by Samsung. Chaebol values rooted in Confucianism continued, of course, to play a large role—ironically, in sustaining the speed and efficiency for rapid decision-making processes more typical of a start-up venture than a company run in the old boardroom and stockholder management style. And then there were also the anachronistic union-busting strategies that worked in Samsung's favor well into the twenty-first century. Samsung, unlike Apple, did not need a Chinese offshore manufacturing company to justify banning union activities or deny corporate responsibility for injuries and deaths resulting from its failure to maintain workplace safety. Instead, the Korean government protected its interests by looking the other way for almost half a century. Because Samsung never permitted unionization in any of its subsidiaries, the company has never lost a single day of work due to labor disputes, which is particularly surprising insofar as most other major industrial manufacturing plants in Korea since the late 1980s have experienced significant social upheaval due to the actions of militant labor unions. Lee Kun-hee closely duplicated the principles of his father, who often declared, "I will have earth cover my eyes before a union is permitted at Samsung."[23] It has taken Samsung more than thirty years, after Lee Byung-chul's death in 1987, to recognize labor unions in its workplace after the public apology from Samsung's current leader, Lee Jae-yong, who admitted past violent and illegal union-busting strategies widely adopted by its managers.[24]

APPLE VERSUS SAMSUNG IN THE US SUPREME COURT

Of all the legal cases fought in the United States over the past twenty years, perhaps the one most intensely monitored by the Korean media was the case that featured the two giant tech companies Apple and Samsung.[25] The dispute dragged on for years in a prolonged series of court hearings, up and down the US District Court (Northern District of California), the US Court of Appeals for the Federal Court, and finally the US Supreme Court. Although the Supreme Court agreed to one hearing in 2016, it refused to hear a second appeal from Samsung in 2018 and the case was eventually settled out of court. While the exact amount that Samsung ended up paying Apple remains unknown, the official verdict in the dispute was the one delivered by the US District Court, which ordered Samsung to pay Apple $539 million in damages. By paying Apple, Samsung averted its worst nightmare, the injunction of sales against its Android phones, while Apple was able to reestablish its close partnership with Samsung, which continues to play a double role in Cupertino as both competitor and supplier of iPhone's memory chips.

One of the legal facts that remained mostly veiled in the heavy Korean media coverage of the US court hearings was the fact that Samsung was not challenging Apple on the grounds of design plagiarism. Samsung had already acknowledged that several of its Galaxy phones had violated the patent protection rights of the iPhone's rectangular design with its rounded corners, its app icon layout, and its home button on the bottom. Instead, Samsung's lawyers insisted that the district court ruling had been "overinclusive." The point of legal contention was not whether Samsung should be exculpated from Apple's claim of infringement on copyrighted design but exactly how much it should pay for the damages incurred by that infringement.

Samsung's lawyers argued that even though Samsung may have copied the iPhone's design, it did not consequently owe Apple the entirety of the profits generated from the total sales of its Galaxy phones. In considering this question, the Supreme Court justices were therefore forced to wrestle over the broader question of whether the value of a product's ornamental design can be separately quantified from its entire value. Perplexity over this question echoed through the chamber throughout the hearing.

During the proceedings, which took place on October 11, 2016, Justice Sonia Sotomayor asked, "But how do we announce the right test for that? Because the phone could be seen by a public—a purchasing consumer as being just that rounded edge, slim outer shell. That might be what drives the sale. I don't know." Her comment came in response to the Samsung lawyer's argument that a further test was required to clarify the value of "an article of manufacture" and thereby better calculate a precise (and much smaller) profit than the one determined when Apple was awarded its judgment in the lower court. Sotomayor's exasperated "I don't know" summarized the confusion of the other seven justices as well—Antonin Scalia had died in February 2016 and would not be replaced until 2017, leaving the Supreme Court one justice short at the time—and their perplexity ultimately led to the verdict of "no opinion" and handed Samsung its momentary reprieve.[26] Of course, common sense tells us that multiple factors drive the commercial success of any product—be it an electronics device or an iconic car such as a Volkswagen Beetle, wherein monumental design can only be just one of those factors. The Supreme Court sent the case back to the Northern California District Court to give the jury another opportunity to review Samsung's claim as to whether a particular iconic design can be uniquely defined as an "article of manufacture" and whether the "quantum of damages, quantum of profits in this case (Samsung's infringement of Apple's design patent)" can be determined from that single "article."[27]

The legal battle between Samsung and Apple dragged on in the US courts for almost a decade partly because the quantum of value of design innovation has become impossible to determine for even the greatest of legal minds. Formerly clear, swift, and routine verdicts against criminals who forge counterfeit products against innovative copyright holders have been replaced with courtroom trials filled with questions that sound like knives cutting through thick smoke. Pang argues that ideas, or "creative labor," are crucial to the understanding of the new economy and must be considered in addition to the "tangible commodity" that Karl Marx identified as the necessary core of capitalist production along with raw material and industrial labor. "Intellectual property" derived from creative innovation and design therefore designates "creativity" as a necessary new element that must be distinguished from the triad of "raw material," "manufacturing labor," and "tangible commodity" in the classic capitalist economy.[28] Samsung's concession that it had copied an American company's iconic product was simply not sufficient to generate a punitive measure of injunction. The Korean company's insistence that the damage penalty be reduced because consumers purchase smartphones based not only on design but also on other factors like cost, durability, and utility garnered sympathy from the Supreme Court justices.

The ambiguity of distinction between original and counterfeit is emblematic of the broader flows and tensions in the global economic and cultural structures in which Korean industrial and entertainment products have claimed a place as ironic inflections of both hegemony and mimicry. Samsung, despite putatively paying Apple hundreds of millions of dollars for copyright infringement, will still continue to exercise its hegemonic status as a global tech industry leader. Its products are marked by a legitimacy that muscled its way through charges of piracy and counterfeiting. Justice Samuel Alito seemed to agree with Samsung when he stated, "I can't get over the thought that nobody buys a car, even a Beetle, just because they like the way it looks. What if it, you know, costs, I think $1,800 when it was first sold in the United States? What if it cost $18,000? What if it got 2 miles per gallon? What if it broke down every 50 miles?" Samsung was bolstered by a reputation that its Galaxy phones do not break down after fifty calls or last only a couple of minutes on a full charge.[29] The company's phones, like its other products such as home appliances, could not be legitimately described as mere counterfeits, despite the District Court ruling of limited design imitation, insofar as countless hours of dedicated employee labor at Samsung had gone into perfecting globally successful products that were outselling any other company in the world. Samsung's Galaxy phones, not unlike many K-pop songs and idol groups, had achieved a hegemonic stature that far exceeded their mimetic attributes. Much like the fandom of K-pop is moved by the dedicated passion and hard work of K-pop performers who strive to achieve perfection through their choreography, Samsung cultivates its loyal consumer base by exuding a brand image of reliability rather than originality and innovation.

I opened this book with a reflection on the fictional script of a post–World War III dystopia where current hegemonic relations between the United States and South Korea become totally inverted. The imagined scenario in question was a historically subversive one, given that the political, economic, and cultural power imbalance between the United States and South Korea was entirely one-sided during the decades after the Korean War. Today, however, the relationship between the two countries has become more convoluted, not only because BTS can dominate American charts and *Parasite* can win an Oscar for the Best Picture in 2020 but also because the complexity of distinction between original and copy can make a mimicked product also a hegemonic one, as Samsung's courtroom dispute with Apple demonstrates. South Korea's response to COVID-19 has also demonstrated that the country is able to become a "fast follower" at adapting new technologies and products in electronics and biomedical technology. Although the polymerase chain reaction is a method in molecular biology that was invented in the United States, as noted by almost every major global news media outlet, it was Korean scientists who promptly adapted it for the development of the world's leading DNA analysis test kits after the pandemic broke out in 2020, and Korea subsequently led nearly every nation in muting the deadly virus spread, within weeks of the outbreak.

South Korea is the perfect context for demonstrating how the relationship between mimicry and hegemony has been complicated. Apple's IT workers engaged in producing "intellectual property" are literally worlds apart from the actual manufacturers of their "tangible commodities." Apple's extravagant offices in Cupertino that provide "creative labor" must be shielded from or even blinded to the grim realities of Shenzhen's Foxconn factories, where Chinese workers making iPhones still get paid only $3.15 per hour and suicide nets must be installed to protect the factories from their workers' self-destructive impulses.[30] This radical divide between haves and have-nots (even among the employed) is in a way reflective of the symbolism used in recent thriller hit films such as Jordan Peele's *Us* and Bong Joon-ho's *Parasite*, where poor families mirror wealthy families as either ghosts or parasites living behind closed doors. However, in a country like South Korea, where bold late capitalist maneuvers have been unable to shrink the manufacturing sector or effectively segregate the urban poor from the extremely wealthy, the effort to neatly divide the two classes, manufacturing labor and creative labor, has been impossible.[31] Not only is the research and development center for Galaxy phones located in the same campus as the Samsung corporation's semiconductor production plants, but protests—for instance, against the premature deaths of young female workers—have been everyday occurrences in front of Samsung's executive office buildings throughout the 2010s. The protest signs wielded by the manufacturing class do not have to be memed, tweeted, or translated in order to reach the creative class; they are right there, sharing the same geographical and linguistic space.

MEME-IFICATION OF K-POP VIDEOS

Samsung is extremely visible virtually everywhere in Korea. Its boring blue logo appears not only in the palms of people's hands holding their electronic devices but also on electronic appliances such as air conditioners, washers and dryers, elevators, cars, apartment buildings, designer apparel, medical research centers, credit cards, insurance company advertisements, amusement parks, and even toilet bowls and door-locking systems.[32] Samsung's ubiquity in Korea is so overwhelming that it almost evokes a scene from the apocalyptic movie *Demolition Man*, starring Sylvester Stallone, set in the year 2032 when every restaurant is literally a Taco Bell. Samsung's seeming omnipresence is partly due to the fact that the company still believes in the physical world—appliances, apartment buildings, doors, and bathrooms—for which the perfection of manufacturing skills is still required, as opposed to, for instance, a world such as Google's, which is based on internet search and online advertisement.[33] Samsung still remains closer to Fordist principles than to the high-tech strategies that propelled Jobs and Zuckerberg to fame. Google, Apple, and Facebook do not have to flaunt their company logos in the physical world, or on "tangible commodities," in order to sustain their money-raking universe built around interconnectivities between humans and cyberspace. Although Samsung obviously services a conceptual model and content that is essential in the internet world, it still needs to be present in the real, physical spaces of human interaction. In other words, rather than fully or exclusively participating in the order of simulacra and pleasure in order to drive the company's vision, Samsung's world is still realized through perfecting the processing and efficient use of raw materials for computerized products.

Four decades have elapsed since Baudrillard pronounced that Disneyland's miniaturized, frozen, childlike world stood as the perfect emblem of "all the entangled orders of simulacra."[34] If the era of internet, digital technology, and social media expedited this process of Disneyfication that irreversibly shifted the world from the real to the hyperreal where memes, hashtags, and other forms of simulacra now rule the day, Samsung, despite its prowess in the IT industry, is an anomaly sandwiched between the real and the hyperreal, pleasure and work, and national and postnational. Just as the status of South Korea itself seems permanently ensconced between the developing nations and the elite leading ones, between high-tech industry and manufacturing, and finally between a Cold War order and a post–Cold War one, Samsung likewise finds itself ambiguously situated vis-à-vis the orbit of the hyperreal simulacra that fuel today's imagination. If Sony and Apple, Samsung's main competitors in the global electronics and tech industry, have built their dream universe by withdrawing from the manufacturing sector and instead finding their own stakes of "Disneyfication" by purchasing and expanding their entertainment operations through music, movies, game content and consoles, and streaming, Samsung's base continues to be, in large part, in the manufacturing and updating of twentieth-century electronic and telecommunication technologies.[35]

A 2012 *New York Times* article remarks on Samsung's expedient corporate decision-making processes that have given it an advantage in a rapidly moving tech world. The article declares that Samsung's "strategy has been to build something similar to another company's product but make it better, faster, and at lower cost." In effect, this strategy *is* the innovation.[36] On the other hand, as Michael Breen observes, there are also other factors behind Samsung's success. Breen, who works as a foreign journalist in Seoul, Korea, and was sued by Samsung in 2009 for publishing a newspaper column that ridiculed the corporation's practice of gift giving to prosecutors and the political establishment, points out that "the *chaebol* problem refers in business to the inequalities and bullying that occurs everywhere in a society that . . . cannot stop viewing people hierarchically and therefore as fair game for abuse. Thus a large company in Korea means something different from a company in an egalitarian place like, say, Australia. Status allows for different rules."[37] Perhaps it was the South Korean government's preferential treatment of Samsung—one of the few original chaebols that has remained standing today—that enabled it to blow past its competitors in virtually every field it entered; perhaps, as the *New York Times* and other pro-Samsung pundits declare, it was the company's small family-style ruling structure that contributed to its success, by allowing it to ignore the encumbrances of boardroom- and shareholder-oriented decision-making processes otherwise better suited to the fast-moving and efficient venture capital–driven IT industry; or perhaps it was the company's union-bashing policies, which came to an end only in late 2019, that allowed Samsung to keep manufacturing costs down and thereby contributed to its global success.[38]

Much less transparent are the ways in which South Korea's long-standing pro-American military, political, and economic alliances have given Samsung a real advantage even in the tech market. In explaining the first deal between Samsung Electronics and a US cell-phone carrier, Elizabeth Woyke, one of the top industry experts reporting today on the tech industry, writes, "Korea was one of the few countries outside the United States that decided to deploy CDMA for its 2G networks . . . and in 1996 this lucky coincidence led Sprint to offer Samsung a $600 million contract to provide cellphones for its CDMA network."[39] But this was no "lucky coincidence." Almost every economic and technological decision made by South Korea following the Korean War had to suit the American way. Just as Korea's military and economic alliance with the United States inevitably led Korean networks to choose the National Television System Committee (NTSC) color-encoding system over the Phase Alternating Line (PAL) system during the analog television era, although more countries had favored PAL as the clearly more advanced system, Korea's decision to choose the Code Division Multiple Access (CDMA) network system of the United States over the Global System for Mobiles (GSM) adopted in the European Union was not a coincidence but a politically motivated choice with deep roots in the industrial and political history of the Republic of Korea. Even as Europe conformed to the GSM mobile standard throughout the 2G and 3G era and Japan remained obsessed with its i-mode mobile operating system, Korea became "the first country to commercialize the CDMA technology."[40] Although CDMA technology was licensed from Qualcomm and touch screen technology was first invented by Apple (both American companies), once they were licensed to Korean companies like LG and Samsung, the doors were open for hegemonic mimicry to unfurl. Not unlike the first generation of Korean rock musicians, who, as noted in chapter 1, were both lucky and unlucky to be first associated with American rock music right around the time of the Korean War, Samsung engineers knew how to manipulate available technology in order to become industry leaders, not by innovation but by creative mimicry. By 2000, South Korea, brimming with new youthful energy in both globalization and democratization, was a "great test-bed" for mobile companies like Samsung, which would soon bury Motorola, Nokia, and Eriksson. These early leaders simply could not compete with the ironic alliance Apple and Samsung had built under the rubric of the CDMA family of standards in smartphone network service.

Of course, much as an act of mimicry alone cannot guarantee viral popularity for a YouTube music video, Korea's decision to network its smartphones exclusively through CDMA could not alone generate success for Samsung in the US market. Just as K-pop acts miraculously forsook individuality in order to promote group identity in the search for global success; or in the same way that the construction and acceptance of large, nondescript apartment buildings helped Koreans develop the country's rapid and urgent urbanization during the desperate postwar years, Samsung was able to build a viable bridge between its anachronistic, imperial chaebol system and its global tech industry aspirations.[41] It was a strange match: a total convergence between a neo-Confucian management system and the Internet of Things. Samsung's strategy to maintain a balance between its labor-intensive production and the world of internet connectivity without becoming too involved in innovative internet technologies ended up working. The strategy in question would then be mirrored in the K-pop industry, which has built its success by legitimating youth labor exploitation and internet tools to simulate the best in global pop without necessarily innovating the genre itself. Unlike players in professional sports leagues or workers in mature industrial economies, K-pop has no unions to represent the human rights and well-being of its vast numbers of trainees, who sacrifice their normal lives in order to pursue dreams in entertainment. K-pop locks in the best human entertainment workers by nabbing them at a young age and retaining them in its neo-Confucian mogul-run system, using the best available technological means — plugged into various bot and troll processes — to spread viral video. Suk-Young Kim points out that K-pop's success was established through liveness and describes it as a medium that "blurs the concepts of liveness, community, and commodity and treats them as interchangeable, rather than antithetical."[42]

Prioritizing liveness in the age of simulacrum was possible in K-pop because of its emphasis on perfectly synchronized human choreography founded on the premium of entertainment labor. Performers' dedication to their fans and their docility in accepting orders from the moguls comprised this liveness on stage and beyond.[43] Across many media platforms, Kim argues, whether they be live stages, TV stations, or KCON conventions where live high-five and meet-and-greet sessions between fans and stars take place, it is affective labor that undergirds the relationship between K-pop stars and their fans.[44] The KCON is a meeting event that feeds off energy, like a Disneyland for the young consumers and lovers of hallyu. Just as the Disneyland smartphone app is now one of the tools visitors must download in order to enhance their experience in the amusement park — for seamlessly navigating and updating daily schedules around pleasure rides and meet-and-greet sessions with animation characters — social media technologies can surely help the facilitation and commercialization of K-pop and its merchandise. However, just as a visitor must physically be at Disneyland in order to fully experience the pleasure of the amusement park, it is the intense physical public activities of K-pop stars that make possible both the physical and online meetings that maximize the screen simulation and simulacra of the K-pop experience. Many top K-pop acts perform at KCON each year, where fans are allowed to interact not only with images, music, and merchandise but also with the physical bodies of the performers, which actually move beyond the screen. K-pop does not conceal its stars in the simulated space of virtual reality but requires them to make themselves readily available to fans by physically attending fan meetings, conventions, and award shows programmed throughout the year. K-pop, not unlike Samsung with its sphere of operation somewhere between the industrial manufacturing world and the high-tech IT industry, therefore defies the cyberscape logic of pop music today by prioritizing the necessity of live interaction between artists and fans.

I concur with Suk-Young Kim's view that the "corporeal and affective dimensions of labor in tandem with how technology augments the 'intimate' nature of such labor" underscores the complex layers of convergence between stars and fans, and between industry and consumers in K-pop.[45] Although Kim suggests that labor in K-pop is both physical and interactive, her insight does not fully account for the fulfillment of real physical labor that legitimates the K-pop aesthetic that sets the global standards of pop culture today. Indeed, labor in K-pop is largely driven by the impulse of the "meme-etic." Julie Choi has analyzed Psy's "Gangnam Style" using several critical tropes of modernity theory, including Siegfried Kracauer's notion of "mass ornament." Central to this notion are the "Tiller Girls" dance synchronizations, which Kracauer equated with the regulation of corporeal movements on industrial assembly lines. The synchronized choreographies performed by boy and girl K-pop groups also correspond to the human desire to organically connect with what is now a postmodern cyberspace condition dominated by emojis and internet-inspired exclamatory expressions.[46] These young Asian bodies that execute "cute" body movements in K-pop performances are perfect human-based ideograms of internet-era memes and other popular forms of text messages that prevail in today's communication forms. So just as the "Tiller Girls" sought a convergence between entertainment and factory work in the previous era, the corporeal synchronicity achieved in K-pop dance may be the best form of mimicry of human expressions in today's internet culture dominated by emojis, memes, and hashtags (see figure 6.3).[47]

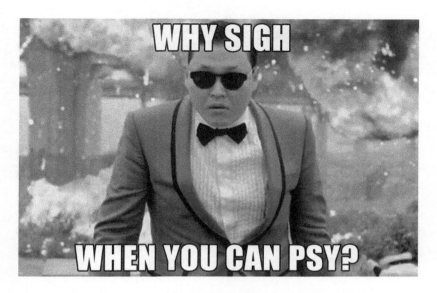

6.3 Just one of the viral memes generated from Psy's "Gangnam Style" (2012).

If the Beatles during the early 1960s dominated the charts with songs inspired by epistolary puppy love, such as "P.S. I Love You" and "From Me to You," and if another idol group, Blondie, produced hits during the late 1970s and early 1980s, such as "Hanging on the Telephone" and "Call Me," that featured direct references to telephones precisely at a moment when teenagers were beginning to have access to their own phones, it is not surprising that many K-pop songs with global teen appeal are inspired by emoticons, instantly manipulated selfies, and new internet slang that is part of a lingua-scape of the era of message apps such as WeChat and KakaoTalk. TWICE's "TT" (an emoticon that suggests falling tears), Apink's "Eung Eung %%" (an emoticon/visual pun on the Korean hangul 응 "Eung," meaning "okay yes"), BIGBANG's "Zutter" (Dope), Blackpink's "Don't Know What to Do," and 2NE1's "Maenbung" (MTBD; Mental breakdown) literally and physically illustrate popular internet-generated emoticons or newly coined internet terms by *in*-corporating them through the motions and alignments of their bodies. All four female members of Blackpink, for instance, make wide shoulder shrugs in order to replicate the widely used emoticon that signifies "Don't Know What to Do"; several members of TWICE use their thumbs and index fingers to form the shape of the double *T*s, dragging down the letters from their eye level in order to re-create the universally accepted text sign of weeping ("TT"); and the members of another girl group, Apink, visually re-create the two circles

6.4 TWICE performing the TT dance, 2018.

and divider slash within the symbol % in their choreography to form the human reinscription that makes up the special characters in "Eung Eung %%." These and other examples are abundant in K-pop (figures 6.4 and 6.5).

The origin of the use of human hand movements to re-create alphabet letters or symbols in popular songs predates K-pop, of course. Constant bending and outstretching of the arms is vital in forming the four letters of the alphabet in a Village People song that became a hit during the early 1980s disco era. For several decades, American cheerleaders have also been enacting group choreograph movements to depict the letters of the teams they represent. However, just as North Korean mass game performers have elevated such spectacles to another level, with dramatic performances where human bodies and ideograms of political chants and slogans converge, South Korean K-pop performances have perfected the mimicry of internet chatroom codes into a form of what I am calling *meme-icry*. The formation of the human-embodied letters *YMCA* was perhaps only a primitive precursor to a broader internet communication mode. Now, more sophisticated and complicated memes that propose asignifying and amusing internet communication forms go viral every day through enactments of mimicry at various levels of convergence between images, human movements, and words. What K-pop choreography aims at is the full embrace of contemporary meme-generated culture that becomes both the very source and the target of meme-icry by reinscribing and restoring the human in the age of computer graphics and social media algorithms. K-pop girls and boys therefore fulfill the mission of bodily transcribing smartphone-era quick-type codes while also providing

6.5 A young Korean schoolgirl imitating the same TWICE dance, 2018.
Photo by Kyung Hyun Kim.

the labor-intensive art form that best reinterprets computer-generated fonts and exclamation points. Not unlike Samsung, which provides a technology halfway between IT-droid culture of the twenty-first century and human manufacturing of the twentieth century, K-pop's affective labor draws from the intensity that recaptures human activity in the hopes of connecting it back to computer symbols and expressions through music and dance. In order to mimic or reanthropomorphize what are clearly simulacra of the smartphone era, tens of thousands of Korean youth are recruited to serve as dedicated, immaculate, and yet, ironically, instantly disposable idols, much like the poor aspiring musical talents of the war-ridden peninsula were once required to don revealing American dresses and smiles in order to spread the Pax Americana in Korea and beyond.[48]

LETHAL WORKPLACE

Every now and then, Korean studies scholars who have written on the subject of Korean popular culture, myself included, receive email requests from journalists from major news networks around the world asking for commentary on the suicides that are claiming the lives of Korean celebrities in the world of K-pop. Sulli, formerly of the girl group f(x), was a recent victim, choosing to end her life at the age of twenty-five in 2019. A couple of months earlier, Goo Hara, another female star, of the K-pop group Kara, had ended her life at twenty-eight.[49] Their lives and deaths, equally sensational, have drawn the attention of the foreign media, since there is a growing concern that behind the glitter of the K-pop industry, darkness and depression loom. Foreign journalists constantly ask: How is it possible that these young stars, who competed all their lives while developing a mentality tough enough to survive cutthroat auditions and achieve stardom, have so easily fallen prey to self-destruction? How could these stage icons, who preach self-love to their fans, have chosen a path that would eventually lead them to take their own lives? Sulli's outspokenness on feminist topics, such as the pro-choice and "free the nipple" movements, may have provoked many bloggers and fans of K-pop to target her. In a CNN article that reported on the rising suicide rate among K-pop stars, CedarBough Saeji, an expert on Korean culture, is quoted as saying that Sulli "was brave. . . . The fact that [she] repeatedly did things that misogynists didn't like, and refused to apologize, is how she really stood out."[50]

While the attacks of online misogynist trolls may have played a significant role in Sulli's suicide, cyberattacks alone cannot fully explain the suicidal wave among K-pop stars, insofar as some of the victims, male or female, were never heavy social media users or simply were not targeted by internet haters. What I am particularly interested in is the precarious line of work of K-pop idols, with careers—just like others in global pop music production and sports—that peak early before the individual is spit out of a system that deems them disposable after a short period of time. K-pop stars' career spans are even shorter than those of their peers in other sports and entertainment industries, averaging only three or four years of primetime even for those who make it as stars.[51] Furthermore, K-pop idols' high reliance on the immaculate movements of their bodies requires them to cultivate their skills as both singers and athletic dancers. Once they are forced to retire early, after long years of abuse—under a neo-Confucian ordinance that requires them to subjugate themselves to management company moguls and submit themselves to a public scrutiny that forces them to constantly live lives of apologies and self-abasement—they are likely to fall into a deep abyss of depression. In "Mourning and Melancholia," Sigmund Freud suggests that the "so interesting—and so dangerous" phenomenon of melancholia, the obsessive feeling of not being able to let go of a lost object, can be part of the solution to solve the puzzle of a suicidal tendency.[52] As is widely known, most K-pop stars begin their training in management company boot camps. They start as early as their preteen years in order to become successful as dancers and singers. However, just as an American football star's career can often be cut short by a head injury or a concussion, the lives of K-pop stars, particularly of females, which require around-the-clock schedules, constant social media engagements with fans, and the need to maintain ridiculously waif-like figures and youthful looks while performing with athletic prowess as powerful dancers, usually come crashing to a halt in their mid to late twenties. Both Sulli and Goo Hara had reached this age and were seeking careers beyond the K-pop performance world when they claimed their own lives. Their respective groups, f(x) and Kara, had already disbanded after being usurped in the popularity charts by younger groups such as Red Velvet and AOA.

The K-pop industry has cultivated a collective psychological syndrome of overvaluing what Freud called object-cathexis. The obsession of object-cathexis, which drains one's emotional energy, is known to lead to symptoms of melancholia. The fear and anxiety of K-pop stars stems, of course, from the fact that one's slim late teenage and early twenties superbody cannot be sustained forever. Celebrities in the United States frequently fall prey to drug overdose when they are unable to cope with the frivolity of idol life or the post-idol melancholia induced by an obsessive relation to the effusive object of one's own youth. In Korea, because cases of drug and other substance abuse are rare, not to mention the fact that professional therapeutic treatment is inadequate to cope with such psychological distress, depression and melancholia inevitably become viral forms of a lethal energy that comes to threaten one's own life. Partly because of the short cycle of a K-pop idol career, the number of retired idol-cum-television personalities is excessive, and these individuals are disposable in the scheme of Foucauldian biopolitics. Just as the National Football League (NFL), an enormous money-making business in the United States for the media and for team owners, for decades systematically misclassified the medical effects of chronic traumatic encephalopathy (CTE) caused by head injuries even as many young (often black) athletes fell into chronic depression and/or fell victim to suicide, the K-pop industry and its profit-churning mechanism continue to force young children to leave regular schools and remain for years in the intensely competitive environment of talent boot camps.[53] The K-pop industry, which authorizes and justifies countless hours of institutional training for young children, working in tandem with government policies that seek to elevate the nation's global soft-power image, is an institution that could not be duplicated in other parts of the developed world, for its agents would likely be charged with child abuse. As such, K-pop is a highly unethical industry fueled by the innocent dreams of young children and the aspirations of their parents to escape mediocrity, both of which are freely purchased by entertainment moguls for ruthless profit. The immaculate meme-icry performances have bathed K-pop in an international spotlight, but the industry continues to dispose of one young talent after another in a process that fits with what Mbembe has characterized as the necropolitics of "living dead."[54]

Such a disregard for the precarity of life is what remains as the central account in the documentary film *Factory Complex*, which depicts the lethal work that female Korean factory workers have endured throughout past decades of industrialization. In telling the veiled story behind the glory of the Miracle of the River Han, in which Samsung also played a pivotal role, director Im Heung-soon focuses on two generations of female workers in Korea who endured the hazardous and sometimes deadly workplaces at the heart of the Korean export-driven economy. "I don't know if undernourishment at the time has led to tuberculosis, or if it was the poor working conditions, but there were many girls at the factory who contracted it," recalls Kim Yeongmi, who worked at Hyosung Textiles from 1983 until she was fired in 1985 for attempting to form a labor union. "You had to quit work if you came down with the disease." Im's documentary also features interviews with three other young women who contracted cancer while working at Samsung Electronics plants. "The production lines where we worked were very clean," explains Park Minsuk, who was employed at one of these plants from 1991 until she had to quit in 1998 after a breast cancer diagnosis; "the problem was the Isopropyl alcohol we used to clean the lines." Lee Seongok, who worked from 1995 until she became pregnant, echoes the same concern with working conditions: "Working on semiconductors was known to be harmful for pregnant women." Fearing the negative impact of toxic chemicals on her pregnancy, she was forced to quit her job in 2002. Despite her efforts to protect herself, however, she was later diagnosed with thyroid cancer. If the wages of nonunion female workers were low, the costs of their death were even lower. Even after Samsung admitted to a practice of negligence with regard to its workers' illnesses and deaths and to issuing threats against the families of deceased workers, the company agreed to pay affected employees the measly sum of KRW 150 million (about US$130,000) for illnesses including leukemia and other forms of cancer and even for cancers found in the children of some of the workers.[55] Park Minsuk leaves viewers with the following comment: "It's just weird. Samsung feels like a lover who has left you, but he's still someone you simply cannot hate because of this fondness that lingers." Her words are surprisingly warm considering that they come from a woman who survived a terrible disease she contracted while working at Samsung. Although Sulli, Goo Hara, and other K-pop victims of suicide, depression, and drug addiction did not leave us with words comparing their line of work to a loving boyfriend who abandoned them, if they were given the chance, I am confident they would have similar words of affection for K-pop, even though it ended up destroying their lives with a stressful working environment of hard training bordering on early child abuse, cut-throat competition during one's formative years, and long working hours where management leaves no room for privacy. The freedom of K-pop stars to choose who to date, befriend, and live with are tightly regulated and enforced for years. Former Samsung employee and cancer survivor Park makes this final comment in Im's documentary: "I wish there are no more sick workers there [at Samsung]." The same hope can only be dreamed of for the idols and artists of a K-pop industry that has made Korea relevant in the global entertainment world today.

7 Reading *Muhan Dojeon* through the *Madanggŭk*

HAN, HŬNG, AND SSAEMT'ONG

The Korean word *mat* (taste) has always been closely aligned to its approximate homonym, *mŏt* (beauty, elegance, refinement), which defines the aesthetic experience of a Korean.[1] Both words, *mat* and *mŏt*, unlike many other terms that are central to the Korean aesthetic, such as *han* (恨, resentment) and *hŭng* (興, joy), are not Chinese-derived words. Even in English, the word *taste* has a double meaning that stands for the oral sensation as well as the ability of a person to differentiate aesthetics. In Korea, similarly, a person who has a good sense of mat (oral sensibility) is better able to judge mŏt (beauty). This mŏt, which first appeared in nineteenth-century p'ansori and then became a fashionable term during the latter part of the twentieth century, is an important criterion that overrides the Korean aesthetic experience that previously focused on han and hŭng.[2] Of course, it was han, because of the pains and trauma Korea had experienced as a nation during the twentieth century, that emerged as the best-known theme among the minjok-ian aesthetic discourses. In the past century, director Im Kwon-taek, quite possibly the last figure of Korean national cinema, cinematically expressed Korea's national pathos of han. As Chungmoo Choi explains, both the South Korean government's official cultural nationalism during the Park Chung-hee era and Im Kwon-taek's best-known film, *Sopyonje*, about an itinerant p'ansori musician who chooses to blind his own daughter to advance his perfection of art, equally share both "cinematic *han*."[3] As much as han was a collective emblem that reminded Koreans that there is a common and unifying reference to the shared tragic past, hǔng is a communal concept of joy that is deeply felt among Koreans. As Suk-Young Kim notes, hǔng may have been born well before the modernization of Korea took place, but the "playful spirit of the community [of hǔng] still persists—over the pixel screens as well as face-to-face in a live concert—to explain one significant aspect of K-pop's liveness."[4] Kim may not have been too far off when she made her attempt to link K-pop, the ultimate art form of the postmodern era, to hǔng, with which Koreans came to pair during the premodern era through the communal activities of harvest cele-brations, shamanistic rituals, and peasant theater. Chief among them were of course p'ansori and mask dance theater, which were largely unscripted and relied heavily on the communal celebration of the spirits rather than narrative arcs featuring individual identities and heroes.

I essentially agree with these two Korean American scholars, who have argued that the Korean communal experience of han and hǔng may have been exploited as the basis for the Korean popular culture that today in-cludes K-cinema, K-pop, and Korean variety shows, content that almost rivals the individualized romantic-genius artist model that has dominated Western-style pop music, drama, and comedy.[5] As I have argued in earlier chapters, all the successes abroad thus far found by K-pop and Korean com-edy programs are driven not by the almost mythological cult of individual genius common to most artistic and cultural production originating in the West but by Korean idol groups and entourage comedy troupes in variety shows and talk shows who emphasize a group identity that embraces the communal spirit of han and hǔng. Much comedy in Korea plays a social and communal role where celebrities take opportunities to learn more about the plight of Korea's countryside (*One Night, Two Days*), cope with the difficulty of running a restaurant business (*Kang's Restaurant*), or pro-vide therapy to small business owners who are suffering from mental and financial difficulties (*Baek Jong-won's Alley Restaurant*). As I discussed in chapter 4, cooking—rather than politics or gender wars—has become one of the most important elements of comedy in Korea today. For any Korean comic or comedy show to engage in political satire or invoke sensitive gen-der issues would be at the risk of alienating half its audience. This move toward overt social critique would require courage and brazenness on an individual level, which the Korean entertainment industry has markedly moved away from since the days of military dictatorship in the 1960s and

1970s.[6] Korean comedy shows are half Oprah and half game shows that focus less on satire and more on a collective empathy that aligns itself with these themes of han and hŭng. Yet making people laugh and cry is not necessarily a domain exclusively reserved for Korean aesthetic tradition. One could also make a case that Oprah Winfrey's ascendance to stardom in the United States is impossible to comprehend without understanding the link between her personal story of triumph and the public therapeutic confessions in which she reveals overcoming oppression as an abused and impoverished African American girl on a small Mississippi farm without her parents. In other words, even on an *Oprah* show, the communal acknowledgment of sorrow and trauma (han) and its intermixing with humor and joy (hŭng) is constantly conveyed to the viewers. I am particularly drawn to Korean comedy and the discourse around K-pop that attempt to uncode a post-traumatic jouissance for their viewers and fans.

Just as *blackness* not only represents racial wounds dating back to the nineteenth century and earlier but also signifies a new signature of cool that engages and sets contemporary global cultural trends, Koreanness had to overcome its han during the previous era in order to extend its power of mŏt to the rest of the world today. When Mbembe insisted in his discussion of blackness that "the twenty-first century is, of course, not the nineteenth century" in order to make a distinction between the modern-day welfare of black people and that of the days of slavery, he could have well been talking about Koreans, who may not have been enslaved and emancipated as black people were in past centuries but who nonetheless suffered massive psychological and physical pain during and after colonial domination.[7]

The double consciousness of Koreans and the inability to shake loose the indignation of being mocked as a pro-Japanese or pro-American collaborator even when one simply seeks to make an honest living leads us to pair the German term *Schadenfreude* (taking joy in others' failure) with a Korean term, *ssaemťong*, or *kkol choťa*, which can be translated roughly as "I am delighted by his misery because he deserves it." Though the German term is more closely aligned with an automatic, childlike delight in looking at others' misfortunes rather than a feeling of moral superiority when a form of justice is served, the Korean feeling of joy induced by others' troubles is simply inexplicable. In a classic novel from the 1930s colonial era, Ch'ae Man-sik's *Peace under Heaven* (*T'aep'yŏng ch'ŏnha*), the main character, Yoon Chik-won, a despicable wealthy man who has amassed his fortune through his loan shark business, gives one of the most exemplary lines from the history of modern Korean literature. Calling the era under Japanese colonialism a "peace under heaven," because law and order under colonial rule protected an opportunistic man like himself, he scoffs at others' misfortunes and sufferings, exclaiming, "Everyone should fail, with the exception of us!"[8] Yoon's laughter serves almost as a cynical way of interpreting the world; it is not an emotion of negativity, which is rare in the Korean sensibility, but actually the expression of derision, or contempt, prevalent in a country that has long suffered from division into two warring camps—the ones who have accepted the fate of being subjugated by foreign rule and the ones who have resisted it. Even among South Koreans who have accepted these conditions of subjugation and being cast as secondary citizens on their own soil, the trope of *ssaemt'ong* or *Schadenfreude* has become one of the most dominant motifs in many genres of Korean popular culture, including comedies, hip-hop, and cinema.

What I am interested in is how madanggŭk, which Namhee Lee calls "a form of 'people's theater' that combined Korean folk dramas with elements of Western drama," not only helped build a counterpublic culture based on the satirical principles of *kkol chot'a* and *sinmyŏng*, which shamed corporate bosses, corrupt officials, and greedy landlords during the early stage of the pro-democracy minjung movement of the 1970s and the 1980s, but also became the principle of what I call Koreanness in the television comedies of the global era—ranging from *Muhan Dojeon* (*Infinite Challenge*), which was quite possibly the most popular comedy program ever to have aired in the history of Korean television, to the music video and dance choreography of the viral song "Gangnam Style."[9] Though it was rarely a political satire, *Muhan* followed the structure of the spirit of a madanggŭk, which is essentially an open-air play that is reliant on the blurring of the boundaries between work and play, scripted acting and improvisation, and the staged space and its perimeters where the audience sits. Often drawing its satirical power from improvised witticism, earthy and vulgar expressions, and nonsensical wordplays, the best comedy moments in Korean television and social media were delivered when power was ridiculed and even self-parodied by the cast members and performers, who would often challenge their own bubbly sense of celebrity status. Audiences worldwide would be drawn to these episodes not only because of the unscripted and unpredictable nature of *Muhan Dojeon* but because of the guest appearances of K-pop idol stars who poked fun at their own power and broke loose from their stage persona. The Koreanness accumulated and showcased on *Muhan Dojeon* as a global stage can be traced from the spirits of resistance that owes its genealogy to the protest minjung theater and even further to peasants' mask dance (t'alch'um) from the premodern days.

Muhan Dojeon, undoubtedly the most popular nondrama program on television aired over the past twenty years, was part situational comedy and part absurd competition that required all cast members to participate in a challenge (scavenger hunts, travel, music, art, and sports) with celebrity guests each week.[10] After initially floundering for the first three years, it drew its highest ratings when it aired on Saturday evenings from the latter years of the first decade of the twenty-first century until it permanently went off the air in 2018—spurring many copycat programs in China and other Asian television markets.[11] Not only did *Muhan Dojeon* rely on the aforementioned tragicomedy elements to reach its top ratings slot, but it also continued to produce entertainment based on an ensemble cast whose members constantly negate their individual identities to project the group's collective hŭng. At first glance, because of its reliance on situational comedy, where cast members are assembled to provide comedy sketches or scavenger hunt games, it feels as if it is no different from the American comedy variety show *Saturday Night Live*, one of the longest-running non–soap opera programs in American television history. However, on Western comedy programs such as *Saturday Night Live* or the UK's *Monty Python's Flying Circus*, cathartic release is achieved through the ripping away of political power as represented in satirical situations. Presidents, celebrities, members of the royal family, or prime ministers are often targets of Western comedy sketches' parodies and pranks, for the arrogance of these targets produces ripe opportunities for comic hilarity. In addition, American humor rests firmly on the individual comic's ability to deliver a stand-up monologue, and SNL is no exception to this rule, since guest stars are obligated to deliver an opening monologue. Korean comedy programs, including *Muhan Dojeon*, provide a radically different perspective on comedy by providing content that is less politically targeted and less individually focused, and yet more unpredictable.

In Korea, as in many other neo-Confucian countries, cultural sensitivity and governmental censorship make political satire impossible. In American situational comedies, even when there is an absence of politics, there is always a prankster or trickster who takes center stage to fill the central role of the narrative. For instance, during SNL's heyday of the late 1990s and early 2000s, the focal point of almost all key ensemble sketches was the highly popular Will Ferrell, who performed carnivalesque, erotic comedy and political satire in his lampooning of President George W. Bush.

Whereas politics, sex, and sociological problems occupied central themes in these American or British comedy programs, *Muhan Dojeon* would try to minimize the role of these issues and instead create its hŭng and sense of fun and comedy by retaining and commenting on the collective sense of the ensemble. Yoo Jae-suk, the main MC of the program, has become a star by displaying characteristics of deferment and humility. He rises above others and refrains from exploiting the childlike ssaemt'ong, but uses his persona of comedy god (he's often referred to as Yooneunim [God Yoo]—a wordplay from *haneunim*, which means "Lord God" in Korean) to rehabilitate a sense of others' mocking at his failures to exercise godlike perfection. Schadenfreude, in other words, does function in this comedy program, but usually it is Yoo Jae-suk's sidekicks, Park Myung-soo and Jeong Hyung-don, who set up Yoo as a godlike figure in order to mock his failure to produce laughter. Rather than focusing on spectacles, fussiness, or impersonations, he constantly refers to others to perform or exhibit their talents and comedy skills. The group's ability to bond as an ensemble requires the leader to constantly direct attention toward others. The entire pathos of *Muhan* is drawn from the cast members' ordinariness and mediocrity rather than their extraordinariness as comedians or the political nuances and sophistication of their line delivery or situational satire. Yoo becomes a star of mŏt by diffusing rather than brandishing the sexual energy and narcissism central to Western comedy programs. As Kevin O'Rourke, a literary scholar and translator of Korean poetry, has insisted, "Mŏt is more in the heart than in the mind; more platonic than sexual; more in looking for love for others rather than inward-looking in perpetual preoccupation with the self."[12] Even in the twenty-first century, with Yoo, Korea has developed a star during the postmodern, transnational era whose spirit is heavily endowed with the traditional, almost neo-Confucian sense of mŏt.

Recent Korean scholarship has scrutinized the relationship between this twenty-first-century reality-television comedy program and Korean traditional theater. Where *Muhan Dojeon* lacks political satire, the comic landscape is filled instead with endless wordplays and improvisational, unscripted gags and humor served up by cast members. Yoon Tae-il, Kim Sae-eun, Kim Sooah, and Sohn Byung-Woo argue that sinmyŏng (exalting joy), which is a central trope of many Korean folk traditions such as p'ansori, t'alnori (mask dance-drama), and *kkokttugaksi norŭm* (traditional puppet play), lays the foundation for the unpredictable plotlines and nonformalized format behind *Muhan's* narratives. These Korean media scholars insist that the elements of pent-up energy—unscripted hilarity; wordplays of both verbal lines and written subtitles that constantly subvert the oral dialogue; and constant games that sometimes involve crew, writers, and accidental bystanders, and require audiences to self-reflexively engage the program—are derived from the *"sinmyŏng* narrative" form that has long occupied Korea's aesthetic tradition.[13] *Muhan's* varied formats of survival game, makeover/renovation, reality dating, hidden camera, and travel mission began in European and Japanese television as early as the late 1970s and the 1980s. In *Muhan,* however, the thematic foundation of sinmyŏng allows it to retain innately Korean characteristics within the medium of what has become global reality TV. This Koreanness that lurks underneath the various formats of reality television that cast members play helps the American hegemony in Korean culture remain ambivalent and transnational.

According to playwright Kim Chi-ha, who, along with Chae Hŭi-wan, Im Chin-t'aek, and Kim Min-gi, among others, pioneered the madangguk (open-air theater) by reinventing the traditional rituals and peasant dance performances during the 1970s. Kim Chi-ha writes, "The new *madang* theater [a wordplay between *guk* (theater) and *gut* (shamanistic ritual)] must create an aesthetics of 'white shadows' that completes the contradictory aesthetic structure that possesses both negative elements and positive ones. For the training goal of an artist, one must understand that the principles of *surisŏng* (a throaty, husky, voice) can only be achieved through the throwing up of bowls and bowls of blood in order to best mix dark han and spirited sinmyŏng."[14] Not only is the principle behind madangguk seeking this exultation spirit of sinmyŏng through its overcoming of the trauma of han, but it is also attempting to work through other binaries, such as order and chaos, performer and audience, and even fiction and reality. Kim Chi-ha may not have realized this in the 1970s, but what he was insisting on through *surisŏng* was a becoming-Korean identity that sought an alliance with the black aesthetics that gripped America at the time. Since madangguk became popular in the 1970s around college campuses as a form of political satire against the then military dictatorship, one can perhaps argue that the elements of post-han sinmyŏng were available just as television became iconic in Korea.

Madangguk's plotline is loose, and senseless situations of farce continue to overwhelm the classical dramatic structure's pressure to neatly divide the spectacle into a beginning, a middle, and an end. The purpose of this theater is neither to impress the viewers with the thespian talents of the actors nor to momentarily suspend the audiences' disbelief in order to maximize the

Aristotelian catharsis that a standard drama proposes to invoke; it is simply to produce laughter in order to release pent-up emotions. Sinmyŏng, an ecstasy, is crafted through the overcoming of han, which for many decades prior ruled as just about the only Korean archetype of national sentiment. The Korean surisŏng or the husky voice that must be cultivated in order for it to adequately produce either sinmyŏng or mŏt in the Korean p'ansori structure may not be categorically dissimilar to the spirit of the "song of sorrow" of which Du Bois spoke regarding the African American music that conveys this essence of American beauty. Speaking about the condition of black people at the turn of the previous century, Du Bois states, "And so by fateful chance the Negro folk-song—the rhythmic cry of the slave—stands to-day not simply as the sole American music, but as the most beautiful expression of human experience born this side the seas."[15] Du Bois may not have lived long enough to appreciate the screechy rumbling voice of Little Richard or the deep and syrupy rap tones of The Notorious B.I.G., but the booming surisŏng that lends acoustic distinction to both Korean peasant music and African American pop sounds of the twentieth century would surely have impressed Du Bois. Whether in the form of James Brown's howls or Whitney Houston's high soprano bursts of "ah," undoubtedly the African American voice of exile in the "song of sorrow" serves as the popular currency that resonates with working people around the globe today. This sense of mŏt—both universal and convincingly captivating—can also be translated in the Korean theatrical and performative experience.

"MUHAN SANGSA"

"Muhan Sangsa" (Infinite company) is one of the recurring motifs of *Muhan Dojeon* (*MD*). It is perhaps the most successful segment, along with the wrestling special (where the regular cast learns professional wrestling moves to perform in front of a live audience), the music festival (where cast members compete with each other by learning to compose and sing a new song with the aid of a professional musician), and the chase drama. In each of these segments, the sense of postgrief enjoyment (sinmyŏng) is particularly dramatized. After debuting as just a brief segment, "Muhan Sangsa" evolved into a two-episode-long sitcom to be repeated twice a year since 2011, until *MD* ended in 2018. In the summer of 2016, it was given a feature-film treatment that runs about one hundred minutes with a professional film director, crew, and actors involved in its production.[16] In a typical

"Muhan Sangsa" episode, all seven members of MD are cast as employees of a fictive company. What exact product they are producing or selling is left intentionally vague. Yoo Jae-suk occupies the role of the head of the department. The rest of the cast each sit at a desk in their shared fictive office space—in downward hierarchical order. So, the older members, Jeong Joon-ha and Park Myung-soo, would occupy the desks closest to MC Yoo, while the youngest employee (G-Dragon) would occupy the desk furthest from the department head.

"Muhan Sangsa," or consequently, the *Muhan Dojeon* format itself, markets itself as no-format reality TV, which departs from other SNL-type comedy programs such as *Gag Concert*, also a long-running comedy program that is strictly based on prescripted skits. Without a scripted framework, and without even explicitly outlining what the cast's missions are, "Muhan Sangsa" creates banal situations such as what food to order for lunch, or how to best make a spreadsheet using an ordinary office application like the Microsoft Word program, in order to create comedy. Though they are on a set, they do not even attempt to facilitate the illusion of creating a world where the audience's suspension of disbelief is required. In other words, the deliberate low production value removes the cumbersome necessity of the mimetic reproduction of reality. This low-value production background allows the actors to be more improvisational and challenging. Actors will often yell, "What kind of work are we supposed to do?" Sometimes their arguments over what to eat for lunch will become so intense that they forget that they are pretending to be a character on a sitcom and will start calling each other by their real names instead of character names that are based on the title of their position, such as vice head (ch'ajang) or office worker (sawŏn), or begin dropping the honorific that must be used between all company workers. Instead of recognizing the heroic qualities of an ordinary man, which sets up almost all romantic drama traditions, or what Benjamin in his assessment of Plato's *Phaedo* stated as the exposing of the undramatic qualities of an excellent man or a sage, MD perhaps creates a folly by extolling the "mediocre qualities" of the ordinary human.[17] They lose their tempers over trivial matters, curse at each other, reject humility, exercise abusive power over those who rank below them, and condone jealousy over other employees. If madanggŭk had usually cast generic servant characters, Malttugi and Soettugi, who ridicule the hypocrisy of landlords in the tradition of peasant theater or t'alch'um, *Muhan* presents a satire of both a company office hierarchy and the chair of the department, played by MC Yoo, by making his sidekicks Park Myung-soo and Jeong Hyeong-don an essential part of the drama. They, along with other cast members, constantly take turns playing updated office versions of Malttugi and Soettugi as a way to—in the words of Namhee Lee—"recover 'a life of community' through the common sharing of *nori* and to recover the meaning of *nori* as life-giving, life-based art."[18]

In one of the first episodes of the "Muhan Sangsa" series, G-Dragon, the leader of the K-pop act BIGBANG, makes his guest appearance (figure 7.1). He makes an entrance first as a young man who is trying to get his first job as an employee of "Muhan." He is able to beat the odds by impressing the three senior members of the company, MC Yoo, Park Myung-soo, and Jeong Joon-ha. His three competitors seeking the same job are awkwardly played by the other members of the comedy company, Haha, Kil, Jeong Hyeong-don, and Noh Hong-chol, who are all doubly cast as job seekers though they are already playing long-term employees in the company. Without the pressure to impress the audience with their dramaturgical achievements, these comedians, along with the guest, G-Dragon, are able to radically shuffle across the stringent boundaries between reality and fiction. G-Dragon, for instance, constantly slips out of his character as a novice white-collar employee and into his identity as the K-pop star that he actually is. The plot, which really doesn't exist except in a loose form, foregrounds G-Dragon as the intern office clerk who is exploited as a rookie to service other employees who outrank him. His day is simply filled with reminding others to take breaks, upload social media posts, and make business-related phone calls.

Overwhelmed with menial tasks such as faxing, copying, and other miscellaneous assistant work, he briefly disappears from the office. When G-Dragon exits, Director Yoo reads on the news of how the son of the company head is serving as a special inspector to improve the condition of the company. The special royal inspector (*amhaeng ŏsa*) is one of the best-known figures from children's fables that take place during the Chosun Dynasty. While traveling incognito, they would serve a secret mission for the king who seeks justice in faraway places where local magistrates are corrupt and unjust. Often working undercover disguised as a beggar or a commoner to improve the lives of ordinary citizens, the amhaeng ŏsa would be cast as a frequent recurring character also in madanggŭk in order to build to a dramatic climactic scene, not unlike that of the p'ansori *Chunhyang*, to punish the corrupt officials and dismiss them.

As much as it would be erroneous for us not to consider *Muhan Dojeon* as a form of comedy verité, it would equally be controversial not to consider

7.1 G-Dragon, the leader of the K-pop idol group BIGBANG, guest stars on the "Muhan Sangsa" series of *Muhan Dojeon*, 2012.

"Muhan Sangsa" as well as other popular segments such as the wrestling special as a form of madanggŭk. However, there are differences. After all, since *MD* is a television program, not a theater performance, the boundary between performers and spectators cannot be physically transgressed as it can in the space of the madang. Although, throughout the program, there is an abundance of interaction between the performers and the crew members, and also bystanders who are constantly solicited to interact with the stars, unlike the actual madanggŭk audiences who can themselves enter in and out of madang, television audiences can only watch pre-edited programs, although they could choose to leave real-time comments on fanzines and also participate as users in re-creating their own Muhan-kind of plays through social media.[19] In order to compensate for this lack of physical intermingling of the bodies of the participants and the performers, what Korean television has done is to cultivate an ubiquitous utility of on-screen captions that serve the voice of neither the performers nor the audience. It is this subtitled commentary that defies a traditional perspective—it belongs exclusively to neither the author (producer, performers, writers on the show) nor the audience. They do sometimes take up the authority of the first-person narrative of Kim Tae-ho, the longtime producer of *Muhan*, who, interestingly enough, occupies the void of narrator-auteur left empty by Yoo Jae-suk and other MCs. These subtitles are almost always freefloating, like those of a silent film narrator (what Koreans called *pyŏnsa* or what Japanese called *benshi*) or those which were once famously employed by Woody Allen in his film *Annie Hall* (1976), constituting a special type of subjectivity—an asubjectifying subjectivity that becomes a mindscreen of its own and takes the place of the voice of both the subconscious of the character and the desire of a spectator. Rather than simply clarifying the live dialogue, the Korean subtitles employed for *Muhan Dojeon* were far more creatively disruptive and innovative than for any other program in Korea.[20]

However much the rituals of *Muhan* have become interwoven into the fabric of everyday life in Korea through its Saturday evening program during the first two decades of the twenty-first century, it would also be a stretch to define it as a space of radical utopian imagination where social hierarchy is totally reinterpreted in order to usher in a revolutionary agenda in the same vein of madangguk as a form of political theater during the 1970s. The ending of "Muhan Sangsa" exemplifies this nonrevolutionary, or even antirevolutionary, spirit when the newbie employee (played by G-Dragon) is revealed as the company president's son, who wanted to witness for himself what the company office culture was really like. The transformative power of subversion here at the end of the drama does not ignite a true sense of revolution since it affirms, rather than denies, the feudal order around which a conglomerate hierarchy is built: the founder and its heir apparent who is benevolent and kind. *Muhan*, as had *Chunhyang* before it, dreams of a coup, but in a manner that refuses to critique the existing feudal hierarchy. Therefore the satire of the office culture that ridicules all forms of social network that is built on meaningless work and oppressive hierarchy must also come to an end rather than igniting the possibilities of real resistance. Yet the madangguk spirit is still what gels and radicalizes the form of this particular kind of comedy verité and retains its spontaneity.

I conclude here with two images—Choe Sŭng-hŭi's dance piece "Eheya Nohara" from the first half of the twentieth century, when Korea was still a colony of Japan (figure 7.2); and Psy's concert at New York City's Times Square at the height of "Gangnam Style" popularity (figure 7.3). Choe was one of the most famous dancers of the twentieth century, who studied modern dance with Ishii Baku and toured around the world—first as a Japanese citizen in the Western world and then as a member of the North Korean dance troupe in Eastern Europe. Choe reached the status of perhaps the most popular female icon during the colonial era not through her standard modern dance repertoire but through her reinvention of the traditional dances such as "Eheya Noara," which was disparaged by Korean critics who found her signature repertoire where she plays a drunk aristocratic man unable to find his way home to be vulgar and ridiculous but

7.2 Ch'oe Sŭng-hŭi dancing in drag during the colonial period, late 1930s.

7.3 *Muhan Dojeon* performing in New York City's Times Square, New Year's Eve 2012.

was extremely popular with Japanese critics, including the writer Kawa-
bata Yasunari.[21] When Choe Sŭng-hŭi, under her Japanese name Sai Shoki,
famously toured the United States, she inspired cultural dignitaries like
Robert Taylor and Pablo Picasso to come and enjoy the show in 1938 and
again in 1939, but she also reconstructed the condition of colonialism that
legitimated both modern norms to the colonies, including hygiene, education, and now an aesthetic accomplishment. But, despite the fact that she
was an exemplary product of the then Japanese campaign of its "civilizing
mission" in Korea, Choe adopted not only Western dance or the austere
kisaeng dance but satirical peasant dance rooted in t'alch'um. Though the
visual archival documents of her dance scarcely survive, American reviews
of her concerts proclaim that many dances in her repertoire were funny
and humorous.[22] In "Eheya Noara," performing a modern dance in what
is unmistakably male yangban (aristocratic) garb, Choe is poking fun at
both Korean masculinity and upper-class decorum—stripping them down
to the vulgar core. Choe's parody is unacceptable to both Korean rightists
and leftists, for her gestures upset the distinction between original and its
quotation. She is the authentic Korean dancer, but she also mimics and ridicules the authentic Korean gestures. It is the ultimate realization of what
I identified in the introduction as Signifyin(g) that cuts through several

social divisions through the power of mimicry. Choe's meticulous ability to shuffle between several social identities—gender (male and female), class (aristocrat and commoner), and nationality (Japan and Korea)—is what enabled the Korean tradition of sinmyŏng to be transplanted to the modern dance stage in New York.

Korea, or the place of Korea in the world today, is very different than it was in 1940, when the country was still a colony of Japan. But in 2012, when *Muhan Dojeon* set its mission to send its cast members, including Noh Hong-ch'ol and Yoo Jae-sok, two of its cast members who appeared in Psy's "Gangnam Style" video as respectively the Elevator Guy and the Yellow-Suit Guy, to Psy's concert in Times Square to participate onstage as dancers, they invoked a new postcolonial, opaquely racial, and ambivalently hegemonic moment through the double gesture of mimicking and transforming the widely ridiculed off-white and blackish "horse dance." The neo-American horse-dance was once again revived in 2019 by black rapper Lil Nas X who had surely grown up watching the Korean musician Psy on YouTube. In the 2020 Grammys, Lil Nas X performed his hit song, "Old Road Road" with BTS. This new dance that is, according to Julie Choi, "an invitation to recreate an alternative pastoral in the city," now dominates the cyberspatialized, *Gangnam*-ish simulation of both Korean mimicry and the Koreanization of miguk.[23] Spliced between these two images are the hegemonic ambitions of Koreans who attempted to legitimate and expand—however ridiculously tiny their national-ethnic boundaries have defined and restricted them during the colonial and postcolonial era—their performative acts through gestures of hegemonic mimicry that serve the double roles of both simulation and authentication.

Noh Hong-chol and Yoo Jae-sok sing and dance with Psy and his boyhood black idol MC Hammer. Ch'oe Sŭng-hŭi's roots in the satire of t'alch'um, when performed outside Korea, might not have been recognized by her American spectators in the 1930s. In the 2010s, *Muhan*'s connection to the madanggŭk would also have been lost to the tens of thousands of spectators, not to mention the millions of worldwide television viewers of this ABC New Year's Eve gala in Times Square. By taking the madanggŭk to Times Square, Psy and his friends from *Muhan* had finally fulfilled the dream of Ch'oe Sŭng-hŭi, who first saw the satirical potential in t'alch'um and other Korean farmers' traditions that have a place in the global open square. *Madang*, after all, literally means "square." Most New York City audiences gathered that day probably would not have realized the hypocrisy of the capitalist or landlord class that was always at the core of the spirit of madanggŭk that had once belonged to the Korean peasantry. The outrageous and vulgar corporeal movements of MC Yoo and Noh Hong-ch'ol and their strong connection to Malttugi and Soettugi, the stock servant characters of t'alch'um who help ridicule the high learning and noble pedigrees of Yangban aristocrats and present-day Gangnam chaebols, may have also been lost in translation. However, the Korean performers' satire and parody of hegemonic American codes would have been understood, and particularly with regard to the conventions of the Western in the historical context of popular culture, from Doris Day's *Calamity Jane* in the 1950s to, more recently, black rapper Lil Nas X's "Old Town Road," as a gesture that ridicules the white, patriarchal, and racist establishment of the American frontier myth, if little else. Strutting and wading through the off-white, blackish, and sometimes mottled ethnic upbringing as well as through a lengthy postwar tutelage under the American military occupation, Koreans had finally come of age. By claiming the center stage of the American special in front of screaming American fans, Psy and the future generation of K-pop stars who would continue to grace the American cover for another decade fulfilled the very dream that Patti Kim and Shin Joong-hyun might have concocted long before these young stars were even born—to become the very origin of the cultural hegemony that they had grown up mimicking in the poverty-stricken, war-ridden camptowns. After all, *Muhan* could mean both "no limitation" and "no more *han* (sorrow)" that will hopefully move Korea into a post-grief, twenty-first century filled with laughter and levitation.

NOTES

Preface

1. Thompson, "What's behind South Korea's COVID-19 Exceptionalism?"

2. Millar, "South Korea."

3. Hall, "Local and the Global," 180.

4. In one of the most interesting books to date about Korean popular culture, Joseph Jeon argues that the ascendance of Korean cinema coincided with the end of the American century. Jeon adopts the theory of Giovanni Arrighi, an Italian economist who theorized that the hegemonic American empire's signal crisis (the beginning of the end) began in the 1970s, with the terminal crisis (the end of the end) occurring sometime in the early years of the twenty-first century. Korean cinema starting in this period, and more broadly even hallyu, which began after Korea had undergone an intense economic restructuring mandated by the IMF bailout in 1997, was both a marker of "a shift toward a program of free trade and liberal capital markets . . . and an economic response to the declining productivity of the industrial sector." Jeon, *Vicious Circuits*, 19.

5. Luce, "American Century."

6. If all the global cultural sensations born outside North America and Europe over the past seventy-five years since the conclusion of World War II, such as Jamaican reggae, New Latin American cinema, or India's Bollywood, have proven both an innovative mix of local brands of beats, edits, and footprints combined with the dominant pop structure of rock 'n' roll and Hollywood films, the Korean brand of cinema, music, and television over the past twenty years, which has more recently captured global attention, stands out as falling short of innovatively integrating the local flavor of Koreanness into its cultural output. Even the most popular form of Korean culture has found success by repressing and making opaque its own national and ethnic subjectivity.

7. Zheng, "Black Lives Matter."

Introduction

1. The year 1968 was the peak for the number of American troops deployed to Vietnam. The increased demand for entertainment for the US troops deployed in Vietnam forced some of the Korean sho-dan members to seek jobs in Vietnam—leading to the demise of the local sho-dan industry in Korea. Many Korean entertainers, including the best bands led by, for instance, Shin Joong-hyun, went to Vietnam for an extended period of time throughout the late 1960s and early 1970s. They were called Wolnam ch'amjŏn migun wimun kongyŏndan (Entertainment Band for the US Military Serving in the Vietnam War).

2. I have actually extrapolated the first couple of pages in this chapter after closely reading Patti Kim's biographical account as a young performer growing up in Seoul, dreaming of performing on the big stage of Manhattan. See Cho Yŏng-nam and P. Kim, *Kŭ nyŏ, Patti Kim*.

3. In 1948 President Harry S. Truman signed Executive Order 9981, which abolished discrimination "on the basis of race, color, religion, or national origin" in the United States Armed Forces. Of course, this new order hardly made a dent on eradicating racism in the US military, as Truman himself declared, "I wish to make it clear that I am not appealing for social equality of the Negro. The Negro himself knows better than that, and the highest types of Negro leaders say quite frankly, that they prefer the society of their own people. Negroes want justice, not social relations." The Korean War was the first war that tried to phase out all-black units in the US military. However, many personnel in the military refused to desegregate the army, and the last of the all-black units in the US military was terminated in 1954—one year after the cease-fire agreement was signed in Korea. Jon Bauer, "Truman and Executive Order 9981: Idealistic, Pragmatic, or Shrewd Politician?," Harry S. Truman Library, accessed February 3, 2020, https://www.trumanlibrary.goFebv/education/lesson-plans/truman -and-executive-order-9981-idealistic-pragmatic-or-shrewd-politician.

4. Fifty black soldiers from Camp Humphreys, in protest of segregated clubs in the nearby town of Anjong-Ni, Pyeongtaek, destroyed several bars there. The Korean National Police and the American military police were called in to break up the rioters and the Korean villagers, who were also angry because of the damages. Some Koreans were rumored to have been killed during the race riot aimed at the camptown segregation. A black American soldier was severely injured and several Koreans were reportedly stabbed—prompting the military police to use tear-gas grenades to disperse the angry Korean mob that was protesting the violence and damage of property in the camptown. Freeland and Lea, "Black GIs on Rampage."

In a blog that reports on Korean modern history, *Gusts of Popular Feeling*, this same article from the Anjong-Ni race riot is uploaded. In the comments section, Robert Gardner, an African American who claims to have been stationed in Korea during this race riot, comments that four clubs were in operation in Anjong-ni, the camptown that served Camp Humphreys: the "T" Club, the Lower 7 Club, the Triple 7 Club, and Duffy's. Gardner writes, "Of the four clubs[,] only the Triple 7 Club catered to the Black G.I. This was done by the type of music played and the friendliness of the club girls." It was the closing of the Triple 7 Club for renovation that had forced the black soldiers to patronize other clubs that did not play R&B and soul—the preferred music among African Americans—and the refusal of club girls to sit with them that eventually led to the escalation of the tensions. "The 1971 Anjeong-ri Race Riot, Part 2," *Gusts of Popular Feeling*, July 8, 2011, http://populargusts.blogspot.com/2011/07/1971-anjeong-ri-race-riot-part-2.html.

5. Katharine H. S. Moon writes, "Throughout 1971, racial tensions between black and white servicemen increased, spread through various camp areas in Korea, and exploded on the weekend of July 9, 1971, in the village of Anjongni in Pyeongtaek County, the site of Camp Humphreys. The demographics of Anjongni at the time of the July racial riots was as follows: 4,759 Korean villagers, including an estimated 970 prostitutes; 1,700 US military personnel at Camp Humphreys, including approximately 500 black servicemen." Moon, *Sex among Allies*, 71.

6. Lea and Brown, "GIT: Key to Racial Equality," 12.

7. Lea and Brown, "GIT: Key to Racial Equality," 10.

8. Constante, "25 Years after LA Riots."

9. Though prostitution was outlawed in South Korea in 1961, by 1964, 145 districts were specially designated for legal prostitution. All were in camptowns. When venereal diseases became a constant complaint made by the US military, then president Park Chung-hee initiated a five-year cleanup campaign in 1971 that "intensified and expanded existing efforts to control VD . . . and teaching club owners and hostesses how to equitably treat black and white soldiers. At each step of the way, the U.S. military prodded the Korean government into action. . . . This creates the illusion that it is primarily the Korean government that regulates prostitution and the camptowns, but in reality such regulation is demanded and orchestrated by the American military, with a weak Korean government able to do little but acquiesce." Yuh, *Beyond the Shadow of Camptown*, 26–27.

10. Korean citizens were often caught between black and white soldiers during the era of the civil rights movement of the 1960s and 1970s. As Ji-Yeon Yuh reports, rejection of black soldiers by Korean prostitutes was common, but Korean "club owners and camptown women countered that it was the prejudices of white soldiers that dictated camptown segregation." Yuh, *Beyond the Shadow of Camptown*, 28.

11. Mbembe, *Critique of Black Reason*, 6.

12. J. Lee, *Service Economies*, 19.

13. Henry Em notes that the Japanese pronunciation of the "compound *minzoku* (K: *minjok*), understood as *ethnic nation*, began to circulate in Korea in the early 1900s." This was well after the neologism of minzoku began to circulate in Japan following Miyazaki Muryu's translation of "French Assemblée Nationale as *minzoku kaigi*." Em, *Great Enterprise*, 67.

14. Foucault writes, "New mechanism of power applies primarily to bodies and what they do rather than to the land and what it produces. It was a mechanism of power that made it possible to extract time and labor, rather than commodities and wealth, from bodies." Foucault, *Society Must Be Defended*, 35–36.

15. J. Lee, *Service Economies*, 15, 7.

16. Yi Yong-u, "Miguk k'ŭrop so hŭnryŏn patŭn taejung ŭmak."

17. Lee, *Service Economies*, 6. Although I support Lee's thesis, which stems from equating Korean service labor for the American military with disposable and necropolitical labor, I would also suggest that missing from her analysis is not only the enormous and rather conspicuous (*mi-p'al-gun*) sho-dan (the US Eighth Army Entertainment troupe) but also the possibility that many of these forms of sex service labor resisted condemnation to death and ended up reviving and reproducing life. Some of the best-known Korean American biracial star athletes and singers, ranging from former NFL star Hines Ward to rapper Yoon Mi-rae, have African American fathers and Korean mothers who first met in US military camptowns in Korea during the 1970s and 1980s. Although it cannot be speculated that these stars' mothers were sex workers, their difficult childhoods due to the lack of paternal support might suggest that their mothers' lives were in some way construed as "disposable" and necropolitical. However, the successful lives not only of these stars but also of many more offspring reared between Korean mothers and American military servicemen throughout the twentieth century are testaments to a (re)*productive labor* on the part of Korean sex workers, which extended well beyond a condition of disposability and necropolitics in the US military throughout the twentieth century. For more on this, see chapter 2.

18. Neves, *Underglobalization*, 3.

19. N. Lee, *Making of Minjung*, 202.

20. One of the arguments that John Lie makes in his book *K-Pop* is that K-pop, while embracing a commercial music route, defies the "elements of authenticity, autonomy, and originality [which] are the essence of the Romantic ideology of the artist." Lie, *K-Pop*, 142–43. Of course, perhaps this era in which "Romantic ideology of the artist" ruled the day may have vanished—not only in K-pop but also in the global pop music scene dominated by hip-hop and electronic dance music (EDM).

21. Cillizza, "Donald Trump's 'Parasite' Critique."

22. J. Park, "K-Pop Stardom Lures Japanese Youth."

23. Homi K. Bhabha, "Of Mimicry and Man," in Bhabha, *Location of Culture*, 86.

24. I thank the anonymous reviewer who has urged me to think broadly and deeply into the distinction of two United States ("Murrica" and miguk)—one without a Korean other and another that produces the Korean mimicry—and how they seek to transform the paradigm of minjok.

25. This is not to suggest that some of the careless or unthoughtful tweets or postings by K-pop or hallyu stars were never found to be racially insensitive. Lack of cultural

understanding of American racist history has led to, for instance, blackfacing that continues to pop up on the media scene as some Korean celebrities try to explicitly and insensitively become comically black.

26. Bhabha, "Of Mimicry and Man," 89.

27. Caillois, *Man, Play and Games.*

28. Antonio Gramsci's concepts of "civil society" and "hegemony" are probably understood best in "State and Civil Society," 206–76.

29. Hall, "Local and the Global," 175.

30. As a matter of fact, South Korea today is often caught without alliance to its more powerful neighbors — China and Japan — despite the popularity of its cultural content in these nations. The relationship between Korea and China has significantly cooled since South Korea's deployment of Terminal High Altitude Area Defense (THAAD), which propelled China to ban Korea's cultural products in 2016. As of February 2021, despite signs of diplomatic improvements between the two countries, China continues to officially ban many Korean television and film exports. In 2019, Japan began its economic retaliation against South Korea for the same year's court rulings that found Mitsubishi and several other Japanese companies liable for damage during the war and responsible for compensation.

31. One of the greatest ironies of the postwar Korean War era is that the Syngman Rhee regime was unable to block the Japanese-language radio broadcaster NHK from reaching almost the entirety of the Korean peninsula even though it had effectively banned Japanese cultural products and films throughout the 1950s. This was possible because the Voice of America (VOA) and the Voice of United Nations Command (VUNC), which were quickly mobilized after the Korean War had broken out on June 26, 1950, in order to combat the North Korean propaganda that had taken over the Korean-language broadcast stations in the South, had to rely on Japanese AM broadcasting transmitters. During the Korean War, pro–Republic of Korea (ROK) (anti-Communist) radio broadcasts were only available in shortwave radio broadcasts, while the largest AM broadcasts (Korean Broadcasting System [KBS]) in South Korea began broadcasting pro–Democratic People's Republic of Korea (DPRK) (Communist) programs. The powerful transmission of Japanese radio airwaves from Tokyo and Fukuoka sent not only the US military radio channels but also NHK broadcast radio that carried news programs as well as sports and entertainment programs that many Koreans at the time understood. Yun Sang-kil, "Naengjŏnki KBS," 13.

32. Korean national identification of *yuhaengga* (trendy songs) of the twentieth century, which are frequently charged as originated from Japan, warrants further discussion. Many aesthetics of the two neighboring countries, Japan and Korea, including music, historically resemble each other. As Min-Jung Son explains in an essay, Koga Masao, a Japanese composer who helped establish the enka genre and has a museum built in honor of his achievements in Shibuya, spent his formative years in Korea (from ages seven to eighteen) from 1912 to 1923 and has acknowledged that he was "heavily influenced

by traditional Korean music and that the *enka* melodies he created originated from Korean tradition." Son, "Young Musical Love of the 1930s,," 265.

33. Kwon, "Shin Joong Hyun's Sonority," 125.

34. Cho Kwan-woo's remake of the song also became a big hit — one of the best-selling songs of all time in the 1990s — and then in 2008, it became the title song and the title for a blockbuster film about the Korean army's dispatch to Vietnam directed by Lee Joon-ik and starring Soo Ae: *Nim ŭn mŏngot e* (English title, *Sunny*).

35. Among many of Shin Joong-hyun's classic tunes is "Arŭmdaun kangsan" (Beautiful mountains and rivers), composed in 1972, which remains beloved by both North Koreans and South Koreans even after almost fifty years since its original release. Though the song is not composed in the pentatonic scale, it combines a simple rock music ballad with the stoic German marching music beats that reportedly caught the attention of North Korean music students. Singer Lee Sun-hee remade the song in 1988 and sang it during her Pyongyang concert in 2018. According to Chu Sŏng-ha, one of the *t'albukja* (North Korean defector) reporters working in South Korea, it was one of the songs that was well received by the North Korean audiences. Ironically, the song was composed in protest of Park Chung-hee's military dictatorship after Shin had refused to write a propaganda song that praises Park's Yushin Constitution that guaranteed him a lifetime presidency. Chu, *Pyongyang chaponchuŭi Paekkwa chŏnsŏ*, 181–82.

36. Iwabuchi argues that most of the cultural and consumer products Japan has made during the postwar years attempted to be "culturally odorless." These odorless products include "consumer technologies (such as VCRs, karaoke, and the Walkman); comics and cartoons (animation); and computer/video games." Iwabuchi, *Recentering Globalization*, 27.

37. That Shin Joong-hyun shared the same kind of influence as did Robert Plant and Jimmy Page of Led Zeppelin is probably not surprising since they come from the same generation of musicians (Shin was born in 1938 and Jimmy Page in 1944) and grew up listening to black music broadcast over the American military forces radio network. "We didn't have the same cultural exchange you had. We didn't have Black America," Plant stated on *Late Night with David Letterman*: "We couldn't turn our dial and get an absolutely amazing kaleidoscope of music. (In the UK) now and then, if you were lucky, there was this American Forces Network radio coming out of Germany. If you were lucky, you could hear Muddy Waters or Little Richard coming through the waves." Smith, "Airwaves Carry U.S. Culture." The unintended audience in places as far removed as Western Europe and East Asia included both Page and Shin, who quite possibly ended up developing their own brand of African American music using the blues chord structure of Buddy Guy and Muddy Waters, inspired by the same radio program broadcast over the American Forces Network (AFN).

38. Jang Sa-ik, a popular *kugak* (traditional Korean music) singer, remade "Nim" in 1995. Also, it was sung by a trot singer, Na Mi-ae, in 2014; the song helped her win the *Trot X* audition program that year.

39. Throughout documentaries on the subject of the Korean War, such as PBS's *The American Experience: The Battle of Chosin* (dir. Randall MacLowry, 2016), black soldiers are seen integrated among the American military forces.

40. The 2015 data from the US Department of Defense (DOD) indicates that black soldiers made up 17 percent of the active-duty military compared to their percentage of the US population, ages eight to forty-four, which stands at only 13 percent as documented in 2015. Parker, Cilluffo, and Stepler, "6 Facts about the US Military."

41. *Swing Kids* is an extravagantly made musical drama set during the Korean War in the Geoje Prison Camp. It centers around a friendship that develops between a young North Korean prisoner and an African American officer, Jackson, who teaches him tap dancing. It was perhaps the first Korean film that featured a black character as one of its main characters, but it failed to do well at the box office.

42. Bridges, "In the Beginning," 326.

43. Kim Ŭn-kyŏng, "Yuhŭi ro sŏ ui nodong," 34. All translations are mine unless otherwise indicated.

44. Shin Joong-hyun, perhaps the most famous guitarist and composer during the entire history of Korean pop, used to peek out from backstage when he played for the sho-dan at the American military camps during the 1960s. If he saw that the majority of the crowd was black, he knew that he had to give a first-rate performance that night. Shin's father was Korean and his mother Japanese. Before 1945, he also lived in Manchuria, where he grew up listening to Chinese music. During the Korean War, his biggest musical influence was Korean traditional folk music. He admits that his diverse musical tastes—country music, black music, Japanese music, Korean music, and Chinese music—gave the foundation to cultivate his composition style, which often was the fusion of many different music genres: "Among all of the music I have listened to, I thought the Korean farming music and folk music was the best. It is because the best music is born naturally from the working people. It is because of this root I think that people insist that my music is very Korean. 'The Woman in the Rain' ["Pi sok ŭi yŏin"] from 1964 feels a little bit Western, a little bit Japanese, but inside there is a deep culture of tradition." Shin Joong-Hyun and Ki-t'ae Kim, "Majimak mutae aptun rokŭi taebu Shinjunghyŏn."

Patti Kim also found black music to be much more advanced than nonblack music. As musicians from this period, including Tommy Shim, attest, the sho-dan bands catered to the diverse musical tastes of the American military personnel—"the Beatles or the Beach Boys for the white GIs, country music for the old white NCOs, and soul music of the Temptations or James Brown at the black clubs." Hyunjoon Shin and P. Kim, "Birth, Death, and Resurrection," 277.

45. Bhabha, "Of Mimicry and Man," 85.

46. Yi Jum, "Tŭlgukhwa, Kim Hyŏn-sik."

47. K. H. Kim, "Korean Cinema and Im Kwon-Taek," 25.

48. K. H. Kim, "Korean Cinema and Im Kwon-Taek," 34.

49. Despite the fact that theatrical and video releases in Korea did not provide dubbed versions of foreign films—only subtitles—voice actors for television were in heavy demand. For instance, Park Il, born in 1949, was a big star during the days when American television series were extremely popular in the 1970s and 1980s. Park was so popular as a voice actor, he actually took on other roles, as a television variety show MC and radio DJ, during the 1980s.

50. Well before Nelson Shin and his Seoul-based company, Akom, infamously provided the tedious animation labor needed for *The Simpsons* and other American animation films and TV programs, such as *The Transformers* and *X-Men*, for the past three decades, it was Japanese animation companies that first saw the potential to engage in offshore Korean animation labor during the latter half of the 1960s, even before the ink dried on the 1965 ROK-Japan Normalization Treaty. A Korean broadcasting company founded by Samsung, TBC, set up an animation sweatshop with Japanese animation creators and helped Fuji TV produce *Golden Bat* (黄金 バット *Ōgon Batto*; Korean, *Hwanggum pakjwi*) and *Humanoid Monster Bem* (妖怪人間ベム *Yōkai Ningen Bemu*; Korean, *Yogwe ingan*) in 1966 and operated in a close collaboration effort. Such joint ventures in animation between South Koreans and Japanese gave many of these television animation programs exemption status from banned import goods from Japan before the cultural ban was lifted in the 1990s. Many Korean children grew up watching *Mazinger Z* as well as the other titles mentioned here as dubbed animation programs—not knowing that they had originated from Japan. See Kim Jong-ok, "Sanŏphwa sidae hanguk hach'ŏng aenimeisyŏn e taehan yŏngu."

51. Jin, *New Korean Wave*, 151. As I elaborate further in the final chapter, these companies maintained an anti-union policy well into the twenty-first century.

52. With the combination of fourteen basic consonants and ten vowels that make up the alphabet system of hangul, Korean is very simple to use. Its simplicity has made both South and North Korea today virtually 100 percent literate countries. As an *Economist* article explains, "Advances in computing [in Korea] may also have been boosted by the ease with which Hangul can be entered into PCs and phones." S.C.S., "How Was Hangul Invented?"

53. John Lie writes, "The South Korean entrepreneurs (of SM Entertainment, YG, and JYP)—by using new Internet-based technologies to market a new musical style, and by devising a new business model that relied more on the Internet than on pressed records—made South Korea the first country where sales of digitized music exceeded sales of music in nondigital formats." Lie, *K-Pop*, 119.

54. Shin Joong-Hyun and Ki-t'ae Kim, "Majimak mutae aptun."

55. From the postwar years through the late 1990s, the Japanese cultural ban prohibited Koreans from importing from Japan almost all popular culture content, including popular magazines. However, Japanese influence dominated Korean popular culture well into the 1990s. During the 1970s and 1980s, many Korean magazines, especially many

teen and children's magazines published in Korea, plagiarized their Japanese counterparts cover to cover. So widespread were the copycat magazines in Korea that, by the early 1990s, several news reports were made on this phenomenon, including one by MBC *Nightly News* under the headline "Waesaek yua chapji to ilbon chapji kŭdaero pekkyŏ silt'ae" [Even baby magazines copy Japanese ones—cover to cover].

56. Even one of the best-known Korean literary critics, Kim Yun-shik, who taught for many years at Seoul National University, could not be free of the charges of plagiarizing from Japanese literary critics. There are reportedly more than seven paragraphs in his book *Hanguk kŭndae sosŏlsa yŏngu* [Study of the history of modern Korean literature], published in 1986, that were plagiarized from Karatani Kojin's original Japanese publication of *Origins of Modern Japanese Literature*. Yi Myong-won, a young literary critic in Korea, criticized Kim Yun-shik in his research, which earned him a place on the blacklist in the literary circle in Korea in 2000. See Yi Myŏng-won, *T'anŭn hyŏ*.

57. Fanon, *Black Skin, White Masks*, 7.

58. Fanon, *Black Skin, White Masks*, 17. Fanon is trying to state that the lost German or Russian still fares far better than a black man. In the next paragraph, he reminds you that "'there is nothing comparable when it comes to the black man. He has no culture, no civilization, no 'long historical past.'"

59. Such was also the fate of my grandfather's old photographs from the colonial period. I once found them in the attic in the early 1970s—locked away in a chest.

60. In another work, I discuss the rampant copying of Japanese manga by Korean *manhwa* artists that "saturated the [Korean] market up to the late 1980s" as a "matter of historical record." K. H. Kim and Choe, *Korean Popular Culture Reader*, 39.

61. Klein, "AFKN Nexus." Christina Klein here argues through her interview with director Bong Joon-ho that he and other New Korean Cinema filmmakers of his generation may have learned genre conventions of Hollywood filmmaking through the AFKN broadcasts during the 1970s and 1980s.

62. An, *Parameters of Disavowal*, 35.

63. The popularity of AFKN probably peaked in the mid-1970s and remained strong for another decade. By the late 1980s, the dissemination of VHS machines and the liberalization of the Hollywood film market made American movies and television programs aired on AFKN less novel. Because AKFN broadcast longer hours—for children and women during the day (*Sesame Street, Electric Company*, and daytime soaps) in the afternoon, (American sporting events such as NCAA, MLB, NFL, professional wrestling, and NBA) and during late-nights (talk shows and movies)—it was a channel that many youth, especially those who came of age during the 1970s and 1980s, fondly remember as a source of cultural growth.

64. Yu Chae-yong, *AFKN K'idŭ*.

65. Kim Chu-hŭi, "Migun kijich'on," 42.

66. Park Yong-gyu, "AFKN-TV ŭi tŭksŏng," 108. Even after 1996, when AFKN discontinued its service through Channel 2, Koreans could access it through UHF and also the cable network. It took American media companies' petition (not Koreans') to the US military for AFKN not to be available for free to Korean audiences. By the dawn of the new millennium, sitcoms such as *Friends* and dramas such as the *CSI* series were popular among young audiences who also spoke some English. American television companies wanted to sell these products to Korean television for broadcasting rights. Permitting AFKN to be accessible to all Koreans with a subscription to a cable network put their sales negotiations at a disadvantage.

67. Through an interview survey conducted in 2014 of people who grew up watching AFKN, Park Yong-gyu found that several of the interviewees had commented on how they would stay up past midnight during the 1960s watching movies broadcast on AFKN because it was the only network in Korea that would broadcast past midnight and also because AFKN broadcast more "sexually explicit" content than anything available on Korean television. Music programs like *Soul Train* were popular especially among young people because you could easily be entertained by music and dance programs without comprehending a word of English. By the 1970s, newspaper columns began to appear in the Korean language to criticize the sensational content allowed on AFKN. Park Yong-gyu, "AFKN-TV ŭi t'ŭksŏng," 117–18.

68. Hyunjoon Shin and S. Lee, *Made in Korea*.

69. Lie, *K-Pop*, 119.

70. Ministry of Culture, Sports, and Tourism, "Podojaryo."

71. John Lie criticizes the exported-oriented development strategy the Korean government has used in cultivating its brand of K-pop. But just as much as the Brazilian government cannot be faulted for its export of soccer players, finding South Korea culpable for the overseas success of its pop stars seems to me a misguided criticism. Lie, *K-pop, 114.*

72. Du Bois, *Souls of Black Folk*, 7.

73. The sensational 1995 Japanese hit song "Da.Yo.Ne" by mixed-gender hip-hop group East End X Yuri seemed to have influenced mainstream Korean hip-hop groups such as Roo'Ra, which ended up being accused of plagiarizing Japanese songs in 1996. However, early Korean hip-hop scenes since the late 1990s were dominated by Korean American rappers who were more familiar with American rappers than the Japanese ones.

Chapter One. K-Pop, K-Cinema, and K-Television

1. The rise of K-pop has positively impacted the study of Korean in educational institutions around the world. Even in the United States, where almost all languages taught in higher education had shown a precipitous decline in recent years, Korean showed an impressive growth of 13.7 percent: from 12,256 students enrolled in 2013 to 13,936 in 2016. Looney and Lusin, "Enrollments in Languages Other than English."

2. Dancing replaced the balladic nature of Korean music, producing idol syndrome after idol syndrome. The emphasis of visual presentation eventually gave way to what John Lie calls "body beautiful," which became "normative for South Korean music stars" (*K-Pop*, 107). During the same phase of paradigm shift, Lie argues that the K-pop impresarios "seized commercial opportunities rather than projecting their artistic vision" (120). Though it is difficult not to agree with Lie that considerations for K-pop are largely decided by market forces and visual criteria rather than by musical integrity, he further suggests that K-pop essentially rejects the essence of any Romantic pursuits of an artist by completely "eschew[ing] the independent musician-artist" (124). BIGBANG's leader, G-Dragon, is quite possibly an anomaly to this rule since he is one of the greatest singer-songwriters to have ever graced the center stage of the Korean pop world, and his fame in other cultural spheres such as art and fashion challenges Lie's argument that there is no trace of Romantic versatility in K-pop.

3. From the mid-1990s through the early years of the following decade, the South Korean government's cultural policy was heavily impacted by the report that *Jurassic Park*, Steven Spielberg's sensational film released in 1993, had earned US$850 million in one year, which was equivalent to the export sales of 1.5 million motor vehicles. As Inkyu Kang reports, "at that time, Korea was exporting barely 700,000 automobiles per year." Kang, "Political Economy of Idols," 51.

4. The 2018 report conducted by HRI, "Economic Effect of BTS," was widely reported in Korea and elsewhere. It projected that close to 800,000 foreigners on average visited South Korea for BTS-related reasons every year since the group's rise in 2015. The report claimed that BTS is estimated to have been responsible for 7.6 percent of the 10.4 million foreign tourists who visited South Korea and 1.7 percent of consumer exports in 2017. Of course, with the popularity of BTS soaring even higher since 2018, its economic impact on South Korea may be even larger. See Choi, "K-Pop Group BTS."

5. See Maliangkay, "Popularity of Individualism."

6. Maliangkay reports that some of the reasons for which Seo Taiji was banned from television stations were petty; for example, "the dreadlocks of Seo's band members led to a ban by KBS-TV" (Maliangkay, "Popularity of Individualism," 301). Also, "Kyosil idea" (Classroom ideology), which was released in 1994 and criticized the education system in Korea, was famously banned from television and radio.

7. Well known for its education fever, South Korea ranks first among Organisation for Economic Co-operation and Development (OECD) countries, in the percentage of secondary school graduation rates between twenty-five- and thirty-four-year-olds. Intense competition for entrance into top universities and top high schools has dramatically spurred an increase in private tutoring and the after-school system over the past two decades. Chon Sun Ihm and Hee Jung Choi report that "according to a recent estimate, more than 80 percent of students receive tutoring from for-profit private institutes." Ihm and Choi, "Early Study Abroad," 34–35.

8. In *K-Pop: Popular Music, Cultural Amnesia, and Economic Innovation in South Korea*, Lie posits K-pop as the antithesis of Confucianism, which probably is the reason why *cultural amnesia* appears in his book's subtitle. However, what Lie fails to recognize is that Confucianism is perhaps the single-most-important reason behind the unique structural underpinning of K-pop that depends on training teenaged girls for years before the groups are put together by the heads of entertainment agencies. Emphasis on the collective qualities of the group, which mold and pound individual identities of each of the team members, makes you wonder where this tradition of the group emphasis would stem from if it isn't derived from Confucianism. Yes, the visual appearance of K-pop, replete with its risqué wardrobe and sexually suggestive dance moves, may appear un-Confucian and unchaste. However, the ideological spirit that forsakes individualism in the agency-driven structure that relies largely on patriarchal, chaebol-like leadership of the entertainment company founders such as Lee Soo-man, Park Jin-young. and Yang Hyun-suk makes K-pop's spirits closely aligned with neo-Confucianism rather than anti-Confucianism.

9. When Seo Taiji's "Nan arayo" debuted on MBC's *Tŭkjong Yonae News* (Extra! Entertainment news) on April 11, 1992 (https://www.youtube.com/watch?v=tY23D2bbL4I), a panel of four judges that included songwriters as well as established singer Jeon Young-rok was asked to comment on the song. All criticized the song and ranked it a 7 or 8 on a 10-point scale.

10. Erica Vogel discusses the linguistic challenges some of the Mexican fans of K-pop face in "K-Pop in Mexico," 69.

11. Hyunjoon Shin and P. Kim, "Birth, Death, and Resurrection," 285.

12. Since 2010, the Korean government agency that oversees the labor contracts between talent and management companies has limited contract terms to seven years.

13. Gooyoung Kim, for instance, argues that K-pop artists are neoliberal agents that have been shaped by "biopolitical aspects of neoliberalism." G. Kim, *From Factory Girls*, xxi.

14. During both 2PM's Jay Park's feud with JYP and TVXQ's members' high-profile discontent with SM Entertainment's treatment of the stars that took place around 2008–9, the term *noye kyeyak* (slave contract) was commonly used by the fans supporting the stars and the media who were sympathetic to the musicians whose prime days of their career were locked into a contract that was typically signed when stars were only in their teens. Because of the media and the fans' protests against such an unreasonable length for an idol's standard contract, during the late 2010s, the contractual obligation of a performer was shortened to seven years.

15. Herman, "BTS Break Three Guinness World Records."

16. Chion, *Audio-Vision*.

17. Steintrager, "Sound-Objects," 1.

18. Steintrager, "Sound-Objects," 4.

19. The year before *JSA* was released, *Shiri* opened in theaters. It portrayed a North Korean soldier who is sent as a spy to South Korea to assassinate its own president. However, played by Ch'oe Min-sik, this North Korean soldier falls into the category of a villain.

20. Noh, "Korean President Park Geun-hye."

21. This is a point I raised in "Mea Culpa: Reading the North Korean as an Ethnic Other," a chapter in *Virtual Hallyu*.

22. Youngmin Choe's *Tourist Distractions* discusses this interaction between moviegoing and travel in fuller detail.

23. More than 80 percent of all screenings during the first weekend of May 2019 in Korean movie theaters were occupied by *Avengers: Endgame,* which began the political discussion for the writing of a new law that would limit such monopolistic release and distribution of films in Korea. See Nam In-yŏng, "Avengers."

24. See the 2019 theatrical market statistics compiled by the Motion Picture Association of America (MPAA), available at https://www.motionpictures.org/wp-content /uploads/2020/03/MPA-THEME-2019.pdf. Out of the world's $42.2 billion market, the United States' and Canada's share is about $11.4 billion, while China's $9.3 billion is a distant second—but much closer than it was a few years ago. The United States/ Canada box office market had shrunk in 2019 from the previous year by 4 percent while the Asia Pacific market led by China and South Korea had grown by 4 percent in the same period. South Korea's market is fourth at $1.6 billion.

25. Yu Chae-hyŏk, "CJ E&M '2020nyŏn kkaji haeoe rok'ŏl yŏnghwa yŏn 20-p'yŏn kaebong.'"

26. See *The World Wide Web Foundation*'s official site, "Internet Users in the World," accessed February 22, 2021, https://www.internetlivestats.com/watch/internet-users/.

27. UNESCO Institute for Statistics, "Feature Films: Exhibition—Admissions & Gross Box Office," accessed February 22, 2021, http://data.uis.unesco.org/index.aspx?queryid =59.

28. According to the 2014 annual report of the Korean Film Council (KOFIC), only Iceland boasts a better moviegoing rate per capita in the world at 4.28. South Korea recorded 4.19 in 2014. In 2015 and 2016, the US/Canada admissions per capita was 3.8. In 2019, it further slipped to 3.5. MPAA, "Theatrical Market Statistics 2019."

29. Deleuze and Guattari, *Anti-Oedipus,* 4.

30. In the record-setting year, more than 1.5 billion movie tickets were sold in the United States in 2002. In 2019 this number, despite the rise of overall US population, declined to sales of 1.24 billion tickets. Box Office Mojo, accessed February 13, 2021, https://www.boxofficemojo.com/yearly/?view2=domestic&view=releasedate&p =.htm. See also MPAA, "Theatrical Market Statistics 2019."

31. Kim Ko-ŭn, "Pangsongsa maech'ul . . ."

32. An, "Naver, Kakao."

33. Paek, "Google and Facebook."

34. Paek, "Google and Facebook."

35. Lynn Spigel writes that over the course of a single decade, from 1948 to 1955, in America, "television was installed in nearly two-thirds of the nation's homes." Spigel, *Make Room for TV*, 1.

36. Kim Yong-ju, "Hanguk, pangsong cont'ench'ŭ."

37. Jin, *New Korean Wave*.

38. Caillois, *Man, Play and Games*, 14–26.

39. Sam Kim, "South Korea Set to Break Own Record."

40. Jiang, "'Running Man.'"

41. Lee Kyung-min, "I'm Satisfied Living Alone."

42. Hyunjoon Shin and P. Kim, "Birth, Death, and Resurrection," 291.

43. See Statista, "Box Office Revenue in South Korea from 2004 to 2019," accessed January 31, 2021, https://www.statista.com/statistics/625439/south-korea-cinema-ticket-sales-box-office/.

Chapter Two. The Souls of Korean Folk

I dedicate this chapter to Nahum Chandler, a friend, a colleague, and an intellectual guiding light, for providing me opportunities to present portions of this material at his conferences and for allowing me to scurry, ramble, and rap about Du Bois and his Korean soul.

An earlier version of this chapter was published as "Becoming-Black: Exploring Korean Hip-Hop in the Age of Hallyu," *Situations* 12, no. 1 (2019): 23–46.

1. For *Sopyonje*, see K. H. Kim, *Remasculinization of Korean Cinema*, 60–66; K. H. Kim, *Virtual Hallyu*, 23–37; and K. H. Kim, "Watching *Sopyonje*."

2. Jeff Chang, in his *Can't Stop, Won't Stop*, claims that "Boyz-n-the Hood" became "an anthem for the fatherless, brotherless, state-assaulted, heavily armed West Coast urban youth, a generation of Jonathan Jacksons." Jackson was a real-life black martyr who was only seventeen years old when he was killed in a shootout after kidnapping a Superior Court judge and prosecutor from the courtroom in Northern California in 1970 when he demanded that several of the black activists be released from prison. This led to the famous court case where Angela Davis was tried in court because the guns used by Jackson and other kidnappers were registered under her name. Davis was later acquitted. Chang, *Can't Stop, Won't Stop*, 306.

3. In *Straight Outta Compton*, screen time compresses real historical time. Eazy-E had to walk through every four bars of the songs over two full days of recording. In the film, he gets it right, after only several tries and putting on his sunglasses at night.

4. Dongho is actually not a biological child of Yubong but an adopted child. However, the fact that he remains an unremarkable musician is almost shocking given the fact that he grew up under the tutelage of Yubong. *Sopyonje* denies the theory that family tradition plays a major factor in the cultivation of musical talent.

5. While discussing *Snowpiercer* (2013), a transnational sci-fi film directed by Korean filmmaker Bong Joon-ho, Seunghoon Jeong writes that the film's ending with a catastrophe reaffirms the common notion that "it is easier to imagine the end of the world than the end of capitalism. . . . The negation of the negative status quo does not necessarily lead to a positive synthesis, but rather serves as a warning criticism of all different alternatives." Jeong, *Global Auteur*, 370. Fredric Jameson states that Theodor Adorno's negative dialectics is a "negativity that ceaselessly undermines all the available positivities until it has only its own destructive energies to promote." Jameson, *Valences of the Dialectic*, 57. In many ways, both *Snowpiercer* and *Sopyonje* can be favorably compared as they continue to cancel out all the positivities (able bodies, successful revolution, perfection of aesthetics, etc.) until they both reach less-than-satisfying endings.

6. Although many of these musicians who have given birth to the genre of gangster rap are no longer associated with poverty, it is very difficult to claim that these black stars are illegitimate due to having lost their ties with their black community. Rap stars such as Jay-Z and Dr. Dre and basketball players such as LeBron James and Magic Johnson are largely regarded as heroes in African American neighborhoods and black communities around the world, for they have overcome hardship from the 'hood in order to achieve a commercial success that has built important links between white mainstream businesses and urban ghettos.

7. P'ansori, almost invisible in regular television or radio programming in Korea, is mostly sustained through the Kugak Broadcasting System, which is operated entirely through government funding. More than US$6 million is spent each year on maintaining this channel's activity, funding that is often challenged in the National Assembly due to conservative opposition. It is also a channel that has yet to provide a single hit program in its twenty-year history. Song Ch'ang-han, "Pangt'ongwi, kugak pangsong yesan 67ŏkwon."

8. Glissant, "Transparency and Opacity."

9. As Raquel Rivera has argued, the participation of Latinos and Puerto Ricans was critical in the formation of hip-hop culture in urban areas. See Rivera, *New York Ricans*.

10. In his article, Thomas answers his own question, "Can the Japanese rap?": "Is it possible for the subculture which by societal standards should not exist, and which is unsure itself if it should exist, to speak with the same unreflective abandon and freedom that rock exists? It is not impossible. It might be achieved passively: perhaps with time, some of the perceived 'blackness' will fall away from the genre of hip-hop, as it largely has with jazz." Thomas, "Can the Japanese Rap?," 236.

11. Du Bois, *Souls of Black Folk*, 7.

12. Du Bois, *Souls of Black Folk*, 7.

13. After meeting with North Korean leader Kim Jong-un in a historical summit in Singapore on June 12, 2018, Donald Trump discussed the eventual withdrawal of 28,500 US troops from the Korean peninsula. Trump is only the second US president (Jimmy Carter is the other) to suggest the possibility of pulling US military personnel from Korea. US forces have been stationed in Korea for seventy-five years, since the conclusion of World War II.

14. As discussed in the introduction, Dohee Kwon notes that television stations and radio stations in South Korea often faced a choice between AKPM and JCS. Kwon, "Shin Joong Hyun's Sonority," 125.

15. Du Bois, *Souls of Black Folk*, 192.

16. In addition to Kwon, "Shin Joong Hyun's Sonority," see Hyunjoon Shin and P. Kim, "Birth, Death, and Resurrection."

17. In a study of hip-hop culture titled *Appropriating Blackness: Performance and the Politics of Authenticity*, E. Patrick Johnson claims, "In contemporary society, one of the most palpable examples of the arbitrariness and politics of authenticity is in language use." He cites both fallacies and authenticities of the claim that "talking 'white' is equivalent to speaking Standard English and talking 'black' is equivalent to speaking in the black vernacular." Johnson, *Appropriating Blackness*, 5. Since the "black vernacular"—real or manufactured—is crucial to almost all rappers who are trying to associate their authentic value to what essentially is entangled in the African American experience, I ask, how does the need to perform "black" signifiers by non-American rappers who may lack any experience of communicating in "black (English) vernacular" help abet or destroy one's agency to authenticate? Is the inability to authenticate the linguistic "black vernacular" the real reason behind so many Korean rappers choosing to braid their hair in cornrows, as if to emulate black men in a penitentiary, as a bodily compensation for their lack of authentic 'hood rhetoric?

18. Michael Eric Dyson has written that "rap music is emblematic of the glacial shift in aesthetic sensibilities." Dyson, "Culture of Hip-Hop," 63. While Dyson here mentions "shifts," he is referring to intergenerational shifts among African Americans and shifts in the economic base from middle- and upper-middle-class to poor urban black people. The depression of urban communities over the past fifty years and the political demoralization that have impacted African American communities are what have raised rap music to its present popular status. However, perhaps equally important in this shift in aesthetic sensibilities, which he fails to mention, is the fact that the sound of raw beats and the scratches that fall between the beats of hip-hop further devalued the importance of melody as the principal criteria for popular music. One could go as far as to claim that the waning of melodies and the exhaustion of rock 'n' roll paved the way for the ascension of hip-hop—new music that was not at all reliant on melodies and instead favored the beats of the street. Listening to the latest rap sensation, Kendrick Lamar, for instance, will make you realize that the last hurdle of eliminating melody in hip-hop—the hook—has almost all but disappeared. Lamar's best songs from the

album *Damn* (2017), "DNA" and "Humble," are simple, loopy, and perhaps most importantly hookless.

19. Glissant, "Transparency and Opacity," 112. I am here indebted to the anonymous manuscript reviewer who recommended Glissant's work to me.

20. Though the first innovation in Korean rap music is usually identified with the arrival of Seo Taiji, it would be difficult to claim that he is revered as the king of hip-hop to the generation of Korean rap artists today. Seo stayed in the pop genre and spent much time as a choreographer of b-boy dance. Even though he rapped, his songs were better known for their soft melodies. In "Nan arayo," a ballad, rather than rap, occupies the centrality of the song. The element of rap is short. Certainly, the accentuation on the first syllable of "arayo" is what pronounced the early rap in Korea, but it is still difficult to see him as a rapper above everything else. See Maliangkay, "Popularity of Individualism."

21. Maliangkay writes, "More than 1.5 million copies of the debut album [that contained the single 'Nan arayo'] were sold within a month from the date of its release and at the end of the year the band had taken all the music awards." Maliangkay, "Popularity of Individualism," 298.

22. Morelli, "Who Is a Dancing Hero?," 250.

23. Katja Lee, "Reconsidering Rap's 'I,'" 353.

24. The identity construction of Korean American rappers' self-posturing that ties them to the underdog victim from the ghetto is complicated because they are obviously already a privileged subject compared to most people who live in Korea. Korean American rap superstars Tiger JK and Tablo of Epic High fame had upper-middle-class family backgrounds and had attended prestigious universities in the United States, UCLA and Stanford, respectively. The only kind of struggles that they had to offer were their antiestablishment alienation and rejections they faced from the producers in mainstream television and radio broadcast in South Korea, as Korean Americans who largely spoke broken Korean, which could not earn sympathy from the masses. The posturing of the "bad boy" image itself was fraught with limits, without the kind of upbringing of ghetto racist adversities that African Americans had historically faced. On the kind of personal attacks on internet and social media blogs that Tablo has suffered because he graduated from Stanford, see Haerin Shin, "Dynamics of K-Pop Spectatorship."

25. See the music video for G-Dragon, "Ni-ga Mwŏnde" [Who you?], YouTube, November 13, 2013, https://www.youtube.com/watch?v=doFK7Eanm3I. Suk-Young Kim devotes about twelve pages in her book *K-Pop Live* to discuss this video. While she focuses on the putative "live" element of the music video, interestingly enough, she refrains from commenting on how the song's title and the lyrics point to the fictive black figure through the wordplay. Suk-Young Kim, *K-Pop Live*, 115–27.

26. A popular female K-pop icon, Jimin of AOA, drew negative attention from her fans when she tweeted a line from Nicki Minaj in a song by Nelly called "Get Like Me," which featured the words "my nigga spend money like coke price free." She later had

to apologize for posting the inflammatory "N" word on her account. See Koreaboo, November 15, 2016, https://www.koreaboo.com/buzz/jimin-receives-backlash-saying-n-word-cover/.

27. Quinn, *Nuthin' but a "G" Thang*, 34.

28. Yoon Mirae has spoken frankly about her experience of living in both the United States and Korea as a mixed-race child. Born in Fort Hood, Texas, near the US military compound, she dropped out of high school at age fifteen because of the racial discrimination she faced. She has candidly rapped and sung about these traumatic experiences in tracks such as "Black Happiness." See Yoon Mirae, "Black Happiness," YouTube, December 23, 2015, https://www.youtube.com/watch?v=1DK-MPh7vKk.

29. See Drunken Tiger, "A Great Birth," YouTube, April 19, 2012, https://www.youtube.com/watch?v=HP4IY-hz_hI.

30. Ongiri, "'He Wanted to Be Just Like Bruce Lee,'" 32.

31. Hall, "Notes on Deconstructing the Popular," 228.

32. Seabrook, *Song Machine*, 127.

33. Song Myŏng-sŏn, *Hiphap hata 2*, 165–67.

34. Lee Woo-young, "Han Dong-chul."

35. Thewesterngirl, "'Show Me the Money 4.'"

36. Of course, it could be argued that mandam did continue to survive in the late 1980s and the 1990s in American-style comedy talk shows such as *Johnny Yoon Show* (1989–90), *Joo Byong-jin Show* (1993, and again in 1995 on MBC), and *Seo Se-won Show* (1996–2002 on KBS2-TV). More recently it is the weekly late-night program *Radio Star* (2007–present) that allows more adult-themed mandam to be featured on broadcast television. However, unlike American-style stand-up comedy, or the earlier form of mandam performed by Sin Pul-ch'ul and, after the Korean War, Kwak Kyu-seok and Pae Sam-yong as a structured routine of storytelling, mandam is completely free-form talk that has very little form or structure and therefore cannot be classified as an aesthetic performance the way a rap song or a stand-up comedy routine can be. It can be argued that Kim Ou-Joon, a radio talk show host and an original member of the Nanŭn Kkomsuda (I am a weasel), a popular podcast that provided anti-conservative commentary during the Lee Myung-bak regime, is the only legitimate mandam-ga left in Korea today.

37. Yi Sang-won, "Sho'mi."

38. As of May 26, 2018, it had sold more than one million downloads. It was the best-selling hip-hop track of 2017—topping the download chart two weeks in a row in the early weeks of September as *SMTM* was coming to the season finale. "List of Gaon Digital Chart Number Ones of 2017," Wikipedia, accessed February 24, 2021, https://en.wikipedia.org/wiki/List_of_Gaon_Digital_Chart_number_ones_of_2017.

39. See Yun Kwang-ŭn, "Hanguk hiphap."

40. For many years, the National Institute of Korean Language, which is operated by the South Korean government, did not recognize the spelling of the popular black bean noodles in Korea as *tchajangmyŏn* (짜장면) and instead only permitted the use of *chajangmyŏn* (pronounced as *jajangmyeon*) (자장면), despite the fact that most Koreans call the inexpensive Korean-Chinese noodles the former. Only in 2011 did the institute officially recognize the dual spelling of the word after not allowing it for several decades. The battle between *tchajangmyŏn* (aspirated tense sound derived from the double consonant) and *jajangmyeon* (plain sound) exemplifies the effort by the government to encourage the use of plain sounds in Korean because the double consonants and aspirated consonants sound were perceived to be uncultured and "foreign." See Sin, *Ŏnŏ ŭi chultariki*, 244–61.

41. Gray composed the beats for the song and served as a contracted producer for rapper Jay Park's label AOMG.

42. See Woo Won-jae, "Sich'a" [We are], YouTube, September 6, 2017, https://www.youtube.com/watch?v=vdwEE1mwjOo.

43. According to Johannes Helmbrecht, only the languages of East and Southeast Asia such as Japanese, Burmese, and Thai have a strong sensitivity to politeness in language usage and within their grammars. Speakers have to account for a variety of social distinctions linguistically. Social distinctions between speaker and listener may reflect relative age, kinship, social ranking, intimacy, and other social features. Helmbrecht, "Politeness Distinctions in Pronouns."

44. The biggest controversy relating to this matter involved the British translator Deborah Smith, who failed to grasp on several occasions the true meaning behind the omitted *you* in the novel *The Vegetarian*, by Han Kang, and mistranslated it as *I*. See Armitstead, "Lost in (Mis)translation?" For a list of mistranslations that include the examples of non-Korean speakers or translators who incorrectly designate the subject behind the omitted *you*, see Wook-Dong Kim, "'Creative' English Translation."

45. Jin, *Smartland Korea*, 153.

46. A recent book on this subject is Myungji Yang's *From Miracle to Mirage: The Making and Unmaking of the Korean Middle Class, 1960–2015*. In it, she describes how in Korea "a small number of young people are able to acquire decent, full-time jobs, while the rest become non-regular workers who are underemployed, leading a precarious, insecure life" (108). The precarious condition of the "spec" generation who are driven to pressure themselves with strengthening their résumés is part of the reason why Korea suffers from one of the highest suicide rates and lowest fertility rates in the world today.

47. See John Lie's *K-Pop* and my discussion of the book in the introduction.

48. See Vinxen's performance on the final episode of *High School Rapper* Season 2, YouTube, April 13, 2018, https://www.youtube.com/watch?v=ACnh9zlmPNE.

49. Though not much is known about Sin after the Korean War, he may have lost his life during the purge of colonial-era artists carried out by Kim Il-sung in the 1970s.

50. Song Kwang-ho, "Mandam-ka 'Sin Pul-ch'ul' ŭl asinayo?"

51. Gates, *Signifying Monkey*, 52.

52. Gates, *Signifying Monkey*, 62. Gates also cites Harold Bloom, a literary critic who defines metalepsis as a "trope-reversing trope, a figure of a figure." Gates, *Signifying Monkey*, 52.

53. Hŭksujŏ means "dirt spoon" and refers to people who have not inherited any wealth. Of course, dirt here symbolizes not only the earth, and therefore the lower economic class, but also the color code of black. Notice that in the latest Korean film sensation, *Parasite*, the darkest-skinned character in the film is Geun-sae, who has been occupying the basement bunker—despite the fact that he has rarely seen the sun during his four-year-plus hideout—while all members of the rich Park family are fair-skinned. This is not a coincidence or a creative liberty exercised by the film's director, Bong Joon-ho. He has used different shades of skin color to classify class positions of haves and have-nots even though they are all putatively same-race people. See also chapter 5.

54. Du Bois, *Souls of Black Folk*, 227.

55. "그까짓 천대 받는 소리를 해봤자 앞날이 뻔한디 . . ." is the original in Korean words that Dongho spits against his father. Noteworthy here is his lamentation of his birth right that is already predetermined as *ch'ŏndae* (vulgar). It is not only his personal birth as an abandoned orphan and the adopted son of a poor, itinerant musician that leads him to declare himself as a "misbirth" but also his national identity, whose musical soul is tied to a Korea that had to suffer because of foreign occupations and invasions.

56. "모두 비웃었던 동방의 소음이 어느새 전국을 울려대" is the original Korean verse. Woo Won-jae is actually here parodying the line from Tagore's poem published in *Tong-a Ilbo*, a Korean newspaper, in 1929. When visiting Japan, the Indian poet declared that Korea, the nation that was then struggling for its independence, was the "lamp of the East." Tagore's original lines are "In the Golden Age of Asia / Korea was one of the lamp-bearers / That lamp waits to be lighted once again / For the illumination of the East." English original available in Sharma, "New Trends in Modern Literature," 96–97.

Chapter Three. Dividuated Cinema

1. Jeon, "Memories of Memories," 88.

2. Citing the demise of traditional analog photography as a major factor, Sweden's Stockholm Water Authority declared in 2005 that toxic silver ion pollution had been radically reduced in the sewage system. The rise of digital photography has reduced not only chemical waste but also paper waste, since most people now print only the photos they need. See Parkman, "Swedish Capital Sees Less Silver Pollution."

3. Steve Lohr's book *Data-ism* argues that improved methods of analyzing data, backed by powerful machines that employ super algorithms, are transforming how decisions are made and the ways in which we live.

4. Jameson, *Geopolitical Aesthetic*, 26.

5. "We live in a society where *all the time* we meet men and women who aren't there. Acquaintance used to be face-to-face, a firm handshake, getting the cut of someone's jib. Trust was a matter of direct, personal acquaintance. But the needs of a complex society, and a set of new technologies, changed all that." O'Hara and Shadbolt, *Spy in the Coffee Machine*, 1. These words ring true even more after having endured sixteen months of social-distanced protocols.

6. Foucault, *Discipline and Punish*, 214; Deleuze, *Negotiations*, 177.

7. Deleuze, *Negotiations*, 181.

8. Brooks, *Reading for the Plot*, 22.

9. *Indexicality* originates from the index, which was used by Peirce during the latter half of the nineteenth century to underscore less-than-clear-cut signs that bear little resemblance to their original objects. His examples included a footprint, a weathervane, the word *this*, and a photograph. See Peirce, *Essential Peirce*. More recently, the term has been adopted by visual studies scholars to determine, in the words of Tom Gunning, "a physical relation between the object photographed and the image finally created." See Gunning, "What's the Point of an Index?," 24.

10. Lukács, *Historical Novel*, 33.

11. Lukács, *Historical Novel*, 33.

12. Lukács, *Historical Novel*, 32.

13. There are two directors in particular whose work lends them a kind of "middle way" that both mourns and celebrates the downfall of a monarchic rule or an aristocratic orthodoxy: Lee Joon-ik and Kim Dae-woo. Lee Joon-ik became a hit filmmaker of the decade with the enormous success of *The King and the Clown* (2005), set during the period of Yeon-san's rule of terror, and another Oedipal drama, *The Throne* (*Sado*, 2015), in which King Yeong-jo infamously killed his crown prince by detaining him in a race chest for eight days in 1762. In addition, Kim Dae-woo emerged in the decade as one of Korea's most talented writer-directors through two successful sagŭk films: a fictional romance between the queen and an erotic genre writer, *Forbidden Quest* (*Umran sŏsaeng*, 2007), and *The Servant* (*Pangjajŏn*, 2010), a revisionist interpretation of the classic romantic tale of Chunhyang. Both films focus on characters who are neither yangbans of great scholarship nor warriors of immense courage. In *Forbidden Quest*, the protagonist is a son of a prominent yangban but shirks the tedious political war between families and instead chooses to find success as an erotic novel writer. In *The Servant*, it is Bangja, the facetious servant of Mongryong, who emerges as the hero in the story and ends up getting the "prized girl," Chunhyang, at the end. This revision, which is rooted in *namsadangp'ae* satire, leaves viewers to wonder if *Romeo and Juliet*

could be just as dramatic, had Juliet fallen not for Romeo but for Mercutio. See K. H. Kim. *Virtual Hallyu*, 200–212.

14. Yoshimoto, *Kurosawa*, 98; Burch, *To the Distant Observer*, 72.

15. Yoshimoto, *Kurosawa*, 100.

16. Michel Chion uses the term *acousmatic* to explain sound that is "heard without its cause or source being seen" and distinguishes it from a "visualized situation." Chion, *Voice in Cinema*, 18–19. See chapter 1 for more discussion of K-pop and its visualized music.

17. Dolar, *Voice and Nothing More*, 60.

18. The best example Baudrillard offers as a model of "all the entangled orders of simulacra" is Disneyland. Baudrillard, *Simulacra and Simulation*, 12.

19. Historian Christian Parenti uses the term *soft cage* to describe how America has built a twenty-first-century digital surveillance system by expanding its technology developed over the past two centuries—from the need to monitor slaves in the South to tracking immgrants and early criminals. See Parenti, *Soft Cage*.

20. Coincidentally, actress Han Hyo-ju plays both the queen of Kwanghae in *Masquerade* and Yi-soo in *Beauty Inside*.

21. Martin-Jones, "Decompressing Modernity," 56.

22. Magnan-Park, "*Peppermint Candy*," 161.

23. McGowan, "Affirmation of the Lost Object," 171.

24. Barthes, *Camera Lucida*, 1.

25. Barthes, *Camera Lucida*, 43.

26. Deleuze, *Cinema 2*, 129.

27. Not only does South Korea register the highest moviegoing rate in the world, but it also defends the title of the most overwired nation in the world—ever since the meaning of "wired" changed from electricity and steel to DSL and 5G. Seoul, particularly, has also been called the bandwidth capital of the world, and it leads the number of DSL connections per head worldwide.

Chapter Four. *Running Man*

I thank Tian Li, a former graduate student, who pointed out *Running Man*'s immense popularity in China. She also translated the blog from the Chinese social media site Weibo. Her comments on an earlier version of this chapter were valuable.

Portions of this chapter appeared as "Running Man: The Korean Television Variety Program on the Transnational Affective Run," *Telos* 184 (Fall 2018): 163–84.

1. In late 2016, there were several rumors that SBS was considering either canceling the show or replacing some of the permanent cast members. However, despite these

reports, as of June 2021, the show remains on the air with most of the main cast intact.

2. Spigel, "Introduction," 3.

3. Gerow, "Kind Participation," 134–35.

4. *Hurry Up, Brother*, despite the pandemic, finished airing its eighth season in August 2020. The Chinese spin-off *of Running Man* did go through a couple of title changes. It was first changed to *Running Man China* and then finally to *Keep Running* (奔跑吧, *Bēnpǎo Ba*).

5. Streamside, "'Running Man' Remake."

6. E. Jung, "Transnational Korea," 75.

7. There are some recent reality-television shows, such as *The Great British Baking Show*, that do not select winners and separate them from losers, but these certainly are not American and are very rare in the context of even Western television.

8. Bauwens, Kostakis, and Pazaitis, *Peer to Peer*, 1.

9. Lie also writes, "One thing is certain: had Confucianism survived and thrived in South Korea, K-pop would not have been possible." Lie, *K-Pop*, 69.

10. George A. De Vos, "Confucian Family Socialization: The Religion, Morality, and Aesthetics of Propriety," in *Confucianism and the Family*, edited by Walter H. Slote and George A. DeVos (New York: State University of New York Press, 1998), 364.

11. Baudrillard, *Simulacra and Simulation*, 23.

12. Gregory J. Seigworth and Melissa Gregg, "An Inventory of Shimmers," in Gregg and Seigworth, *The Affect Theory Reader*, 9.

13. I am borrowing the term *spreadability* from the book title of Jenkins, Ford, and Green, *Spreadable Media*.

14. Ahmed, "Happy Objects," 38.

15. Ahmed, "Happy Objects," 38, emphasis added.

16. Ahmed, "Happy Objects," 38.

17. Kim Ha-nŭl, "'Running Man' Is Exported." On the global success of *American Idol*, see Bochanty-Aguero, "We Are the World."

18. Jameson, *Postmodernism*, 5.

19. Chen, "Imperialist Eye.."

20. K. H. Kim, "Part Four," 250.

21. Choe's *Tourist Distractions* discusses how the experience of travel, for instance, brings out new viewing complexities that suggest a new East Asian affective economy. Jenkins, "Transmedia Storytelling 101."

22. Actress Song Ji-hyo is one of the only female MCs who have had a permanent place among the cast members not only in *Running Man* but also in popular action comedy

shows. *Muhan Dojeon*, in its entire thirteen-year broadcast history, for instance, never had a female MC. Though Song's role is small, compared to the main MCs Yoo Jae-suk or Haha, she, understated in her beauty and erotic appeal, has always been an asset to the program and perhaps the secret recipe to the show's long-term success.

23. Gerow states that Japanese critics of screen captions (what he calls "telop") have expressed "fears that its overuse will 'rob viewers of the ability to sense the delight of turns in conversation or figures of speech' or eliminate forms of 'thinking humor' with the audience itself left stupid." Gerow, "Kind Participation," 123. Korean television critics initially responded to screen captions in a similar fashion.

24. Derrida, *Of Grammatology*, 41.

25. Koreans, partly because of Confucian principles and learning, are sensitive as to how to address each other by name. Such sensitivity placed on names also often produces humor. On a recent episode of *The Tonight Show Starring Jimmy Fallon*, Jimmy Fallon, an American talk-show host, asks BTS members about their "secret career dreams." Despite his limited English, Suga jokes about Jimin's childhood dream of becoming a talk-show host. When Fallon playfully yells, "Don't take over my job!" Suga, seated next to Jimin, quickly quips, "Maybe [a] Ji*min* Fallon." "BTS on First Impressions, Secret Career Dreams and Map of the Soul: 7 Meanings," YouTube, February 24, 2020, https://www.youtube.com/watch?v=v_9vgidPJ8g. Such a humorous reorganization of Western names to follow the Korean three- or two-syllable rules of nomenclature is very common in Korea. Korean fans of NBA basketball, for instance, call the former star player of the Houston Rockets, Russell Westbrook, Sŏ Pŭruk (Seo Brook), which fulfills the three-syllable name rule in Korean. It is a playful game of localizing the name of the star point guard's "West" into "Sŏ," which in Korean means *direction west* and is also a popular Korean surname.

26. Wang, *Politics of Imagining Asia*, 95. Wang examines the phonocentric scheme in China that, throughout history, tried to regulate and standardize the proper pronunciation of Chinese that became the basis of Mandarin along with the modern language unification movements that took place in both Japan and Korea. While pursuing this line of thought, Wang is attentive to Kojin's discussion of Derrida's *Of Grammatology* in his article "Nationalism and *Écriture*," which was translated into Chinese: "Minzu zhuyi yu shuxie yuyan," *Xueren* [The scholar] 9 (1996).

27. In fact, a phonetic writing system had existed in Korea for 550 years, ever since King Sejong the Great devised a Korean alphabet that prioritized phonetic sound in the writing system introduced in 1443, although the system in question remained largely uncirculated until the 1890s.

28. Karatani, "Nationalism and *Écriture*," 18.

29. Bong Joon-ho made this comment while accepting the Best Foreign Language Film award during the Seventy-Seventh Golden Globe Awards ceremony, January 5, 2020.

30. Wada-Marciano, "Global and Local Materialities of Anime," 242.

31. Wang, *Politics of Imagining Asia*, 13.

32. Cartwright, *Moral Spectatorship*, 25.

33. Dargis, "Scorsese's Hall of Mirrors."

34. Lucy Mazdon reports that when Luc Besson's French action film *Nikita* was remade into an English-language film titled *The Assassin*, the prolific British film critic Barry Norman penned these words: "Another example of Hollywood's unfortunate tendency to remake fine Continental fare and turn it into sensationalist pap." Mazdon, *Encore Hollywood*, 1.

35. Li, "Guonai Zongyi."

36. Kim, with Li, "Running Man," 180.

37. Mazdon, *Encore Hollywood*, 5.

38. Sŏ, "Chunggukp'an 'Running Man.'"

Chapter Five. The Virtual Feast

1. Box office earnings of $127 million place *Extreme Job* in first place for any film released in the country. In terms of actual number of tickets sold, it trails only *The Admiral: Roaring Currents*, a period film about Admiral Yi Sun-shin's naval battles against the Japanese navy in the late sixteenth century.

2. Kroll, "Kevin Hart to Star in English Remake."

3. See my essay "Crossing Borders," included in the Criterion Collection Blu-ray release of *The Housemaid*.

4. I here also invoke the term *virtual*, which I have used in my *Virtual Hallyu*, to indicate "artificial," along with its original meaning of "truthful" and "potential."

5. Chŏng Ŭn-jŏng, *Taehanminguk ch'ik'in chŏn*, 18.

6. Peterson and Rie, "Korean Fried Chicken."

7. It was reported in 2015 that the number of fried-chicken restaurants in Korea had surpassed the number of McDonald's worldwide. Kim Nam-kwŏn, "Hanguk ch'ik'injip Sam-man-yuk-chŏn-kot."

8. Jameson, *Valences of the Dialectic*, 424.

9. Lee Kyung-min, "I'm Satisfied Living Alone."

10. Sloterdijk, *Critique of Cynical Reason*, 3.

11. Gallup, "What Is the World's Emotional Temperature?," accessed February 26, 2021, https://news.gallup.com/interactives/248240/global-emotions.aspx.

12. Manning, "'And You Know This, Man!,'" 244.

13. Hye-jin Kim, "'Spoon Theory.'"

14. See K. H. Kim, *Remasculinization of Korean Cinema*, 27–30.

15. Myungji Yang argues that "since the economic crisis in 1997, the socioeconomic landscape in Korea has been completely overturned. . . . Membership in the middle class, a symbol of social and economic possibility and confidence in the 1970s and 1980s, is now a challenging status to maintain and is increasingly characterized by heightened anxiety and frustration." Yang, *From Miracle to Mirage*, 2.

16. Sloterdijk, *Critique of Cynical Reason*, 4.

17. Sloterdijk, *Critique of Cynical Reason*, 7.

18. See Gates, *Signifying Monkey*.

19. Fanon, *Black Skin, White Masks*, 36, emphasis added.

20. Fanon, *Black Skin, White Masks*, 110.

21. Donald Trump tweeted on February 27, 2019, that "The potential [of North Korea] is AWESOME, a great opportunity, like almost none other in history, for my friend Kim Jong Un." This was widely reported since it was tweeted right before his second summit with Kim in Vietnam. Yee Nee Lee, "Trump Says."

22. You, *Writing in the Devil's Tongue*; Bizzell, "Who Owns English in South Korea?," 72.

23. Homi K. Bhabha, "DissemiNation," in Bhabha, *Location of Culture*, 139–70.

24. Deleuze and Guattari, "What Is a Minor Literature?," 16.

25. Another film that foregrounds the Korean relation to the English language is *I Can Speak* (dir. Kim Hyun-seok, 2017), the story of a former wartime comfort woman who struggles to come to terms with the trauma of her past and in which learning English, the topic of a supplemental plotline, becomes more essential than the main plotline itself. The priority of the supplemental plotline is already suggested in the Korean title (*Ai k'aen supik'u*), which is a hangulization of the English title phrase. The drama is loosely based on the life of an actual comfort woman, the halmoni (grandmother) Lee Yong-soon, who in 2007 testified in a US congressional hearing prior to the passing of Resolution 121, which demanded that the Japanese government apologize for past crimes against comfort women and incorporate curriculum materials on the subject in Japanese schools. In *I Can Speak*, the story focuses on the relation between Ok-bun, a cantankerous older woman known to torment low-level clerks working in her district office, and Min-jae, a young male civil servant. Min-jae reluctantly agrees to teach Ok-bun English and subsequently learns that her determination to learn the language stems from her desire to find her brother, who immigrated to the United States before the Korean War. But he also discovers that she has a second motivation: her friend Jeong-sim, a former comfort woman like her, has made a commitment to learn English in order to testify in Washington against Japanese war atrocities on behalf of Korean comfort women, but she has fallen ill and cannot make the trip. The duty of giving the testimony now falls on Ok-bun, who, during the story's climax, flies to Washington, DC, to deliver a speech in English

to American congressmen prior to the vote on Resolution 121. *I Can Speak* proved to be a hit in Korea, striking an emotional chord with audiences still angry and frustrated over Japan's failure to issue an acceptable form of apology and reparation for these war atrocities.

I Can Speak in fact exemplifies a failure to effectively use a "minorization" of English that might question both this language's hegemonic role in world affairs and the responsibility of the United States in resolving the historical tension between Korea and Japan. Ok-bun works very hard to perfect her English pronunciation, and the film promotes the problematical message that justice and reconciliation in international courts can only be obtained if Koreans can speak standard English. It is not plausible that an octogenarian halmoni would learn English in order to deliver a speech in a foreign court, nor is it desirable for someone bearing witness to trauma to speak in any language other than their native tongue. (In fact, in the actual story from which the film was adapted, Lee Yong-soon testified in Korean.) The film's misguided agenda, then, encages the Korean subject in a colonized linguistic space where English rules as the master language and no discourse of cynical reason is allowed to enter.

26. For an excellent dissertation on this topic, see Asokan, "Breaking the Retrospective Curse."

27. Bong Joon-ho, during his first of the three speeches during the Ninety-Second Academy Awards, thanked "South Korea," by which he meant people of South Korea, who have, for the past two decades, supported his films. Miky Lee, during the final speech at the Academy Awards, thanked the South Korean moviegoers who have led her to continue to invest in South Korean films. In my lunch conversations with Lee, she has repeatedly told me that more money can be found if her company, CJ Entertainment, simply distributes Hollywood movies and collects fees from it rather than taking a risk by investing in Korean movies. The South Korean film industry's success can be attributed to both filmmakers' bold commitment to make daring films and Korean fans' support over the years.

28. See K. H. Kim, *Virtual Hallyu*, 42–54.

29. Jin, *Smartland Korea*, 127.

30. Sloterdijk, *Critique of Cynical Reason*, 14.

31. See Gilbert and Gubar, *Madwoman in the Attic*.

32. Deleuze and Guattari, "What Is a Minor Literature?," 22. See also the chapter on Park Chan-wook in my *Virtual Hallyu*, where I argue that by employing clues such as *gunmandu* (Chinese dumplings), Park's film *Oldboy* underscores a sense of the unknowable that is exemplary of a postmodern condition. Kim, *Virtual Hallyu*, 178–98.

33. Deleuze and Guattari, *Anti-Oedipus*, 49.

Chapter Six. Korean Meme-icry

1. I currently live in Irvine, California, a city that notoriously underfunds and under-supplies accessible and affordable public transportation in an effort to curtail flow between Irvine and other less privileged neighborhoods and encourage the use of private cars for commutes and other daily activities. Irvine ranks seventieth among US cities in "accessibility and convenience." McCann, "Cities with the Best." Although antiseptic and safe, Irvine, which was planned and is still managed by a single giant real estate company (the Irvine Company), has maintained its corporate-friendly reputation by resisting efforts to construct an accessible public transportation system or incorporate pedestrian-oriented features such as a public town square. Stepping into the Samsung Digital City in the middle of Korea gives me the same eerie sense of dystopian reality that I feel in Irvine, as both cities are built on a privatized, monolithic, *Truman Show*–like dream.

2. Pang, *Creativity and Its Discontents*, 203–30.

3. The original three stars in the Samsung logo were replaced with the company's present-day blue oval design in 1993. As Bruce Cumings notes, "Samsung ('Three Stars') is a play on Mitsubishi's 'Three Diamonds,' which probably modeled its logo on Mercedes's." Ironically, Mitsubishi was ordered by a Korean court to pay damages for forced wartime labor to several of the surviving Korean victims. Many Koreans were subject to unjust labor at the Mitsubishi shipyard and machine tools factory during Japan's occupation of Korea during World War II. The Korean court ruling in 2018 ignited tensions between Japan and Korea that still persist. Cumings, *Korea's Place in the Sun*, 328.

4. Even during the peak of Nokia's global dominance in the cellular phone era, which helped establish Finland's reputation "as the most wired nation in the world" (Ibrahim, "Cell Phones Make Nokia a World Player"), Nokia accounted for only 16 percent of Finland's exports. Nokia reached the peak of its sales in 2006, one year before the first-generation iPhone was released on the market, leading to Nokia's precipitous decline. Woyke, *Smartphone*, 11.

5. Bevin Fletcher, "Will the Apple/Samsung Smartphone Duopoly Continue with 5G?"

6. Reuters, "Jury Awards Apple $539 Million."

7. Lee Shin-Hyung, "Samsung Takes on Huawei."

8. King, *Seoul*, 226. While I agree with King on the basic principles he notes with regard to the similarities between Samsung and K-pop, two of the most iconic interfaces that Korea offers the contemporary world, my analysis departs from his because I find these two Korean icons to be similar due to their focus on labor-intensive, mogul-driven, and export-led initiatives—factors King never delves into. Another Korean studies scholar, John Lie, also compares Samsung and K-pop, and in so doing, almost follows the logic of the Supreme Court Justices verbatim. Lie writes, "People would not purchase Samsung cell phones if the devices were not functional and dependable, presentable and

pleasurable. In the same way, popular-music fans would not download a track or attend a concert if they didn't get their money's worth, so to speak." Lie, *K-Pop*, 142–43.

9. As discussed in the introduction and chapter 1, K-pop was deeply and historically rooted in the act of mimicking African American hegemonic culture after the Korean War.

10. Pang, *Creativity and Its Discontents*, 29. Here it is also useful to think about Ackbar Abbas's concept of "fake globalization," where the original can no longer be distinguished from the counterfeit. Abbas, "Faking Globalization."

11. Bruce Robbins writes, "You have heard, for example, about the suicides at Foxconn and perhaps also about the anti-suicide nets that were subsequently installed." Robbins, *Beneficiary*, 6.

12. Livesey, *From Global to Local*, 36.

13. Galaxy phones are no longer assembled in Korea, but unlike Apple, which completely outsources its production and purchases its components from other companies around the world, Samsung continues to be responsible for the supply of raw materials and components for its Galaxy phones.

14. Song Yu-jin, "Samsung, LG Ssaumyŏn?"

15. Lee Jae-yong, the de facto corporate head, actually issued a public apology in May 2020 for Samsung's past wrongdoings, which included years of sabotaging efforts to organize unions and bribing government officials for favoritism and tax evasion. Whether this public promise to ban any anti-union activities and to clean up Samsung's way of doing business holds up or not remains to be seen. Because of the rise in the polls of left-leaning president Moon Jae-in in 2020, Samsung was under a lot of pressure to come clean. Choe Sang-hun, "Samsung Heir Apologizes."

16. The average monthly wage in 2019 in the region of urban Hanoi and Ho Chi Minh City was about $180. Das, "Vietnam Hikes Minimum Wages." In South Korea, the average monthly salary was about $3,700 per month in 2019. "Average Salary in South Korea in 2021," destinationscanner.com, accessed February 21, 2021. https://destinationscanner.com/average-salary-in-south-korea/.

17. When Samsung opened America's largest wafer plant in Austin, Texas, in 2007, it boasted that its new $3.5 billion facility would be the first to produce semiconductors on a twelve-inch wafer. Samsung announced that the "12-inch wafer can typically hold about 1,200 standard 256-megabit memory chips, compared to about 500 such chips on an eight-inch wafer." "Samsung Opens Largest Wafer Plant."

18. The defect ratio of Samsung Electronics' semiconductor production line is miniscule. However, in order to maintain its low defect rate, the facility must be spotless, because even a single particle of dust on a wafer can cause computer chip defects. Humans are responsible for ensuring the cleanliness of the plant, which ironically often leads to the contraction of illnesses. As reported by Chŏng Ae-chong, whose testimony is featured in the book *Samsung Semiconductor and Leukemia*, cowritten by Pak Il-hwan and the Organization to Protect the Human Rights and Health of Semiconductor Workers:

"If [a dust particle] falls onto a wafer chip (holding 1200 microchips), it has to be thrown out due to the high probability that it will cause a defect. There is so much pressure [applied by the machines]. If you have to work in that environment, you just get sick so easily. All of the women workers suffer a great deal from premenstrual syndrome while working." Pak, *Samsung pandoch'e wa paekhyŏlbyŏng*, 35.

19. Cook and Agence France-Presse, "Samsung Apologises to Workers."

20. J. Song and K. Lee, *Samsung Way*, 23.

21. J. Song and K. Lee, *Samsung Way*, 38.

22. In an independently written biography of Lee Kun-hee, the third son of Samsung's founder, Lee Byung-chul, who expanded his father's vision for Samsung Electronics starting in the 1990s, Yi Kyŏng-sik notes that "Kun-hee was an obsessively curious person even when he was young. But he was not focused on one single area. Among his areas of interest, machinery was one of his favorites. The fact that Lee Kun-hee was a machine fanatic is widely known. . . . When he was studying how to run the company with his father starting in 1967, he would often wrestle with machines after work. He would study the mechanics and performance of machines or appliances by taking them apart and putting them back together. Hundreds of Japanese technicians paid visits to his house during this period, for he solicited explanations from mechanics and engineers themselves." Yi Kyŏng-sik, *Yi Kŏn-hŭi Sŭt'ori*, 62.

23. Cumings, *Korea's Place in the Sun*, 328.

24. The Moon Jae-in government found guilty Samsung's board chair Lee Sang-hoon in late 2019 for his active role in the company's union-busting actions. Porter, "Samsung Electronics Chairman Found Guilty." Though about thirty former and present Samsung executives were found guilty for their roles in union busting in a January–February 2021 trial and received sentences that ranged from a year to two years, Lee Sang-hoon was found not guilty verdict after a retrial. Kim Hyŏn-jŏng, "'Samsung nocho wahae.'"

25. From the moment Apple filed its lawsuit against Samsung in 2011, Korean media decried injustice using sensational headlines such as "Apple Falsely Accuses Samsung of 'Plagiarism' Using Doctored Photos." However, very little detail was actually reported by the Korean media when it came to the actual proceedings of the case. Chŏng, "Sosongnaen aep'ŭl 'kaellŏkshi' sajindo chojak."

26. In fact, the court was two justices short. During the entire hearing process, Clarence Thomas did not utter a word, as is his usual practice.

27. Samsung Electronics Co., Ltd., et al., Petitioners v. Apple, Inc., Respondent, The Supreme Court of the United States No. 15-177 (Washington, D.C., October 11, 2016) at 16–17.

28. Neither the production structure of Samsung nor the configuration of K-pop allow us to clearly distinguish intellectual property from tangible commodity. The process of capitalist production in Korea today emphasizes a combination of creative labor

and intensive human labor, as seen in the K-pop industry as well as the hybrid cluster characteristic of companies such as Samsung. Most K-pop artists acquire a quasi-artist status as both creative laborers and traditional laborers who must endure intense, long work hours in exchange for enjoying a short career span, which is disposable once their youth comes to an end.

29. Quite possibly the largest threat to Samsung's smartphone business was not Apple's lawsuit but the technical debacle that took place when more than one million Samsung Galaxy Note 7 phones had to be recalled in late 2016 because of faulty SDI batteries. See Cain, *Samsung Rising*, 25.

30. Nicas, "Apple's Plan to Buy $75 Billion."

31. Over the eleven-year period from 2008 to 2018, the manufacturing sector in Korea shrank by only 0.5 percent, declining from 25.49 percent of the entire working force in 2008 to 24.96 percent in 2018. On the other hand, Korea's agriculture sector continued a precipitous decline—falling from 7.18 percent in 2008 to 4.73 percent in 2018. Plecher, "Employment by Economic Sector." By comparison, the manufacturing sector in the United States suffered its worst performance in history during the first decade of the twenty-first century. From 2000 to 2010, 33 percent of manufacturing jobs were lost. That decline has been cited as a factor in the particular resonance of Trump's "Make America Great Again" campaign in the Rust Belt states. Atkinson et al., "Worse than the Great Depression."

32. Harlan, "In S. Korea."

33. Google's mission is "to organize the world's information and make it universally accessible and useful." In other words, Google (or its parent company, Alphabet) is not in the business of *producing* information; it simply organizes that information so that the public can better search for the products and knowledge it needs. Google, "About," accessed February 21, 2021, https://about.google/. For a company that is valued in the top five in the world today, Google's vision statement represents a clear departure from the world that was dominated by manufacturing in the twentieth century.

34. Baudrillard, "Precession of Simulacra," 23.

35. Lee Kun-hee was originally solicited to invest in the early formation of Dream-Works SKG, the studio built by Steven Spielberg, Jeffrey Katzenberg, and David Geffen. The Korean magnate, who was also a movie buff, attended a dinner meeting with these founders at Spielberg's house. However, Lee's focus on semiconductors supposedly turned the American movie moguls off, and the $900 million investment deal fell through. In a *New York Times* article, Geffen recalled, "If we were only interested in making money, we'd also build semiconductor plants." The canceled Korean-side investment was replaced by Lee's niece, Miky Lee, who wrote a check for $300 million. Pollack, "International Business." Miky Lee would go on to become a movie mogul in Korea by assuming de facto ownership of CJ Entertainment, which ended up producing many Korean blockbusters over the past two decades, including Bong Joon-ho's *Parasite*.

36. Quoted in King, *Seoul*, 226.

37. Breen, *New Koreans*, 223. In "What People Got for Christmas," his Christmas article for the English version of the *Korea Times*, Breen wrote satirically on the nature of political corruption in Korea. Samsung dropped its charges against Breen only after he publicly apologized for the column. In his list of "Christmas gifts" given by Korean corporations, politicians, and celebrities, Breen listed two items pertaining to Samsung: "Samsung, the world's largest conglomerate and the rock upon which the Korean economy rests, sent traditional year-end cards offering best wishes for 2010 to the country's politicians, prosecutors and journalists, along with 50 million won in gift certificates." He continued, "Employees received two framed photographs of Lee Jae-yong, the new Chief Operating Officer at Samsung Electronics Co., with instructions to place one in their children's bedroom and the other in their living rooms beside but slightly below the one of his father, Lee Kun-hee."

38. Jeong Eun-Young, "Samsung Chairman Sentenced to Jail."

39. Woyke, *Smartphone*, 56.

40. Jin, *Smartland Korea*, 49.

41. I. Jung, *Architecture and Urbanism in Modern Korea*, 51.

42. Suk-Young Kim, *K-Pop Live*, 50–51.

43. K-pop defies the odds in today's pop world not because it rebels against Confucianism but because it conforms to it. If anyone knows a thing or two about the spirit of rock 'n' roll, it is all about "sticking it to the man," as Dewey Finn, played by Jack Black in the hit movie and musical *School of Rock*, puts it. Successful pop or rock bands very often disband at the peak of their success due to internal feuds among band members or between a band and its managers. Only once in the history of K-pop has this been the case. At the pinnacle of their success in 2009, three members of the five-boy group Tong Bang Shin Ki (TVXQ)—Jaejoong, Yoochun, and Junsu, who would go on to combine their initials and form the group JYJ—filed a lawsuit against their management company, SM Entertainment. Their highly publicized lawsuit and the subsequent injunction given by the court to void their contracts with SM "shed light on the exact terms of the contract that had provided the basis for a relationship between the management company and the idol. The thirteen year contract essentially meant a lifetime contract." Seung-Ah Lee, "Of the Fans," 113.

44. In *K-Pop Live*, Suk-Young Kim reports on her experience attending KCON LA in 2015, persuasively attesting to the fact that this affective labor constitutes the greatest impulse driving about one hundred thousand fans who gather to attend concerts, panels, and meet-and-greet sessions with artists and to explore exhibition booths featuring Korean fashion, beauty, and K-pop culture.

45. Suk-Young Kim, *K-Pop Live*, 182.

46. Julie Choi, "Right to the City."

47. While I applaud Choi's attempt to embrace the modernist theory of Kracauer and Walter Benjamin in her analysis of the viral song and choreography of "Gangnam

Style," I ultimately cannot endorse her view that K-pop choreography underscores the "additional compulsion of consumption as the new labor" (Julie Choi, "Right to the City," 95). Certainly, Baudrillard's characterization of "ego Consumans," not unlike Deleuze and Guattari's "body without organs" or "line of flight," is the asignifying symptom of today's consumerist society. However, what Choi then fails to further elaborate is precisely how K-pop best approximates the Baudrillardian "ego Consumans." Could one not argue that black hip-hop or DJ-inspired techno-pop are just as complementary to the Baudrillardian "hysterical lack" as K-pop is?

48. Although he refrains from claiming that female K-pop idols are "disposable," Gooyoung Kim argues that "in tandem with the state's supports, the K-pop industry has implemented its . . . public agenda of national development, exercising Foucauldian biopolitics which (re)produce and proliferate neoliberal subjects. A concept of discipline, especially docility-utility . . . is permeated in K-pop idols who have been conditioned through years of training, and audiences who internalize and glorify their favorite K-pop stars." G. Kim, *From Factory Girls*, 19. While I disagree with Kim's conception of a totality in which both the production and the consumption of K-pop music and performances are realized, I do concur with him that K-pop idols are largely obedient subjects who are required to actively internalize the agenda of idol-manufacturing processes sought by management companies in what has become a highly export-oriented industry for the Korean government.

49. S. Choe and S. Lee, "Suicides by K-Pop Stars."

50. Hollingsworth and Seo, "Death of K-Pop Star Sulli."

51. TWICE and Blackpink are the latest girl groups to headline the K-pop industry. After parading a score of hits for about three or four years, however, girl groups—which typically have shorter life spans than boy groups—begin to lose their mass appeal. These two young girl groups, TWICE and Blackpink, replaced Wonder Girls and 2NE1, respectively; their music and style closely resemble their predecessors because their songs are written by the same company of men that also manages them both. Unless its members can transform themselves into mature solo performers, TWICE and Blackpink are likely to have been forgotten by the time this book is published.

52. Freud, "Mourning and Melancholia," 588.

53. On sports concussions, see Hardes, "Governing Sporting Brains."

54. Mbembe, "Necropolitics," 40.

55. *Another Promise* (*Tto Hana ŭi yaksok*, dir. Kim T'ae-yun, 2014) is a South Korean film based on the true story of a legal battle that took place between Samsung and the family of a young employee who died of leukemia. In the film, the company uses every coercive method possible in order to persuade the family to drop their case, including pressuring other sick employees and their families to refrain from testifying, falsifying medical records, and spying on current workers and families.

Chapter Seven. Reading *Muhan Dojeon*

1. Kevin O'Rourke, a translator who spent more than forty years in Korea, writes, "Professor [of Korean literature] Kim Chonggil tells us . . . that *mŏt* is a phonetically corrupted form of *mat* (taste), and that the word first occurred as late as the second half of the nineteenth century." O'Rourke, *My Korea*, 173.

2. On mŏt's connection to p'ansori, see O'Rourke, *My Korea*, 173.

3. C. Choi, "Politics of Gender," 113.

4. Suk-Young Kim, *K-Pop Live*, 19–20.

5. Lie, *K-Pop*, 142.

6. Kim Je-dong is the only active comedian known for stand-up shows that feature political satire that mock conservatives. The late Shin Hae-cheol, Kim Chang-hoon, and Yoon Do-hyun are some of the socially conscious singers who took a political stance, especially during conservative political rule (2008–17). They were, however, without exception, blacklisted during the Park Geun-hye presidency (2013–17), and their appearances on mainstream media were severely restrained.

7. Mbembe, *Critique of Black Reason*, 20. Of course, this is not to suggest that racism has ended. Twenty-first-century racial discrimination remains intense, especially during the Trump era, as evidenced by increased border patrols, surveillance, security, and the war on terror. Mbembe's idea of necropolitics and his fungible sense of "black" signals not only a series of traumatic and excruciating historical experiences but also, once you reverse it, an "act of creation and capab[ility] of living in the midst of several times and several histories at once." Mbembe, *Critique of Black Reason*, 6–7.

8. Though the original text in *Peace Under Heaven* [T'aep'yŏng ch'ŏnha] is "Uri man ppaenotko ŏso manghaera," which was translated as "Let Everyone Else Go to Hell," a more literal translation of this critical phrase, which is also a chapter title in the novel, is "everyone should fail, with the exception of us!" Ch'ae, *Peace under Heaven*, 28.

9. N. Lee, *Making of Minjung*, 11.

10. Though the proper McCune-Reischauer romanization of the popular television program name is *Muhan Tojŏn*, it has been widely circulated on official MBC and other YouTube channels as *Muhan Dojeon*. I am following the more popular form of its romanization.

11. *Muhan Dojeon*'s Chinese remake rights were officially sold to CCTV, China's leading state-owned network. Retitled as *The Great Challenge* (Chinese: 了不起的挑战), it aired in 2015 and 2016. This program could not be renewed for 2017 because of China's ban on Korean cultural content due to Korea's decision in the previous year to deploy THAAD. Lee Miyoung, "'Mun tatko pekkigo'"; Kil, "Korean Variety Show." *Muhan Dojeon* was so popular that there were not one but two Chinese remakes. The unauthorized copycat program, *Go Fighting!* (Chinese: 极限挑战), broadcast on a cable network, SMG: Dragon Television, also became popular around the same time, despite

being threatened with a lawsuit and being pulled off the air for several weeks in 2015. While the authorized remake was pulled off the air because of the tumultuous relations between South Korea and China, the unauthorized version ironically continued to air well into 2018. The Chinese market, despite the recent easing of tensions between the two countries, still maintains the partial ban of Korean cultural exchanges and businesses. Even the popular K-pop group BTS was not able to tour China during its highly successful "Love Yourself" World Tour in 2019. alim17, "MBC Gives Warning."

12. O'Rourke, *My Korea*, 174.

13. Yoon et al., "When Old Meets New."

14. Kim Chi-ha, "Madanggŭk eso madang gut ŭro." Also, Cho Tong-il echoes Kim when he claims that "p'ansori's vocal expression is one that can only be refined after the voice has become hoarse by throwing up blood. It could sound murky, but ultimately it is a sound that is heavy—covering a lot of change." Cho Tong-il, "P'ansori ŭi chŏnpanjŏk sŏnggyŏk," 12.

15. Du Bois, *Souls of Black Folk*, 190.

16. In my personal estimation, this "professionally" directed version of "Muhan Sangsa" is the least successful among these segments. Because it was largely scripted with an editing speed that was more cinematically aestheticized, it was not as interesting as the largely improvised renditions of the televised program.

17. Benjamin, *Selected Writings*, 303.

18. N. Lee, *Making of Minjung*, 199.

19. *Muhan*, just like some of the top idol groups, generated a subculture following on cyberspace, where fandom participated in the form of a "gallery." *Muhan Dojeon* fans actively started to use the bulletin board gallery created on the internet site "DC Inside," which was originally created as a forum to discuss digital camera and other electronic devices. However, by 2007, *Muhan* fans had petitioned to create their own fan site, which was heavily dominated by female users, at the time unusual for a comedy program. It was here that several important online campaigns, including one to drive out one of the earlier members, Jeon Jin, were mobilized after having made an impact offline.

20. In Western television, because subtitles are generally frowned upon, mock documentary interviews of the characters often replace the role captions play in Korean television. This was first successfully incorporated into the British sitcom *The Office*, created by Ricky Gervais in 2001. Since this show was brought successfully into the United States, the "asubjectifying subjectivity" that "mock documentary" scenes serve has become one of the vital tools of reality TV today.

21. S. Park, "Making of a Cultural Icon," 609. The title "Eheya Noara" is translated roughly as "Dance of the Carefree," though in Korean this phrase has no real meaning. Atkins, *Primitive Selves*, 227.

22. Martin, "Sai Shoki Is Seen in Korean Dances."

23. Julie Choi, "Right to the City," 86.

BIBLIOGRAPHY

Abbas, Ackbar. "Faking Globalization." In *The Visual Culture Reader*, edited by Nicholas Mirzoeff, 282–95. New York: Routledge, 2013.

Ahmed, Sara. "Happy Objects." In *The Affect Theory Reader*, edited by Melissa Gregg and Gregory J. Seigworth, 29–51. Durham, NC: Duke University Press, 2010.

alim17. "MBC Gives Warning to 'Infinity Challenge' Rip-Offs in China." June 30, 2015. https://www.allkpop.com/article/2015/06/mbc-gives-warning-to-infinity -challenge-rip-offs-in-china.

An, Jinsoo. *Parameters of Disavowal: Colonial Representation in South Korean Cinema*. Oakland: University of California Press, 2018.

An Hŭi-jŏng. "Naver, Kakao, chaknyŏn maech'ul 20% nŭlŏtchiman yŏngŏp iik ŭn kamso" [Though last year's revenues of Naver and Kakao have increased by 20 percent, the actual profit has fallen]. *ZDNet Korea*, January 29, 2019. https://www.zdnet.co.kr/view/?no=20190129115159.

Armitstead, Claire. "Lost in (Mis)translation? English Take on Korean Novel Has Critics up in Arms." *The Guardian*, January 15, 2018.

Asokan, Sue Heun Kim. "Breaking the Retrospective Curse: Ethical Identity in South Korean Film and Literature." PhD diss., University of California, Irvine, 2020.

Atkins, Everett Taylor. *Primitive Selves: Koreana in the Japanese Colonial Gaze, 1910–1945*. Berkeley: University of California Press, 2010.

Atkinson, Robert D., Luke A. Stewart, Scott M. Andes, and Stephen Ezell. "Worse than the Great Depression: What the Experts Are Missing about American Manufacturing Decline." Information Technology and Innovation Foundation, March 19, 2012. https://itif.org/publications/2012/03/19/worse-great-depression -what-experts-are-missing-about-american-manufacturing.

Barthes, Roland. *Camera Lucida*. New York: Hill and Wang, 1982.

Baudrillard, Jean. "The Precession of Simulacra." In *Simulations*, translated by Paul Foss, Paul Patton, and Philip Beitchman, 1–79. New York: Semiotext(e), 1983.

Baudrillard, Jean. *Simulacra and Simulation*. Translated by Sheila Faria Glaser. Ann Arbor: University of Michigan Press, 1994.

Bauwens, Michel, Vasilis Kostakis, and Alex Pazaitis. *Peer to Peer: The Commons Manifesto*. London: University of Westminster Press, 2019.

Benjamin, Walter. *Selected Writings*. Vol. 4, *1938–1940*. Edited by Howard Eiland and Michael W. Jennings. Cambridge, MA: Belknap Press of Harvard University Press, 2006.

Bhabha, Homi K. *Location of Culture*. New York: Routledge, 1994.

Bizzell, Patricia. "Who Owns English in South Korea?" In *Crossing Divides: Exploring Translingual Writing Pedagogies and Programs*, edited by Bruce Horner and Laura Tetreault, 70–86. Logan: Utah State University Press, 2017.

Bochanty-Aguero, Erica Jean. "We Are the World: American Idol's Global Self-Posturing." In *Global Television Formats: Understanding Television across Borders*, edited by Tasha Oren and Sharon Shahaf, 260–82. New York: Routledge, 2012.

Breen, Michael. *The New Koreans: The Story of a Nation*. New York: Dunne, 2017.

Breen, Michael. "What People Got for Christmas." *Korea Times*, December 25, 2009.

Bridges, William H., IV. "In the Beginning: Blackness and the 1960s Creative Nonfiction of Ōe Kenzaburō." *positions: asia critique* 25, no. 2 (2017): 323–49.

Brooks, Peter. *Reading for the Plot: Design and Intention in Narrative*. Cambridge, MA: Harvard University Press, 1984.

Burch, Noel. *To the Distant Observer: Form and Meaning in the Japanese Cinema*. Berkeley: University of California Press, 1979.

Caillois, Roger. *Man, Play and Games*. Translated by Meyer Barash. Urbana: University of Illinois Press, 2001.

Cain, Geoffrey. *Samsung Rising: The Inside Story of the South Korean Giant That Set Out to Beat Apple and Conquer Tech*. New York: Currency, 2020.

Cartwright, Lisa. *Moral Spectatorship: Technologies of Voice and Affect in Postwar Representations of the Child*. Durham, NC: Duke University Press, 2008.

Ch'ae Man-sik. *Peace under Heaven*. Translated by Chun Kyung-Ja. Armonk, NY: M. E. Sharpe, 1993.

Chang, Jeff. *Can't Stop, Won't Stop: A History of the Hip-Hop Generation*. New York: Picador, 2005.

Chen, Kuan-Hsing. "The Imperialist Eye: The Cultural Imaginary of a Subempire and a Nation-State." *positions: east asia cultures critique* 8, no. 1 (Spring 2000): 9–76.

Chion, Michel. *Audio-Vision: Sound on Screen*. Edited and translated by Claudia Gorbman. New York: Columbia University Press, 1994.

Chion, Michel. *The Voice in Cinema*. Translated by Claudia Gorbman. New York: Columbia University Press, 1999.

Cho Tong-il. "P'ansori ŭi chŏnpanjŏk sŏnggyŏk" [The general characteristics of p'ansori]. In *P'ansori ŭi ihae* [Understanding p'ansori], edited by Cho Tong-il and Kim Hŭng-gyu, 11–28. Seoul: Ch'angjak kwa pipyŏng, 1978.

Cho Yŏng-nam and Patti Kim. *Kŭ nyŏ, Patti Kim: Cho Yŏng nam mutko, Patti Kim iyaki hata* [That woman Patti Kim: Cho Young-nam asks, Patti Kim talks]. Seoul: Tolbaegae, 2012.

Choe Sang-hun. "Samsung Heir Apologizes for Corruption and Union-Busting Scandals." *New York Times*, May 6, 2020.

Choe Sang-hun and Su-Hyun Lee. "Suicides by K-Pop Stars Prompt Soul-Searching in South Korea." *New York Times*, November 25, 2019.

Choe, Youngmin. *Tourist Distractions: Traveling and Feeling in Transnational Hallyu Cinema*. Durham, NC: Duke University Press, 2016.

Choi, Chungmoo. "The Politics of Gender, Aestheticism, and Cultural Nationalism in *Sopyonje* and *The Genealogy*." In *Im Kwon-Taek: The Making of a Korean National Cinema*, 107–33. Detroit: Wayne State University Press, 2002.

Choi, Julie. "Right to the City: The Metropolis and Gangnam Style." *Korea Journal* 59, no. 2 (Summer 2019): 86–110.

Choi Moon-hee. "K-Pop Group BTS Induces Production Worth 4 Tril. Won per Year." *Business Korea*, December 19, 2018. http://www.businesskorea.co.kr/news/articleView.html?idxno=27583.

Chŏng Ŭn-jŏng. *Taehanminguk ch'ik'in chŏn* [The tale of chicken in the ROK]. Seoul: Ttabi, 2014.

Chŏng Yŏng-hwan. "Sosongnaen aep'ŭl 'kaellŏkshi' sajindo chojak" [Apple sues after altering photo of Galaxy S]. *Dong A Daily News*, August 22, 2011. http://www.donga.com/news/article/all/20110822/39699819/1.

Chu Sŏng-ha. *Pyŏngyang chaponchuŭi paekkwa chŏnsŏ* [The encyclopedia of Pyongyang capitalism]. Seoul: Puktotum, 2018.

Cillizza, Chris. "Donald Trump's Fundamentally Un-American 'Parasite' Critique." CNN, February 21, 2020. https://www.cnn.com/2020/02/21/politics/donald-trump-parasite-gone-with-the-wind/index.html.

Constante, Agnes. "25 Years after LA Riots, Koreatown Finds Strength in 'Saigu' Legacy." NBC News, April 25, 2017. https://www.nbcnews.com/news/asian-america/25-years-after-la-riots-koreatown-finds-strength-saigu-legacy-n749081.

Cook, James, and Agence France-Presse. "Samsung Apologises to Workers Who Developed Cancer after Exposure to Toxic Chemicals." *The Telegraph*, November 23, 2018.

Cumings, Bruce. *Korea's Place in the Sun: A Modern History*. New York: Norton, 2005.

Dargis, Manohla. "Scorsese's Hall of Mirrors, Littered with Bloody Deceit." *New York Times*, October 6, 2006, E1.

Das, Koushan. "Vietnam Hikes Minimum Wages by 5.3 Percent in 2019." *Vietnam Briefing*, January 15, 2019. https://www.vietnam-briefing.com/news/vietnam-hikes-minimum-wages-by-5-3-percent-in-2019.html/.

Deleuze, Gilles. *Cinema 2*. Translated by Hugh Tomlinson and Robert Galeta. Minneapolis: University of Minnesota Press, 1989.

Deleuze, Gilles. *Negotiations*. Translated by Martin Joughin. New York: Columbia University Press, 1995.

Deleuze, Gilles, and Félix Guattari. *Anti-Oedipus: Capitalism and Schizophrenia*. Translated by Robert Hurley, Mark Seem, and Helen R. Lane. Minneapolis: University of Minnesota Press, 1996.

Deleuze, Gilles, and Félix Guattari. "What Is a Minor Literature?" In *Kafka: Toward a Minor Literature*, translated by Dana Polan, 16–27. Minneapolis: University of Minnesota Press, 1986.

Derrida, Jacques. *Of Grammatology*. Translated by Gayatri Chakravorty Spivak. Baltimore: Johns Hopkins University Press, 1967.

De Vos, George A. "Confucian Family Socialization: The Religion, Morality, and Aesthetics of Propriety." In *Confucianism and the Family*, edited by Walter H. Slote and George A. De Vos, 329–80. New York: State University of New York Press, 1998.

Dolar, Mladen. *A Voice and Nothing More*. Cambridge, MA: MIT Press, 2006.

Du Bois, W. E. B. *The Souls of Black Folk*. New York: Penguin Books, 2018.

Dyson, Michael Eric. "The Culture of Hip-Hop." In *That's the Joint! The Hip-Hop Studies Reader*, edited by Murray Forman and Mark Anthony Neal, 61–68. New York: Routledge, 2004.

Em, Henry H. *The Great Enterprise: Sovereignty and Historiography in Modern Korea*. Durham, NC: Duke University Press, 2013.

Fanon, Frantz. *Black Skin, White Masks*. Translated by Richard Philcox. New York: Grove Press, 2008.

Fletcher, Bevin. "Will the Apple/Samsung Smartphone Duopoly Continue with 5G?" *Fierce Wireless*, January 15, 2020. https://www.fiercewireless.com/devices/will-apple-samsung-smartphone-duopoly-continue-5g-handsets.

Foucault, Michel. *Discipline and Punish*. Translated by Alan Sheridan. New York: Vintage, 1979.

Foucault, Michel. *Society Must Be Defended: Lectures at the Collège de France, 1975–76*. Edited by Mauro Bertani and Allesandro Fontana. Translated by David Macey. New York: Picador, 2003.

Freeland, Jim, M. Sgt., and Jim Lea. "Black GIs on Rampage: Riot-Torn Anjong-ni—Why It Happened." *Stars and Stripes*, July 16, 1971. http://populargusts.blogspot.com/2011/07/1971-anjeong-ri-race-riot-part-2.html.

Freud, Sigmund. "Mourning and Melancholia." In *The Freud Reader*, edited by Peter Gay, 584–88. New York: Norton, 1989.

Friedberg, Anne. "The End of Cinema: Multimedia and Technological Change." In *Film Theory and Criticism: Introductory Readings*, edited by Leo Braudy and Marshall Cohen, 802–13. New York: Oxford University Press, 2009.

Gates, Henry Louis, Jr. *The Signifying Monkey: A Theory of Afro-American Literary Criticism*. New York: Oxford University Press, 2014.

Gerow, Aaron. "Kind Participation: Postmodern Consumption and Capital with Japan's Telop TV." In *Television, Japan, and Globalization*, edited by Mitsuhiro Yoshimoto, Eva Tsai, and JungBong Choi, 117–50. Ann Arbor: University of Michigan Press, 2010.

Gilbert, Sandra, and Susan Gubar. *The Madwoman in the Attic: The Woman Writer and the Nineteenth-Century Literary Imagination*. New Haven, CT: Yale University Press, 2000.

Glissant, Édouard. "Transparency and Opacity." In *Poetics of Relation*, translated by Betsy Wing, 111–20. Ann Arbor: University of Michigan Press, 1997.

Gramsci, Antonio. "State and Civil Society." In *Selections from the Prison Notebooks*, edited and translated by Quintin Hoare and Geoffrey Nowell Smith, 206–76. New York: International Publishers, 1983.

Gray, F. Gary, dir. *Straight Outta Compton.* Los Angeles: Universal Pictures, 2015.

Gunning, Tom. "What's the Point of an Index? Or, Faking Photographs." In *Still Moving: Between Cinema and Photography*, edited by Karen Beckman and Jean Ma, 23–40. Durham, NC: Duke University Press, 2008.

Hall, Stuart. "The Local and the Global: Globalization and Ethnicity." In *Dangerous Liaisons: Gender, Nation, and Postcolonial Perspectives*, edited by Anne McClintock, Aamir Mufti, and Ella Shohat, 173–87. Minneapolis: University of Minnesota Press, 1997.

Hall, Stuart. "Notes on Deconstructing the Popular." In *People's History and Socialist Theory*, edited by Raphael Samuel, 227–40. London: Routledge and Kegan Paul, 1981.

Hardes, Jennifer. "Governing Sporting Brains: Concussion, Neuroscience, and the Biopolitical Regulation of Sport." *Sport, Ethics and Philosophy* 11, no. 3 (2017): 281–93.

Harlan, Chico. "In S. Korea, the Republic of Samsung." *Washington Post*, December 9, 2012.

Helmbrect, Johannes. "Politeness Distinctions in Pronouns." *World Atlas of Language Structures Online.* Accessed January 15, 2019. https://wals.info/chapter/45.

Herman, Tamar. "BTS Break Three Guinness World Records with 'Boy with Luv' Video." *Billboard*, April 18, 2019. https://www.billboard.com/articles/news/bts/8507811/bts-break-3-guinness-world-records-boy-with-luv.

Hollingsworth, Julia, and Yoonjung Seo. "Death of K-Pop Star Sulli Prompts Outpouring of Grief and Questions over Cyber-Bullying." *CNN*, October 15, 2019. https://www.cnn.com/2019/10/15/asia/kpop-sulli-death-aftermath-intl-hnk-scli/index.html.

Ibrahim, Youssef M. "Cell Phones Make Nokia a World Player." *New York Times*, August 13, 1997.

Ihm, Chon Sun, and Hee Jung Choi. "Early Study Abroad: A Survey and Demographic Portrait." In *South Korea's Education Exodus: The Life and Times of Study Abroad*, edited by Adrienne Lo, Nancy Abelmann, Soo Ah Kwon, and Sumie Okazaki, 25–39. Seattle: University of Washington Press, 2015.

Im, Kwŏn-t'aek, dir. *Sŏp'yŏnje.* Taehung Pictures, 1993.

Iwabuchi, Koichi. *Recentering Globalization: Popular Culture and Japanese Transnationalism.* Durham, NC: Duke University Press, 2002.

Jameson, Fredric. *The Geopolitical Aesthetic: Cinema and Space in the World System.* Bloomington: Indiana University Press, 1992.

Jameson, Fredric. *Postmodernism, or, The Cultural Logic of Late Capitalism.* Durham, NC: Duke University Press, 1993.

Jameson, Fredric. *Valences of the Dialectic.* New York: Verso, 2010.

Jenkins, Henry. "Transmedia Storytelling 101." March 21, 2007. http://henryjenkins
    .org/blog/2007/03/transmedia_storytelling_101.html.
Jenkins, Henry, Sam Ford, and Joshua Green. *Spreadable Media: Creating Value and
    Meaning in a Networked Culture.* New York: New York University Press, 2013.
Jeon, Joseph. "Memories of Memories: Historicity, Nostalgia, and Archive in Bong
    Joon-ho's Memories of Murder." *Cinema Journal* 51, no. 1 (Fall 2011): 75–95.
Jeon, Joseph. *Vicious Circuits: Korea's IMF Cinema and the End of the American
    Century.* Stanford, CA: Stanford University Press, 2019.
Jeong, Eun-Young. "Samsung Chairman Sentenced to Jail for Violating Labor Laws."
    Wall Street Journal, December 17, 2019.
Jeong, Seunghoon. *The Global Auteur: The Politics of Authorship in 21st Century
    Cinema.* New York: Bloomsbury, 2016.
Jiang, Ada. "'Running Man,' 'I Am a Singer' and 8 Other Korean Reality TV Shows
    That Got a Chinese Remake." *South China Morning Post,* August 15, 2018.
    https://www.scmp.com/magazines/style/news-trends/article/2159596/remade
    -china-tom-cruise-korean-tv-show-running-man.
Jin, Dal Yong. *New Korean Wave: Transnational Cultural Power in the Age of Social
    Media.* Urbana: University of Illinois Press, 2016.
Jin, Dal Yong. *Smartland Korea: Mobile Communication, Culture, and Society.* Ann
    Arbor: University of Michigan Press, 2017.
Johnson, E. Patrick. *Appropriating Blackness: Performance and the Politics of Authen-
    ticity.* Durham, NC: Duke University Press, 2003.
Jung, Eun-young. "Transnational Korea: A Critical Assessment of the Korean Wave in
    Asia and the United States." *Southeast Review of Asian Studies* 31 (2002): 69–80.
Jung, Inha. *Architecture and Urbanism in Modern Korea.* Hong Kong: Hong Kong
    University Press, 2013.
Kang, Ingyu. "The Political Economy of Idols: South Korea's Neoliberal Restructuring
    and Its Impact on the Entertainment Labour Force." In *K-Pop: The International
    Rise of the Korean Music Industry,* edited by JungBong Choi and Roald Maliang-
    kay, 51–65. New York: Routledge, 2017.
Karatani, Kojin. "Nationalism and *Écriture.*" *Surfaces* 5 (1995). https://www.erudit.org
    /en/journals/surfaces/1995-v5-surfaces04904/1064990ar/.
Karatani, Kojin. *Origins of Modern Japanese Literature.* Edited and translated by
    Brett de Bary. Durham: Duke University Press, 1993.
Kil, Sonia. "Korean Variety Show 'Infinite Challenge' to Be Remade by China's CCTV."
    Variety, March 17, 2015.
Kim Chi-ha. "Madanggŭk eso madang gut ŭro" [From madang theater to
    madanggŭt]. *Pressian,* August 27, 2008. http://m.pressian.com/m/m_article/?no
    =56749#08gq.
Kim Chu-hŭi. "Migun kijich'on e taehan kiŏk ŭi chŏngch'i wa pyŏnmo hanŭn
    minjŏkjuŭi" [Politics of memory of US military camptown and changing nation-
    alism]. *Hanguk yŏsong hak* [Journal of Korean women's studies] 33, no. 4 (2017):
    39–76.

Kim, Gooyoung. *From Factory Girls to K-Pop Idol Girls: Cultural Politics of Devel-opmentalism, Patriarchy, and Neoliberalism in South Korea's Popular Music Industry*. Lanham, MD: Lexington Books, 2019.

Kim Ha-nŭl. "'Running Man' Is Exported to Nine Different Asian Territories includ-ing Taiwan, Thailand, China, and Japan." *EKNews*, November 22, 2011. http://www.eknews.net/xe/kr_politics/193744.

Kim, Hye-jin. "'Spoon Theory' and the Fall of a Populist Princess in Seoul." *Journal of Asian Studies* 76, no. 4 (November 2017): 839–49.

Kim Hyŏn-jŏng. "'Samsung nocho wahae' chŏn, hyŏnjik imwŏndŭl yujŏe hwakjŏng . . . Yi Sang-hun sajang mujŏe" [Executives involved in 'Samsung union-busting scheme' Found Guilty . . . Sang-hoon Lee found not guilty]. *Maeil Kyŏngje*, Febru-ary 4, 2021. https://www.mk.co.kr/news/society/view/2021/02/117311/.

Kim Jong-ok. "Sanŏphwa sidae hanguk hach'ŏng aenimeisyŏn e taehan yŏngu: 1970–80-nyŏndae aenimeisyŏn ŭl chungsim ŭro" [A study on subcontract animation in Korea during the industrialization era—Centered around anima-tions in the 1970s–80s]. *Manhwa aenimeisyŏn yŏngu* [Cartoon and animation studies], June 2016, 47–75.

Kim Ko-ŭn. "Pangsongsa maech'ul nŭrŏtchiman 'chŏkcha' JTBC man usŏtta" [Though the revenues of broadcasting companies have risen, they are losing money, only JTBC laughs]. Hanguk kija hŏyphoe [Journalists Association of Korea], June 28, 2019. http://www.journalist.or.kr/news/article.html?no=46380.

Kim, Kyung Hyun. "Crossing Borders." Liner note to *The Housemaid*. Blu-ray. New York: Criterion, 2013.

Kim, Kyung Hyun. "Korean Cinema and Im Kwon-Taek: An Overview." In *Im Kwon-Taek: The Making of a Korean National Cinema*, edited by David E. James and Kyung Hyun Kim, 19–46. Detroit: Wayne State University Press, 2002.

Kim, Kyung Hyun. "Part Four: Strut, Move, and Shake." In *The Korean Popular Cul-ture Reader*, edited by Kyung Hyun Kim and Youngmin Choe, 249–54. Durham, NC: Duke University Press, 2014.

Kim, Kyung Hyun. *The Remasculinization of Korean Cinema*. Durham, NC: Duke University Press, 2004.

Kim, Kyung Hyun. *Virtual Hallyu: Korean Cinema of the Global Era*. Durham, NC: Duke University Press, 2011.

Kim, Kyung Hyun. "Watching *Sopyonje* in the Era of Hallyu." Liner note to *Sopyonje*, Blu-ray. Seoul: Korean Film Archive, 2017.

Kim, Kyung Hyun, and Youngmin Choe, eds. *The Korean Popular Culture Reader*. Durham, NC: Duke University Press, 2014.

Kim, Kyung Hyun, with Tian Li. "Running Man: Korean Television Variety Program on the Transnational, Affective Run." *Telos* 184 (2018): 163–84.

Kim Nam-kwŏn. "Hanguk ch'ik'injip Sam-man-yuk-chŏn-kot . . . chŏnsegye McDonald maejang poda manta" [36,000 chicken restaurants in Korea . . . more than McDonald's in the entire world]. *Yonhap News*, October 5, 2015. https://www.yna.co.kr/view/AKR20151003056000009.

Kim, Sam. "South Korea Set to Break Own Record on World's Lowest Birth Rate." *Bloomberg*, November 26, 2019. https://www.bloomberg.com/news/articles /2019-11-27/south-korea-set-to-break-own-record-on-world-s-lowest-birth-rate.

Kim, Suk-Young. *K-Pop Live: Fans, Idols, and Multimedia Performance.* Stanford, CA: Stanford University Press, 2018.

Kim Ŭn-kyŏng. "Yuhŭi ro sŏ ŭi nodong, nodong ŭro sŏ ŭi yuhŭi: Mi p'algun sh'odan yŏkasu ŭi kyŏnghŏm ŭl chungsim ŭro" [Labor as amusement and amusement as labor: Focusing on the experiences of female singers performing for the Eighth United States Army]. *Asia yŏsong yŏngu* [Journal of Asian women] 56, no. 2 (November 2017): 7–45.

Kim, Wook-Dong. "The 'Creative' English Translation of *The Vegetarian* by Han Kang." *Translation Review* 100, no. 1 (2018): 65–80.

Kim Yong-chu. "Hanguk, pangsong cont'ench'ŭ such'ul segye 3'wi . . . il chech'yŏ" [Korea ranks third in the export of broadcasting contents, surpasses Japan]. *etnews*, April 11, 2017. http://www.etnews.com/20170411000356.

Kim Yun-shik. *Hanguk kŭndae sosŏlsa yŏngu* [Study on history of modern Korean literature]. Seoul: Ŭlyu munhwasa, 1986.

King, Ross. *Seoul: Memory, Reinvention, and the Korean Wave.* Honolulu: University of Hawai'i Press, 2018.

Klein, Christina. "The AFKN Nexus: U.S. Military Broadcasting and New Korean Cinema." *Transnational Cinema* 3, no. 1 (2012): 19–39.

Klein, Christina. *Cold War Cosmopolitanism: Period Style in 1950s Korean Cinema.* Berkeley: University of California Press, 2020.

Kroll, Justin. "Kevin Hart to Star in English Remake of Korean Comedy 'Extreme Job' for Universal." *Variety*, April 29, 2019.

Kwon, Dohee. "Shin Joong Hyun's Sonority and Korean Pentatonicism in 'Miin.'" In *Made in Korea: Studies in Popular Music*, edited by Hyunjoon Shin and Seung-Ah Lee, 123–32. New York: Routledge, 2017.

Lea, Jim, and Len Brown. "GIT: Key to Racial Equality." *Pacific Stars and Stripes*, October 24, 1971, https://starsandstripes.newspaperarchive.com/pacific-stars-and -stripes/1971-10-24/page-11/.

Lee, Jin-kyung. *Service Economies: Militarism, Sex Work, and Migrant Labor in South Korea.* Minneapolis: University of Minnesota Press, 2010.

Lee, Katja. "Reconsidering Rap's 'I': Eminem's Autobiographical Postures and the Construction of Identity Authenticity." *Canadian Review of American Studies* 38, no. 3 (2008): 351–73.

Lee Kyung-min. "I'm Satisfied Living Alone." *Korea Times*, October 7, 2018. https:// www.koreatimes.co.kr/www/biz/2018/11/488_256506.html.

Lee Miyoung. "'Mun tatko pekkigo'—hanchung ent'ŏ ŏpkye amulhaetta [hanhallyŏng 1nyŏn]:" [Shut down and plagiarized . . . depressing Sino-Korea entertainment in- dustry]. *Joynews 24*, November 4, 2017. http://www.joynews24.com/view/1057777.

Lee, Namhee. *The Making of Minjung: Democracy and the Politics of Representation in South Korea.* Ithaca, NY: Cornell University Press, 2007.

Lee, Seung-Ah. "Of the Fans, by the Fans, for the Fans: The JYJ Republic." In *Hallyu 2.0: The Korean Wave in the Age of Social Media*, edited by Sangjoon Lee and Abe Mark Nornes, 109–30. Ann Arbor: University of Michigan Press, 2015.

Lee Shin-Hyung. "Samsung Takes on Huawei in Race for 5G Dominance." *Asia Times*, November 20, 2019. https://www.asiatimes.com/2019/11/article/samsung-takes-on-huawei-in-race-for-5g-dominance/.

Lee Woo-young. "Han Dong-chul, Mastermind of Korean Hip-Hop Boom." *Korea Herald*, April 12, 2016. http://www.koreaherald.com/view.php?ud=20160412000578.

Lee Yen Nee. "Trump Says There is 'AWESOME' Economic Potential for North Korea—if Kim Abandons Nukes." *CNBC*, February 27, 2019. https://www.cnbc.com/2019/02/27/trump-on-north-korea-potential-if-kim-jong-un-agrees-to-denuclearize.html.

Li Xiazhi. "Guonei Zongyi Jinbanyou Jiyin Guanzhong Tucao: 'Paocai yuelai yuenongle'" [Nearly half the domestic variety shows have Korean DNA and the audience complains: "Kimchi is getting stronger"]. *Beijing Daily*, April 17, 2015. http://www.xinhuanet.com/politics/2015-04/17/c_1115004949.htm

Lie, John. *K-Pop: Popular Music, Cultural Amnesia, and Economic Innovation in South Korea*. Berkeley: University of California Press, 2015.

Livesey, Finbarr. *From Global to Local: The Making of Things and the End of Globalization*. New York: Pantheon, 2017.

Lohr, Steve. *Data-ism*. New York: HarperBusiness, 2015.

Looney, Dennis, and Natalia Lusin. "Enrollments in Languages Other than English in United States Institutions of Higher Education, Summer 2016 and Fall 2016: Preliminary Report." 2018 Modern Language Association of America. https://www.mla.org/content/download/83540/2197676/2016-Enrollments-Short-Report.pdf.

Luce, Henry. "The American Century." *Life*, February 17, 1941, 61–65.

Lukács, Georg. *The Historical Novel*. Translated by Hannah Mitchell and Stanley Mitchell. Lincoln: University of Nebraska Press, 1983.

Magnan-Park, Aaron Han Joon. "*Peppermint Candy*: The Will *Not* to Forget." In *New Korean Cinema*, edited by Chi-Yun Shin and Julian Stringer, 159–69. New York: New York University Press, 2005.

Maliangkay, Roald. "The Popularity of Individualism: The Seo Taiji Phenomenon in the 1990s." In *The Korean Popular Culture Reader*, edited by Kyung Hyun Kim and Youngmin Choe, 296–313. Durham, NC: Duke University Press, 2014.

Manning, Brandon J. "'And You Know This, Man!': Love, Humor, and Masculinity in *Friday*." *Black Camera* 8, no. 2 (Spring 2017): 243–54.

Martin, John. "Sai Shoki Is Seen in Korean Dances: Young Oriental Artist Offers Her Second Program Here." *New York Times*, November 7, 1938, 22.

Martin-Jones, David. "Decompressing Modernity: South Korean Time Travel Narratives and the IMF Crisis." *Cinema Journal* 46, no. 4 (Summer 2007): 45–67.

Mazdon, Lucy. *Encore Hollywood: Remaking French Cinema*. London: British Film Institute, 2000.

MBC *Nightly News*. "Waesaek yua chapji to ilbon chapji kŭdaero pekkyŏ silt'ae" [Even baby magazines copy Japanese ones—cover to cover]. April 16, 1992. http://imnews.imbc.com/20dbnews/history/1992/1913392_19402.html.

Mbembe, Achille. *Critique of Black Reason*. Translated by Laurent DuBois. Durham, NC: Duke University Press, 2017.

Mbembe, Achille. "Necropolitics." Translated by Libby Meintjes. *Public Culture* 15, no. 1 (2003): 11–40.

McCann, Ann. "Cities with the Best and Worst Public Transportation." WalletHub, September 10, 2019. https://wallethub.com/edu/cities-with-the-best-worst-public-transportation/65028/.

McGowan, Todd. "Affirmation of the Lost Object: *Peppermint Candy* and the End of Progress." *symploke* 15, nos. 1–2 (2007): 170–89.

Millar, Abi. "South Korea: The Rise of a New Medtech Giant?" *Verdict: Medical Devices*, August 4, 2020. https://www.medicaldevice-network.com/features/south-korea-the-rise-of-a-new-medtech-giant/.

Ministry of Culture, Sports, and Tourism, Republic of Korea. "Podojaryo: munch'ebu 2019-nyŏndo yesan 5cho 9,233ŏk wŏnŭro ch'oejong hwakchŏng" [2019 budget is confirmed at five trillion, nine hundred, thirty-three won]. December 10, 2018. https://www.mcst.go.kr/kor/s_notice/press/pressView.jsp?pSeq=17025.

Moon, Katharine H. S. *Sex among Allies: Military Prostitution in U.S.-Korea Relations*. New York: Columbia University Press, 1997.

Morelli, Sarah. "Who Is a Dancing Hero? Rap, Hip-Hop, and Dance in Korean Popular Culture." In *Global Noise: Rap and Hip-Hop outside the USA*, edited by Tony Mitchell, 248–58. Middletown, CT: Wesleyan University Press, 2001.

Nam In-yŏng. "Avengers, Sk'ŭrin tokkwajŏm, kŭriko kwankaek sŏnt'aekkwŏn." [Avengers, screen monopoly, and spectators' freedom to choose]. *Joongang Ilbo*, May 23, 2019. https://news.joins.com/article/23476582.

Neves, Joshua. *Underglobalization: Beijing's Media Urbanism and the Chimera of Legitimacy*. Durham, NC: Duke University Press, 2020.

Nicas, Jack. "Apple's Plan to Buy $75 Billion of Its Stock Fuels Spending Debate." *New York Times*, April 30, 2019.

Noh, Jean. "Korean President Park Geun-hye Implicated in CJ Chief Miky Lee's Exit." *Screen Daily*, December 11, 2016. https://www.screendaily.com/korean-president-implicated-in-cj-chiefs-exit/5112104.article.

O'Hara, Kieron, and Nigel Shadbolt. *The Spy in the Coffee Machine: The End of Privacy as We Know It*. Oxford, UK: Oneworld, 2008.

Ongiri, Amy Abugo. "'He Wanted to Be Just Like Bruce Lee': African Americans, Kung Fu Theater and Cultural Exchange at the Margins." *Journal of Asian American Studies* 5, no. 1 (2002): 31–40.

O'Rourke, Kevin. *My Korea: Forty Years without a Horsehair Hat*. Kent, UK: Renaissance Books, 2013.

Paek Tae-woo. "Google and Facebook Take Heavy Fire during Parliamentary Audit." *Hankyoreh* (English version), October 11, 2018. http://english.hani.co.kr/arti/english_edition/e_business/865443.html.

Pak Il-hwan, and Pandoch'e nodongja ŭi kŏnkang kwa inkwŏn chik'imi (Organization to Protect the Human Rights and Health of Semiconductor Workers). *Samsung Pandoch'e wa paekhyŏlbyŏng* [Samsung semiconductor and leukemia]. Seoul: Sam ui poinun ch'ang, 2010.

Pang, Laikwan. *Creativity and Its Discontents: China's Creative Industries and Intellectual Property Rights Offenses.* Durham, NC: Duke University Press, 2012.

Parenti, Christian. *The Soft Cage: Surveillance in America, from Slavery to the War on Terror.* New York: Basic Books, 2003.

Park, Ju-min. "K-Pop Stardom Lures Japanese Youth to Korea despite Diplomatic Chill." Reuters, May 8, 2019. https://widerimage.reuters.com/story/k-pop-stardom-lures-japanese-youth-to-korea-despite-diplomatic-chill.

Park, Sang Mi. "The Making of a Cultural Icon for the Japanese Empire: Choe Seung-hui's U.S. Dance Tours and 'New Asian Culture' in the 1930s and 1940s." *positions: east asia cultures critique* 14, no. 3 (Winter 2006): 597–632.

Park Yong-gyu. "AFKN-TV ŭi t'ŭksŏng kwa munhwa jŏk yŏnghyang (1957–1996)" [Characteristics of AFKN and its cultural influences in Korea, 1957–1996]. *Ŏnron kwahak yŏngu* [Journal of communication science] 14, no. 3 (September 2014): 101–34.

Parker, Kim, Anthony Cilluffo, and Renee Stepler. "6 Facts about the U.S. Military and Its Changing Demographics." *Facttank: News in the Number,* April 13, 2017. https://www.pewresearch.org/fact-tank/2017/04/13/6-facts-about-the-u-s-military-and-its-changing-demographics/.

Parkman, Helena. "Swedish Capital Sees Less Silver Pollution Thanks to Digital Photos." *Environmental News Network,* November 25, 2005. https://www.enn.com/articles/3134-swedish-capital-sees-less-silver-pollution-thanks-to-digital-photos.

Peirce, Charles Sanders. *The Essential Peirce: Selected Philosophical Writings.* Vol. 1. Edited by Nathan Houser and Christian Kloesel. Bloomington: Indiana University Press, 1992.

Peterson, Cecilia, and Crystal Rie. "How Korean Fried Chicken, AKA 'Candy Chicken' Became a Transnational Comfort Food." *Smithsonian Magazine,* October 18, 2017.

Plecher, H. "Employment by Economic Sector in South Korea 2019." *Statista.* Accessed January 29, 2020. https://www.statista.com/statistics/604702/employment-by-economic-sector-in-south-korea/.

Pollack, Andrew. "International Business; Unlikely Credits for a Korean Movie Mogul." *New York Times,* July 5, 1996.

Porter, Jon. "Samsung Electronics Chairman Found Guilty of Union Sabotage: Lee Sang-hoon Has Been Sentenced to 18 Months in Prison." *The Verge,* December 17, 2019. https://www.theverge.com/2019/12/17/21025874/samsung-electronics-chairman-union-sabotage-prison-sentence-priguilty-south-korea.

Quinn, Eithne. *Nuthin' but a "G" Thang: The Culture and Commerce of Gangsta Rap.* New York: Columbia University Press, 2004.

Reuters. "Jury Awards Apple $539 Million in Samsung Patent Case." *New York Times,* May 24, 2018.

Rivera, Raquel. *New York Ricans from the Hip Hop Zone.* New York: Palgrave Macmillan, 2003.

Robbins, Bruce. *The Beneficiary.* Durham, NC: Duke University Press, 2017.

"Samsung Opens Largest Wafer Plant in Austin, Texas." June 14, 2007. https://www.samsung.com/semiconductor/newsroom/news-events/samsung-opens-largest-wafer-plant-in-austin-texas/.

S.C.S. "How Was Hangul Invented?" *The Economist,* October 8, 2013. https://www.economist.com/the-economist-explains/2013/10/08/how-was-hangul-invented.

Seabrook, John. *The Song Machine.* New York: Norton, 2015.

Seigworth, Gregory J., and Melissa Gregg. "An Inventory of Shimmers." In *The Affect Theory Reader,* edited by Melissa Gregg and Gregory J. Seigworth, 1–28. Durham, NC: Duke University Press, 2010.

Sharma, Ramesh. "New Trends in Modern Literature of East Asian Countries with Special Reference to Modern Korean Poetry." In *East Asian Literatures: An Interface with India,* edited by P. A. George, 95–110. New Delhi: Northern Book Centre, 2006.

Shin, Haerin. "The Dynamics of K-Pop Spectatorship: The Tablo Witch-Hunt and Its Double-Edged Sword of Enjoyment." In *K-Pop: The International Rise of the Korean Music Industry,* edited by Jung Bong Choi and Roald Maliangkay, 133–45. New York: Routledge, 2014.

Shin, Hyunjoon, and Pilho Kim. "Birth, Death, and Resurrection of Group Sound Rock." In *The Korean Popular Culture Reader,* edited by Kyung Hyun Kim and Youngmin Choe, 275–95. Durham, NC: Duke University Press, 2014.

Shin, Hyunjoon, and Seung-Ah Lee, eds. *Made in Korea: Studies in Popular Music.* New York: Routledge, 2016.

Shin Joong-Hyun and Ki-t'ae Kim. "Majimak mutae aptun rok ŭi taebu Shinjunghyŏn" [Shin Joong-hyun, the godfather of rock, who looks forward to his last stage]. *Han'gyŏre,* June 26, 2006. http://www.hani.co.kr/arti/culture/music/135922.html.

Sin Chi-yŏng. *Ŏnŏ ŭi chultariki* [Language's tug of war]. Seoul: 21st Century Books, 2018.

Sloterdijk, Peter. *Critique of Cynical Reason.* Translated by Michael Eldred. Minneapolis: University of Minnesota Press, 2001.

Smith, George A. "Airwaves Carry U.S. Culture to Unintended Audience." Army.mil, July 10, 2013. https://www.army.mil/article/107168/airwaves_carry_us_culture_to_unintended_audience.

Sŏ Pyŏng-gi. "Chunggukp'an 'Running Man' kongdong chejak han Cho Hyojin PD ŭi k'ont'ench' ŭi such'ul choŏn" [Advising of Cho Hyo-jin PD, who has coproduced Chinese version of *Running Man*]. *Herald Business,* December 2, 2014. http://biz.heraldcorp.com/view.php?ud=20141202000005.

Son, Min-Jung. "Young Musical Love of the 1930s." In *The Korean Popular Culture Reader*, edited by Kyung Hyun Kim and Youngmin Choe, 255–74. Durham, NC: Duke University Press, 2014.

Song Ch'ang-han. "Pangt'ongwi, kugak pangsong yesan 67ŏk won . . . chiyŏk pangsong 43kaesa nŭn" [Committee on Broadcasting Communication Funds Kugak Broadcasting Company 6.7 billion won]. *MediaUs*, October 27, 2019. http://mediaus.co.kr/news/articleView.html?idxno=165415.

Song, Jaeyong, and Kyungmook Lee. *The Samsung Way: Transformational Management Strategies from the World Leader in Innovation and Design.* New York: McGraw-Hill, 2014.

Song Kwang-ho. "Mandam-ka 'Sin Pul-ch'ul' ŭl asinayo?" [Do you know the comedian Sin Pul-ch'ul?]. *Chu-gan Dong-A* [Dong-A weekly], May 15, 2009. http://weekly.donga.com/List/3/all/11/87547/1.

Song Myŏng-sŏn. *Hiphap hata 2.* Seoul: Annapuruna, 2016.

Song Yu-jin. "Samsung, LG Ssaumyŏn, kukmin yŏngum nuku p'yŏn?" [If Samsung and LG were to fight, whose side would social security support?]. *Chosun Ilbo*, December 6, 2019. https://biz.chosun.com/site/data/html_dir/2019/12/06/2019120600076.html.

Spigel, Lynn. "Introduction." In *Television after TV: Essays on a Medium in Transition*, edited by Lynn Spigel and Jan Olsson, 1–34. Durham, NC: Duke University Press, 2004.

Spigel, Lynn. *Make Room for TV: Television and the Family Ideal in Postwar America.* Chicago: University of Chicago Press, 1992.

Steintrager, James A., with Rey Chow. "Sound Objects: An Introduction." In *Sound Objects*, edited by James A. Steintrager and Rey Chow, 1–19. Durham, NC: Duke University Press, 2018.

Streamside. "'Running Man' Remake 'Hurry Up, Brother' Is a Huge Hit in China." soompi.com, January 12, 2015. http://www.soompi.com/2015/01/12/running-man-remake-hurry-up-brother-is-a-huge-hit-in-china/.

Thewesterngirl. "'Show Me the Money 4' Viewer Ratings Keep on Rising." July 11, 2015. https://www.allkpop.com/article/2015/07/show-me-the-money-4-viewer-ratings-keep-on-rising.

Thomas, Dexter, Jr. "Can the Japanese Rap?" In *Traveling Texts and the Work of Afro-Japanese Cultural Production: Two Haiku and a Microphone*, edited by William H. Bridges IV and Nina Cornyetz, 223–38. London: Lexington Books, 2015.

Thompson, Derek. "What's behind South Korea's COVID-19 Exceptionalism?" *The Atlantic*, May 6, 2020.

Tsai Ming-liang. Interview. *Cine 21 PIFF Daily*, November 11, 2001. Reprinted in Kyung Hyun Kim, *The Remasculinization of Korean Cinema* (Durham, NC: Duke University Press, 2004).

Vogel, Erica. "K-Pop in Mexico: Flash Mobs, Media Stunts, and the Momentum of Global Mutual Recognition." In *Pop Empires: Transnational and Diasporic Flows of India and Korea*, edited by S. Heijin Lee, Monika Mehta, and Robert Ji-song Ku, 55–71. Honolulu: University of Hawai'i Press, 2019.

Wada-Marciano, Mitsuyo. "Global and Local Materialities of Anime." In *Television, Japan, and Globalization*, edited by Mitsuhiro Yoshimoto, Eva Tsai, and Jung-Bong Choi, 241–58. Ann Arbor: University of Michigan Press, 2010.

Wang Hui. *The Politics of Imagining Asia*. Edited by Theodore Huters. Translated by Chris Berry. Cambridge, MA: Harvard University Press, 2011.

Woyke, Elizabeth. *The Smartphone: Anatomy of an Industry*. New York: New Press, 2014.

Yang, Myungji. *From Miracle to Mirage: The Making and Unmaking of the Korean Middle Class, 1960–2015*. Ithaca, NY: Cornell University Press, 2018.

Yi Jum. "Tŭllgukhwa, Kim Hyŏn-sik, Siin kwa ch'onjang twi e nŭn kŭ ka issŏtta: Tong-A Kihoek Kim Yŏng Int'ŏbyu" [Behind Deulgukhwa, Kim Hyon-sik, and Siin kwa ch'onjang, there was him: Interview with Dong-A Management's Kim Young]. *Channel Yes*, November 11, 2018. http://ch.yes24.com/Article/View/37415.

Yi Kyŏng-sik. *Yi Kŏn-hŭi Sŭt'ori: saengae wa ritŏsip* [The Lee Kun-hee story: Life and leadership]. Seoul: Human and Books, 2010.

Yi Myŏng-won. *T'anŭn hyŏ* [Burning tongue]. Seoul: Saeum, 2013.

Yi Sang-won. "Sho'mi tŏ mŏni ka mandŭn hiphap k'aesŭtŭ" [The hip-hop cast made possible by Show Me the Money]. *Sisain.co.kr*, August 2, 2017. http://www.sisain.co.kr/?mod=news&act=articleView&idxno=29724.

Yi Yŏng-t'ae. "Yanggŭkhwa, taehanminguk I kalrajinta" [Polarization, the Republic of Korea is splitting in two]. *Hanguk Ilbo*, July 12, 2010. https://www.hankookilbo.com/News/Read/201007121353788323.

Yi Yong-u. "Miguk k'ŭrop so hŭnryŏn patŭn taejung ŭmak" [Popular music trained in American military clubs]. *Hangyoreh*, July 6, 2005. http://www.hani.co.kr/arti/culture/culture_general/47952.html.

Yoon, Tae-il, et al. "When Old Meets New: An Analysis of Korean Traditional Narrative in the Contemporary Reality TV Show *Infinite Challenge*." *Acta Koreana* 20, no. 2 (December 2017): 423–48.

Yoshimoto, Mitsuhiro. *Kurosawa: Film Studies and the Japanese Cinema*. Durham, NC: Duke University Press, 2000.

You, Xiaoye. *Writing in the Devil's Tongue: A History of English Composition in China*. Carbondale: Southern Illinois University Press, 2010.

Yu Chae-hyŏk. "CJ E&M '2020nyŏn kkaji haeoe rok'ŏl yŏnghwa yŏn 20-p'yŏn kaepong.' . . Global chejaksa toyak" [CJ E&M targets to release 20 overseas local films per year by 2020, launches a global production company]. *Hanguk kyŏngje* [Korean financial times], September 13, 2017. https://www.hankyung.com/economy/article/2017091343911.

Yu Chae-yong. *AFKN K'idŭ ŭi miguk tŭryŏdapoki* [AFKN kid's peeking at America]. Seoul: Nanam, 2007.

Yuh, Ji-Yeon. *Beyond the Shadow of Camptown: Korean Military Brides in America*. New York: New York University Press, 2002.

Yun Kwang-ŭn. "Hanguk hiphap ŭi changrŭ jŏk rok'alraijing kwa Woo Won-jae" [Korea's localizing of hip-hop genre and Woo Won-jae]. *Huffington Post*,

September 14, 2017. https://www.huffingtonpost.kr/kwangeun-youn/story_b
_17991102.html.

Yun Sang-kil. "Naengjŏnki KBS ŭi 'chayu taehan ŭi sori' pangsong kwa taeil ratio
pangsong" [Voice of Free Korea's Japan-targeted radio broadcasting in the period
of Cold War: Ruptures and convergence of the East Asian cultural cold war].
K'ŏmmunik'eisyŏn iron [Communication theories] 15, no. 4 (December 2019):
5–43. http://www.dbpia.co.kr/journal/articleDetail?nodeId=NODE09276748.

Zheng, Crystal. "Black Lives Matter: How Should Asian Americans Answer the Call?"
The Lens, July 26, 2020. https://thelensnola.org/2020/07/26/black-lives-matter
-how-should-asian-americans-answer-the-call/.

INDEX

Page numbers followed by f refer to illustrations.

Astro Boy (animated television program), 156
audio-vision, 57. *See also* Chion, Michel

"Bae Bae" (song), 36, 50, 91
Baek Ji-Young (musician), 56
ballad, 16, 20, 36, 56, 91, 103, 171, 241n35
Bang, Si-Hyuk (music producer), 26, 56
Barking Dogs Never Bite (Bong Joon-ho, film, 2000), 181
Barthes, Roland, 137–39
Baudrillard, Jean: Disneyland and, 208, 258n18; ego Consumans, 269n47; hallucinatory resemblance, 145; simulacrum, 97, 116, 130, 199, 208, 209, 211–12, 215, 258n18
Bauhaus (Walter Gropius), 187–88
Bazin, André, 33, 160
Beatles, The (music group), 20, 37, 52, 60, 82, 83, 111, 115, 213, 243n44
Beauty Inside (film, 2015), 122, 124, 130–35, 258n20
Bhabha, Homi K., 10, 12, 19, 179; pedagogical vs. performative, 179–80
Bicycle Thief (1949, film), 184
BIGBANG (music group), 36, 45, 46, 50, 55, 61, 91, 96, 213, 229, 230f, 247n2. *See also* G-Dragon
Big Hit Entertainment, 26, 56
Billboard, xi, 55, 56. *See also* music: chart
birth rate, 42, 53, 78, 79f, 112, 168, 255n46
Bizzell, Patricia, 177
"Black Happiness" (song), 254n28
blackness, 2, 5, 11, 17–18, 19, 26, 29–30, 31, 32; 49–50, 59, 89, 91, 95–97, 116, 171, 177, 178–79, 243n39, 243n41, 252nn17–18; "becoming-black of the world," 5–6, 88, 93, 116; humor and, 30, 92, 96–97, 99–100, 114, 170, 176; off-white/blackish 8, 11, 13, 19, 30, 80, 89, 96, 115, 171, 185–86, 199, 234–35, 256n53. *See also* hip-hop: authenticity; United States: racism in
Blackpink (music group), xvii, 61, 213, 269n51

Blondie (music group), 213
body beautiful, 54–55, 107–8, 109–10, 132–37, 213–14, 247n2
body switch. *See* genre: body switch
Boney M, 56
Bong Joon-ho (film director), ix, 15, 26, 33, 63, 70–71, 119, 155, 165, 171, 180–82, 193–94, 245n61, 251n5, 260n29, 263n27
border between North and South Korea, 23, 67, 148f. *See also* DMZ, North Korea
"Boyz-n-the Hood" (song), 85–88, 91–92, 250n2
Breen, Michael, 209, 268n37
Bridges, William H., IV, 18
Britishness, 11, 15, 20, 36, 79, 81, 242n37, 255n44
Brown, James (music group), 227, 243n44
BTS (music group), xi, xvii, 14, 15, 16, 22, 29, 36, 39, 41, 45, 46, 48, 56, 58–62, 82–84, 91, 96, 207, 247n4, 260n25, 271n11
Buñuel, Luis (film director), 168
Burch, Noel, 127–28
Busker Busker (music group), 82

Caillois, Roger, 77
Calamity Jane (film), 235
camptown, xii, 3–4, 7, 27, 38, 50, 166, 235, 238n4, 239n5, 239nn9–10, 240n17
Candy Candy (animated television program), 156
Cannes Film Festival, 165, 180
capitalism, capitalists, xi, xii, 5, 20, 46, 81, 122, 123, 143–44, 168, 172, 181, 185–86, 192, 246n66; consumerism and, 41–42, 82–83, 160–61; critique of, 7, 46, 64, 160–61, 171–72, 176, 181–94, 217–18; 234; BTS and, 60–61, 247n4; Gamestop and, 61; living crypt of capital, 5, 7, 218. *See also* economy; economic divide; necropolitics; *Parasite*; Trump, Donald; slave contract

captions, 77, 128, 144, 151–55, 230–31, 260n23. *See also* fansubs; subtitles

Cartwright, Lisa, 158–59

CDMA (Code Division Multiple Access) vs. GSM (Global System for Mobiles), 210

celebrity, celebrities, xi, 3, 7, 78, 89, 141, 145, 146, 150, 160, 166, 216–18, 221, 223, 224, 241n25, 268n37. *See also* idol

Celebrity Apprentice (reality television program), 80

censorship, 20, 25, 26, 41, 66, 92, 104, 145, 158, 224–25, 242n35, 246n67

chaebol, 21, 33, 38–39, 51, 144, 167, 191, 195–219, 235, 248n8

Ch'ae Man-sik (writer), 222, 270n8

Chan, Jackie (comedian), 152–55

Chang, Jeff, 250n2

Chen, Kuan-Hsing, 147

Chicago Cubs, 60. *See also* sports

China, Chinese, 169; audience and viewers, 159–63; ban on Korean contents, 147, 159–63, 170, 241n30, 270n11; coproduction with Korea, 70, 162–63; cinema, 70–73, 75, 142, 249n24; Netflix in, 74; *hallyu* and, 49, 53; hegemonic mimicry and, 8,13, 159–63, 224; manufacturing in, 199–200; Ming Dynasty, 127; phonocentricism and, 260n26; remake, 32–33, 78, 79, 142–43, 150–51, 158–63, 224, 270n11; United States and, 79, 80, 147–48, 160, 161, 163, 199–200. *See also* affect Confucianism; East Asian; *Hurry Up! Brother*; kimchi imperialism; THAAD

Chion, Michel, 57, 128, 258n16

Cho, Dong-jin (musician), 7

Cho, Hyo-jin (television producer), 162

Cho, Kwan-woo (musician), 242n34

Cho, Yong Pil (musician), 7, 43

Choe Sŭng-hŭi (Sai Shoki, dancer), 33–34, 231–35

Choe, Youngmin, 149–50, 249n22, 259n21

Choi, Chungmoo, 220–21

Choi, Julie, 212, 268n47

Choi, Sun-sil, 144, 174, 198. *See also* Park, Geun-hye

choreography. *See* dance

Chosun (Chosŏn), 27, 123–29, 142, 155, 229–30

Chow, Rey, 57

Chun Doo-hwan (past president), 92

Chunhyang (folktale) 229, 231, 257n13

"Cider Song" (song, early 1970s), 92

cinema and films: American and Hollywood, 21, 27, 51, 65, 67, 72, 110, 127, 155, 160–61, 245n61, 249n23, 249nn28–29, 261n34, 263n27, 267n35; box office, 63, 70–74, 82–83; 142, 165, 171–73, 249nn23–24, 249nn28–29, 261n1; French, 33, 160, 168, 190–91, 261n34; Holocaust and, 69; Hong Kong, 49, 159, 173–74; Japanese, 42, 127, 194; Korean, ix, 20, 62–74, 82–83, 118–39, 164–94; neorealism, 184. *See also* China: cinema; genre; Netflix; *names of actor, actress, film, film director and film producer*

CJ E&M, xviii, 64, 71, 110, 263n27, 267n35

"Classroom Ideology" (Kyosil idea, song, 1993), 41, 96, 106, 247n6

classroom tyranny. *See* education fever

Cold Eyes (*Kamsijadŭl*, film, 2013), 123

Cold War. *See* United States: Cold War

"Come Back Home" (song, 1993), 41, 107

comedy, comedians, 32, 54–55, 80, 92, 153, 157, 220–35, 254n36, 270n6; African American, 30, 92, 114, 164, 170, 176; censorship, 224–25; code-switching, 165, 176, 194; 233–34; films, 32, 164–94; gender-war, 64, 221, 233–35; laughter, 168–69, 170, 178–79, 223, 225, 227; television, 32–33, 54, 76–78, 140–63, 254n36; wordplay, 55, 97, 113–14, 151–55, 179–80, 223. *See also* mandam; *names of comedian and television comedy program*

comfort women, 262n25

Compton, 85–89, 92, 116

G-Dragon (musician), 91, 96, 157, 228–31, 247n2, 253n25. *See also* BIGBANG

Gag Concert (television comedy program), 228

gaming, games, 12, 21, 28, 46, 61, 77, 122, 140–63; punishment and, 142, 151, 158, 222–23. *See also* television: variety game shows

"Gangnam Style" (song), 22, 34, 53–54, 56, 149, 212, 213f, 223, 231, 233f, 234–35. *See also* dance: horse-dance

Gangnam, 54, 55, 235

Gates, Henry, Jr., 12–13, 114, 176, 256n52. *See also* Signifyin(g)

genre (film), body switch, 32, 70, 72, 118–39; crime mystery, ix, 119, 122–23; food drama, 76, 164–68, 182–84; Korean War and Cold War, 66–69, 70, 178–80, 243n41; melodrama, 63, 66, 68, 70, 76, 113, 164, 165, 169; *saguk*, 64, 123–29, 257n13; thriller, 63, 65, 67–69, 70; time-travel, 32, 76, 132–33. *See also* comedy

Gerow, Aaron, 141, 260n23

Gervais, Ricky (comedian), 271n20

Get It Together (GIT), 3

Get Out (film, 2017), 176

Girls' Generation (musician group), 50, 55

Glissant, Édouard, 89, 93. *See also* opacity: of language

g.o.d (music group), 40, 56

Goo, Hara (musician), 216–19

Google and Googleplex, 196, 208, 267n33

Gramsci, Antonio, 14

Grandpa over Flowers (*Kkotpoda halbae*, television comedy program), 26, 77, 78

"Great Rebirth" (*Widaehan t'ansaeng*, song), 99–102

Groundhog Day (film, 1993), 131

"Growl" (*Ŭrŭrŏng*, song), 16, 48

hagwŏn, 46, 50

Haha (comedian), 157, 260n22

Hall, Stuart, x, 14, 100

hallyu (Korean Wave), discourse of, xiv, 63, 76–84, 141, 183, 237n4, 241n30; government policy on, 22, 28, 37–39, 41–42, 51, 64, 75, 81, 89, 217–18, 246n71, 247n3, 248n12, 269n48; North Korea and, 163, 242n35. *See also* China; hegemonic mimicry; Japan: reception of *hallyu*; *Jurassic Park* theory; K-drama; K-pop; music

han, 6, 116–17, 220–27, 235

Han, Dong-chul (television producer), 104

Han, Hyo-joo (actress), 132, 258n20

Han, Kang (writer), 255n44

Han, Myung-sook (singer), 18–19

hangul, 1–2, 19–20, 21, 24, 45, 47–49, 55, 93–94, 96–97, 100, 109–10; 152, 153–55, 178–79, 244n52, 255n40, 255n43, 260n27, 262n25. *See also* homonym; *ŏnmun ilch'i*

happiness, 168–69, 175

happy object, 146–47

Harlins, Latasha, xv

Hart, Kevin (comedian), 164

"Hayeoga" (song, 1993), 30

Hegelian history of the spirit (*Geistesgeschichte*), 124, 190

hegemonic mimicry, ix–xiii, 1–9, 14, 24, 26, 28–31, 33–34, 149, 162–63, 183, 210, 231–35

Hell Chosun, 104, 112

heroism, 32, 180, 228–30, 251n6

Hide and Seek (*Sumpakkokjil*, film, 2013), 123

hip-hop: Asianness and, 99, 251n10, 256n56; authenticity, 89–97, 251n10, 252n17, 253n24; autobiography in, 95–96, 98, 105–17; education ghetto, 59, 95–96, 104–13; ghetto and, 32, 95–96, 251n6, 253n24; Japanese, 89, 104, 108, 112, 246n73, 251n10; Korea and, 41, 47–49, 59, 85–117, 174, 246n73, 256nn55–56; Koreanness and, 86–90, 95, 116, 252n17, 253n24;

Latinos and, 251n7; rap and rhyming in, 30, 48–49, 88–117, 252n17; storytelling in, 87, 90, 92–93, 96–97, 100–102, 108–10, 112–17. *See also* blackness; United States: racism

Hŏ, Kyun, 125–26

Hollywood. *See* cinema: American

homonym, 113–14, 220

Host, The (film), 63, 181, 189

H.O.T. (music group), 40, 41, 46

Housemaid, The (film, 1960), 165, 261n3

Houston, Whitney (musician), 56, 227

Huawei, 198

hŭng (joy), 34, 157, 220–22, 225

Hurry Up, Brother (Bēnpǎo Ba Xiōngdì, television comedy program), 142, 160

Hyun, Jin-young (musician), 47

Hyundai, 29, 39, 51, 197

I Can Speak (film, 2017), 262n25

Ice Cube (musician), 85, 87, 88–89, 98, 170

idol, 36, 37, 39–53, 56–62, 104, 247n2, 269n48, 269n51, 271n19; suicide of, 216–18

"Idol" (song), 91

Im Kwon-Taek (film director), 70, 117, 220–21

indexicality, 124, 126, 257n9. *See also* Peirce, Charles S.

Infernal Affairs (film), 159

Infinite Challenge. See Muhan Dojeon

International Monetary Fund (IMF) bailout, 38–39, 42, 79, 166, 174, 186, 197–98, 237n4

internet, 71, 137, 142, 163, 181, 208, 212–15; algorithms, 32, 214, 257n3, 267n33; Chollian, 45, 59; cyberattack, 216, 253n24, 253n26; emojis and emoticons, 111, 154, 155, 199, 212, 213; fandom and, 40–41, 43, 59–62; Google Korea, 75; Hitel, 45, 59, 98; KT, 21; Naver, 75; music and, 43, 45–46, 213–14; netizens, 127; serial novel, 134; spreadability, 146, 259n13; technology

in Korea, x, 21, 43, 45, 75–76, 208, 258n27; viral on, 22, 45, 54–55, 60–62, 142, 199, 210–15, 217, 223. *See also* Kakao talkscape; language: online; meme; smartphone, television: OTT

"In the Sentimental Past" (Dang nian ching, song), 173–75

Irvine, 264n1

Ishii, Baku, 231

Itaewon (Yongsan), 4, 7, 9, 10, 26, 27, 28, 30, 50

Ivanhoe (novel, 1820), 32, 124–25. *See also* Scott, Walter

Iwabuchi, Koichi, 17, 26, 242n36

Jackson, Michael (musician), 39, 54

"Jakdu" (song), 91

Jameson, Fredric, 120, 147, 167, 251n5

Jane Eyre (novel), 188

Jang, Beom-joon (musician), 82. *See also* Busker Busker

Japan, Japanese, 239n13; anime, 21, 24, 156–57; ban on, 42, 170, 244n50, 244n55; blackness and, 179; cultural color and odor (waesaek), 17, 26, 156, 242n36, 244n50, 245n55; J-pop, 16, 39–40, 49, 50, 51, 53; colonization of Korea, 24, 30, 33–34; 37, 62–63, 90, 91, 113, 170, 178, 222–24, 241n32, 245n59, 256n56; 264n3; and Korea, 154, 170, 194, 241n31, 241n32, 244n50, 246n73, 266n22; reception of hallyu, 52; television, 76, 151, 155, 260n23; whiteness and, 156. *See also* cinema: Japan; East Asia: de-Asianization; enka; JCS

Jay-Z, 251n6

JCS (Japanese-colored songs), 16–18, 90, 252n14

Jeanne Dielman, 23, quai du commerce, 1080 Bruxelles (film, 1975), 189–90, 191

Jenkins, Henry, 149

Jeon, Joseph Jonghyun, 119, 237n4

Jeon, Young-rok (musician), 248n9

Jeong, Hyun-don (comedian), 225